Pushing

THE STORY OF
THE MIDDLESBROUGH DIOCESAN
PILGRIMAGE TO LOURDES

By
Paul Farrer
with
Mike McGeary and Ged O'Connor

Middlesbrough Diocesan Lourdes Pilgrimage
All proceeds from this publication to Middlesbrough Diocesan Lourdes Sick Fund

Published in 2003 by
Middlesbrough Diocesan Lourdes Pilgrimage
Diocese of Middlesbrough Curial Office
50a The Avenue, Middlesbrough, England, TS5 6QT

www.middlesbroughlourdes.co.uk
www.middlesbrough-diocese.org.uk

ISBN 0-9544822-0-4

British Library Cataloguing-in-Publication Data
A catalogue record for this book is available from the British Library

Middlesbrough Diocesan Lourdes Sick Fund
Part of the Diocese of Middlesbrough
Reg. Charity No. 233748

Designed and Printed By
Hillprint Ltd – evolution through design
Prime House, Park 2000, Heighington Business Park, Newton Aycliffe, Co. Durham DL3 6AR

Acknowledgements

The production of this book is the result of real teamwork over 18 months. Thanks are due to very many people without whom this work would not be. Jim White provided the foundations for the project through tireless research of the Gazette archives. Angela, Anne-Marie and Maureen are to be thanked for their typing skills, time and patience. We are indebted to Barney Connelly and Pat McGeary for their critical advice and support and to Janet and Matt O'Connor, who proof read the appendix, checking that it is an accurate reproduction of original documents. Dave Allan provided expert advice and support allowing us to give you something worth reading. Teresa Atkinson cooked our tea as we worked. Stephen, John and Anthony at Hillprint have made our work look good. Nicola Collins and Eamonn McClurey provided artwork for the back cover, while Julie Allinson willingly took on the task of distributing the book.

We gratefully thank the Evening Gazette, Middlesbrough for reporting so well on the Lourdes Pilgrimage over the years and granting us permission to use its reports and pictures in this book. Similarly we thank Henri Lacaze for taking so many wonderful pictures of the Pilgrimage and allowing us to use some of them here. Most importantly of all, we record our thanks to all of the people who have shared their Lourdes stories and pictures with us so that we may share them with you. They have helped us build an accurate picture of the history of the first 50 years of the Middlesbrough Diocesan Pilgrimage to Lourdes.

Finally, if you have enjoyed reading this book do not lend it to your friends. Please ask them to buy a copy too and help send a deserving person to Lourdes.

Cover photo shows Bill and Barbara Boyes arriving at the baths in Lourdes.

CONTENTS

FOREWORD

My first memory of Lourdes is as a young lad – probably about 11 or 12 – travelling with my parish to Lourdes by boat train from Victoria. How excited I was, and what a thrill to arrive in Lourdes by night and see the illuminated cross, as it then was, on the mountainside. Thereafter over the years I have returned to Lourdes periodically, but it wasn't until being made Bishop of Middlesbrough that I began to go every single year. This May sees my tenth consecutive pilgrimage with the diocese, and, happily, that small anniversary coincides with a much bigger one of our Diocesan Golden Pilgrimage to Lourdes. Incidentally, my very first visit to Lourdes coincided as regards the year with the first Middlesbrough Diocesan Pilgrimage in 1952.

Many memories of the last ten years crowd my memory, but the highlight has to be the experience of prayer at the Grotto. For me personally I love to spend time facing the Grotto from the other side of the fast flowing Gave. How often have I found a place on those stone seats near the low river wall and gazed across to the place where it all began. My prayer almost invariably is "Mary, place me close to your Son". Those were the words which St Ignatius of Loyola prayed after his conversion, and they have become mine over the years. They are words which sum up the role of Mary, not least at Lourdes. It always fascinates me to realise that the millions of pilgrims who come to Lourdes each year are 'invited' by Mary and yet, once there, are led by her straight to her Son. Just to consider some of the major events of any Lourdes pilgrimage – the celebration of Mass at the Grotto, the Blessed Sacrament procession, the anointing of the sick, the Sacrament of Reconciliation, the Stations of the Cross – all these are gateways into closer union with Jesus, her Son.

How much I look forward to being with the Diocese in Lourdes on this Golden Jubilee Pilgrimage. Whether it is a first visit or the latest in a series of many, our desire is a common one, namely that Mary our Mother will 'place us close to her Son'.

Bishop John Crowley
BISHOP OF MIDDLESBROUGH

Chapter One

DEDICATED TO MARY

DEVOTION to Mary the mother of Jesus is perhaps older than the Church itself. That is to say her place as the mother of the wonderful prophet of Nazareth was well respected by many of those who followed him. Long before the birth of the Church at Pentecost, those who knew her venerated Mary, perhaps sensing something of the importance of the part she plays in our salvation. Even before the birth of Jesus, Elizabeth greets Mary with these words: "Of all women you are the most blessed and blessed is the fruit of your womb. Why should I be honoured with a visit from the mother of my Lord?"

To some it may seem that the way we express our faith today is a far cry from its early beginnings. And yet when we contemplate Mary the mother of Jesus, we have never been far away from that ancient expression of faith made by one mother to another. It is perhaps the simplicity of the expression of Mary's faith that we all find so alluring. It is her simple, 'Yes' to God's plan for her that we, as people of faith, wish to emulate. But it is not only Mary's relationship with God that is to be marvelled at and copied. Her relationship with God affected in a very definite way her relationships with those around her.

How heartbreaking and challenging it must have been for her to stand outside that house waiting for Jesus to come out and speak to her and through the open door hear him say: "Here are my mother and my brothers." The beauty of Mary's instant and dignified embrace of the whole plan that God had for her is possibly the bedrock of our devotion to her. It is this that puts us in close contact with her Son. As we meet Jesus, the son of Mary, the words she spoke to the wedding servants at Cana ring in our ears: "Do whatever he tells you."

On September 25 2002, for the first time in the history of the Diocese of Middlesbrough, a group of pilgrims, led by Bishop John Crowley, celebrated Mass in the Church of St Alphonsus in Rome.

History will mark this Mass as one of little significance beyond the fact that once again, by the grace of God, those pilgrims took part in the Last Supper with Our Lord. However, those who were there know that in many ways this Mass marked a return to the very roots of the Diocese and its devotion to Our Lady. It was, by common consent, the only place that a Middlesbrough Diocesan Pilgrimage to Rome could have started. It is in this place, above the high altar, that the Byzantine icon of Our Lady of Perpetual Help hangs. Mounted simply in clear glass secured in a stone arch, its relatively small size in a city full of huge works of breathtaking art belies the importance of the icon for our Diocese.

It is this icon and the popular devotion to Our Lady of Perpetual Help which inspired a young student for the Priesthood to step out of the Venerable English College and into the Via Monserrato to pray for healing. The icon was taken in solemn procession to the Church of St Alphonsus on April 26 1866 and as it passed the student's home he seized his opportunity. By the intercession of Our Lady the student was cured and his lifelong devotion to Our Lady secured. Richard Lacy went on to be ordained priest and at the age of just 38 became the first Bishop of the brand new Diocese of Middlesbrough. We can assume that he placed our Diocese under the patronage of Our Lady of Perpetual Help without hesitation. He even insisted that every church in the Diocese displayed the icon.

Photo: Diocesan Archive

Bishop Richard Lacy, whose cure in 1866 led him to dedicate the Diocese of Middlesbrough to Our Lady.

The icon of Our Lady of Perpetual Help which Bishop Lacy saw in 1866.

The Catholic Encyclopaedia tells us something of the history of the Icon:

The picture of Our Lady of Perpetual Succour is painted on wood, with background of gold. It is Byzantine in style and is supposed to have been painted in the 13th Century. It represents the Mother of God holding the Divine Child while the Archangels Michael and Gabriel present before Him the instruments of His Passion. Over the figures in the picture are some Greek letters which form the abbreviated words Mother of God, Jesus Christ, Archangel Michael and Archangel Gabriel respectively. It was brought to Rome towards the end of the 15ᵗʰ Century by a pious merchant, who, dying there, ordered by his will that the picture should be exposed in a church for public veneration. It was exposed in the church of San Matteo, Via Merulana, between St Mary Major and St John Lateran. Crowds flocked to this church, and for nearly 300 years many graces were obtained through the intercession of the Blessed Virgin. The picture was then popularly called the Madonna di San Matteo. The church was served for a time by the Hermits of St Augustine, who had sheltered their Irish brethren in their distress. These Augustinians were still in charge when the French invaded Rome in 1812 and destroyed the church. The picture disappeared. It remained hidden and neglected for more than 40 years, but a series of providential circumstances between 1863 and 1865 led to its discovery in an oratory of the Augustinian Fathers at Santa Maria in Posterula. The pope, Pius IX, who as a boy had prayed before the picture in San Matteo, became interested in the discovery and in a letter dated December 11 1865 to Father General Mauron, CSSR, ordered that Our Lady of Perpetual Succour should be again publicly venerated in Via Merulana, and this time at the new church of St Alphonsus. The ruins of San Matteo were in the grounds of the Redemptorist Convent. This was but the first favour of the Holy Father towards the picture. He approved of the solemn translation of the picture on April 26 1866, and its coronation by the Vatican Chapter on the June 23 1867. He fixed the feast as duplex secundae classis, on the Sunday before the Feast of the Nativity of St John the Baptist, and by a decree dated May 1876, approved of a special office and Mass for the Congregation of the Most Holy Redeemer. This favour later on was also granted to others. Learning that the devotion to Our Lady under this title had spread far and wide, Pius IX raised a confraternity of Our Lady of Perpetual Succour and St Alphonsus. He was among the first to visit the picture in its new home, and his name is the first in the register of the arch-confraternity. Two-thousand-three-hundred facsimiles of the Holy Picture have been sent from St Alphonsus' church in Rome to every part of the world. At the present day not only altars, but churches and dioceses, Leeds and Middlesbrough in England and in the United States Savannah, are dedicated to Our Lady of Perpetual Help.

What we are about to see spread out before us is the development of a huge devotion to Our Lady of Lourdes in the Diocese of Middlesbrough. We can point to many external factors, which help us on our way, and they all have a place in the story. The Marist Fathers, the Faithful Companions of Jesus, the Sisters of Mercy, personal cures and inherited devotion all have a part to play. However, without Bishop Lacy's personal devotion to Our Lady, which he passed on to the whole Diocese, the connection may not have been made.

Bishop Lacy was perhaps affected by his encounter on the Via Monserrato more than we might first realise. It was he who inaugurated the huge Corpus Christi procession in Middlesbrough, the only Catholic procession in England which carried the Blessed

Sacrament. Bishop Lacy did make a pilgrimage to Lourdes at least once, in 1928, just a year before his death. But it was his eventual successor, Bishop Thomas Shine, consecrated Bishop in 1921, who was to be one of the earliest regular pilgrims from our Diocese to the shrine. He made his first pilgrimage in 1924.

On that same pilgrimage was a man called Tom Hoy of Wellington Street, Middlesbrough. He was a big man, born into a large family in Glasgow in 1900. His family moved to Middlesbrough during World War I as his father sought employment in the steelworks. Tom himself was tall and fit and was apprenticed to the shipyards, but his life changed dramatically when he was involved in an horrific accident at the age of 17. Tom was late for work, which meant that he would have lost a day's pay. For his over-stretched mother this would have been a serious matter. In an attempt to make up time, Tom jumped from a moving bus and fell under it, dislocating his hip and breaking the upper leg. Despite the pain he managed to get to work but collapsed soon after his arrival. Treatment was delayed and Tom was permanently disabled.

Tom Hoy, who in 1924 became the first Middlesbrough pilgrim to be cured in Lourdes.

It is difficult now to be sure of just how much damage Tom's injury caused him, but we are sure that his bad leg was considerably shorter than the other. Walking was difficult and he had a pronounced limp. There was even talk, at the time, of "an aperture big enough for a man to put his fist in". Needless to say he was out of an industrial job for good. His injured leg was supported by a surgical boot. In time he was helped with casual work, which included part-time caretaker at St Mary's School. Tom also served Mass regularly at the Cathedral and became sacristan, at first casually and then on a full-time basis.

Tom joined the 1924 pilgrimage without expectation and travelled as a sick pilgrim. He sent two telegrams back to England during his pilgrimage and they were to be the beginning of another story which inspired so much of our early devotion to the Shrine. At 8pm on June 4, Sampson Grainger, Tom's father-in-law and then landlord of the Windmill Hotel, also in Wellington Street, received the simple message: "GOOD NEWS – TOM." This was followed by a telegram to the Knights of St Columba in Southfield Road stating: "TOM HOY DEFINITELY CURED." According to the Evening Gazette of June 5: "The news spread with lightning rapidity and the town was agog with excitement".

The Gazette reporter of the time took up the story.

Middlesbrough rejoices over a Lourdes miracle in which one of her townsmen is central figure. Mr Thos Hoy of Wellington Street, who has suffered from a fixed hip for about 11 years, today returned from the pilgrimage completely cured. His hip trouble arose through a fall at the Linthorpe-Dinsdale Ironworks, for which he was awarded compensation. It resulted in a shortening of the limb by one-and-a-half to two inches, causing a pronounced limp and depriving him of all movement in the hip. Three operations and specialists' treatment at Newcastle, Sunderland and South Shields availed nothing, but Mr Hoy had sufficient faith in the powers of Our Lady of Lourdes to make the long journey to the Pyrenean village. Sceptics have always doubted reports of cures, but seeing is believing, and those who knew Tom Hoy before he made that wonderful journey can vouch for the genuineness of his cure. Ever since the accident that was the cause of his trouble, he has had to rely on the good offices of his relatives for such little services as the lacing of his boots, but a Gazette representative who visited him today, found that he was not only able to perform that task, but could do all manner of physical jerks.

For actual detail we have the benefit of the family history handed down to his great-granddaughter, Ann, of Middlesbrough, as well as Tom's words recorded in the Evening Gazette. "It all happened last Sunday," he said. "I was waiting for the procession of the Blessed Sacrament to pass the stretcher cases when a thought flashed through my mind that I was cured." As this happened Tom felt immediately well and as if his injury had simply disappeared. Tom said to Harry: "I want to run." Harry replied: "Don't be daft, you can't even walk." But he could. He removed the surgical boot and never used it again. "I went to a private room and found that I could move my leg. It was wonderful." From that moment everything went well and on the way home he was able to assist in carrying stretcher and chair-cases and luggage aboard. Except for a slight limp, Tom's leg was completely cured and free from pain. Having thrown away his boot he had to borrow a pair of sandshoes to come home!

It is easy to look back at cures from the early part of the century and explain them away in the light of modern medical knowledge. However, the story of Tom's disability was a well-known one and upon his return home his much-improved state was there for all to see.

Although the pilgrims were timed to arrive at the early hour of 5.45 to-day, hundreds of people gathered at the station and were able to witness for themselves the miracle that had been wrought. Tom Hoy stepped out of the train and walked with normal ease and comfort. He received an overwhelming welcome. Women were moved to tears, but they were tears of joy, while his friends showered congratulations upon him.

Tom was overwhelmed by his fame and always very casual about his recovery, not really wanting all the attention it brought. Although he returned to Lourdes in 1952 he then stopped going. It was years before he returned to Lourdes but he arranged and paid for someone to go every year. Tom was listed among the pilgrims on the Diocesan Pilgrimage of 1954, just a year before his death.

There are people in Middlesbrough today who remember Tom with great affection, not only because of his years of service as altar server, sacristan and caretaker. Because he came from a family of publicans, Tom had played mine host in various pubs around central Middlesbrough. There are some who have the distinct memory of being introduced to him as, 'The man who was cured in Lourdes'. Although his cure was never officially recognized, he did tell his story to those waiting back home. In 1919 Tom married Elizabeth Grainger, becoming brother-in-law to a man called Johnny Coleman, who has his own part to play in the pilgrimage tradition of the region. It is difficult to know exactly what the cure of Tom Hoy means for the pilgrimage tradition which has grown up in our Diocese. But if we simply look back to the welcome home Tom received it would seem that the already strong devotion to Our Lady, established by Bishop Lacy, was fuelled beyond anything we may come to have expect.

Chapter Two

LOURDES CALLING

THE first Middlesbrough Diocesan Pilgrimage to Lourdes was an eight-day adventure from August 4 to 12 1952. But this is far from the beginning of our story. Indeed, in terms of the history of the Pilgrimage, starting at the very beginning is a very difficult thing to do. At first glance it would seem that rather than being a great new innovation that would become one of the spiritual cornerstones of annual Diocesan life, it was just simply bound to happen. If we look back as far as 1950 we can see that there are strands of various stories that begin to come together in a way that, even if the people caught up in them didn't realise it at the time, would lead to the founding of the Diocesan Pilgrimage. But tracing these threads takes us back very much further.

The short answer to who it was that founded the pilgrimage is Canon Gerard T Rickaby. His influence is without question and history will show us that present day pilgrims from the Diocese of Middlesbrough would perhaps not be gathered together as we are now without his early zeal. But his huge contribution is far from the whole story. He did not simply pluck the notion of a Diocesan Pilgrimage to Lourdes out of the ether. He in his turn was influenced by the pilgrimage tradition that had already begun, not only in our own Diocese, but also in its very near neighbours and beyond.

The pilgrimage tradition that we pick up at the very start of the 20ᵗʰ Century in the Diocese of Middlesbrough was the natural response of a faithful few to the message of Lourdes. It goes without saying that the story of Bernadette Soubirous and her conversations with the lady who told her *"I am the Immaculate Conception"* would have already been well reported throughout Europe. And yet it would seem that something more was needed to get people moving. What we see is a beautifully simple ripple effect. Just as we watch waves ripple away from a stone dropped into a pool hit the side and then, having grown and gathered force, return to where they began, so it is with the beginnings of pilgrimage to Lourdes.

It was from Lourdes itself that ripples were sent out all over Europe and the world and by the turn of the century those ripple, were flowing back to Lourdes with great force. Those first ripples set out from Lourdes after two events; the publication of a history of the apparitions written by Henri Lasserre called *Notre-Dame de Lourdes* and the founding in France of the Assumption Movement's pilgrimage to Lourdes. Lasserre was a journalist and devout Catholic. His book, written with the earnest piety of the time, romanticises not only the story of the apparitions but also the main characters and even the place itself. He painted a picture of a place and people so untouched by the modern world as to be beyond reproach regarding the reliability of the events he detailed. He used his gifts as a journalist to great effect. His book, first published in 1896, became known as The Bible of Lourdes and was among the bestsellers of the 19th Century. It was translated into at least 80 languages by 1900 and sold well over a million copies.

Lasserre was well known in Lourdes as his eyes had been cured while he himself was on pilgrimage there in 1863. This led to his work receiving the approval of the Lourdes authorities. Henri Lasserre had hyperaemia, a congestion of the pupil. The two most distinguished eye specialists of the time, Dr Demarres and Dr Giraud-Teulon, diagnosed the lesion of the retina and took all possible steps to prevent its development. Absolute rest for the eyes, a change to the country, hydrotherapy and tonics were all prescribed and taken without success. Gradually the sight grew weak and at last failed altogether. Several months passed. Lasserre felt he was growing blind. Trusting in the power of God, he asked for some Lourdes water, bathed his eyes in it and was cured. His history of Lourdes was a hymn of thanksgiving.

Faithful people all over the world read The Bible of Lourdes and resolved to go there themselves. We simply don't know for sure if this publication ever made it into the hands of those first pilgrims from Middlesbrough but it certainly had an influence. The style of his book made Lourdes a very attractive place and promoted the idea that somehow the apparitions were a call to action for every person of faith. Add to this the fact that Lasserre himself had been cured at the shrine and the net result was a work that had people all over Europe keen to temporarily make themselves a part of the beatific vision he described at Lourdes.

The Bible of Lourdes was not the only attempt to write such a book at the time. The tendency to extreme piety won the book many critics who worried that its lack of objectivity would harm the message of Lourdes. And yet Lasserre's book remained the most popular and influential work of its time. Indeed, a leather bound copy of the French edition of the work was in due course to be presented to Bishop Lacy by the staff and pupils of St Patrick's School in Middlesbrough. Ruth Harris, in her book Lourdes, *Body and Spirit in the Secular Age*, tells us how important Lasserre's work was, but she is keen to point out that this is only half the story.

The publication of Lasserre's text in 1869 brought an image of Lourdes into national and international consciousness that was almost impossible to change. No amount of scientific history could undermine the beatific vision of contact with the divine that he so brilliantly constructed. But the rituals of pilgrimage that are now commonly associated with Lourdes – the trains, the stretchers, the crippled and the dying escorted to the Grotto and the massive Eucharistic processions – were still to be established.

The year 1839 saw the birth of the Assumptionist Order in Nimes but it wasn't until the 1870s that the popularity of the order blossomed in Paris. By then France had lived through the fall of Louis Napoleon's Second Empire after a war with the German Reich. France had lost its domination of the European political scene and the order was set up to try to re-establish the link between the Church and the Crown. The order grew in popularity, particularly among the working classes. It was based on personal relationships, especially those relationships that formed around spiritual direction.

As the order grew so did its popularity. Its horizons broadened and it began to influence the rich aristocracy. These people, along with their priestly directors, began to raise money to send the sick to the Grotto. It would not be long before the development of organised pilgrimage. As the order continued to develop it seemed more and more inevitable that small groups of pilgrims travelling on an *ad hoc* basis to Lourdes would give way to a more organised and formal pilgrimage experience.

The French National Pilgrimage was born in 1872, the idea of Fr Francois Picard, a member of the Assumptionist Order. It was not a successful affair. The pilgrimage that first year was to La Salette, where a child named Melanie Calvat had also seen Our Lady. By the time the Lourdes apparitions began Melanie was a Carmelite sister in the convent at Darlington. But the French pilgrims at La Salette found themselves looking with envious eyes at the shrine of Lourdes. The following year, 1873, saw them switch to Lourdes and the town became their centre of pilgrimage for many years. As many groups of people have found throughout history, the pilgrimage bug is a powerful one. Numbers of pilgrims grew, as did the National Pilgrimage's influence. It was Fr Picard who began the Blessed Sacrament Procession in Lourdes as he looked to enhance the spiritual experience afforded by such a pilgrimage.

By the mid 1870s the spiritual notion of a pilgrim people was a hugely important concept. It became obvious that as the Church considered itself the Pilgrim Church on Earth, people should actually make a physical pilgrimage too. There is no doubt that before the founding of the French National Pilgrimage the pilgrimage tradition was strong and vibrant. However, there was a much deeper spirituality to be gained by actually making the journey to Lourdes together, rather than travelling individually and joining fellow pilgrims at the shrine. Ruth Harris takes up the story.

It was in these years that the special mission of tending the sick at Lourdes emerged. Only then did the numbers of sick pilgrims rise, requiring the organisation of special trains and the institution of the Hospitalites, the lay organisations designed to transport the sick from the train to the Grotto, tend them in the hospitals and bathe them in the pools. In this enterprise the sick began to take centre stage. The rituals of pilgrimage created a community of extraordinary solidarity in which the poor and the weak were serviced by the rich and the strong.

Of course, the French National Pilgrimage was just like any other human organisation. It was full of internal power struggles and differing opinion but its development is a milestone in our story. As early as 1864, 20,000 people gathered in Lourdes and processed from the parish church to the Grotto to inaugurate the statue of Our Lady placed in the niche where it remains today. But they had not necessarily journeyed to Lourdes together. It was the equal importance of the journey made together as well as actually getting to Lourdes that was to become so attractive. Without this no modern day pilgrimage would value the journey as much as the arrival.

It is easy to see the effect that these ripples had in our own country. By the time we enter the 1900s Lasserre's book was available in English. It painted a hauntingly attractive picture of Lourdes for the faithful, who would have known well the story of Bernadette but little of what their own personal response should be to Our Lady of Lourdes. *The Bible of Lourdes* told them of pilgrims, processions, cures and great demonstrations of faith by ordinary folk like them. The existence of the French National Pilgrimage, the Hospitalites and an ever-developing communication system began to make the possibility of a pilgrimage to Lourdes from England a very real goal. At the same time these events were unfolding in France, the Diocese of Middlesbrough was being born. In the mid 1800s the Catholic population of North Yorkshire and the East Riding blossomed. This was due to two factors, Irish immigration and the development of the ironworks in the Cleveland region. Local historian David Simpson tells us more.

By 1851 Middlesbrough's population had grown from 40 people in 1829 to 7,600 and it was rapidly replacing Stockton as the main port on the Tees. In 1850 iron ore was discovered in the Cleveland Hills near Eston to the south of Middlesbrough and iron gradually replaced coal as the lifeblood of the town. The ore was discovered by John Vaughan, the principal ironmaster of Middlesbrough who along with his German business partner Henry Bolckow had already established a small iron foundry and rolling mill at Middlesbrough using iron stone from Durham and the Yorkshire coast. The new discovery of iron ore on their doorstep prompted them to build Teesside's first blast furnace in 1851. Iron was now in big demand in Britain, particularly for the rapid expansion of the railways being built in every part of the country. More and more blast furnaces were opened in the vicinity of Middlesbrough to meet this demand and by the end of the century Teesside was producing about a third of the nation's iron output. By the 1870s, steel, a much stronger and more resilient metal was in big demand and Middlesbrough had to compete with Sheffield and the rest of the world. In 1875 Bolckow and Vaughan opened their first Bessemer Steel plant in Middlesbrough.

This was a crucial moment in the story of Middlesbrough, as before the Bessemer furnace was invented the local iron would not make steel.

The expanding iron and steel industry of Middlesbrough in the 1860s and 1870s spurred on

THE BIRTH OF THE DIOCESE

On June 2 1938, the Evening Gazette focused again on the Catholic heritage of the town.

"Middlesbrough is a modern town, the product of a great modern industry, iron and steel, and St Mary's Cathedral, though a comparatively modern building, has behind it a great wealth of local Roman Catholic History.

It seems there has been a Catholic church in Middlesbrough since the year 686, before Danish invaders eventually destroyed it. We know for sure, thanks to ecclesiastical documentation, that at the beginning of the 12th Century, Middlesbrough was the site of a priory church dependant on the Abbey of St Hilda in Whitby.

At that time, the church of St Hilda at Middlesbure was given by Robert de Brus, of Skelton Castle, founder also of Guisborough Priory, to the Monks of St Benedict at Whitby. This was on condition that there should always be monks at Middlesbrough and a fine set of stone buildings was built to accommodate 12 monks. The church was the principal cell of Whitby Abbey and Roger de Scarborough, the eighth Abbot of Whitby, spent his early monastic life there.

During the dissolution of the monasteries, the monks were turned adrift and the church was allowed to become a ruin. The ruins were transported to Newport in 1730 to be used in the reconstruction of a chapel, but the re-build never took place. Much of the unused stone remained on the site and was used for the first buildings of the new town.

It was almost a hundred years later that a revival in the Catholic faith in Middlesbrough happened as the town boomed due to the expansion of the iron and steel industry. In 1838 Fr Dugdale of Stockton came to Middlesbrough and celebrated Mass in an upper room in West Street. It was the first for 300 years. In 1841 the people welcomed their first resident priest, Fr Walsh, who said Mass in a hired room in Dacre Street and later moved to larger premises in Suffield Street. Here, the small community had their first mission given by two Rosminian Fathers, Fr Gentili and Fr Furlong.

In 1848 Fr Walsh was able to erect a small chapel on the site that was to be the Cathedral in Sussex Street. Around this time the discovery of ironstone in the Cleveland Hills caused the mushroom growth of the town and, attracted by visions of steady work and regular income, many Irish Catholics arrived in Middlesbrough.

By 1854 Fr Burns had followed Fr Walsh as Parish Priest and he was forced to extend the chapel so that it would hold 700 people. In 1871 a young curate, Fr Richard Lacy, came from Bradford to replace Fr Burns and he was soon to be consecrated first Bishop of the brand new Diocese of Middlesbrough."

According to the Gazette: "The young Bishop had to provide accommodation for 1,200 Catholic children and St Patrick's School in Lawson Street and St Mary's School were the result of his initiative." He also began the building the church of St Mary, which eventually became the Cathedral Church in Sussex Street. Dr Cornthwaite, Bishop of Beverley, laid the foundation stone and Cardinal Manning opened it on August 21 1878. The design and construction of the church cost £10,000, although the towers were never added to the building. In the following year the Diocese of Beverley was reorganised and Middlesbrough and Leeds became separate Diocese.

the growth of Middlesbrough with a population of 19,000 in 1861 increasing to 40,000 only ten years later. The residents of this early town came mainly from neighbouring Yorkshire and the North East, but later from Cheshire, Ireland, Scotland, Wales and some European countries. At the turn of the century Middlesbrough's population had more than doubled to 90,000 and it must have been hard to believe that only 70 years earlier the town did not exist. Today Middlesbrough has a population of 150,000 and is undoubtedly the heart of the Teesside conurbation and the modern capital of the area. In English history nothing compares to Middlesbrough's rapid growth. It is no wonder that Middlesbrough has been described as the 'oldest new town in England.'

Crucially for Catholic life in this old new town, another development was taking place at the same time. The traditionally Catholic farming communities of North Yorkshire were losing their young people. These faithful youngsters abandoned the countryside and headed into Middlesbrough, taking up the new opportunities offered by the development of heavy industry.

This growth did not go unnoticed by the Church. In 1872 Reverend Richard Lacy was entrusted with the charge of the Middlesbrough Mission. In August 1878, Cardinal Manning and Bishop Cornthwaite of Beverley opened St Mary's Church. In December that year St Mary's became the Cathedral of the new Diocese of Middlesbrough. "The Diocese of Beverley conterminous with Yorkshire" was by the authority of apostolic letters of Leo XIII dated December 20 1878 divided into the Dioceses of Leeds and Middlesbrough. However, it was not until December 11 1879 that the Papal Brief was received notifying the appointment of the new bishop, the Reverend Richard Lacy. He was just 38 years old. Bishop Lacy made a pilgrimage to Lourdes in 1928. It would seem he was not the first Bishop of the Diocese to make the trip; that honour fell to Bishop Shine. But as we have seen, Bishop Lacy's personal devotion to Our Lady is a key part of our story.

Chapter Three

ANSWERING THE CALL

ON May 27 1924 the Middlesbrough Evening Gazette reported remarkable scenes at Victoria Station, London. The reporter was very probably unaware of the nature of the story and how it was the beginning of something very special that would touch the lives of thousands of people from the Diocese of Middlesbrough for generations to come.

Over 200 sick people, including 67 who were unable to walk, six doctors, 30 trained nurses and over 50 handmaids of the sick left Victoria (for Lourdes) at eight o'clock this morning in the first of three special trains. The pilgrimage, promoted by the Society of Our Lady of Lourdes, was headed by Archbishop Mostyn of Cardiff and the Bishops of Leeds, Plymouth and Brentwood and the co-adjutor-Bishop of Middlesbrough (Dr Shine); about 74 priests also accompanied the pilgrimage.

By 1924 there was a great devotion throughout Britain to the shrine of Our Lady at Lourdes. And while it would seem no diocese took the decision to journey alone, large numbers of people from across the country were keen to make their own pilgrimage of faith. A total of 1,430 people journeyed together from Victoria to Lourdes. But why was Bishop Shine there? Simply because more than 100 of the number were from the Diocese of Middlesbrough. The Gazette takes up the story:

Scenes of such remarkable fervour as to leave an impression both lasting and poignant among over 1,000 witnesses occurred last night (May 26) in Middlesbrough Railway Station. The occasion was the departure of Teesside pilgrims to Lourdes, an event marked with all the depth and sincerity of the Catholic faith and involving the assembly of many hundreds of their relatives and friends to wish the pilgrims God-speed.

Shortly after seven o'clock the South platform began to assume a congested appearance, whilst ambulance vans, drawing up at the main entrance, waited the arrival of the train that was to take the last batch of 50 pilgrims from Middlesbrough, South Bank, Grangetown and Port Clarence, on the final stages of their long journey.

Among the 16 incurable invalids forming part of the pilgrimage were four stretcher cases – one, a young woman who had lain helpless for six years, and others whose implicit faith has swayed almost reluctant medical advice. Pending the arrival of the train the invalids and their fellow pilgrims and friends gathered in a pressing crowd in the station.

Faith of Our Fathers was taken up by over 1,000 voices and added a deeper hymnal solemnity to a spectacle in its humanity intensely moving. The train having entered there were many willing hands to assist aboard pilgrims of faith, but the hymns continued until the last carriage had disappeared down the long line to Lourdes.

Altogether, more than 100 devout Catholics of Middlesbrough and district will meet at the famous shrine this year. The invalids who departed last night are being sent by the Middlesbrough Institute of the Knights of St Columba, whose representative in charge – Mr Muir – was busily attending their requirements last night.

Piecing the story together is far from easy. Very little is written down and we find ourselves relying on the memories of the few remaining pilgrims from that era. We certainly know that Tom Hoy was one of the expectant pilgrims on the platform that night. But he was unaware he was beginning a journey that would transform his life forever. Sadly, the modern day Knights of St Columba possess no record of those years. And sadly there are no documents detailing the relationship between the Society of Our Lady and the Knights of St Columba. This link would be very interesting to uncover simply because the Society made its first pilgrimage in 1922, just two years before the first Middlesbrough pilgrims made the journey. Present day Knights are aware of their heritage and continue to tirelessly fundraise and send sick pilgrims to Lourdes. Indeed, many continue to make the pilgrimage every year as brancardiers.

This much is clear. In Middlesbrough and its surrounding district, including Stockton and other southern parts of the Diocese of Hexham and Newcastle, it was the faith of the lay people and their desire to pray at the shrine at Lourdes that became a reality as early as 1924. By then, the people of the Cathedral Parish, The Holy Name of Mary Parish and, crucially for sick pilgrims, the Institute of the Knights of St Columba on Southfield Road in Middlesbrough, had begun to firmly established the tradition of pilgrims travelling from Middlesbrough to Lourdes.

Building up a complete picture is a risky business as living history has much to do with perception and opinion. What is utterly convincing is that if one single piece of the jigsaw that emerges before we get to August 4 1952 had been missing, then that day would have been just like any other and no more noteworthy than the next. Although we don't know exactly how the link

JOSEPH SCOTT: KNIGHT OF COLUMBUS

Joseph Scott, personal friend of Pope Pius X, was an extraordinary man. Although a resident of Pasadena, Joseph Scott was so prominent in the civic affairs of Los Angeles that he became known as "Mr Los Angeles". The son of an Irish Catholic mother and a Scottish Presbyterian father, he was raised as a Catholic and one leaving Ushaw College in County Durham, aged 22, he went to the United States. After working for six months as a labourer in a Massachusetts paper mill, he obtained a position at St Buenaventure's College in Allegheny, New York, teaching rhetoric and English literature. Scott moved to Los Angeles three years later. There he studied Law and was admitted to the Bar.

As a lawyer, he was involved in several highly-publicised cases, including participation in the defence of the McNamara Brothers, who were accused of blowing up the Times building in 1910. As a national figure he nominated Hoover for the presidency. As a community leader, Scott was a member of the Los Angeles School Board, President of the Chamber of Commerce, a founder of the Southwest Museum and a member of the museum's board of trustees for 50 years, chairman of the local draft exemption board during World War I, a founder and then president of the Community Chest and after World War II, a charter member of the Advisory Board of the local chapter of the National Conference of Christians and Jews.

He was deeply involved in Catholic activities and helped form the Knights of Columbus, as the organisation is known in the States, in Southern California in 1902. In recognition of his services, he was decorated by three Popes and received numerous honours from Catholic organizations. Without doubt he left his mark on Jackie, who, after this meeting, would return to Middlesbrough and emulate Scott's commitment to the community and Catholic causes.

between the Middlesbrough Knights and the Society of Our Lady of Lourdes was established, it is interesting that this dynamic partnership which ushered in a new era in our Diocesan devotion to Our Lady happened within about a year of the almost simultaneous birth of the Knights in Middlesbrough and Stockton.

Here we meet two of the first of the characters who picked up the pilgrimage tradition of our Diocesan family and took it in a new direction. Tom Connelly and, crucially, Jackie Muir. These two men were responsible for the founding of the Knights of St Columba in Stockton and Middlesbrough respectively in around 1921. The driving force was Jackie and he looms large in the early history of not only the Knights in Middlesbrough, but also of pilgrimage to Lourdes.

Jackie Muir was a time served joiner and ship's carpenter who emigrated to Canada with his family. While there, he was present at a convention of the Knights of Columbus, to this day the American spelling of the Order's name. The convention president was a lawyer from Los Angeles called Joseph Scott who, Jackie discovered, was not only Grand President of the Order but also related to the Scott family of Stockton-on-Tees. By the time he attended the convention it seems Jackie had already decided the Muir family would resettle in Middlesbrough and spoke to Joseph Scott about establishing a Council of Knights upon his return. Joseph simply pointed him in the direction of the Scott household in Stockton and in particular to a member of the family by marriage, Tom Connelly.

According to one of Jackie's daughters, Teresa Condren, Jackie met Tom around 1921, the year of the Muir family's return to Middlesbrough. The two men began to help each other start a club in each of their hometowns. The Middlesbrough Council was established first, followed by Stockton. Jackie ran things from the beginning. Upon his return to these shores he gave the whole of his time to the Church in so many ways, as well as raising a large family. This is the man who organised the first Lourdes venture. Teresa remembers: "We were all in on it, the whole family. In those days the Knights never posted a letter anywhere in town. Dad would send us out to hand deliver everything."

Jackie had a great deal of help from the first Middlesbrough Knights also. Charlie Brown was one of the very first Grand Knights in Middlesbrough. He was eventually to serve as head teacher of St Mary's School. He was joined in the Order by his brother Bernard and John Quinn, who became the first headmaster of St Richard's. They, along with Jackie were powerful characters.

The Knights of St Columba is a fraternal organisation which participates in the work of the Lay Apostolate, assisting in all matters concerning the progress of the Catholic Church. The Order promotes the moral, intellectual and material welfare of its members and of the Catholic community generally and encourages all in the practice of the faith. Jackie and those who joined him took all of this to heart. Within three years of establishing the Knights on Southfield Road, Jackie was managing a busy and effective group of volunteers. The Knights quickly became the focal point for much good work in the town. This work would be evident nowhere more than at Middlesbrough Station on May 27 1924, where Jackie was to be found tending to the needs of the sick pilgrims sponsored by the Knights.

Tom Connelly, for the purposes of our story, remains in the background as aide and confidant of Jackie. And yet he has a larger part to play. Tom is the father of Bernard Connelly, who will play bigger part in the story of Middlesbrough pilgrims in Lourdes than any other single person. Barney possesses a great knowledge for and love of Lourdes, which is both self evident and infectious. Still a very active pilgrim in his 80th year, his love of Lourdes is rooted in his early years.

"My maternal grandmother, Agnes Scott, was three times a pilgrim with The English National Pilgrimage, which seemed to me to be based in Liverpool," he says. "She travelled with the contingent from the Knights Club in Middlesbrough. They organised the trip and the club was the gathering point. I think she went in 1924, 1926 and 1928. Since I was born in 1922, I really only remember the last trip. I remember before she went that time she talked to us endlessly about Lourdes. She had brought us all souvenirs from her other trips, a statue in gold that played the Lourdes Hymn, medals, pictures, her badge and a huge glass bottle bound in wicker-work which always went out empty and came back full."

This English National Pilgrimage mirrored what the Assumptionist Order had done in France some years earlier and was the product of The Society of Our Lady of Lourdes. Founded in March 1912 the Society organised its first Pilgrimage to the shrine in 1922. Despite the General Strike in 1926 and the depression of the 1930s, it established a regular programme of annual pilgrimages, disrupted only by the Second World War. The Society was set up "To promote devotion to Our Lady of Lourdes. To organise pilgrimages to Lourdes and services in Her honour. To provide financial and other assistance to enable pilgrims who cannot afford the cost to go to Lourdes."

Pilgrimages such as the English National became a logistical possibility in the 1920s thanks to the First World War. During the 1914-18 conflict it had been necessary to manufacture a way of transporting large numbers of injured men over great distances. Hospital Trains were born and after the War ended it became possible for pilgrimage organisers such as the Society of Our Lady to hire the specially designed rolling stock. Interestingly, World War II also plays a huge part in our story. The post-War pioneers in the travel agency business during the 1940s were, for the most part, ex-army transport officers. One such character was Barney Connelly, who followed his employer John Peckston out of the services and into the shipping and travel agency business in 1948. Barney soon

Photo: Diocesan Archive

Bishop Thomas Shine, whose many visits to Lourdes in the 1920s inspired hundreds of others to follow.

had pilgrimages to Lourdes on his mind as Lourdes had been at the heart of his family upbringing since the 1920s.

"We lived in Stockton until 1929 and my grandmother was a retired publican, badly crippled with arthritis and chair-bound," recalls Barney. "I remember she was a very generous lady, giving most of her savings to good causes and spending the rest on herself. I think she died leaving only three pence behind. She loved Lourdes and passed that love on to the family. By the age of six I could sing the Lourdes Hymn. I can remember going with her in a horse-drawn cab late at night as a special treat. We took her to the Knights Club in Middlesbrough where she joined the other pilgrims who took the night train down to Victoria to join the National Pilgrimage. The year after this my family moved to Middlesbrough."

Bishop Shine became a regular pilgrim with The National, his attendance over the next seven years being recorded regularly by the Gazette. The style of reporting suggests that part of this pilgrimage was seen as its Middlesbrough Diocesan 'arm' - even if only by the people of Middlesbrough. In the paper's Town Talk column on May 23 1933, correspondent Margot noted: "Still happily enjoying the health and vigour of a young man, Dr Shine, the Roman Catholic Bishop of Middlesbrough, is leading the Middlesbrough Section of the National Pilgrimage to Lourdes, which left England today. This is, of course, by no means Dr Shine's first visit to Lourdes. Indeed he seems disposed to make this an annual pilgrimage. He is accompanied by Mgr McCabe of Whitby, Canon Lynn of Scarborough and Canon Gryspeert of Redcar." Despite his apparent health and vigour in 1933, research indicates this may have been the last time Bishop Shine made the pilgrimage. However, this is not certain. He had become the second Bishop of Middlesbrough on April 11 1929 after the death of Bishop Lacy.

In more recent times we have become used to the Gazette reporting on our mishaps as pilgrims, most notably airport delays - we have even made the front page occasionally! However, over the years the reporting has been gentle and sympathetic, always interested in this slightly odd phenomenon of pilgrimage which has gripped so many in the town for generations. By 1925 the Evening Gazette seemed to have lost interest in the fact that pilgrims from Middlesbrough were travelling to Lourdes and it would seem that no report of their departure from the town's station was made. Far more interesting was the prospect of meeting them as they returned, hoping to be able to report a miraculous cure to rival that of Tom Hoy the previous year. On May 28 the anxious reporters were rewarded as the headline read: "Middlesbrough Cripple Now Able To Walk.". This was good news for Mrs Wright of Costa Street, but the paper seems disappointed that the cure was not recognised by the Lourdes authorities. "Interviewed by Gazette representatives, Teesside pilgrims who have just returned from Lourdes were unanimous in reporting the beneficial results of their pilgrimage, although no actual cures were reported at the bureau."

It may seem slightly patronising to sick pilgrims today, but in its time this journalistic curiosity was only natural. The previous year the initial story had been the sheer number of pilgrims heading for that place in France where the sick were cured. The fact that a cure actually happened to a Middlesbrough pilgrim seems to have made the press hungry for more. Perhaps in 1924 nobody realised this exodus was to become a regular event. The fact that it happened again was bound to send the reporters looking for a story. Amusingly all Mrs Wright could tell them was: "I haven't felt this good for ages!" Not quite as dramatic as the cure of Tom Hoy, but as pilgrims down through the years have come to realise, little miracles happen every day in Lourdes.

In 1927 the Pilgrimage left on May 24 and returned on June 1. From the Gazette reports it is clear that a few changes had taken place. Jackie Muir is not mentioned, replaced by another key character

Early pilgrims enjoy a day trip to Gavarnie in the mountains near Lourdes.

Photo: B Toolin

in those early years, Jim Kelly, also of the Knights and father of Harry Kelly, who would become the Diocesan Pilgrimage's first Head Brancardier. Jim replaced Jackie as the Knights' representative at Middlesbrough Station. In his turn, Jim was replaced by James O'Brien, also of the Knights, in 1933.

The night train left Middlesbrough, not for Victoria but for King's Cross, to meet up with the ever increasing numbers of the National Pilgrimage, this year thought to be in the region of between 2,000 and 3,000. The pattern seems to be well established now. The focal point was the Knights Club, where much of the fundraising was done. From here the volunteer helpers came and it was here pilgrims met before heading to Middlesbrough Station to catch the first of the trains that would take them to Lourdes. Judging by the tone of the Gazette, the town had become accustomed to the pilgrimage and now regarded it as a noteworthy annual event rather than something to be sensationalised. The report for this year concludes: "Whether or not cures will have been affected it is certain that the hearts of the pilgrims will have been comforted, and to all those who have made this possible by their practical support, the promoters wish to give their sincere thanks."

The next few years would seem to have little of interest for us in terms of the Pilgrimage's development, but we should note that 1928 is the only year we can positively identify that Bishop Lacy made the journey. This is particularly poignant as the following year marked his death and the enthronement of Bishop Shine.

Disaster struck in 1931. The Pilgrimage left on May 12 and all was going well until the return journey. As the pilgrims left Boulogne heading for Folkestone, a 50mph gale swept across the English Channel. "The special staff of doctors and nurses travelling with the pilgrims worked incessantly attending and comforting those who suffered from the effects of the rough sea. When the steamer Engadine berthed it looked like a hospital ship. Sick women and children lay helpless on the decks and the disembarkation occupied a considerable time." Passengers later told how the steamer had rolled so badly in the rough seas that those caught on the top deck had found themselves level with the sea. The Archbishops of Cardiff and Birmingham, along with Bishop Shine and the Bishops of Menevia and Plymouth, were aboard and suffered along with their fellow pilgrims.

Mary Walsh of Eston, who was to become a key member of the nursing team in the early days, made her first pilgrimage to Lourdes in 1939. Although this was about the time Fr Walter O'Connor began to organise pilgrimages in earnest, Mary found herself there with the Geordies! "I will never forget my first pilgrimage to Lourdes. It was with Hexham and Newcastle and I was with my mother and aunt," she says. "I had just qualified as a State Registered Nurse in the June of that year and my aunt promised £5 to spend in Lourdes provided I could save the £10 fare."

We have now been introduced to some of the key players in the history of pilgrimage to Lourdes from Middlesbrough. Jackie Muir set up the Knights, where a popular tradition of sending pilgrims to join the National Pilgrimage was nurtured. These pioneers made sure pilgrimage to Lourdes was a constant part of Catholic life in the Middlesbrough area. Their part in our story is almost over but their influence will be enduring. Harry Kelly and Barney Connelly we will meet again. But for now we must pick up the main strand of the story of the Diocesan Pilgrimage, and here we find Dr Bill Boyes and his wife Barbara, who took Canon Rickaby to Lourdes for his first pilgrimage in 1949.

Chapter Four

UNDER ONE BANNER

An historic milestone: The sick pilgrims and helpers of the first official Diocesan Pilgrimage to Lourdes in 1952.

THERE are many people without whom the first Middlesbrough Diocesan Pilgrimage to Lourdes would not have happened, that much is certain. Sadly, it is just as certain that some will remain hidden, some who worked hard and played vital roles yet do not figure here. What we know for sure is that without Bill and Barbara Boyes we would not have seen pilgrims walking behind the Middlesbrough banner at Lourdes at all. The first child of John and Mary Wordsworth, Mary

Barbara Wordsworth was born in Leeds on October 24 1920. Older sister to Marjorie and John, Barbara, as she became known, grew up with them first in Wetherby and later in York after the family moved there. Barbara attended the Bar Convent School and during her time there had her first experience of a Lourdes pilgrimage. It was a very private affair. At the age of 15 she travelled to Lourdes along with the National Pilgrimage in 1936. This is a very small but important part of our jigsaw, for she would carry a love of Lourdes and a desire to return there into her adult life. Her first pilgrimage was to have a profound effect.

"I travelled privately with the school French Mistress, Miss Catcheside," recalled Barbara. "She asked me if I would like to go to Lourdes. It was the summer of 1936 and I had to ask permission from my parents. Once they had agreed I discovered that I would have to make my own way to London because I would be joining the pilgrimage there. Then I discovered that I would have to look after a sick lady who was to be put on the train at Newcastle. I was joining the train at York and was supposed to care for this lady who I had never met until we reached London. When I got on the train I had to look for the sick lady everywhere. Eventually I found her in a stretcher on the floor of the guard's van. I was only 15 and didn't really know what to do. To make matters worse I discovered the lady couldn't speak. I only had to get her to London, but my goodness me, it was a long enough journey! I had to work out what to feed her so I had to get the chef from the restaurant car to come and see her. It's funny how things stick in your mind. That certainly does. All I remember about the rest of the trip is that in France the train would often stop in the middle of nowhere and we would be allowed to alight to stretch our legs."

Now a fully-trained secretary working for the Railway Hotels, Barbara married Bill, then a non-Catholic, and they moved up to Middlesbrough during the Second World War, buying a house in Lambeth Road. William Boyes was born in York on November 8 1917, the son of George and Alice and younger brother to a sister whom he never knew as she died aged nine months. Having attended the Knavesmire Primary School and then St Peter's School, Bill went to the University of Leeds from 1937 to 1944 to study Medicine. He held the post of House Officer in Harrogate for six months in 1944 and during this time he and Barbara married. Their move to Lambeth Road was to accommodate Bill's new post at Middlesbrough General Hospital, were he worked for a period of only six months again. From here Bill moved to West Lane Hospital, then the Infectious Diseases Hospital, and after two years he joined Joe Maccabe's General Practice.

The part played in the foundation of the Diocesan Pilgrimage by Dr Maccabe and his wife Phyllis has proved difficult to clarify, but it should not be underestimated. They themselves were very active Catholics of some standing locally. Indeed, it seems Joe was at the right hand of Bishop Shine and also Bishop Brunner in many of their undertakings. Joe was a natural leader and to say Phyllis was a powerful personality is an understatement. Joe Maccabe found himself and his wife in this position not simply because of their social standing in a relatively small town. Joe was the president of the Middlesbrough and district Council of Catholic Action, which was an official Church body formed in 1937. With the threat of war in Europe yet again, Pius XI ordered the foundation of such an organisation in each diocese. Catholic Action was essentially a lay organisation formed to ensure the Church's survival in Europe if the Nazis persecuted the clergy. Joe's position here led to other local responsibilities which made him a force of some considerable power.

Living in Lambeth Road put the Boyes family within the parish boundaries of the Sacred Heart - then called St Philomena's - on Linthorpe Road. The parish the Maccabe's called home was the Marist Parish of The Holy Name of Mary on The Avenue, in Linthorpe. Barbara's warm practice of her faith was having a lasting effect on Bill. Father Rickaby, later to become Canon Rickaby and known to many as 'Ric', was curate at St Philomena's and in 1949 when, after completing his Military Service, Bill made enquiries about becoming a Catholic, it was he who instructed him.

Bill tells us what happened next. "Fr Rickaby was in our house one night and Barbara asked him if he had ever been to Lourdes. He said he hadn't but would love to go. So Barbara and I looked at each other and told him we would take him. We booked on a Catholic Association trip on a 'No Night Travel Group', hoping we would get a night's rest in a proper bed along the way. We made our way down to London and then took a train to the coast. We arrived in Paris fairly late in the evening and when we got to the Hotel we found they had prepared a meal for us.

There were about 30 people in our group by now. After the meal I remember we were looking forward to our beds but the Hotelier announced he had arranged for us all to go on a sightseeing tour of Paris. We all went and it was very interesting but we got back to the hotel at about 3am and had to be up to get the train at 5am. So much for no night travel! We did everything in Lourdes. I was very fortunate, I had been received into the Church by then. We had Mass in the Grotto and Mass at the Twelfth Station, which in those days was quite something. Also Canon Rickaby was able to say Mass in one of the private side altars in the Upper Basilica. It was a very special week. While we were there Ric said he thought it would be a good idea for us, the Diocese, to have a Pilgrimage of our own. Of course we agreed. He told us he would go and see Bishop Shine when he got back."

This decision of Father Rickaby's is the keystone for all the other events in this book. Although we know Bishop Shine had been a keen Lourdes pilgrim, it is far from certain that Canon Rickaby would have known that as he arranged to see him in 1949. Bill Boyes had already agreed to act as Medical Officer for the pilgrimage providing Bishop Shine approved the whole idea. The meeting took place within a week of their return.

Bill recalls: "A week or so after we got back I asked Ric if he had seen the Bishop and he said he had. I think he went in a state of fear and trepidation because I remember Bishop Shine as a very autocratic man. Ric told me he had told the Bishop that he thought,

Canon Gerard T Rickaby heading for the Grotto at Lourdes.

in his own humble way, that there should be a Diocesan Pilgrimage to Lourdes. Apparently the Bishop never said a word but listened intently as the whole idea was unfolded before him. In the end he told Canon Rickaby that if he thought it was a good idea, he'd better get on and organise it! That was in 1949 and we got the thing off the ground in 1952."

Fr Rickaby had taken up his appointment as Curate at St Philomena's after returning from a spell as Secretary to the Apostolic Delegate in London. This is a crucial appointment for our story. If he had not been appointed here he would not have met Bill and Barbara. But he also found himself in the middle of a political situation which probably helped his ambition of establishing a Diocesan Pilgrimage more than he could have realised at the time. His Parish Priest, Mgr Dunne, was also the Vicar General and great friends with the Maccabes. Although only speculation, it is likely that as standard procedure Bishop Shine would consult his Vicar General regarding Fr Rickaby's proposal. The fact that the Vicar General was also Rickaby's Parish Priest can only have helped his cause.

Fr Rickaby, newly returned to the Diocese from London, was certainly one of the stronger characters on the Middlesbrough scene at the time. This, along with the fact that he had proved himself during his time with the Apostolic Delegate as one well able to organise, led to his appointment as Pilgrimage Director. It seems only natural that when looking for a Medical Director he should turn to his friend Bill Boyes. The fact that Bill was part of Joe Maccabe's Practice aides the establishment of the Pilgrimage. Joe not only gave Bill the time he needed to spend on the Pilgrimage, he was keen to be a part of the Pilgrimage himself. It cannot have been easy for Bill to work alongside Joe Maccabe, but he was of a naturally sunny disposition.

As soon as the word was given the organisation began. It is clear to see that there were plenty of people around with experience of Lourdes and these people were called into play. Canon Rickaby appointed Mary Mulholland as Matron. Mary's brother John was a priest in the Southwark Diocese and she had been to Lourdes many times with him. She knew all about the medical equipment that would be needed and gave this new venture a solid grounding. Eileen McElhatton was the first Head Handmaid and Harry Kelly was the Head Brancardier. Dr Maccabe joined Bill Boyes on the medical team. Although Bishop Shine had endorsed the establishment of the Diocesan Pilgrimage, he never actually joined them. He was now in his 80s and passed on many of his duties to Bishop Brunner, his Auxiliary.

Three years to bring the idea to fruition may seem like a long time, but Barbara pointed out: "Nothing had been done in this way before, at least not by us and we wanted to make sure we were doing it right. That mattered for all of the pilgrims but especially for the sick." By 1952, Fr Rickaby had left Middlesbrough for St William's School, Market Weighton, towards the South of the Diocese. The years between Rickaby's first visit to Lourdes and 1952 saw much movement of clergy within the Diocese. Many of the priests on the move in those years are key figures in the development of the Pilgrimage. Mgr Dunne, Rickaby's former Parish Priest and the Vicar General, had died in 1951. Bishop Brunner, who had been appointed Auxiliary Bishop in 1946, succeeded him as Vicar General in that same year. By this time Bishop Shine had become very frail and moved to the Convent at Whitby to be cared for by the sisters there. Bishop Brunner was in Hull at the time and was great friends with Fr Walter O'Connor SM, also in Hull living in the Marist Community there along with Fr Walter Symes SM.

As we shall see, these three from the south of the Diocese were as keen as those in the north to develop a Diocesan Pilgrimage because of their own experiences, but before they could do so they would all be on the move. After his appointment as Vicar General in 1952 because of the incapacity of Bishop Shine, it became necessary for Bishop Brunner to move to Bishop's House in Middlesbrough. He was soon to be joined in the town by Fr Walter O'Connor and Fr Walter Symes, who found themselves moving back to the parish of the Holy Name of Mary.

Fr O'Connor was a huge supporter of the venture. He was an experienced pilgrim who had taken a small party to Lourdes privately, without the assistance of the National Pilgrimage or the Catholic Association, in 1948. He was as keen as Bill, Barbara and Canon Rickaby to see a Diocesan Pilgrimage established. He was also very friendly with the Boyes family and was a patient under Bill, who remembers a visit to his surgery by Fr Walter in 1951. "He came to me complaining of chest pain," he says. "I sent him for an X-ray and the specialist found shadows on Fr Walter's lung. He was told he would be seen very quickly by a consultant. Fr Walter told the specialist he would not be seen that quickly because he was going to Lourdes. Of course, the specialist advised against it, saying he needed urgent attention. Fr Walter won the day and went to Lourdes. Upon his return he reported to the consultant, who could find nothing wrong with him. A new X-ray showed no shadows on the lung at all."

The itinerary for the first Middlesbrough Diocesan Pilgrimage to Lourdes sets out the Pilgrimage Organising Committee as it was then. It was a very clerical affair. The Pilgrimage Leader was The Rt Rev Bishop Brunner VG, and the Organising Secretary was Rev G T Rickaby. Two area representatives supported them, Rev W O'Connor SM in Middlesbrough and Rev W Symes SM in Hull. The Marist Fathers play a huge part in the early life of the Pilgrimage. Indeed, from their base at 50a The Avenue, Linthorpe they provided help, expertise and support of every kind from the earliest days. They even allowed all the equipment to be stored in their cellar. Today that same building is the home of the Diocesan Curial Offices and the Marists are long gone but the cellar still remains the Lourdes Store. The Marists' devotion and dedication to the place of Our Lady in the life of the Church is as important to our Diocese as Bishop Lacy's devotion to Our Lady of Perpetual Help. Fr Michael Coleman SM, son of Johnny Coleman, the man who persuaded Barney Connolly to make his first air pilgrimage, is the inaugural Director of The Marist Way, and continues to organise pilgrimages to many shrines across Europe. Lourdes is one of the cornerstones of his continuing work.

In a similarly effective way their devotion rubs off on others. Indeed, Harry Kelly, the first Head Brancardier of the Diocesan Pilgrimage was influenced by none other than Fr Walter O'Connor SM.

Eileen, Harry's daughter, tells us more. "My parents, Harry and Betty, were both natives of Middlesbrough and spent most of their lives teaching in the town's Catholic schools," she says. "The majority of their time was spent on the staff of St Mary's College, the grammar school run by the

Marist College staff pictured in the early 1950s including Harry Kelly (back row fourth left) and Fr Walter O'Connor SM (front row fourth left).

Marist Fathers. One of the Marist Fathers, Fr Walter O'Connor, who had spent time in Marist foundations in France, was an aficionado of Lourdes. His enthusiasm communicated itself to many, including my parents, who had been friends of his for many years. Consequently the very first time my brother and I were taken abroad was in 1951 when we drove in the family Vauxhall 10 from Middlesbrough to Lourdes, calling at Lisieux, Paray le Monial and Nevers en route. At the time my brother was five and I was ten. We were amazed at the greetings proffered by the French as we travelled: plainly the GB plate on the car gave the stimulus for the many waves and Victory V signs we received. My mother had visited Lourdes as a schoolgirl with a party from St Mary's Convent FCJ but this was my father's first visit. We all returned uplifted by the experience, as is so often the case."

During her recollections Eileen provides another piece of the jigsaw that is the origin of the Pilgrimage. She says: "It was about this time, as I understand it, that Bishop Brunner, who had been a fellow pupil of my father's at St Mary's College and who was the Auxiliary Bishop of the Diocese, decided to make use of the enthusiasm arising from Fr Walter's ardent devotion to Lourdes and thus the first Diocesan Pilgrimage to Lourdes was scheduled for August 1952."

Rather than discount any of the stories that point to how the pilgrimage was founded, it is probably best to include them all in what is a fascinating historical landscape. The story of pilgrims from the Diocese of Middlesbrough to Lourdes is a fascinating one based on growing devotion to Mary, the message of Our Lady of Lourdes, miraculous cures and the faith of many ordinary people. What we have pieced together here and even those tales that are gone and lost all helped to build up sufficient momentum in 1952 to begin what has become both an annual pilgrimage and an epic journey.

Josie Coughlan was half of a great Lourdes husband and wife team. She was Matron while Jim was Head Brancardier, and he was also Fr Walter O'Connor's nephew. Josie, who remembers Tom Hoy as caretaker of the Cathedral School, has a similar view to Eileen when she recalls the first Pilgrimage.

"Bishop Brunner requested a Pilgrimage and Fr Rickaby was appointed as director," she says. "He was fortunate to have a great deal of help from Fr O'Connor, a South Bank boy. Fr Walter had a wonderful personality and terrific kindness and rapport with the sick pilgrims. He loved Lourdes, it was no trouble for him to go and visit prospective sick pilgrims in their homes encouraging them to make a pilgrimage."

Josie is one of many women who have given service to the Middlesbrough Pilgrimage over the years. It began in an unlikely way in 1951 under the influence of the Marists, with whom she first visited Lourdes. She says: "It was a pilgrimage organised by Fr Jones SM. We travelled by train, boat and coach and visited the Shrines of France on our way down to Lourdes. We stayed there a few days and I left vowing I would not return. I found the French pilgrims very pushy, they seemed to regard the shrine as their property and consequently have to be the first at everything. This upset me greatly and I had no desire to return."

But Josie's wish to stay far away from Lourdes was a vain one as she herself admits. "I possibly hadn't reckoned on the power of Our Lady as I have now completed 51 years of pilgrimages. Naturally, in 1952, many volunteer staff were needed to look after the sick while travelling and for the five days spent in Lourdes. I was asked to go to work as a nurse and I must have forgotten my vow never to return as I said a most decided 'Yes'."

A minimum of 300 passengers was needed to make the pilgrimage work. A decision regarding the viability of the venture was to be made on December 31 1951, a date which explains the years between the Boyes' trip to Lourdes with Fr Rickaby and the work that had to be done before August 4 1952. The Evening Gazette of that day tells us that all the work paid off.

Middlesbrough Station must have been one of the busiest in the North East today when hundreds of Roman Catholics saw the start of the Middlesbrough Diocesan pilgrimage to Lourdes. The pilgrimage headed by the Auxiliary Bishop of Middlesbrough (the Rt Rev G Brunner) who joined the special train at its start in Middlesbrough, included 30 sick people, some of them stretcher cases, who hoped to be healed.

Over 250 people went from Middlesbrough and at Northallerton and York the train was joined by others taking part. Among the Northallerton party were sick people from the St John of God Hospital at Scorton. The train will take the pilgrimage to London, where they will be joined by more people from the North East, and the party will then go on to Newhaven from where they sail to Dieppe before the journey overland to Lourdes.

Director of the pilgrimage is the Rev G Rickaby, of Market Weighton, and formerly of St Philomena's, Middlesbrough. The party was accompanied by Doctors JE Maccabe and W Boyes of Middlesbrough and by 15 nursing sisters.

Many of the sick people are paralysis cases. Among the pilgrims who went from Middlesbrough were three sick children. One of them, a boy of 14, is still suffering from the effects of bomb blast, while a 14-year-old girl in the party has been deaf from birth. They will stay in Lourdes about a week.

A small scrap of paper among Bill Boyes' notes tells us of the numbers more accurately. A total of 454 people made that first Pilgrimage, of whom 30 were sick pilgrims

Photo: David Boyes

A Lourdes Family: Bill and Barbara Boyes with their sons Tim, Dom, Mike and David.

Chapter Five

PLANES

THE development of regular passenger air services across Europe and our use of charter aircraft for the Pilgrimage go hand in hand. It may be surprising for some to learn that the first plane transporting Middlesbrough Pilgrims to Lourdes took to the skies in 1954. But it should come as no surprise to anyone that it was the brainchild of Barney Connelly. Barney did not actually travel to Lourdes until after his marriage in 1949. He and his family had moved from Stockton to Middlesbrough in 1929. Barney says he has only been involved in the Diocesan Pilgrimage to Lourdes since about 1980. He is keen to point out that he was never involved in the organisation of the Diocesan Pilgrimage at all.

"I was very much aware of the pilgrimage and the planning," he says. "Dr Maccabe was my father's best friend and Canon Rickaby was a priest in our parish, so I was very aware of the early plans though I was not involved in any way. I made my first pilgrimage to Lourdes just before the first Diocesan Pilgrimage. I went by air, under the persuasion of John Coleman. We flew from Liverpool, which was the only way to get there by air in those days. We flew on the Wilson Service, who ran Dakotas and a horrible little plane called a Rapide."

At the time Barney was working for the Catholic ship owner and travel agent named Colonel John Peckston. John had unsuccessfully bid to become the carrier for the Diocesan Pilgrimage and according to Barney, once he lost the bid did very little to help in any way. But it was during his time with Peckston that Barney gained invaluable experience. He ran the first ever charter flight from the north of England when he was asked to make arrangements for all the Irish doctors working in the North East to get home to Dublin for the rugby!

This experience, coupled with Barney's first experience of Lourdes other than those hand me down stories from his grandmother, left him wildly enthusiastic to run a pilgrimage by air from

Middlesbrough. He did his best to persuade John Peckston to provide such a service but he refused, saying that it was not a viable proposition. He would be proved right but Barney was so enthusiastic for the project that he eventually left the service of John Peckston to see his dream through.

"There was a firm in Stockton called Roberts Tours who had just begun to operate Dakota aircraft to Jersey," says Barney. "This was the first holiday traffic out of Teesside. Arising from the service I had run to Dublin with Frank Pilling, now of Roberts Tours, I came across three gentlemen called Barnaby, Keegan and Stephens, who belonged to Northampton. They operated a small charter firm called BKS which became the largest of its time. I had arranged that John Peckston would become the agent in this enterprise for BKS, but he wouldn't put the brass in. So I took the whole proposition to Roberts Tours and I launched for them the weekly air service for 11 weeks in the summer. We had to run a service at least half-full out and half-full back 11 times to make any money. We could only afford to have one break and, of course, it didn't work. I ran it for six years and we lost money every year. To be fair to Roberts Tours, they carried the cost. Our downfall was simple; we couldn't fill the aircraft every week. It was then that I realised what John Peckston had recognised as the flaw in the plan all along. The earlier system had failed over here but had been a roaring success in Liverpool, simply because the Irish were using the ferry to get to Liverpool to catch the plane, and so they had a great many more pilgrims."

These very early flights were well documented by the Gazette. The first was reported on June 3 1954.

The first aircraft to fly from the North East to Lourdes was blessed by the Bishop of Leeds, the Rt Rev J C Heenan, before departure at Greatham Airport today. In a short service the Bishop was assisted by the Rev J Gannon, parish priest of St Teresa, Owton Manor, West Hartlepool. The Auxiliary Bishop of Middlesbrough, who will go by train with 400 pilgrims tomorrow, was present. Today's departure was the start of the annual pilgrimage to Lourdes from Middlesbrough and Leeds. After prayers in which the pilgrims joined, the Bishop went round the aircraft, a 36-seat Dakota, sprinkling holy water. The Bishop, himself one of the pilgrims, was flying for the first time to Lourdes. Today's pilgrims went from Leeds. Tomorrow 36 pilgrims from Middlesbrough will fly out.

The flight took five hours and included a 30-minute stop over in Jersey at lunchtime for refueling. By today's standards it was a long haul, but it was almost revolutionary then compared to the 30 hours taken by train and boat. However, the real matters of interest are behind the headlines. Why was the Bishop of Leeds blessing a plane in the Diocese of Hexham and Newcastle carrying Middlesbrough pilgrims? The fact that there was a plane to bless at all is another example of how events have dovetailed so well down through the years to make the pilgrimage work. The plane in question was part of the BKS fleet, which had only very recently begun to operate.

It was not always fixed which of the airports, Greatham, near Hartlepool, Woolsington, just north west of Newcastle, or Yeadon between Leeds and Bradford, was the departure point for the Lourdes flights. Getting customs clearance at Hartlepool in the early days was difficult. Indeed, the flights relied on the good nature of two Middlesbrough customs officials who attended the Greatham flights as a special favour. When their attendance was in doubt flights went from Newcastle and Yeadon. Customs clearance at Greatham was always a problem, which was solved by Roberts Tours providing a taxi for the customs officials and a private fee for their out of hours work. Barney recalls those pioneering flights fondly.

The first Middlesbrough pilgrims to travel by air boarding the BKS Dakota at Greatham Airfield near Hartlepool in 1954.

Photo: B Toolin

"I ran a weekly service and to do that properly I made about six trips out to Lourdes to get to grips with what pilgrims would face upon their arrival," he said. "I had been critical of this part of the trip I'd made from Liverpool. Once we arrived we were left to our own devices, sometimes even without a chaplain. I was keen that a priest should be commissioned for each trip in advance and fully instructed as to what would be expected of him. All of a sudden I found myself very popular with the Diocesan clergy, who cottoned on to the notion that they were in line for a free week in Lourdes in exchange for acting as chaplain. This was difficult because I had to choose them myself! At the time I thought it was very important that they should be able to speak French, which took me to the French Master at Ampleforth, a priest called Fr Basil Hume. He took one group and then booked the plane for the Ampleforth Pilgrimage later in the year."

In the 1930s Barney had become deeply involved in the annual St Vincent de Paul (SVP) Boys' Camp at Ampleforth. The destination was the hockey pitch there and the whole concept was aimed at the welfare of young boys. This became one of the foundations on which the Young Christian Workers (YCW) movement was founded. It wholly occupied Barney for some years and brought him into contact and friendship with the bishops of Leeds, Hexham and Newcastle and Middlesbrough. It is an interesting detail of history that each of these three men were also friends of Joseph Scott, who inspired Jackie Muir to establish the Knights of St Columba in Middlesbrough, all having studied at the priests' training college at Ushaw.

Barney's contact in the Ampleforth Community was Basil Hume. They brought into the YCW some of the young men who attended the Ampleforth event. The founder of the Middlesbrough YCW was Fr Oswin Corboy. On September 3 1939, at St Philomena's in Middlesbrough, Fr Corboy, Fr Rickaby's fellow curate, held the foundation meeting of the YCW. This is important background

REACHING FOR THE SKY

The BKS story is the tale of one man's vision, of how Cyril Stevens and his partners with just a lone DC3 built an airline and placed the three northern airfields of Newcastle, Teesside and Leeds/Bradford firmly on the aviation map. On the February 7 1952, BKS Aerocharter Ltd (the name standing for the initials of the founders, James Barnaby, Thomas Keegan and Cyril Stevens) began flying from Southend Airport.

The aircraft was a DC3 G-AIWE formerly owned by Crewsair. The three founders were offered it in lieu of shares in the company when it encountered difficulties and started to flounder. The DC3 flew livestock to Florence and Milan on that first day. Just two years before the Lourdes charter began the company had only one aircraft.

The DC3 was sold by BKS in April and with the proceeds two DC3s were purchased from the RAF. The sister company, BKS Engineering Limited, was formed in January 1952 and was responsible for the high standard of maintenance applied to the BKS fleet from the start of the company's services. In 1953, at the beginning of the season, another two DC3s were purchased from the RAF. At the end of the season a fifth DC3 was bought.

BKS flew two DC3 services a week from Southend to Corsica for Horizon Holidays, offering 14-day holidays for under £40. On May 18 1953 the first scheduled service began from Greatham Airport, West Hartlepool, to Northolt. This service continued until 1956. In 1953 the company employed about 50 people. At the beginning of 1954 the name was changed to BKS Air Transport Ltd. BKS started running charters for Robert Tours from Woolsington Airport, Newcastle.

as we piece together another part of the jigsaw. When Barney turned his attention to the possibility of a flight from the North East to Lourdes he did so with a lot of advice from Basil Hume. Perhaps then, as much as to Bishop Lacy, Tom Hoy and the Marist Fathers, we also owe a debt of gratitude to the Monks of Ampleforth Abbey. It was Fr Basil who arranged the first air journey with BKS for the Ampleforth pilgrimage.

Barney was keen from the very beginning that he was not to be seen as a travel agent. He had a very real lifelong love of Lourdes and his driving force was a desire for people to experience a pilgrimage there. Very aware of his duty to the Diocese of Middlesbrough, he was also eager to speak to the Bishop and gain his approval for the flights. Of course, potential pilgrims would also come from the Diocese of Hexham and Newcastle and the Diocese of Leeds, so he would have to speak to all three bishops, a task which did not fill him with dread, as he already knew them all!

"I went to see them and put it to them that I wanted to operate the whole venture from Greatham Airport so I could attract pilgrims from all three diocese. I got a very interesting response. Bishop Brunner told me there was no way he could endorse a commercial service. I didn't want him to endorse what we were doing, I wanted him to say we were doing it with his authority. He refused and quizzed me about our proposed itinerary. He wanted to know if we were going to take people up the mountains and to the seaside. I told him very clearly that I was planning a pilgrimage, not a holiday. I had to give Bishop Brunner an undertaking that I would stick rigidly to a pilgrimage programme, in return for which he allowed me to say that he did not object to my proposal."

It was less than Barney had hoped for, but he was over the first hurdle and headed for Hexham and Newcastle to see Bishop McCormack. He too questioned Barney vigorously. "In the end he told me he was satisfied I would do a proper job but that I had to abide by his rules," says Barney. "I had to agree because Greatham Airport was in his Diocese."

A week later Barney received a letter outlining ten conditions he had to satisfy. The letter no longer exists, but Barney obviously managed to satisfy Bishop McCormack as the aircraft did get off the ground. The next visit was to Leeds to see Bishop Heenan. This was to be a much more positive meeting. "I got a marvellous reception from Bishop Heenan and he told me he thought the whole thing was a wonderful idea," he says. "In fact he said he would be on the first plane! This seems to me to be a very interesting response from three very different characters at a moment in time."

Gripping conversation: Cardinal Hume listens to a young Middlesbrough pilgrim's Lourdes story.

Photo: Ita Leahy

These differing reactions explain why it was Bishop Heenan who blessed the plane and Bishop Brunner merely attended. After the service, Bishop Heenan boarded the plane while Bishop Brunner went home and travelled by train the following day.

"Now I was in trouble, as I have been ever since, because this was expressly not part of the Diocesan Pilgrimage! It became part of the Leeds Diocesan Pilgrimage by default as Bishop Heenan and his pilgrimage staff travelled on the aircraft. Curiously, the Middlesbrough party included Mgr Willie Brunner, Bishop Brunner's brother. Both Bishop Brunner and Father Rickaby gave me a lot of help."

This annual series of flights took place for the next six years as a commercial venture on behalf of Roberts Tours run by Barney. He did something nobody else had done at the time. He personally chose the priest for each flight - Fr Louis Collingwood, Fr Roland Connelly SM, Fr Basil Hume OSB, Fr Maurice Hardy and Fr Oliver Plunkett.

"While in Lourdes myself I met an extraordinary character who was to become a large part of my life," says Barney. "He was called Henri Lancien and he was well known in Lourdes. He was a Welshman with a French father and lived in Lourdes, working as a freelance guide. He was a pious man with a great devotion to St Bernadette. If I got my devotion to Our Lady of Lourdes from my grandmother, my devotion to Bernadette comes directly from Henri. He became my agent at the other end. He met every plane, got them through customs and organized them. The real idea for a regular air service was Johnny Coleman's. I discussed it with Father Rickaby, Bishop Brunner and Dr Maccabe in the Hotel De La Grotte in Lourdes, because that was always where Bishop Brunner

CARDINAL HUME AND LOURDES

The man who eventually became Cardinal Hume is a character who certainly plays his part in our story. Not only was he one of the people who helped make things happen for pilgrims before 1952, but he helped instigate the Ampleforth pilgrimage and was always a welcome visitor to the Middlesbrough ward at the hospital when his time in Lourdes coincided with ours. In his book, *Ampleforth: The Story of St Laurence's*, Anselm Cramer, monk of Ampleforth, tells us a little more:

"One particular way in which the faith took practical form was the pilgrimage to Lourdes, which combined the joys of expedition with an extremely valuable and very much appreciated service to the sick. There were school groups which visited Lourdes between the wars: individuals had of course gone before that period. But after the Second World War travel became increasingly easier, and in 1953 Fr Basil, ten years before he was Abbot, joined Fr Martin Haigh in establishing what was definitely an Ampleforth pilgrimage. The first pilgrimage was notable for its difficulties of travel, since while they were there all France became strike bound. Beginning every other year and later annually, an ever larger group of monks, bys, sisters, parents, friends and relations accompanied an ever growing number of sick, often very sick people, and helped them to have a memorable spiritual experience, as indeed the helpers found they had themselves. Fr Martin led the pilgrimage arrangements for 25 years, before other duties took him from it, but the annual event in July had for a long time been an established fixture, and a source of grace for all."

stayed. The owner of the Hotel, Louis Guingene, wanted to be in the forefront of improving the services of Lourdes. He was ambitious to bring people to Lourdes by air. One must remember we were working with Dakota aircraft, no others, because they were able to take off and land on grass. This was the ground surface at both Greatham and Tarbes. Louis Guingene was keen to be involved in the airport and he saw me as a way of doing that. He was enormously generous. I booked a group of 36 people for 11 weeks without paying a deposit and he charged me the same price as a two-star hotel, so I owe a strong personal debt to him. He even came to Middlesbrough several times to attend meetings. The inspiration for the air service came from Johnny Coleman, but I got practical advice and lots of help from Fr Walter O'Connor."

Despite not being part of the Official Pilgrimage as such, the Pilgrimage Handbook for 1954 does list all 36 of the air passengers, including the Vicar General, Fr Walter O'Connor SM, and his sister, who was Mother General of the Irish Assumption Sisters. This trend would continue as long as the flights did. However, Barney found he would soon have to stop being involved with the flights. He was being employed on a meagre wage by Roberts Tours and he now had four children. Had the flights been a commercial success, Barney would have received a pay rise. It was not to be.

"Fr Walter O'Connor introduced me to a lady called Bernadette McGrogan, now Mrs Toolin," he says. "She was a high-ranking private secretary to one of the directors of Dorman Long. When I needed any kind of help in organising Lourdes she helped me. Although Roberts Tours could no longer afford to pay me, they did pay her, although much less than she was paid by Dorman Long."

Bernadette was of such a calibre that she soon took it on. So it continued to be a service with which I was involved but Bernadette did everything. She developed it and it led to her forming her own travel agency when Roberts Tours gave up the Lourdes service as non-profitable."

Bernadette McGrogan joined the staff of Roberts Tours at their office in Middlesbrough's Finkle Street in April 1954. She took on much of the work Barney had done as he began to canvas for parliament. She recalls the early years of her involvement. "The BKS service usually left Newcastle Airport in those days, although we chartered another service from Leeds Airport, as at that time Middlesbrough and Leeds Diocesan Pilgrimages travelled together."

Newcastle Airport was twice the size of Lourdes Airport - the entire complex consisted of two tin sheds while Lourdes only had one! Bernadette recalls how this affected the process of checking in and boarding the aircraft. "It makes me laugh now to think of all the pilgrims standing around on the airfield waiting for the steps to arrive so they could get on the plane," she says. "I remember Barney never travelled to Lourdes at the same time as me, but we were always on the photo together. He would just saunter around to the plane and line up with the rest of us. Try doing that today and I'd be visiting him in jail! What a changing world."

Although this air service was not part of the official Pilgrimage, Bernadette speaks with affection of the Pilgrimage officials at the time. She certainly enjoyed a close working relationship with them. "I think one of the Grangetown Walshes was the Matron," she says. "Eileen McElhatton was in charge of the handmaids, strongly supported by Mildred Raw."

The first year of Bernadette's involvement was memorable because of a railway strike which began in England while the pilgrims were in Lourdes. "I had to ask some of the air passengers to give up their seats so the sick could return by air," she recalls. "I then led a contingent of volunteers home overland. I recall that Fr Walter gave the Gazette a glowing report about it."

Fr Walter O'Connor was so supportive of the air service that he travelled back with them on several occasions, taking groups quite separately from the Diocesan Pilgrimage in the month of September. In 1972 Bernadette took the risk and booked the first Jumbo Jet for the Pilgrimage, with Barney acting as courier.

"I can recall being on the inaugural flight for travel agents from Teesside Airport," she says. "Shortly after that I chartered the same aircraft for Lourdes. The same year the Diocesan Pilgrimage chartered a similar aircraft. Mine went with Getaway Travel and Fr Rickaby was none too pleased with me. In the event both aircraft were filled."

The railways were beginning to scrap their wartime Ambulance Cars and this alone would eventually close the rail service for sick pilgrims. Eventually all heavy traffic to Lourdes would be by air. The airports at both ends now had concrete runways and the world of the travelling pilgrim had changed. The future was air travel. However, it would be many years before the pilgrimage trains were finally abandoned, allowing sick and able-bodied pilgrims all to take to the skies together.

Of course, these flights were not the only ones to be operated even in those early days. And the founding of the Diocesan Pilgrimage did not automatically mean all pilgrims travelled that way. Flo

WHEN IS A JUMBO A JUMBO?

Today there are 1,193 Boeing 747s in service. This unique giant of aviation has transported 2.2 billion people, which equals 40% of the world's population. But is this the aircraft the pilgrims of the early 70s called a Jumbo Jet?

The 747 story began in 1965, when Pan American World Airways asked Boeing to develop a commercial airliner which could transport 400 passengers over a distance of 5,000km. The first 747 into service, Jumbo 001, received its certification on 30 December 1969. From 1970 Boeing expanded its program by taking on the 747-200 with wider range and bigger payload.

However, it seems unlikely that the huge demand for this new giant of the skies would have allowed it to be used by our pilgrims so shortly after it had come into service. Surely a small number of passengers from a small regional airport could not have hoped for one of these aircraft.

Much more likely is the possibility that the plane referred to as a Jumbo Jet was a Boeing 727 or 737. This would tally with the fact that according to the records of Teesside International Airport, the first time a 747 landed there was for the Lourdes Pilgrimage of 1990. That particular Jumbo was operated by Air France and made all the local papers at the time simply for being the first.

McCunnell, who was one of the pilgrims who celebrated Mass in Rome before the icon of Our Lady of Perpetual Help in 2002, recalls her first journey to Lourdes. "Peter, my husband, took out our first passport so we could go," she says. "We travelled with a firm called Pilgrim Tours and met our Spiritual Director at the Brompton Oratory, where we had our first Mass. I can't remember which of the London airports we used, but I remember the aircraft was a Dakota. It carried 31 pilgrims.

"We took our 14-year-old daughter Christine. She is now 57. We will never forget the trip. We were supposed to stay at the Hotel Rotundo but when we got there they only had one spare room. This was given to our priest and we were spread all around town. We were put over a butcher's shop and I remember him glazing pigs' heads all the time we were there.

"The group photo from that pilgrimage still hangs on the hall wall in my home alongside the group photo for the 1994 Diocesan Pilgrimage, which Peter and I made to celebrate our diamond wedding anniversary. Sadly, Peter died in 1997, but I have continued to go to Lourdes. I am hoping to be accepted as a sick pilgrim this year as I now cannot manage in a hotel. I would not be able to do a full pilgrimage without the wonderful children who help us all."

Teesside Airport was first used by Lourdes pilgrims in 1965 when an Argonaut aircraft picked up pilgrims including Bishop Wheeler. By 1967 it seems to have been the preferred departure point for the now ageing Bishop Brunner. The Evening Gazette reports peace and quiet at Middlesbrough Railway Station.

For the day on which Teesside's pilgrims set off on their journey to the Holy Shrine at Lourdes, the No.1 platform on Middlesbrough railway station was remarkably quiet at 7.59 this morning.

Instead of the usual large crowd which have featured pilgrimage days for quite a few years, there was a party of 18 schoolchildren, a priest, a nun, and a mere handful of adults today. Surprising absentees were the sick. But there has not been a drop in interest in the Lourdes pilgrimage.

For many of the pilgrims from Teesside are this year making use of Teesside Airport. The Rt Rev George Brunner, 77-year-old Bishop of Middlesbrough is leading a party which will fly from Middleton St George tonight, a party which includes the sick. Others left by coach this afternoon.

Leading a party of ten boys from St Mary's College, Middlesbrough, by train, was the Rev Reginald Riley, a French teacher at the school. He told a reporter: "We will be in Lourdes by eight tomorrow morning. Naturally we are all looking forward to it. I understand that the sick on this pilgrimage are all able to walk. In the past we have had people on stretchers and in wheelchairs."

Some of the pilgrims leaving in Teesside parties came from as far away as Hull. There were a number from the North Riding and from County Durham.

In 1985 the Diocesan Pilgrimage was forced to abandon the train for air travel *en masse* for the first time. Far from being the solution to all the challenges the train had caused over the years, it simply created its own problems. Fr Nicholson recalls some of the ups and downs of air travel.

"The plane notion grew and grew. We really have been through joys and sorrows with planes," he says. "Many pilgrims will be aware of the delays we have suffered, but there have been other crises along the way. One year the actual plane was changed the day before we were due to begin the pilgrimage. The times hadn't changed but the aircraft was not the one we had been expecting. Each year the medical team works hard to pre-seat all of the sick pilgrims near the front of the aircraft, placing them near nurses, brancardiers and handmaids so that they can be watched and cared for during the flight. Getting such a seating plan together

Photo: Middlesbrough Evening Gazette

Ready to pick up Middlesbrough pilgrims in 1990, the first Boeing 747 Jumbo Jet to land at Teesside dwarfs the airport terminal.

takes hours and hours. When the plane changed at the last minute our plan was out of the window and we had to start from scratch."

Modern day experiences of making the pilgrimage by air have been marked by triumph and disaster. Few people who experienced them will forget the severe delays caused by technical problems with our chartered aircraft in both 1997 and 2001. Yet few people will forget that the first Jumbo Jet ever to fly into Teesside airport was operated by Air France and came to take pilgrims to Lourdes.

The Evening Gazette of June 24 1997 made a little bit of history. It reported such a serious delay to the departure time that pilgrims read about their ordeal in the paper before they finally left for Lourdes.

More than 200 pilgrims faced misery at Teesside Airport. They were due to fly out to Lourdes at 9am but faced a gruelling nine-hour delay. Their Air Holland plane had been hit by technical difficulties outside the UK.

Airport staff opened another departure lounge for the stranded travellers, some of whom were ill or disabled, as they were told there was no chance of a plane arriving before 5pm. The flight out was chartered for the Middlesbrough Diocese by Tangney Tours, who desperately tried to find another plane. They finally took off just after 6pm once their original aircraft was fixed.

Airport customer services manager John Waiting said they were in good spirits despite the delay. "There were no problems, staff and helpers looked after the people who were ill or disabled. We never like to see people delayed and particularly not pilgrims going on a special weekend."

Whoever told us lightening doesn't strike twice in the same place has obviously never been to Lourdes and in 2001 history repeated itself. This time the delay was so long that the second flight to Lourdes, which did leave on time, landed in Lourdes hours before the first plane had arrived at Teesside to pick up its passengers. And this time the story managed to make front-page news in the Gazette.

Travellers on a pilgrimage to Lourdes – including several ill or disabled people – were faced with a ten-hour flight delay before their trip. The nightmare delay saw pilgrims fly out at half-past midnight on Saturday, having been scheduled to leave at 2.30pm the previous day.

Almost 500 people flew out to Lourdes on the annual pilgrimage, organised by the Middlesbrough Roman Catholic Diocese. The hitch came on Teesside Airport's busiest-ever day with around 6,000 people due to use the facility.

John Waiting, of Teesside Airport, said: "The delay was due to a technical problem on the aircraft, which was operated by Airtours. As an airport we were concerned and upset. Unfortunately there are delays but this was an exceptional delay. We were very disappointed, with particular concern for the passengers who were pilgrims."

He said airport and Airtours staff ensured waiting passengers were comfortable and provided refreshments and food at regular intervals. "The passengers who were pilgrims were in an area which was fairly calm and comfortable."

A spokeswoman for Airtours International said: "It was an unfortunate delay. As much as possible was done for the passengers. This aircraft had a problem and we got a replacement aircraft as soon as we could. Unfortunately it had a problem and our priority was to ensure passengers were as comfortable as possible. That resulted in a heavy delay."

Such a delay was unacceptable to all concerned. After much hard work everyone on the delayed flight received a financial compensation for the delay later that summer.

Flying is far and away the most popular current mode of transport for pilgrims and the advent of no-frills flying to destinations such as Biarritz followed by a train or bus journey are attractive to many. However, the actual Pilgrimage flight is keystone in the middle of all of the modes of transport as it is the only viable way of moving large numbers of sick people together.

Modern day health and safety issues coupled with travel insurance for the very ill make such a plane a necessity. Thanks to the nurses, brancs and handmaids, this flight has been staffed adequately enough over the years to take a maximum number of sick. Without them on that plane, the Pilgrimage would have no sick pilgrims.

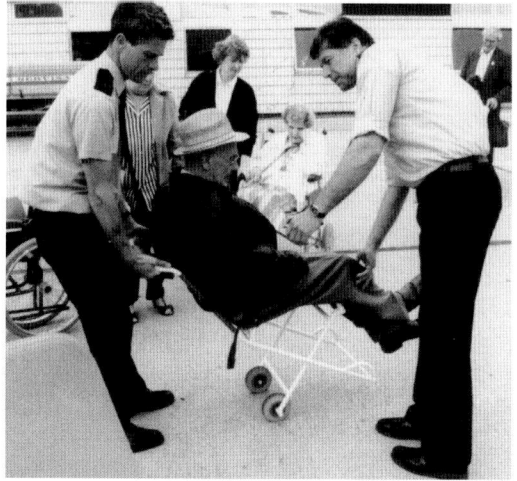

Fireman's lift: Members of Teesside Airport's fire serice help sick pilgrims board the plane for Lourdes.

Photo: Middlesbrough Evening Gazette

Chapter Six

TRAINS

BARRING delays, Lourdes is a 90-minute flight away from our Diocese today. Many of us continue to make the pilgrimage by coach in school and parish groups, while a few pilgrims still regularly travel by train. This tradition has been kept up in recent years by brancardiers Gerard Moxon and Bernard France, who leave Hull Paragon Station along with various members of their families and arrive in Lourdes before the flights. This proves invaluable as they work along with other early arrivals, including former Matron Ita Leahy, to prepare the hospital ward.

Over the years people have used almost every means of transport to make the pilgrimage, but train and boat were the original methods. Using rolling stock of Ambulance Cars from the two world wars was the best way of caring for the sick pilgrims while making the journey, although there were not always enough of them. The journeys were long and sometimes demanding, but through them a great bond was forged between pilgrims and friendships for life were formed.

Liz Boyes of York, who is not related to Bill and Barbara and their family, has made each of the Diocesan Pilgrimages and recalls her first trip as a teenager. "My two sisters and I were able to go on the first pilgrimage as young helpers," she recalls. "The trains were not like they are today. They had wooden seats and we sat bolt upright, facing each other, for the whole 27-hour journey. Some of the sick travelling with us were laid on stretchers and placed in the luggage compartment along with all the equipment. I can remember vividly having to feed one of the sick pilgrims during the journey. Him being on a stretcher, my inexperience and the movement of the train made it a very nervous time for me."

That first pilgrimage cost £27.15.0, which included third class travel in England and on the boat and second class on the Continent, all transfers, certain meals en route, full board and accommodation at second class hotels in Lourdes, pilgrim's prayer books and badges, the service of couriers and interpreters and all normal gratuities. We know this because Bill Boyes has kept every Pilgrim's Handbook for every Pilgrimage and has kept notes along with them of who travelled and when.

All travel and accommodation arrangements were made by the International Catholic Travel Service of Lanseair Travel Service Ltd, 71 Knightsbridge, London. A 'No Night Travel' section was proposed on the booking form at a cost of £33.10.0. The sums of money may seem laughable by today's standards but Agnes McGrogan, who eventually served as the Pilgrimage Matron and first travelled to Lourdes in 1957, points out that it cost about six weeks' wages to go in those days. "I was lucky because the Catholic Nurses Guild paid about a third of my fare, but it was still hard to afford," she says.

Rail tickets were not sent to individual passengers but were held by the courier in charge of the party. All one had to do to board the special train at York was show a Pilgrimage Card. Those first journeys were arduous to say the least. The travel itinerary for 1952 was as follows:

August 4	Dep	York (by Special Train) early afternoon.
		Dinner en route.
	Arr	Newhaven approximately 9pm
	Dep	Newhaven 10.40pm
August 5	Arr	Dieppe 2.10am (Holy Mass if possible).
	Dep	Dieppe approximately 4am
		Breakfast and Lunch in Restaurant Car.
	Arr	Lourdes 7.30pm
		Transfer to Hotels; dinner.
August 11		Breakfast in Hotels. Transfer to Station.
	Dep	Lourdes approximately 8am
	Arr	Dieppe midnight.
August 12	Dep	Dieppe 1.30am
	Arr	Newhaven 5am (Holy Mass if possible).
		Breakfast and Lunch en route.
	Arr	York approximately 3pm

Clearly pilgrims had to get from either Middlesbrough or Hull to York by a more regular service than the special trains. Agnes remembers her first train journey to Lourdes in 1957. She was in the nursing team and describes how work began straight away. "I recall Middlesbrough Railway Station in the cold early hours, with its steamy, coaly smells," she says. "The train made its first stop at Northallerton to pick up the sick pilgrims from the St John of God Hospital at Scorton. They were seriously dependant men and I hadn't a clue how to meet their needs. Mgr Tindall was the priest who accompanied them and he was a figure to be reckoned with. He was enormous and wore a black cassock with a purple fringe and he strode around the place fiercely defending his chaps!"

Josie Coghlan also remembers Mgr Tindall, the first Chaplain to the Sick. "The sick pilgrims from Scorton were a joy to nurse," she says. "Many were stretcher patients accompanied by Mgr Tindall, a good and holy man with a sincere love for those sick people. Many tears were shed at Northallerton Station on our return journey when we said our goodbyes."

One of the exceptional characters who was a key part in the Pilgrimage for many years boarded at Northallerton. He was Archie Coxhead, a remarkable man who from day one was indispensable to the Pilgrimage's smooth running. Everyone would come to know Archie, if only because for years the entire Pilgrimage would line up behind him as he proudly held the banner in place for the Torchlight Procession each evening.

Agnes also recalls another year when she was working in London and joined the Pilgrimage at Finsbury Park. Although she remembers no-one else joining there it seems unlikely that the train would stop to pick up a single passenger. This must have been one of the many comfort breaks needed on those mammoth treks down through England and France. During the train journey the sick pilgrims were allowed no visitors. The first Pilgrimage Handbook tells its readers: "On the journey you may NOT visit the sick without the permission of the Matron. Please keep away from the approaches to the Ambulance Car. Your presence may be obstructive as well as embarrassing."

So, what of the other pilgrims then? Frances McLoughlin, whose father Leo McLoughlin made the first 14 pilgrimages and served as Head Brancardier, travelled herself in 1958. That year the Pilgrimage was a huge affair, a joint venture for more than 1,000 pilgrims from the Diocese of Middlesbrough and the Diocese of Leeds. She was coming to the end of her final years of a French Honours degree at the University of London and at the will of Fr Rickaby, Frances worked on the Pilgrimage as a Catholic Association representative, doubling up as an interpreter.

She recalls: "The total journey time was about 36 hours – there was no Eurostar or TGV then. I remember that the French SNCF railway was very good and each train boasted a suited man who was in charge, le directeur. It was my brief to deal with him on all matters relating to the welfare of the pilgrims and passengers of the SNCF. There were six sittings for each meal on that French train and it was my job to usher the pilgrims on an accurate head count by strict rotation of coaches and carriages towards the Restaurant Car.

"There was an exact number of place settings and allocation of food allowed. When the sixth breakfast sitting had finished the first lunch sitting began almost immediately. The man in the suit would not allow any deviation from the system, no one was allowed to dine earlier or later or swap with a fellow pilgrim, as this would confuse the whole system and people would find themselves without anything to eat. This was a daunting task but I found that a little friendly persuasion kept things running smoothly."

The meals system may have been well regimented, but it didn't always go without a hitch. Brancardier Tom Waterson recalls one year when two of the passengers from Scorton ordered the most expensive bottle of wine on the menu – then disappeared leaving the next occupants of their table to foot the bill!

Fr Michael O'Connor, who later served as Chaplain to the Sick, first travelled to Lourdes by train in the early 1960s. "I'll never forget my first experience of trying to sleep on the top bunk in a compartment with five other people in it," he says. "Actually, I couldn't sleep at all. All I was conscious of was the ringing of the level crossing bells as we passed them. There must have been lots of crossings because I remember the bells ringing all night!

"Another event on the journey I remember vividly was the evening meal. We actually had a four-course dinner served in grand style. It was really enjoyable if you were on the first sitting but by the time you got to the second sitting, in my case anyway, I almost felt I had stopped being hungry."

Earlier this year the Lourdes community lost a much-loved figure with the death of former Head Brancardier John Adams. Thankfully, John wrote down some of his own Lourdes recollections before he died, leaving us an invaluable contribution to our story. "One of my first recollections as a brancardier is from an early Pilgrimage by train," he wrote. "In those days the three pilgrimages - Leeds, Lancaster and Middlesbrough - although travelling by separate trains shared a cross Channel steamer. On this occasion Middlesbrough arrived at Dover first. After moving our sick pilgrims from train to boat, we adjourned to the bar for a well-earned drink. It is as well to remember that in those days things were a lot more strenuous than now. There were very few wheelchairs, so the majority of the sick had to be carried by either stretcher or sedan chair.

"It was a warm, sticky evening and we were looking forward to quenching our thirst. However, before we had settled in the bar there was an announcement over the ship's Tannoy telling us that the Leeds Pilgrimage train had arrived. All of our brancs were required to help them board the boat. So off we went. Between our own and the Leeds brancs it did not take long to get them settled on the boat. We had barely reached the bar for that now overdue refreshment when the Tannoy once more interrupted our anticipation. The Lancaster Pilgrimage had now arrived and our assistance was once more required. After helping them we were all very tired and after eventually partaking of liquid refreshment, we found our way to our compartments for a few hours' sleep."

The journey always threw up plenty of practical challenges for John and his team to grapple with. One was the need to always have a sufficient supply of drinking water available to the handmaids for making tea.

"For the first few years we used an old milk churn carried on a specially-built carrier. This was very cumbersome and extremely heavy to lift back on to the train when filled. In later years strong plastic five-gallon containers were used, making it much easier to refill. One of the big snags was we never knew how long the train was to stop, so it was always a mad dash to find a drinking water tap and get back to the train as quickly as possible. This often occurred in the middle of the night and on more than one occasion it was touch and go as to whether the branc concerned would make it. Fortunately he always did, which was a minor miracle. The reward of having a good supply of plastic containers was that for the journey home they were filled with Lourdes water. Those that had to be used for tea were refilled as soon as possible so some of the Lourdes water could be retained."

Two other incidents stood out vividly in John's memory, both happening at Bordeaux Station one year when Middlesbrough and Leeds shared the French train.

"A request was made of the Middlesbrough brancs to assist a lady in the Leeds portion of the train to a place in the Middlesbrough Ambulance Car. On arrival there, we discovered that the lady in question had collapsed and would need to be carried by stretcher. Not only that, but owing to the lady's size she had to be carried through the open window of the carriage. Once we'd managed that, we had to carry her the length of the platform and, with inches to spare, into the Ambulance Car.

"The second memory also concerns a homeward stop at Bordeaux. It was mid-afternoon on a very hot day. Some brancs visited the wine shop on the station and bought several bottles of red and white wine. The intention was to enjoy it later in the evening along with the packed meals. Unfortunately, the heat of the day did the wine no good at all. By evening the red was barely drinkable and the white was more like vinegar. It all had to be poured down the drain."

Paul Griffiths recalls the gruelling task of transferring luggage from train to ship by trolley was thirsty work. One year branc Ken Frith and a group of nurses, including some from the Welsh National Pilgrimage who we shared the train with, could not be found with the ship about to sail. "Brancs were despatched to search the local hostelries but they couldn't be found," says Paul. "With great concern, the ship left without them. On arrival at Folkestone, the wayward Ken and his nurses were waiting on the quayside with placards reading 'Homeless – please help'. They'd got on to the wrong ferry!"

On the whole, sea crossings over the years were fairly peaceful. There were a few exceptions however, with one in particular sailing from Calais to Dover being lodged forever in the memories of everyone unfortunate enough to have experienced it.

"The wind was gale force and the boat was going up and down like a cork," recalls John. "There were very few people who did not suffer from extreme seasickness. That was the year British Rail was on strike and all pilgrims, including the sick, travelled to and from the coast by bus. Imagine the feelings after being very sick having to face a 300-mile bus journey! However, the knowledge that we were over the worst seemed to work wonders and everyone was soon in good spirits. We arrived home at 2am the following morning."

Ita Leahy confirms that it was easier to recount those who were not sick than those who were. "Everybody was bad except Fr O'Connor and Anne Woods, my sister, Sister Magdalene," she says. "Archie was green, white and gold! There were bottles flying everywhere and you couldn't stand up. When I eventually got into a toilet to be sick I thought, 'Please God, put me through the porthole!'"

There were a few other hardy souls who made it across the Channel intact. Handmaid Pat McGeary was one, although her husband Peter was sick as soon as the boat left Calais and their 15-year-old daughter Anne only succumbed as it reached Dover. "I don't think it was the motion of the boat with Anne but everybody around being ill," says Pat. "The smell was terrible and the floor was awash. We were there with Leeds and there was a Fr Bartley who had a guitar and together with two or three teenagers he went round trying to keep people's spirits up. I really admired them and people tried their best to rise to it."

Canon Dan Spaight recalls that another passenger who did not get sick was, perhaps predictably, the stoical Mgr Peter Storey. "I asked him afterwards how he managed it and he said, 'I just went up on the deck, watched the sea and thought, 'I'll go with the waves.' He was so tough you couldn't knock him down. I wasn't and I was quite badly knocked by it. There were wheelchairs overturned and glasses went flying – it was something else."

To make matters worse, the boat tried and failed to dock twice. But just as the pilgrims were told they might have to move on to another port and it seemed the nightmare would never end, it managed to dock at the third attempt.

Current Pilgrimage Director, Fr Brian Nicholson, made five or six trips by train after his first Pilgrimage as a priest in 1979. "The thing I remember most was the tiredness that swept over everyone as we arrived back at Middlesbrough Station at three in the morning," he says. "Mind you, in my early years we departed Middlesbrough to start the Pilgrimage at a similar time and always had a civic send off! Norman Swash and other Catholic Mayors would be chauffeured to the station from some other function to wave us off. The old Ambulance Cars finally gave up the ghost and we no longer had a means of transporting the sick.

"We tried it without the Ambulance Cars one year as I remember, simply using the old-style carriages but it just didn't work and the plane came into service full-time. Fr Dan Spaight had no option but to make the decision to change from train to plane. This was an interesting time in terms of how we actually made the journey. The train was no longer a viable option and we were about to part company with the Catholic Travel Association, who we had used from the very beginning. The arrangements for travel were changing."

The final transition from train to air as the principal mode of transport for pilgrims was, as Fr Brian remembers, a swift affair but it had been on the agenda for years. It was essentially a simple matter of both British Rail and then later the French Railways retiring their Ambulance Cars from service and not replacing them with rolling stock capable of handling the numbers of sick and disabled people that made the journey all at the same time. The Evening Gazette tells us that as early as 1972 Pilgrimage organisers were beginning to look to the heavens rather than down the track.

Lourdes pilgrims from the Middlesbrough Diocese will very probably make the trip entirely by air from next year, says Fr Michael O'Connor, one of the organisers of this year's pilgrimage.

Father O'Connor, who was referring to the withdrawal of the ambulance coaches by British Rail, said this year would probably be the last time the pilgrims would travel by rail, coach and boat. "A special train from Middlesbrough was fixed some time ago, but last weekend, the rail situation being what it is, British Rail said they could not guarantee it would run."

Now coaches carrying more than 300 pilgrims will leave Middlesbrough tomorrow for the journey to Folkestone and a boat trip to Boulogne, where a special train will take them to Lourdes. A further 150 will fly from Teesside Airport in two flights, one tonight, the other tomorrow afternoon.

Said Father O'Connor: "British Rail's earlier decision on the ambulance coaches meant that three people from the Diocese were unable to make the journey. One sufferer has to be strapped to a chair and the other two, who have artificial limbs, could not have sat in coach seats. On the railway's ambulance coaches there would have been facilities for them to lie down."

It would seem that even then, the economics of keeping the Ambulance Cars running for the very limited use they got were simply unacceptable to British Rail. Maintenance costs were high and there was no guarantee they would be in service the following year. This meant that even as they were setting off on the 1972 Pilgrimage, the organizers had to think long and hard about what would happen in 1973. Charter flights had been operating alongside the Pilgrimage for years and they were growing in popularity. As the safety and comfort of passengers on the train began to be questioned, the safety and comfort of air passengers was continuing to increase year on year. Air travel was also becoming more affordable and people began to look to the skies.

However, despite Fr O'Connor's belief that their day had been and gone, the trains rolled on until 1979 when, for the first time, the entire Pilgrimage travelled by air. It would seem that the forbearance of the sick pilgrims on the train sustained them until they got to France, where SCNF still ran their Ambulance Cars. But by 1979 it was time for a change. Canon Rickaby accepted that change was inevitable but told the Gazette he was sad to see end of the train.

"It's quicker to get there by air, but in many ways it was better when we all went together on the train. British Rail withdrew the ambulance coaches some years ago and flying is the only way we can now take the sick to Lourdes."

Canon Rickaby and Fr O'Connor were both very certain about the future travel arrangements of the Pilgrimage when they spoke to the press. And they were both mistaken! In 1980 the train was back and it was to be the principal mode of transport for the Pilgrimage up to and including 1985. By then no Ambulance Cars existed for any part of the journey, making it unbearably uncomfortable for the sick. This point marks the end of the train as the preferred mode of transport, although it did have one comeback year in the late 1980s. For the main body of the Pilgrimage it was time to leave behind the age of the train and embrace the age of the plane.

While flying is certainly quicker, more comfortable and immensely more practical, without exception those who took part in those momentous journeys of faith by train remember them with a lasting affection. And like any long voyage, the waiting and the hardships endured along the way made the moment the pilgrims reached their destination all the more special.

"Arriving in Lourdes for the first time was a wonderful feeling as we all sang the Lourdes Hymn as we saw the Grotto on our approach to Lourdes Station," says Fr Michael O'Connor. It was when all the months of planning, hard work and saving up seemed worthwhile." As the Grotto would come into view with the candles burning and all the lights it was a wonderful moment," says Ita Leahy. "It didn't matter how tired you were then."

Chapter Seven

AUTOMOBILES

WHILE the attraction of a modern day short-haul flight is obvious compared to more than 24 hours on a coach, there are some who would not travel to Lourdes unless it was by coach. Many of the school groups that make up the youth section of the Pilgrimage today continue to travel by coach as do very many other older pilgrims. It is still the preferred mode of transport for many of the individual parish groups and, of course, the Marist Pilgrims, who travel under the direction of Fr Michael Coleman SM.

A major advantage of the coach is its ability to stop at other shrines along the way and so enhance the spiritual aspect of the pilgrimage. However, this was probably not a consideration the first time coaches were used by some unsuspecting pilgrims in the 1950s. A strike by British Rail drivers in 1955 led to the first use of coaches by pilgrims. The industrial action meant returning pilgrims arriving at Dover had no trains to get them north. Once again the Evening Gazette takes up the story.

About 200 pilgrims from Lourdes were today travelling from Dover to Middlesbrough by coach because the special trains which were to have brought them North were marooned in sidings without engines. The pilgrims were among 1,000 Roman Catholics from Leeds, Middlesbrough and Lancaster who were diverted from Folkestone to Dover. In the trains were some coaches converted to carry stretcher cases. Now, the stretcher cases will be last home. The main body of pilgrims from Middlesbrough expect to arrive on Teesside between 8pm and 9pm. The stretcher cases are expected to leave Dover by ambulance either today or tomorrow. A doctor, a priest and nurses are staying with them in Dover.

KSC GENTLEMEN'S CAMPING CLUB

Eddie Lappin's biggest contribution to our story was probably encouraging Paul Griffiths to go to Lourdes for the first time in 1979. Paul became a regular visitor to Lourdes and now serves the Pilgrimage as Head Brancardier. He takes up the story of his introduction to the KSC Gentlemen's Camping Club.

"Eddie was a committed Catholic with great devotion to Our Lady," says Paul. "He was also a key member of the Knight's of St Columba in Middlesbrough. He and his family took annual holidays touring France and always, within their circular route, stayed over in Lourdes for a period, a practice his family has continued since Eddie's death in 2002. They always camped and Eddie was proficient at organising these trips. In early 1978 he encouraged my father in law, Eddie Collins, to visit Lourdes for the first time and this evolved into a four-man camping trip, including the tour through France. Thus the KSC Gentlemen's Camping Club to Lourdes was formed.

"The following year, Martin Lovell was unable to go and Eddie's powers of persuasion turned to me. Obviously not having visited Lourdes before I was a prime target, but the crafty beggar sold it as a 'holiday'. And so in September 1979 I set off with Eddie Lappin, Eddie Collins and Tommy Waterson on what I thought was going to be basically a simple and inexpensive holiday break. Some holiday! As soon as the car turned south out of Middlesbrough Eddie announced, 'The pilgrimage prayer for a safe and holy pilgrimage' and we duly recited the Rosary!

"As our fairly leisurely journey progressed we must have stopped off at half the cathedrals in France. Eventually we arrived in Lourdes for a couple of days, apparently in order to give Eddie a break from driving. It was late evening and we pitched the tent, sorted our belongings and ate a simple meal. While clearing up, Eddie said to the others, 'Do you fancy popping along to the Torchlight?' They very readily agreed. I didn't have a clue what they meant. I remember thinking, 'Well, in for a penny, in for a pound'. I'd said the Rosary for five consecutive days, I must have visited and prayed in at least three churches or cathedrals every day so far, why not do the Torchlight?

"Off we went on the short drive down the hill from Camping la Forêt. It was dark and we found a parking space near the top of the domain and entered the area above the Rosary Basilica to the strains of *Ave Maria*. The next moment will stay with me forever. I was encouraged to the edge for a view of the esplanade and there before us was an absolutely incredible sea of candles. It appeared to go on for what seemed forever, against the blackness of the night at that time of year, and I realised this was real devotion to Our Lady. Surely most of us have doubts, but I have never felt belief as strong as I did that night.

"By now I had realised that this was a lot more than a simple holiday break, and over the next few days they introduced me into making a pilgrimage, with daily Mass, confession, the baths and the stations. On the way back we saw a vast amount of France and Eddie's knowledge and enthusiasm for the country was only matched by his affection for the Rosary! Making the trip the following year seemed unavoidable and if my memory is correct, the cost was only £60 including ferry, fuel, food and fees. The only thing it didn't include was the cost of beer during our evening sojourns to the local hostelry. It was a Lourdes pilgrimage after all!

"I was fortunate to join this group again and again. After my father-in-law passed away, Eddie introduced more new blood, and the KSC Gentlemen's Camping Club to Lourdes thrived even with plans of taking a second car. I have also learned that as an active member of the Knights of St Columba, Eddie Lappin was instrumental in ensuring funding was put in place to assist young people to visit Lourdes as Hospitalité Stagiares during college holidays. This undoubtedly was a major influence in what we have today, and must have sown many good seeds. Eddie did all of this and many other works. A great many people have a lot to thank Eddie Lappin for, especially me. Thanks Eddie."

These coaches were operated by Beeline Roadways of West Hartlepool and Internet research suggests their entire fleet was made up of second-hand London buses.

The closing of the BKS Service and the start of the Jumbo Jet flights marked a watershed in the Pilgrimage. Being the father of a large family, Barney Connelly became aware of the cost of taking a whole family to Lourdes. He came up with a very popular scheme allowing families to travel cheaply together. Its popularity was based not only on the cost but also on the fact that it was huge fun. He travelled by car with his whole family and camped at La Foret, on the edge of the Forest of Lourdes. He was soon to be joined by other families and 'Families Camping' was born.

Eventually there was enough equipment there for use not just by groups of families but also by school groups. Although very large numbers of schoolchildren had often made the Pilgrimage, it was this venture that led to the development of the system most of the modern day school groups continue to rely on. It was developed with the support of Bishop Harris and for the first time Barney was involved in the Diocesan Pilgrimage to Lourdes. Free from the travel industry and now with a large young family, Barney continued to indulge his passion for Lourdes and to pass it on to his children. Finding Lourdes hotels too expensive for a large family, he took the road up the hill past the Basilica and found the La Foret Campsite. And there he pitched his tent!

"I have not been a very good servant to the Middlesbrough Diocesan Pilgrimage," he says. "I had a fierce ambition to do something for Lourdes and frankly the organisation of the Diocesan Pilgrimage did not need me. By this time Bill Boyes was running it and I continued to go as my children grew up. All my children had walked in the processions at Lourdes, I was very proud of that. Eventually a group of mutual friends grew up and we began to travel together in our own cars and camp at Lourdes because we could not pay the hotel fees. A group from Liverpool came in cars and minivans and we met up and camped." The Connelly and Lappin families blazed a trail to be followed by hundreds of young pilgrims.

Year by year, Barney built up a stock of camping equipment and 12 tents, which was stored year round at the campsite. More and more families began to use the equipment during the whole Lourdes season each year. A company called Sunseeker Holidays, owned by Fr Arthur Dutton's sister, aided the venture. She sold Barney a great deal of surplus equipment cheaply and this was all stored, free of charge, by Jean Carruze at La Foret.

Eventually a more formal system developed with the idea of introducing whole families to Lourdes together. It became known as Families Camping. A coach service was arranged to take families from the UK to La Foret. It ran for six years. The venture was large enough by now that the campsite needed an experienced leader there at all times. As Barney's children grew up and went through university they found themselves taking turns at spending summer holidays on duty at the campsite. Much of this residential work fell to Rory Connelly, who still has extraordinary enthusiasm and involvement and has stayed the course.

The Knights of St Columba, under the influence of John Adams, Derek Brough and Eddie Lappin, set up a Young Brancs' Group and they often travelled out to La Foret during the summer to complete an *etage* – a week working with whichever pilgrimages were in Lourdes at that time.

Many Middlesbrough families spent a fortnight each year at La Foret 'doing the Pilgrimage' and spending time with other families. Travelling together either in their own cars or by coach, each family lived communally at the campsite using Barney's tents and they forged lifelong friendships. They came from all parts of the Diocese and beyond, including Stockton, Derby, St Helen's and Kirby. Many parents of the families had strong connections with the YCW.

A Newlands School group continue the tradition of groups camping at La Foret.

The success of the venture caught the eye of Bishop Harris and he encouraged Barney to make his camping facilities available to the schools of the Diocese so they could join the Pilgrimage in large numbers. In 1983 Barney joined forces with Rita Morris to bring a group of children on what became known as the Schools Service. Rita and Barney shared the driving of a hired minibus packed with schoolchildren and heaped on top with camping equipment. The venture was a great success and the following year a battered coach made the journey. In turn this was replaced in subsequent years by a fleet of ever more modern coaches.

St David's, Newlands, Sacred Heart Redcar, St Mary's College Middlesbrough, St Patrick's Thornaby, and St Michael's Billingham were the pioneers along with a Youth Group from St Stephen's Pastoral Centre in Hull, led firstly by Fr Tom O'Neill in 1983 and then Fr Pat Day, who took over that group and the Centre in 1985. This helped the development of the Diocesan Youth Service's contribution to the Pilgrimage simply because for the first time large numbers of children from many of the Diocese's secondary schools and beyond were able to afford to go to Lourdes and places were available for them.

The tents have sadly succumbed to repetitive, frequent usage and have nearly all been scrapped, but the rest of the equipment is still used each year by Newlands School, who camp in static caravans on the site. The Schools Service which built upon the success of Families Camping is still flourishing today. What we did was a Schools Service and was not the Youth Service," says Barney. "The children were brought in school groups, each with a team of school staff in charge."

Alongside this new Schools Service was a service of coaches for parish groups. These groups have grown and multiplied, some taken by Alcuin Travel, run by Barney Connelly, others with Marist Pilgrimages run by Fr Michael Coleman SM. In recent years Brian Arnold of Compass Travel and Malcolm Campbell have also provided coaches to schools and parishes for this popular service. Despite falling costs, air travel was still out of the reach of many people. Sensitive to this in the early years of official Pilgrimage flight there were also official coaches. Bishop Harris even surrendered the luxury of the plane to journey over land with pilgrims in 1988. The Gazette tells us more.

A record number of Lourdes pilgrims left Middlesbrough's Roman Catholic Diocese today in search of miracles or simply a spiritual blessing. Numbers heading for the shrine in south-west France were up by about 500 on last year, said the Rev David Hogan, from the office of the Bishop of Middlesbrough, the Rt Rev Augustine Harris.

After the Bishop boarded one of the coaches which left Middlesbrough Cenotaph and were later to join a convoy from other parts of the Diocese, Father Hogan said: 'The fact that the Pope has designated this a Marian Year – a special year of prayer last held 34 years ago – probably accounts for the rise in the number of pilgrims.'

'In recent years, we decided to travel by coach, too, and this keeps down the cost compared with flying.' The 1,500 pilgrims, some of them wheelchair-bound, are expected to arrive home next Friday.

The Gazette report the following year illustrates how popular the coach journey had become, while alerting us to the fact that this year for the final time a train figured in the transport plans for sick pilgrims.

A mission of mercy has gone out from a Middlesbrough school to the French shrine of Lourdes – despite a last minute passport hitch. Thirty-five pupils from Newlands School, Saltersgill Avenue, are to help sick pilgrims make the journey to the south-west of France. They are part of a 1,200 strong contingent making its way from the Roman Catholic Diocese of Middlesbrough over the weekend.

Twelve coach loads – four of them filled with children – and 80 seriously or chronically sick pilgrims who travelled in the specially equipped Jumbulance coach, drove from Teesside to Dover before embarking on a special train.

Middlesbrough MP Stuart Bell stepped in to help secure a collective passport after delays at the Liverpool office left them with the 11th hour problems.

Each year since 1987 Canon Eddie Gubbins has travelled to Lourdes by coach with Barney's company Alquin, named after a great Eighth Century teacher and monk whose life took him from York to Tours in France where he became Abbott.

"It is a distance of 1,100 miles there and exactly the same distance back," he says. "The journey by coach has much to recommend it. The many hours sitting together allow pilgrims to really get to know each other as they make their journey. I have, in the past, even cooked up the seating plan for our coach so that people can get to know each other, to share faith and each individual reason for travelling to Lourdes. This, more than anything, makes a long and tough journey worthwhile. Of course, it is all made even more bearable by very many cups of tea and coffee, the odd sing-song and a game of bingo or two. Religious videos occupy the more sedate moments of the trip.

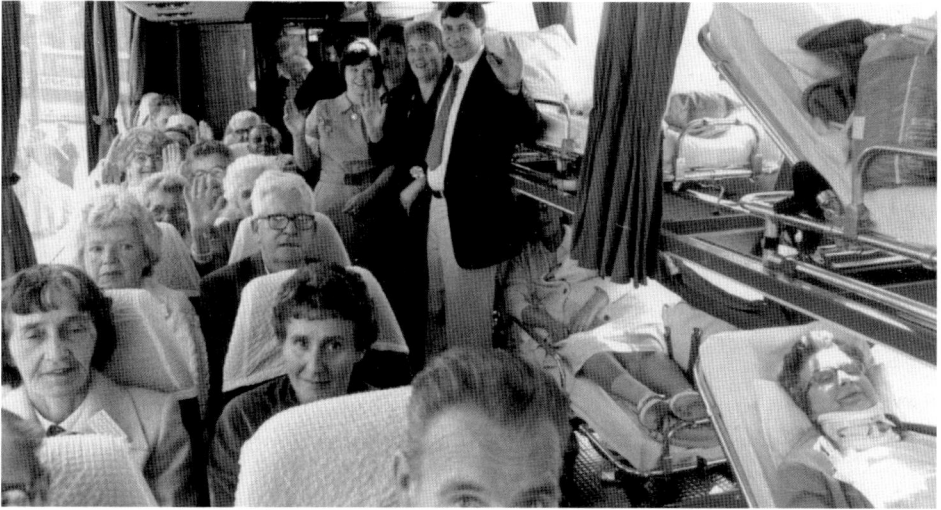

On board the Jumbulance: Dr John Doherty and friends.

For the first six years we travelled straight through with a total journey time of about 26 hours. More recently we have broken our journey overnight at Rheims. On the way back we have traditionally broken our journey home at Nevers, where St Bernadette died. I also recall visiting Taize, Cluny and the fields of Flanders."

Eddie remembers many of the characters he has shared the coach journey with over the years with great joy. "I recall sitting next to Mary Mendoza and listening to her telling me how much she preferred the coach trip to the plane," he says. "She was 87 at the time. Nellie Russon, from Beechwood in Middlesbrough, came for many years and spent the journey charming the coach drivers and providing everyone with much merriment and laughter. I am grateful also to Ken Riley, Eileen Woodhead and Mary Brynn of Saltersgill. They would be like excited children for weeks before we set off."

Obviously Eddie has fond memories of Lourdes, generated in no small part by the actual act of getting there. "Special mention should go to Alison McDermott, who always managed to bring out the best in us all," he says. "I salute everyone who has shared the journey with me over the years."

Another seasoned coach traveller is Fr Kevin Trehy. "For years, I never considered myself a coach traveller. A trip to London by coach was something I would not even consider. However in 1982 I had my first coach Pilgrimage to Lourdes to take part in the Diocesan Pilgrimage. What a great experience! At that time I was a priest in St. Bernadette's Parish in Nunthorpe. Generally the people there were not coach travellers and on that first occasion we managed just less than half a coach full. We agreed to share with St Patrick's Parish in Thornaby. This we did for the next four years and over those trips wonderful friendships were forged between the two communities.

Pilgrims board a Jumbulance at Middlesbrough Cenotaph in the 1980s.

"I have now been to Lourdes at least 20 times," he says. "On four occasions, I travelled by air and enjoyed the plane travel, but it wasn't the same. There is such a tremendous sense of pilgrimage on a coach and a great bonding of people. We have had some wonderful experiences of roadside Masses over the years that are truly memorable. To anyone who hasn't been by coach and is unsure of the idea, I would say try it. I firmly believe you will not regret it.

"This Jubilee pilgrimage we hope to travel from Richmond and share the coach with Sacred Heart Church Middlesbrough. I have no doubt this will be another occasion when there will a gelling of two different communities."

There are many ways of getting to Lourdes. As far as we know no-one from the Diocese has actually walked there, although several, including Agnes McGrogan, her brother Jim and her cousin Frances have all hitch-hiked. Veteran brancardier Tommy Waterson warmly recalls the time he hitched along with his friend Dick Bryan, who sadly died earlier this year. The two were about 27 when they decided to thumb to Lourdes in 1953 – and what an eventful journey it turned out to be. After getting to the south coast easily enough they were offered a lift by a group of gypsies in Calais. They stopped the night in a small hotel but at around 2am were woken by someone trying to force the locked door on their room.

"We got this big wardrobe and pushed it up to the door to keep them out," says Tom. "The hotelier the next day thought the gypsies had been trying to get in to take our passports." In those years not long after the War, a union jack on their borrowed rucksacks usually meant Dick and Tom didn't have to wait too long for their next lift.

Their next hosts were a lot more friendly, a French Canadian and a Jewish American in a flashy

Photo: Margaret Stewart

Canon Eddie Gubbins and a coach full of friends arrive in Lourdes.

car and looking like a pair of film stars.

While they admired Tom and Dick's enamel mugs – ideal for enjoying a bottle of wine to break the journey – the English lads were impressed by their driver's movie camera! Their new friends wanted to take them to Spain with them, but Dick and Tom were determined to get to Lourdes and pushed on. Their final lift of the adventure was a fitting one. They were picked up by the Bishop of Tarbes in his limo and arrived in style, chauffeur driven by a monk!

That was Tom's second trip to Lourdes. He had also gone the previous year, 1952, with a group organised by Jack Donovan with the Boys' Club from the old Cathedral parish. There were around 30 in the party, including current nurse Rachel Forgan's great-uncle Frank Gillespie and current brancardier Joe Harrison's mother, Philomena, and aunt, Theresa. While Mary and Margaret Stead were baking to help send sick pilgrims to Lourdes, Jack Donovan came up with an ingenious scheme to help get his boys there. "He got us to collect scrap and rags, which were sold to help pay our fare," says Tom. "I think it cost us about £40." It was through Jack that Tom was first introduced to the brancardiers, an association that continues right up to the present day.

"When he asked me if I would like to go and be a brancardier I didn't have a clue what he was on about," recalls Tom. "He explained that they helped to look after the sick, so I went with him and got the straps." There were no Middlesbrough sick that year, so Jack and Tom just helped wherever they could. Since then Tom has been to Lourdes countless times, including a memorable trip on the Jumbulance and with the Leeds Diocese the

Sign of the times: Dick Bryan hitching to Lourdes in 1953.

53

Tommy Waterson, now the longest serving branc, flies the flag while hitching with Dick Bryan.

year Middlesbrough didn't go. Another year he travelled by car with Jim Coughlan, John Cassidy and Herbert Smith, and he has also made the journey by road with Eddie Lappin, Eddie Collins and Martin Lovell.

Many have driven to Lourdes over the years and a few hardy pioneers have actually biked there. It is thought the first to do so was Fr Olly Plunkett, while the latest were Joe and Teresa Harrison. Joe tells us what it was like.

"I went to Lourdes for the first time in 1986 with Middlesbrough Catholic Handicapped Fellowship," he says. "The friendship was flawless and the coach was comfortable with an air of excited contentment. My memory tells me the days were sunnier and longer then. Around that time I bought myself a motorbike and from the coach window I saw that France was the place of warm, open roads. It was a gateway to Europe. Over the following years I had a couple of bike rides through France to Germany and beyond so I was becoming quietly confident with the foreign roads. By 1992 it was just the thing to do. I was just turned 30 and I regarded myself as young, free and not quite single, with Teresa riding pillion.

"On a mild Saturday dinnertime, family and friends waved us off from Normanby. Our Honda motorbike was carefully loaded and balanced - for the mechanically-minded, the bike was a CX500ec Eurosport in black, a shaft-driven touring bike with a 500cc engine, two plastic panniers aside of the back wheel and a top box. When the Japanese designed it they must have had Teresa and I in mind because they built it just big enough to carry two travellers with the bare essentials for camping. I even managed a few spanners and spare bulbs strapped in behind the plastic tail panels.

"The weather was mild and the ride down through England was uneventful. I recall the contentment of clocking up mile after mile. By teatime we were having pizzas in Portsmouth and awaiting the evening ferry. Bikers are easily accommodated on ferries. We just turned up at the dockside and bought a ticket for the late night crossing. I was tired but found little rest. The Channel was rough and laid out on the floor between the lounge room seats I managed little sleep, but by 7am we made a bright and enthusiastic start. Leaving Caen there was little traffic and we made great progress. I anticipated that we would be in Lourdes for tea.

"By midday we had reached a McDonald's outside Tours. I was tired and caught an hour's sleep outside on the grass. The day was starting to pass us by. I don't recall any more stops. Again there was the contentment of clocking up the miles, the changing scenery and the warmer breezes. This was France, and that meant sunshine burning down on our black leathers. As the afternoon passed we picked up signposts for Bordeaux. Kilometres meant little to me and I used my speedometer to calculate the miles. I should have been proud of the distance we'd travelled but I focused on how far away Lourdes was. I had thought of Bordeaux as the last milestone but in truth Lourdes was not just around the corner. There were still lots of miles to go.

"As we drove closer to Lourdes the night sky grew darker and everything was damp. Adjacent fields, neighbouring woodlands and passing hedges were collecting the misty rain. The grass verges were wet and the gutters had puddles. The bike surfed them and frequent splashes caught my now not-so-waterproof over-trousers. I longed for my journey's end. I began to feel we had bitten off too much. I started singing *Hail Queen of Heaven the Ocean Star*. I didn't know all the words so I kept singing the ones I knew about guiding the wanderer.

Photo: Teresa Harrison

Riding high: Joe Harrison well on the way to Lourdes by motorcycle.

"After 22 hours of biking, damp, disorientated and weary, we arrived via a minor country back road through the back door of Lourdes. It was 10pm. We rode around to the bridge and the Brickies with its customers standing around the pavement spilling out on to the street. From among the crowd in the damp neon light I saw John Lumley and he saw us. Parking at the kerb, we had completed our journey, a distance of 888 miles. Taking off our helmets John nearly dropped his Stella Artois when he saw it was Teresa and I. Our journey was now complete, but it was only the start of many a return pilgrimage. The next year we went by car with Michael McGeary and Andrew Quinn, then there was a minibus trip with others including Elaine McGeary, Marie and Nicole Kelleher. I suppose the important question is, 'Would I do it again?' By 1995 I had discovered the comforts of flight!"

Chapter Eight

ALL CHANGE FOR LOURDES!

THERE has been a slow and steady development in the ongoing story of our Diocesan Pilgrimage. Experience has made everyone wiser. Many individual pilgrims will have returned home from Lourdes determined to do things slightly differently next year. Similarly the organisers have made refinements each year which all go to make things a little better, especially for the sick. Development on the whole is not planned, but a reaction to a change in circumstance.

The late 1970s and early 80s saw much change. It became apparent that a pilgrimage could be a wonderfully spiritual time, full of prayer and devotion and that the sick could be cared for professionally and in a dignified manner - and that the whole experience could be relaxed and even fun! Certainly this was not a new notion but it was one that had taken second place as everyone worked to do the best for the sick pilgrims, who continued to form the heart of the Diocesan Pilgrimage.

A new Bishop, a new Pilgrimage Director and the formalisation of the role of Deputy Director by Canon Rickaby after the death of Fr Walter O'Connor saw the birth of the biggest change in the organisation of the Pilgrimage to that date. It was a change in mentality as well as practice and it gave birth to the kind of pilgrimage that we experience today. But how did we get to that point?

The Annual Diocesan Pilgrimage to Lourdes was well established by the mid-1950s. It was to be well and truly cemented by 1958, the centenary year of the apparitions in Lourdes. This was the first year that large numbers of schoolchildren joined the pilgrimage on a second special train led by the legendary Mgr Peter Storey. Not only did those early pioneers have to get to grips with how they should transport all of those people down through England and France, but they also had to come to terms with what the Lourdes authorities expected of an organised pilgrimage.

As luck would have it, in the early 1950s American writer Ruth Cranston was researching her famous book, *The Miracle of Lourdes*. Part of her research was an interview with the then Rector of the shrine, who told her how pilgrimages of the day were welcomed by the Lourdes authorities and how they were to be organised. This interview tells us much about what the first organisers of our pilgrimage were up against.

Ruth asks the Rector how an individual who wanted to organise a pilgrimage should go about it. The answer gives away the formality of the time. "An individual can't organise a pilgrimage, no matter how pious or devoted they may be. All pilgrimages must be organised under diocesan authority and under the local priesthood. If a priest wants to organise a pilgrimage, first he gets authority from his bishop. Then he writes to the Secretary-General at Lourdes to say how many pilgrims he wants to bring and about what time. The Secretary-General arranges the schedule for all pilgrimages and when you see the tremendous list – with three or four pilgrimages arriving every day – you realise what a terrific job it is."

As for who makes the arrangements for all of the people, that was again the role of the local pilgrimage priest and director. "He is responsible for all of the arrangements. The Secretary-General simply gives that all important thing: a date. What if a priest or group should arrive without the proper authority? They would not be admitted. You can understand how we would very soon be in chaos if these great numbers of people arrived helter-skelter, without complying with the regulations, or without the necessary staff to look after their sick members."

Of course, this has now changed dramatically and the numbers of individual pilgrims who come to Lourdes alone is increasing year by year. They are warmly welcomed, as are all who visit the shrine, but the majority of people continue to come with organised pilgrimages. The birth of the Pilgrimage in our Diocese certainly took place in Middlesbrough. Fr Rickaby, Bill and Barbara Boyes and the Knights were all strong forces there. There were, as we now know, Bishop Brunner and Fr Walter O'Connor SM down in Hull who were also interested, but before they could make any move to establish a tradition they also found themselves in Middlesbrough.

In practical terms, the Director, the Doctor and the Matron administered the Pilgrimage. They formed a trinity whose word was beyond question. Current Pilgrimage Director Fr Brian Nicholson says: "Because of the way they worked, all their roles dovetailed together and everything was answerable to them one way or another. All other things seemed to be on a lesser plain."

However, pilgrims came from far and wide from the earliest days and as they returned home to their corners of the Diocese they took their stories and enthusiasm with them. It was an infectious concoction, which saw the Lourdes cause taken up in Hull and York and beyond. Characters like Fr Olly Plunkett and Meg Whelan were among the first pilgrims and were keen to assist and promote the Pilgrimage as much as possible in their own corner of the Diocese. Fr Olly got to Lourdes by hook or by crook, one time even arriving there on a motorbike! He and Meg made sure that the early Handmaids never needed to buy tea bags and other necessities. The good people of Hull who followed his lead in doing a small bit to help things along provided them. It was in small ways like this that the people who were far from the centre of the organisational side of the pilgrimage were able to take ownership of a small part of it. Like all things their contribution grew and grew.

Meg was housekeeper at St Charles' Parish. When she was in Lourdes she was befriended by Head Handmaid Mildred Raw and upon her return to Hull she became the focal point during the 1950s for contributions to the Lourdes cause.

A similar story is to be told in York surrounding a man called Terry Gilmartin. He is the brother-in-law of Liz Boyes, who made the first Pilgrimage with her sister. It quickly became clear to them that the only way they could take sick pilgrims to Lourdes was by taking the food, medicine and equipment they needed with them. Together with the handmaids they collected tins of ham, salmon and other foodstuffs. The handmaids also baked cakes which are served with tea in Lourdes. All of this was packed the night before the Pilgrimage set off by the brancs. A team would help the handmaids pack the big wooden boxes in the Lourdes store at the Holy Name of Mary Church. Middlesbrough. Fr Nicholson takes up the story.

"Terry was the caretaker of the Poor Clare's Convent in York," he says. "He started the tradition of placing a huge wooden box on York Station waiting for the arrival of the Pilgrimage train. It was full of food to sustain pilgrims as they travelled."

Fr Olly Plunkett, Lourdes pioneer in Hull, with essential supplies.

Photo: B Toolin

By 1958 Fr Olly Plunkett was Chaplain to the Sick and the organising members of the pilgrimage Committees began to reflect the fact that pilgrims now came from all over the Diocese and beyond. Yet the power base that ran the Pilgrimage continued to be the very close working relationship that had to exist between the Director, the Pilgrimage Doctor and the Matron.

This seemed to suit Fr Rickaby, who Fr Brian remembers was single minded in his approach to organisation. Everything revolved around caring for the sick and allowing them to pray at the Grotto. "All the tales about Rickaby are really apocryphal," he says. "You see, he only ever appeared for the official Pilgrimage events. The only other time you saw him was at the hospital meeting with the Matron. I remember not seeing him for days on my first Pilgrimage, but you have to bear in mind that in those days we didn't have all the big communal services we have now. This meant that wherever the sick were congregating you would find Rickaby. Having said that, he only ever appeared when there was work to be done. He never just hung around and passed the time of day."

Eventually, in 1980, control of the Pilgrimage was to pass from Canon Rickaby to Fr Dan Spaight. In Fr Dan's early years as Director the Pilgrimage was still run essentially by three people; the

Director, the Matron and the Pilgrimage Doctor. Of course, the Deputy Director was always there for Fr Rickaby. What they decreed happened, no more and no less. However, things were changing. We should not make the mistake of thinking that Fr Dan was simply adopting a policy of 'out with the old and in with the new'. He was a pilgrim of long standing and knew the operation well. He recalls his first visit to Lourdes, long before he took over the running of the Pilgrimage.

"My involvement started in 1961 when I first went. I was ordained in 1959 and that was one of the first things I wanted to do," he says. "I think it was because during the 1950s we'd had the Marian Year, the centenary year of the apparitions and also the Rosary Crusade led by Father Patton. From all that there was a tremendous devotion to Our Lady and Lourdes was the place to go. We went on the train with about 350 pilgrims. We joined up with Leeds and met up at Dover, crossed the Channel and shared a French train down to Lourdes. That was a wonderful pilgrimage for me, I was very much a free agent and had no commitments. It was just wonderful. It's true that the first pilgrimage is often the most memorable."

It is clear that from the earliest days of Fr Dan's ministry he is a pilgrim priest. After his first trip to Lourdes he spread his wings. Everywhere he went he took his camera and thousands of photos and slides now back up his stories. "I had one or two other things I wanted to do," he says. "Pope Paul VI went to the Holy Land in 1965 and I had a great desire to go there, I went to Rome in 1967 and Oberamagau in 1970." Eventually he would return to Lourdes, a decade after that first visit. "I felt ready for Lourdes again so I went back in 1971. Quite a lot had changed. The thing I remember is I had moved on from photos to slides."

It was also a tragic year for the Pilgrimage, as one of our founding members died there. "That was the year Fr Walter O'Connor died and he was buried there," recalls Fr Spaight. "I had just greeted him shortly before he died."

The gap left at the heart of the Pilgrimage by Fr Walter's death needed filling. Of all people Canon

---

From the Evening Gazette, June 4 1971

PRIEST DIES ON LOURDES VISIT

A Teesside priest died at Lourdes while he was with the Middlesbrough Diocesan Pilgrimage.

The Rev Walter O'Connor, 67, was buried in the English section of Lourdes cemetery after a Requiem Mass at Lourdes Parish Church, celebrated by the Bishop of Middlesbrough and attended by all the Teesside members of the pilgrimage – over 200 of them.

A memorial service will be held at the Holy Name of Mary, Middlesbrough, next Wednesday, which will also be attended by members of the pilgrimage, which arrives back on Teesside tonight.

Father O'Connor was born at South Bank and was deputy headmaster of St. Mary's College, Middlesbrough from 1946 to 1955. After teaching at Exeter and Hull he returned to Middlesbrough for his retirement.

For the past four years he was a patient at St. John of God Hospital, Scorton, suffering from cerebral thrombosis.

Rickaby would have known this best of all. Fr Walter had been one of the founders of the Diocesan Pilgrimage. Without him there would have been no such thing. His steadfast devotion to Our Lady of Lourdes at the heart of the organisation would be missed. Canon Rickaby needed someone else to stand close by him. Without ever having the title, Fr Walter had been the Deputy Director. Now Canon Rickaby recognised that he needed someone to fill Fr Walter's boots. On the train home from Lourdes in 1971, a chance conversation brought him to the conclusion that Fr Dan was the man, as he remembers.

"On the way home on the train I got into a conversation about my recent trip to Oberamagau and Canon Rickaby was present," he says. "I suppose it was that conversation that led him to ask if I was interested in helping him with the pilgrimage and eventually taking over from him. He was at Filey. He was a bit isolated and probably didn't know the priests that well. He would always be at the solemn Masses where he would be Master of Ceremonies or the cantor leading the singing. I said 'Yes' and he brought me in for the 1972 pilgrimage as Deputy Director. He was still Director but he used to involve me with giving forms for the sick, fundraising events and occasionally attending meetings in Middlesbrough which he was unable to get to."

Although Fr Dan had taken on much responsibility, it seems that Canon Rickaby did not always feel his load had been lightened. Fr Dan tells a story that sums up his outlook. "There was a famous quote from Bishop Brunner on the platform at Middlesbrough Station. He said: 'I think everything is going well because Canon Rickaby looks worried!' It was a typical pose of Canon Rickaby's. He looked sometimes as though the worries of the world were on him."

1979 saw Canon Rickaby call another newly ordained priest into the service of the Lourdes Pilgrimage. Fr Brian Nicholson made his first pilgrimage to Lourdes in 1957. He would not go back again until 1979. This was his first pilgrimage as a priest but he was soon to find himself in the thick of things. Unbeknown to him, Canon Rickaby had lined up Fr Dan as his successor and needed a replacement as Deputy Director. Ric could then retire knowing the Pilgrimage was in safe hands. After his return in 1979, Fr Brian was called to the Curial Office to see Canon Rickaby. "I was ordained in 1978 and went to Lourdes in 1979," he says. "In July that year I was made Diocesan Master of Ceremonies, which opened a number of doorways for those who get impressed with titles. The Pilgrimage Committee knew everything I was doing was accountable to Bishop Harris, who would have certainly made his views known to me if I were getting things wrong.

"Within weeks of getting back for the 1979 Pilgrimage I was summoned to see Rickaby. I was petrified. I had just taken up my appointment as Bishop's Secretary and I had spent much of the Pilgrimage that year in the hospital with the sick pilgrims and their carers. It seemed that everything I did provoked a warning from someone that I shouldn't let Canon Rickaby find me doing whatever it was. I thought he had caught up with me. The office he used was in the Curial Office and was the biggest, best room in the building. In the corner, behind the desk, was the Lourdes banner, pristine and encased in glass. I remember the banner had just been renovated because Canon Rickaby had heard Bishop Harris wanted a new Lourdes banner and it seemed to the Canon that there was nothing wrong with the old one."

Here we get another glimpse of the kind of character Canon Rickaby was. He was a Canon of Lourdes, only becoming a Canon of the Diocese of Middlesbrough much later. And yet he commandeered this prominent office in the Diocesan headquarters in order to get his job done. And get the job done he did.

"By this time Rickaby had moved to Guisborough and so he would come into the office several days a week in the months leading up to the Pilgrimage," says Fr Brian. "There he would summon people to him so he could maintain operational control of all the preparations. I remember going in to the office to see him wondering what I had done wrong. It was then that he offered me the job of Deputy Director. Typically for Rickaby he didn't say Deputy Director, he asked me if I was prepared to help with the organising of the Diocesan Pilgrimage. The next Pilgrimage, 1980, was when he retired and Fr Spaight took over. Although Rickaby never told me, he must have known that this was going to happen as I stood in that office."

Fr Dan and Fr Brian had their work cut out straight away. For the 1980 Pilgrimage they had a problem nobody in the Diocese had been faced with before. How were they to handle the formidable ex-Director now that he was stepping down and would be an ordinary pilgrim, without responsibility, for the first time since 1949? They need not have worried. Canon Rickaby went to his eternal reward before he had the chance to return to Lourdes. He died on February 3 1981.

"He decided he was finishing in 1980 and I took over in 1981," says Fr Dan. "I had been due to meet him for him to handover all the documentation in February 1981. After that, he suddenly realised he hadn't invited me to lunch so he wrote a brief letter saying he should have done so and inviting me to eat with him. I think it's very likely that he went out the next morning to post the letter and stopped at a filling station and died there as he got into the car. I got the letter after he had died. His funeral at the Sacred Heart was very close to the feast of Our Lady of Lourdes. He was buried in Filey."

Of course, at this time Fr Dan was down in Hull as Parish Priest at the Sacred Heart. The person responsible for affairs up in Middlesbrough was Fr Michael Murray. In July 1980 Fr Murray sent a letter regarding Canon Rickaby to all pilgrims. "Canon Rickaby has retired as Pilgrimage Director after many years of devoted service," he wrote. "We thought that a token of appreciation should be shown to him by pilgrims, past and present, for undertaking the tremendous task of organising the Annual Diocesan Pilgrimage over the years. On our return journey from Lourdes this year it was decided, after consultation, that it would be appropriate to present Canon Rickaby with a Spiritual Bouquet and a cheque as a token of our appreciation. A collection on the train realised £160 towards the cheque. We invite you to contribute towards the cheque and the Spiritual Bouquet as indicated in the form below."

The presentation took place at the Lourdes Reunion of that year on September 7. Mass was celebrated in St George's Church, York and then a social was held in the Tramways Club. By the time he came to retire as Director, Canon Rickaby had seen three Bishops come and go. Bishop Brunner, who some would credit with the initial idea of the Diocesan Pilgrimage, died on March 21 1969. Bishop McClean, a regular pilgrim to Lourdes who grew to know Canon Rickaby's scowl very

Photo: Lacaze

Regular pilgrim Bishop Harris, who encouraged the Pilgrimage to evolve into what it is today.

well, succeeded him. Bishop John Gerard McClean died on August 27 1978 and was succeeded by Bishop Augustine Harris.

The first decade of Bishop Harris's time in the Diocese was one of huge change for the Pilgrimage. An evolution that some at the time may have considered to be revolution was going on. Things were about to change and there would be no going back. Fr Brian remembers well those winds of change, blowing at the time of his first involvement. "It seems to me that the unofficial motto of the Pilgrimage is 'Nothing is impossible!' - and we learned that all of a sudden in the early 80s."

It was to be Brian McGowran who would be first to test this unofficial motto. His first year in Lourdes was also 1979. Eventually he would serve as Head Brancardier, replacing John Adams. As the 1980 Pilgrimage was being planned, Brian kick-started a bold initiative. It was a brave move for one so new to the Pilgrimage, and one Brian's close friend Fr Brian Nicholson remembers as one of the key moments of transformation in the Pilgrimage.

"Brian McGowran installed a kitchen on the train," he says. "It was a momentous step and it caused some consternation. I had to convince Barbara Boyes that it would be fine and I remember Bill was very uneasy. Things had changed though, and we had a Director in Fr Dan who was much more easy going that Canon Rickaby had ever been. There was a very strict regimentation to the Pilgrimage, both in Lourdes and back at home in the Diocese. There was a very rigid point of view from the Committee, which had 'done' Lourdes for many years, and they seemed to know what was permissible and what was not. The kitchen challenged that view, but it got the nod from Bill Boyes. The Pilgrimage took a monumental step that year as not only the sick pilgrims but also every person on that train was given a cup of tea and one of the first slices of the now legendary cake! It was like all the miracles of Lourdes had happened all at once - after all, in the past this had been a luxury afforded only to the sick. Imagine the folk who had made that same trip year after year clutching a Thermos and making it last. All of a sudden, this year, they were woken with an early morning cup of tea as the train carried on through France. It was a new and very important statement for the

Pilgrimage - especially when you consider that even as late as the 1980s there were people who would spend all their money on the fare to Lourdes and spend the entire pilgrimage penniless. It was a great thing to witness. Our ability to care for people expanded and we were able to grasp opportunities for service that in the past had not been taken up."

What may seem like a light-hearted attempt to provide a little more comfort than was usual on the journey is a very important step in our pilgrimage story. "It was only common sense really that we should care not only for the sick but for their carers also," says Fr Brian. "The atmosphere created on the train was crucial, as it would be the atmosphere that continued through the whole pilgrimage."

Brian McGowran remembers the raised eyebrows his kitchen caused. "It was a fantastic piece of engineering," he says. "Mike McCullagh fabricated a stainless steel frame which held the water boiler and gas cylinders. We probably broke every rule British Rail had but nobody cared. We all got a cup of tea, or something else."

The 'something else' Brian refers to was kept safely in a wooden chest, painted blue with a large red cross on all sides and its lid. It was carried very carefully and given pride of place. Paul Griffiths claims that as early as his first time working as a brancardier he was counted as responsible enough to carry this heavy load aboard the train.

"Brian told me I had to be very careful with the chest as it was very fragile," he says. "I was really worried about it because it was marked with a red cross. I placed it very carefully near the kitchen where I had been told to put it. Later on as we were well on the way, I passed by and the lid was open. It was full of beer and wine - apparently it was all for medicinal purposes!"

Brian recalls the fact that in those days many pilgrims had less money. "We had a bucket in the kitchen," he says. "It was left so that people could drop in some money if they took anything out of the chest. The bucket was full going out to Lourdes and it was full coming back too. The only difference was that on the way back it was full of buttons and centimes!"

The credit for this development goes in some way to Brian and his mobile kitchen. However, the real credit for the expansion of the Pilgrimage during the 1980s belongs to new Director, Fr Spaight.

"Fr Dan simply allowed all these things to happen, a real turnabout compared to his predecessor," says Fr Brian. "I was given free reign to promote and encourage this change, but Dan would certainly let me know when things perhaps went too far. This evolving scene suited Dan and he was very well aware of it. Much of the change happened as a direct result of renewing our approach not only to caring for the sick and carers, but also the celebrations of the various liturgies. I was in charge of that and this allowed Dan to take a step back and let it happen. In those days the hotel Panorama was the Pilgrimage HQ and both Fr Dan and Bishop Harris stayed there. Both were very aware of these changes and happy to let them run their course. Fr Dan in particular had a constant eye on what was necessary and was happy to let everything else just happen."

Slowly in the 80s people began to arrive in Lourdes with a little more money. This allowed people to continue the more relaxed spirit that had been engendered on the train journey while they were in Lourdes. Added to this was another very important movement away from the hotels immediately opposite St Joseph's Gate and the Domain and into the hotels along the river.

In Bishop McClean's time, The Heinz Hotel was used as the Pilgrimage HQ hotel so many people didn't come very far away from the Grotto. More money and a more relaxed atmosphere brought us a boom period in recruiting helpers - and more helpers needed bigger hotels to stay in. So it was that we moved up towards the very many hotels alongside the River Gave. Of course, this brought pilgrims

Photo: David Boyes

Brian's Kitchen: Brian McGowran (top left) with Mildred Raw and front row, brancardiers Tony Bryan, Albert Adams, George Metcalfe Snr, unknown, Tommy Waterson and Jim Rainey.

close to the bars and cafes and the great social side of the Pilgrimage was born. There was a definite boom period at first, with constant sing-songs each night in the bars. The singing has taken a back seat in recent years, but the socialising has not.

In the early 80s, the Pilgrimage underwent several big changes. 1979 had seen the beginning of the end of the Ambulance Car rolling stock on both BR and SCNF. For the first time the Pilgrimage travelled by air. Following this the Pilgrimage reverted to the train for four years, but the lack of Ambulance Cars made it an impossibly difficult journey for the sick. The demands of this change began to weigh on a Committee that needed restructuring. Bishop Harris, relatively new to the Diocese, decided to actively promote the change that had already begun to happen naturally.

Changes were happening behind the scenes too. The Pilgrimage Committee was changing and expanding. The Pilgrimage was bigger than it had ever been and in the many regions of the Diocese, smaller committees were hard at work raising money to enable local sick pilgrims to make the journey. The organising Committee expanded to reflect this reality and yet another step was taken away from the days when the Director, Doctor and Matron ran everything.

Even in those days there was a Committee, each member appointed by the Bishop. It included area representatives and Pilgrimage officials but the 'trinity' still ruled. What began to make a real difference was the existence of fundraising bodies other than the Diocesan Lourdes Sick Fund. This fund had been established by Josie Coughlan and Barbara Boyes, among others, right at the birth of the Pilgrimage. Barbara acted as treasurer to the fund for years.

As the Lourdes message spread throughout the Diocese, smaller groups of equally committed people began to work to benefit the Pilgrimage in their local areas. The Hull Lourdes Committee was born, as was a similar body in York. Area representatives from these groups were invited to join the organising Committee and were joined in 1986 by members of the newly formed Scarborough Lourdes Committee.

This was a very interesting development. A good cross-section of people were now able to advise the Bishop as to the best way forward. The area representatives met on equal term with the Pilgrimage Officials who were appointed by the Bishop and they worked together to great effect. Thanks to their efforts, the Pilgrimage continued to grow and expand. However, by the mid-80s the difficulties of securing satisfactory transport meant the long-standing working relationship between the Pilgrimage organisers and the Catholic Touring Association was deteriorating fast. This new look Committee had its work cut out.

Only once has the Pilgrimage been cancelled due to the cost. Fr Spaight tells us: "For the first time in 1977 the price being quoted was going to be over £100 and it was feared it would put people off. And so we had a meeting at the end of 1976 and decided that from then onwards we would have the Pilgrimage in alternate years - abandon 1977, go in 1978 and so on. But when we went back we got used to the increase and we just kept going."

By the mid-80s costs had risen to around £250 per person. This was not the only worry for the Committee. The French railway company, SCNF, was unwilling to guarantee that they would provide a special train for less than 400 people. This gave Pierre Barrere, Gerard Perombelon and their colleagues at the CTA problems which they seemed unable to solve to the satisfaction of the Committee. Because SCNF was unable to guarantee a train, the CTA felt it could not underwrite the risk and guarantee the travel arrangements itself. Also, the exchange rate at the time meant that the French Franc was very unstable against the Pound. Again, the CTA would not take on the risk of the fluctuation in the market, preferring to hand a quote to the Committee that did not give a fixed price but rather reserved the right to adjust the price up to three weeks before departure. These conditions were deemed to be unsatisfactory by the Committee and they began to get other quotes.

The Committee at the time - Fr Spaight, Fr Nicholson and Fr O'Connor, Dr Boyes and Dr Doherty, Barbara Boyes, Margaret Stewart, Liz Boyes, Irene Brankley, Margaret Jackson, Margaret Dasey, John Adams, Brian McGowran, Tony Tasker, Brenda Coleman, Sr Dymphna, Dominic Boyes, Anne Broadbent, Margaret Hardgrave and Angela Warren - faced a problem which has dogged the organisers ever since. They needed to find a way of providing suitable, competitively priced travel. They put the Pilgrimage out to tender, inviting quotes not only from the CTA but also from other companies.

On October 2 1986 a small sub-committee gathered at the home of Brian and Kath McGowran in Cowley Road, Middlesbrough, to meet with other possible travel agents. John Tangney and Bridget Moran of Tangney Tours spoke to the gathering for more that three hours about a quote that they had submitted to the Committee.

Once prices had been received from all companies matters were somewhat clearer, but there still remained the problem that seemed to be out of anyone's control - the fact that the French railways would not guarantee a train for less than 400 passengers. In spite of this problem, the CTA submitted a quote after the deadline set by the sub-committee, that was incomplete and subject to change. Tangney Tours submitted a quote that would not change and spelled out that the company rather than the Pilgrimage organisers assumed all risk in terms of costs and guaranteeing travel arrangements.

This would prove a defining decision in the life of the Pilgrimage. Whatever decision the Committee made had to be the right one, otherwise the high numbers of people who were responding to the call of Our Lady to go to the Grotto in procession may have well been lost. It seemed that all the problems faced by the Committee were to be taken off their shoulders by accepting the Tangney tender. Not only that but it was very competitively priced. But the Committee had to get other assurances before they accepted the quote.

Fr Brian Nicholson and Brian McGowran travelled to Lourdes to see the hotels that Tangney Tours was able to provide rooms in and inspect standards. They returned satisfied. At the same time, Dr John Doherty performed a search into the financial stability of Tangney Tours and was also satisfied. After further deliberations, Tangney Tours was appointed as operator for the 1987 Pilgrimage. These deliberations proved very difficult and were perhaps not what anyone would expect to deal with when agreeing to serve as a Pilgrimage official. This part of the Committee's remit was a thankless task for all concerned. And it didn't end there. After a year with Tangney, the Pilgrimage switched to Arena Travel for several years, returned to the CTA and finally back to Tangney and have never used another operator since.

Bishop Harris realised the strain these deliberations put on the Committee very early. He had two problems. He was keen to add to the Committee's skill base but did not want to restructure an organisation that finally had a good representative body of people on it. His solution to both of these problems was to appoint an Executive Director who would work alongside Fr Spaight. He needed someone who understood both the professional world and the Pilgrimage well. Mike Boyes is the eldest son of Bill and Barbara. Two of his brothers, Dom and David, had followed their parents to Lourdes in the early 70s and became regular pilgrims, serving as brancs and musicians for many years. Mike managed to resist Lourdes for much longer but eventually succumbed.

"I first went to Lourdes in 1980," he says. "I had lived with the organisation of the Pilgrimage, it all seemed to go on around me but I paid it no attention. When my wife and I fostered and then adopted our son Michael in 1977, my mother said to me that I should think about taking him to Lourdes because he was suffering from Tricuspid Atresia. Over the years we both became regular pilgrims. Michael became known to lots of the helpers, who cared for him tremendously, and I started to work as a brancardier along with my brothers David and Dominic. When he was 11, Michael underwent his first major operation and following his recovery he went to Lourdes and became a brancardier too. He continued this until he was 16."

Michael is a big part of Mike's continuing involvement in Lourdes. After Michael's death in 1993,

MICHAEL BOYES

Mike Boyes would perhaps not have made a pilgrimage to Lourdes had it not been for his son Michael. Mike recalls how his involvement began.

"We went in 1980 by train. Michael was a very delicate child, almost purple in colour due to his heart condition," he says. "As a four-year-old I'm not sure what he would have remembered from his first trip, but I didn't know what to expect. Everyone was very kind on the train. On the ferry, we had settled down in the lounge for the crossing when Barbara Christie tapped me on the shoulder. She was making the Pilgrimage with her disabled daughter, Lucy. We became firm friends during that Pilgrimage.

"Michael and I stayed in the Hotel Panorama with my parents, while Barbara and Lucy stayed in the hospital. Things were much more strict then and I would supply Barbara with the odd drink in the hospital as she was not allowed out in the evening. Michael enjoyed the whole week and joined in with as much as he could. I was very worried about him not eating - he would not even try French food - but I found out that he would toddle along to the handmaids, who fed him up with biscuits and cake, in the Accuile.

"The highlight for me was taking him to the baths. Normally if Michael was put into very cold water he would go even more blue than he was normally, but I remember that in the baths his colour did not change and he seemed to be in no discomfort at all. I remember that the whole Lourdes experience hit me like a sledgehammer the first time I was there. It was a very emotional week. It was all a learning curve. Barbara and I used to go into the corner of Rosary Square for the Blessed Sacrament Procession. It seemed to be the place where all the children congregated for that particular part of the day. We would stand there and chat every day. One day she asked me how many people I thought were in the square. I told her I thought there were about 10,000 and she turned to me and said, 'They can't all be wrong can they?'

"Michael had a huge operation at the age of 11. It took place in Newcastle. It was a long do, lasting about nine hours, and then he was sent to Intensive Care for recovery. Liz and I were spending the night in a flat they have there for relatives. At about five in the morning one of the nurses called us and asked us to get across there quickly. She told us not to panic and that everything was all right, but they needed us. We dashed across and they told us that Michael had been taken off his ventilator and was trying to speak. They couldn't make out what he was asking for and wanted us to help. I went right up to him and put my ear to his lips. He said to me 'Lourdes water.' I couldn't believe it. I told the sister who, it turned out went to Lourdes with Hexham and Newcastle, and we both began to cry. I couldn't believe how intimately involved an 11-year-old boy had become with the place.

"I am convinced that when he was in Lourdes and got ill he always came through it stronger. He died in 1993. I consider him a child of Lourdes."

Mike continued to make the trip to Lourdes and was working as a branc when Bishop Harris asked him to take on more responsibility. "I had come to know Bishop Harris very early on in my involvement with Lourdes," says Mike. "I was sitting quietly at the stern of the ferry with Michael. The only other people there were John and Marie Adams, who used the ferry crossing to sneak away from everyone else and enjoy a silver service picnic which Marie seemed to produce out of nowhere each year. Bishop Harris strolled around the corner on his own, obviously escaping the crowds too. He watched Michael intently and we began to chat. Before we knew it the whole crossing had passed by. Typically for Bishop Harris, from that day he never passed us by but always stopped for a quick word."

"September 1989 brought a summons from him to Bishop's House. I had no idea what I was to go there for but when I walked in I knew it was about Lourdes because Fr Dan was there. Bishop Harris told me he would like me to run the Committee for him. He was keen to promote teamwork at every level of the Lourdes organisation in our Diocese. From the outside it looked as though everyone had become very entrenched and Bishop Harris took steps to move things along."

1990 saw a few changes of Pilgrimage officials. Dr Sarah Bottom succeeded Dr John Doherty as Medical Director and Agnes McGrogan followed Margaret Stewart as Matron. Agnes had been a regular Lourdes pilgrim in the early years of her nursing career. 1972 was to be a year she would not forget. She was due to fly to Lourdes on one of the two chartered aircraft heading for the shrine that year. The night before the flight her father, Andy Mulligan, himself a Lourdes branc in 1924 and 1926, had a heart attack. This placed him in a similar position to his good friend Mr Wordsworth, father of Barbara Boyes. Barbara's dad was so ill that she did not travel to Lourdes that year. But Agnes was told her father was in fine fettle and so she decided to make her pilgrimage. As she had flown, Agnes volunteered to work the first night shift in the hospital and then retired to bed for the day. At around 6pm she woke to the tragic news that her father had died.

"I didn't go to Lourdes for a few years after that," she says. "I didn't really want to go back. At some stage in the intervening years I did go back for a couple of days as part of a Marist Origins Pilgrimage. That seemed to break the curse for me and I became a regular pilgrim again. Fr Spaight approached me and asked me if I would be the Matron. I had done quite a lot of the donkeywork for it anyway. I agreed and worked as Matron until Teresa Harrison took over."

Changing personnel on the Pilgrimage Committee is always a difficult affair. Finding new people with a flair for innovation who at the same time are steeped in the Middlesbrough Pilgrimage tradition is not easy. "I knew well from living at home with my parents the days when the Pilgrimage was essentially run by three people," says Mike. "I remember hearing mum typing away very late at night and she used to do all the bookkeeping too. Dad did all the selection of the sick pilgrims, obviously involving the Matron as well, and then 'Ric' would appear at our house, sometimes with Fr Spaight, sometimes not. So I was familiar with the way it had worked for years. Then we got the Committee which developed out of groups that had got together principally through Brian McGowran, who was Head Branc at the time. I remember the whole Committee meeting with various travel agents at Brian's house. Bishop Harris's request to me to join the fray was really a way of formalising what was already happening, giving it the seal of approval.

"What was interesting about the birth of the Committee was that all of a sudden people began to think the revolution had come and democracy was here. It was a difficult change to manage because the Pilgrimage is such a complicated affair to pull off year after year. Debate and opinion have to be encouraged, but essentially it has to be left to a rather small group to make the decisions. Appointment of Pilgrimage officials has always been down to the Bishop and that is still the case today. Once that appointment is made I do my best not to interfere with the way they operate. It is my job to simply ensure the smooth running of the Pilgrimage as a whole.

"I first acted as Executive Director on the 1991 Pilgrimage, when Dr Sarah Bottom was the Medical Director. Bishop Harris told me I had to ensure I communicated with people as best I could and that I should try to take a general overview of the whole thing. I have tried to do this even to the extent that I always stand at the back of the very large services that we now have in Lourdes and try to take in the whole thing, from how we get in and out to how the whole experience was perceived by the pilgrims. I also have to take a look ahead every year and keep an eye on how the Pilgrimage continues to change and develop. That's why I am so worried this year about the cost to pilgrims going to Lourdes. I think it will have far reaching consequences."

The 80s and 90s are characterised by a steady growth in numbers of pilgrims over the years, culminating in more than 2,000 pilgrims in Lourdes for the Millennium Year. These pilgrims have benefited both from an ever more relaxed air, promoted by the Committee, which was now big enough to manage the Pilgrimage in a professional manner, and an ever increasing number of clergy who have remained fiercely loyal to Our Lady of Lourdes. While bigger doesn't always mean better, there is no doubt that the very sick and the very young have grown in number over these two decades of the Pilgrimage and have brought with them extra life and vitality which cannot be ignored.

After a minor stroke Canon Dan, as he is now, stepped down as Director after the 2000 Pilgrimage and was succeeded by Fr Nicholson. During the 2001 Pilgrimage, Canon Dan was also made an honorary Canon of Lourdes, to the delight of pilgrims when the news was announced in the Underground Basilica. It seems fair to say that these years of change were managed by teamwork. The Pilgrimage Committee became a much larger body sharing concerns, if not responsibility, and making corporate decisions after much consultation. The days of the trinity gave way to a consultative process involving regional representatives, the Medical Team, Matron, Head Handmaid, Head Brancardier, Chaplain to the Sick, Pilgrimage Director and the new post, Executive Director, who chairs meetings and steers the work of the Committee.

This work is a year round task. During the Pilgrimage each year the Doctor, Matron and Executive Director make an appointment with the Lourdes Authorities and book a set number of beds for the sick for the following year. This is a crucial meeting at which an act of faith is made. The only way to guarantee beds in the *Accueil* is to book them a whole year in advance - but once they are booked they have to be paid for even if they go unused. This means that during each year's Pilgrimage a decision is made over how many sick pilgrims will be able to stay in the *Accueil* the next year.

Current practice is to book one of the larger sections of a whole ward, which holds 63 beds. Added to this are a steadily increasing number of sick pilgrims who stay in hotels.

Pilgrimage Officials also meet for about one hour each day at 6pm during the Pilgrimage, usually in the doctor's room on the hospital ward. There they discuss how each day has gone and make plans for the coming days, dealing with anything unexpected as they go along. They also discuss any information the Director has been given from his daily lunchtime meeting with the Lourdes

Authorities. Shortly after returning home there is a full meeting of the Committee to debrief and begin plans for the next year. Of course, if the Committee does its work properly it should all go unnoticed by pilgrims, but much happens behind the scenes.

The medical team have a huge job to do before anyone gets near a plane. They have to deal with all the applications from potential sick pilgrims, assess each person and then go through a selection process to decide who can be accepted and who is not. Former Matron Teresa Harrison says this process is neither easy nor straightforward.

"The sick pilgrims all have to make a written application to be accepted as pilgrims," she says. "Every year far more people apply than we can manage, so inevitably we have to turn people down. That's very hard. The medical team, the Pilgrimage doctors and some of the experienced Lourdes nurses go through all the applications and weigh them against factors such as how many beds we have been allocated, how many nurses and doctors will be making the Pilgrimage and the skills of those professionals specific to the needs of the sick. We can then make a responsible decision about being able to care properly for each individual applicant while we are in Lourdes and, crucially, on the journey there and back. Ultimately it can be a simple question of how many doctors and nurses are on the official Pilgrimage flight."

This whole selection process takes a very long time. The booking forms and application forms for sick pilgrims are circulated to parishes in early November each year. The first selection conference takes place around January. Each of the sick people is visited by two nurses to be assessed and their own GP is also consulted. Only then can decisions be made.

"Being Matron is very hard work," admits Teresa. "One of the hardest jobs is actually going through the selection process with the rest of the medical team, deciding which of the sick applicants can be taken and cared for properly and who can't and then informing them all of our decision."

This has to be one of the most difficult jobs that Committee members undertake. On this matter the judgement of the medical experts is never questioned by any of the other members, as the safety and comfort of the sick pilgrims continues to be paramount in the Committee's work. However, another difficult job is going on at the same time. Deciding which of the sick people can go to Lourdes on the plane is going on quite often for a long time before we actually have one, or a take off time. Putting both these crucial pieces of the jigsaw into place is a job for the Executive Director, working closely with the tour operator.

"From around February each year I am in daily contact with Tangney Tours," says Mike Boyes. "We monitor how bookings are going and can then begin to work on securing a suitable aircraft for the journey. Our problems in this respect are many and not easily solved. We are a one-off charter from a small regional airport for a small group of passengers, a large number of whom have special needs. The list of companies who judge such a small, potentially problematic charter to be good business is small."

Not withstanding these difficulties, Mike usually has a rough idea of the type of aircraft that will be used and of its projected departure time. All kinds of aircraft have been used in the past and some

A typical scene at Teesside Airport on departure day.

of them present their own problems.

"It can be very exciting for the Pilgrimage to travel all together on a Boeing 747 Jumbo Jet as we have done on several occasions, but it is very worrying to me. The reality is that most of the charter companies we use only have one or two of these aircraft in service and if they break they are very hard to replace at short notice. Other wide bodied aircraft like the Airbus are much better for my blood pressure!"

One of the other things Mike works with the travel agent over is finding out where the aircraft is coming from and when it will arrive at Teesside. The news that the plane will be positioned at Teesside overnight before our departure is music to Mike's ears - but this rarely happens! In recent years the aircraft has often been used to bring the Leeds Diocesan Pilgrimage home, fly from Leeds to Teesside to collect the Middlesbrough pilgrims, and then return to Lourdes. While this makes good economic sense, it also means any delays are handed on down the line.

Other members of the Committee have less onerous responsibilities throughout the year. The Head Handmaid and Head Brancardier keep in touch with existing volunteers and are always on the look out for new people to bolster numbers. They also keep a watchful eye on supplies and equipment, making sure it is all in good order. They get to Teesside Airport the night before departure so it can all be checked in before pilgrims arrive the next morning. The brancs, nurses and handmaids meet regularly throughout the year and it is their hard work and commitment that brings the decisions made by the Committee to life. The Youth Officer does a similar job, liaising with teachers and other youth group leaders.

The work of the Committee is essential to the success of the Pilgrimage. To paint an accurate picture of its existence and development over the years of our Pilgrimage we have to acknowledge that it has had its fair share of both joy and heartache and has come in for both praise and criticism. What has been and continues to be true of every member of the Committee down throughout the years is that they have been deeply committed to Lourdes and getting as many people there as possible. Without that commitment, our Pilgrimage would not have grown to the size it has, nor would it have lasted these 50 years.

Chapter Nine

I BOW MY HEAD IN PRAYER

THERE are some phrases in the Lourdes lexicon that make no sense to anyone who has never visited the shrine. Ask for a branc anywhere but Lourdes and all you'll get is a blank look. No dimension of the Pilgrimage to Lourdes is safe from this. The whole venture has a language all of its own. In terms of liturgy, the Masses and other services we celebrate together, these phrases have grown out of the ever-changing liturgical demands of pilgrims. It may surprise some to discover that the difference between Mass in the Grotto and Mass at the Grotto is huge, big enough to fit several hundred yards of concrete and the width of the River Gave into.

Holy Hours, Penitential Services, even Youth Prayers are all regular features of the modern day Diocesan Pilgrimage, but this was not always the case. Indeed the advent of concelebration, where all priests unite around one altar, was to revolutionise

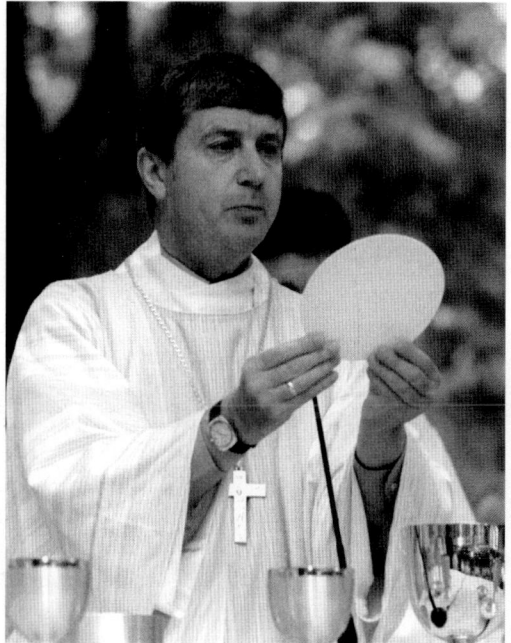

Photo: Lacaze

Bishop John celebrates Mass at the Grotto.

73

Pilgrimage programmes. Until then priests were up at the crack of dawn trying to find a side altar to say Mass at. Once that was done, the only Mass celebrated by the whole Pilgrimage together would have been the one occasion during the trip that they gathered at the Grotto. So what happened for the rest of the day?

The mainstays of each day were simply the processions, the Blessed Sacrament Procession in the afternoon and the Torchlight Procession in the evening. These surrounded by devotions such as the Rosary and the Stations of the Cross made up the spiritual life of any Pilgrimage. Fr Dan Spaight recalls his first experience back in 1961.

"We had to say individual Masses, there was no concelebration then, and we always had the greatest of difficulty finding an altar in the morning," he says. "We would hope to say Mass in the Rosary Basilica where there are 16 altars, or the Upper Basilica, where there are about another 14, while there are quite a number in the crypt as well. But in spite of that it was difficult to get one with so many priests all intending to say Mass."

Demand for altars was so great that some priests had to say their Mass as early as 4am. It would seem that the priests of the larger French and Italian pilgrimages habitually took the more civilised hours around breakfast time.

Fr Dan continues: "There was a Pilgrimage Mass which would have been either at the Grotto or the main altar of the Rosary Basilica or Upper Basilica. One of the rather nice features of that time was when we had a Holy Hour in the Upper Basilica from 11pm to midnight. During that time the priest made themselves available for confession using the side altars and then, at 12 o'clock, the Bishop had a solemn Mass at the high altar while the priests said theirs in the side altars. Concelebration didn't really get going until the late 1960s and even then it came in relatively slowly. In those days the sick were not always present for the Masses because there was no way of taking them into the Basilica."

Fr Brian Nicholson remembers also that the liturgies of the Pilgrimage were not as well structured and thought out as they are today. "We didn't have to deal with the large numbers of people who now make the annual Pilgrimage," he says. "All our services were together and I had a difficult first job as Diocesan Master of Ceremonies. Bishop Harris wanted a renewal of the liturgies that we celebrated in Lourdes. At the time they were basic liturgies for which Canon Rickaby would choose three hymns, one of which would always be a Marian hymn. I remember very vividly that the sick did not walk in the Torchlight Procession in those days. As brancs, some of us had to be on duty in the hospital and get the sick to join in with the singing as the procession passed by. I must admit it seems a bit stupid to me now. We would get them to sing 'Ave!' as best we could and quite often we weren't even allowed to open the window. It seemed to defeat the whole object of the exercise."

Mike Boyes says: "In many ways the old style discipline has gone but the liturgy is much better. Things were much more ritualistic in the old days, there was a great emphasis on the recitation of the Rosary at every opportunity. It was almost as if the liturgy began even before people congregated in the place of worship. People would make solemn procession from their hotels down to Mass and the sick had to be placed in chairs or voitures in very strict and straight columns. Their whole movement was highly controlled. The Torchlight Procession as it is now would be unrecognisable back then. It was very rigidly controlled and marshalled. That has all changed."

Certainly it would seem that the main focus of the liturgies in the early day was on public private devotion, the Rosary and particularly the Stations of the Cross. Fr Dan recalls: "The stations of the cross was a must for everybody in those days – everybody who wasn't sick. When you got to the 12th Station, a priest was allocated to say Mass. The priest used to be fasting for three hours so the handmaids would take him a flask of tea to have after Mass. It was a quick Mass with no singing or preaching and without communion because the pilgrims would have been to an earlier Mass."

Ita Leahy also remembers those Stations with fondness. "A lot of people would do them in their bare feet. We would stop at the 12th Station and Mass was said there and that was absolute heaven. You really felt that you were there."

Of course, fasting overnight was the norm in those days for a priest who intended to say Mass, so a relaxation of the rule seemed to be in place in Lourdes and the fast was reduced to three hours only. There also seems to have been a rule that only those groups who did the Stations in the morning could have Mass at the 12th Station. Presumably this rule was also in place to aid the relative comfort of the celebrant. It would be wrong of us to think the observance of the Stations of the Cross is exclusive to more traditional pilgrims. It is an experience which continues to affect many. Gilly France recalls walking the Stations in 1989 with Hull Youth. "Doing the Stations of the Cross in bare feet absolutely killed my feet," she says. "But Fr Pat was right, I will never forget that special experience."

Prayer such as this seems to have been a much greater part of the Lourdes Pilgrimage than it now is. The proposed programme for the Pilgrimage as recently as 1986 is remarkably sparse:

Saturday	3pm	Opening Mass	St Joseph's
Sunday	9am	Mass	Chapiteau
	3pm	Stations of the Cross	St Joseph's
Monday	9am	Mass of Anointing	St Pius X
	2pm	Baths	
Tuesday	9.30am	Grotto Mass	
	11am	Stations of the Cross	Uphill
	2.30pm	Holy Hour	City of the Poor
Wednesday	10am	Mass	St Joseph's
		Afternoon Free	
Thursday	9.30am	International Mass	
	2pm	Closing Ceremony	

Unlike our itinerary today, there is no indication of which night all pilgrims were expected to walk in the Torchlight Procession or the afternoon they were to walk in the Blessed Sacrament

Middlesbrough handmaids and Children of Mary lead the Blessed Sacrament Procession in the 1950s.

Procession. This was not because they were not expected to do it, but rather because most did it every day. There were no themes to the Mass either. The simple fact that Mass was taking place seemed to suffice, with the notable exceptions of the Anointing Mass and the International Mass. It is also worth noting the use of St Joseph's Chapel, which can hold a maximum of 450 pilgrims and very few sick, giving some indication of the smaller scale of the Pilgrimage then. Other changes have taken place within our own organisation rather than in Lourdes. One huge transformation which has happened slowly over many years is the development of the music group, which plays such a vital role in our modern Pilgrimage. It was preceded in the very early days by a choir organised by Margaret Stead. "Practices were held along the corridors and in the compartments on the French train during the journey," Margaret says.

This was only the start of the grand things which have followed under the leadership of Director of Music David Boyes, who fittingly is one of Margaret's former pupils. The choir did come to have its share of fame, if only by default when one year they led the singing for the Torchlight Procession.

Margaret continues: "A recollection I have is of Canon O'Mahony singing with the choir on the Rosary Basilica steps for the Torchlight Procession. We sang 72 verses of Immaculate Mary in English because we were the only English speakers to turn up that night! It was hard work." The choir seems to have been an *ad hoc* arrangement of whoever happened to be joining the Pilgrimage from year to year. The current music group has continued that tradition, but there is a little more organisation and forethought and even the chance of a rehearsal before the Pilgrimage sets off.

"About 15 years ago we decided that we really should begin to prepare the music for the liturgies before we got to Lourdes," says David Boyes. "There is almost no opportunity to rehearse while in Lourdes so we started the tradition of having a Lourdes Music Day. Fr Brian Nicholson arranged for us to use Nazareth House, as he was Chaplain there at the time. We went there until 2001 and in 2002 we moved to Corpus Christi School in Middlesbrough and were given a fantastic welcome by a group of Year Six children who came to Lourdes to sing."

Mike Boyes gives his view of the impact of the music group on the Pilgrimage. It is interesting to note that music lifts not only the liturgical parts of the Lourdes day, but many other moments too. "The music group has grown from what was a couple of guitarists in the early 70s to a significant grouping within the Pilgrimage," he says. "I believe this has made the liturgies we celebrate much more people-friendly. But the music does much more than simply enhance our prayer. Sing-songs now happen all the time, providing sick pilgrims and the young with so much joy. We even used to get away with a sing on the old wards. Now there is no need, as we can do it either outside the hospital or in one of the lounges in the new building. The music now attracts pilgrims from all over the place and sometimes we have to close down the singing simply for safety reasons! A great atmosphere is created that lasts long after the music has stopped. It hasn't made the Pilgrimage any more or less spiritually rewarding, but it has given it a different spirit."

David Boyes was 18 when he first went to Lourdes in 1971 as a brancardier, along with another of the Boyes brothers, Dominic, then 15. "Mum and Dad treated us to the trip," David says. "Lourdes had been part of our family life from the beginning and now we were going to be part of Lourdes."

They were greatly helped by some legendary brancs like Archie Coxhead, Jack Wilson, Tommy Waterson, and George Metcalfe Snr. As well as developing an interest in Lourdes, David was becoming a keen musician. "I had been interested in music for a while and I had just reached grade five on the organ," he says. "I had begun to play at church back home and I was quite shocked to find there wasn't much music on the Pilgrimage."

David was introduced to Fr Decha, who was the Director of Music at the shrine for many years. Fr Michael O'Connor, who was Chaplain to the Sick, recalls that meeting. "I can remember meeting Fr Decha for the first time," he says. "He was kind enough to introduce David to the keyboard of the outdoor organ on the Basilica steps. That was the start of David's immense contribution to our Lourdes music."

"Fr Decha was a great character," says David. "He used to call himself Fr Pussycat – a play on his name. He was a very assertive Basque priest and composer. He was also a brilliant

Photo: Lacaze

Musical trailblazer: Dominic Boyes sings The Cry Of The Poor.

organist. When I met him he had just been appointed and in his first years he revolutionised the music in Lourdes. Vatican II had changed the liturgy a lot. They had the International Mass and the processions and he created the music for all of them. His music for the International Mass set the standard. It was very accessible, simple music. It was very easy for people of all nations to join in without words or music. There are three unique challenges at the International Mass - the congregation is huge, different every week and international. He devised a formula of creating pieces of music with a very easy refrain, normally in Latin, for everyone to join in. Different cantors sang the verses in different languages. He gave us the *Lourdes Gloria* and the *Lourdes Sanctus*. Sadly Fr Decha retired and died, but his successors have continued to use that formula."

On the 1974 Pilgrimage, Dom brought his guitar. This would prove to be as revolutionary a step as Brian McGowran setting up the kitchen on the train some years later. David tentatively asked Canon Rickaby if they could play one or two guitar hymns at Mass and he agreed. David would also play the organ if Mass was held in St Joseph's Chapel.

"We used to sing things like *Give Me Joy In My Heart* and *My God Loves Me*," he says. "We had a sheet of paper that we'd typed the words to some of these hymns on and we used to give it out and then collect it back in again. That was how it started and it grew and grew and grew. Today we have a music group of more than 50 people and the skills in the group range from professional musicians right down to primary school children taking their first steps in music. They are all welcome. Everyone joins in and we all have a good time."

The first members of the music group were key in fostering this open and welcoming attitude, which embodied Vatican II's maxim of full and active participation in the liturgy above beautifully pristine music. Over the years the music group has produced high quality music but never at the cost of people's participation in the liturgy. This is something that the development of the Lourdes Liturgy Group has helped to develop into all areas of the Pilgrimage's many services. This development has only been possible because of the firm foundations laid by those early musicians.

David continues: "Dominic and Mary Crotty were the very first. Much of what we have today is owed to Mary. She is a gifted guitarist with a lovely voice and she used to come every year. After a car accident Mary decided not to play in the music group any more, although she is still a regular pilgrim and joins the group of singers.

"After Mary came Angela Ward from Hull, who is now Angela Wade, another powerful singer and a key member in a relatively small music group. There are very many others who came and went over the years, making important contributions usually for a year or two and then moving on. Sadly, some members of the music group have subsequently died. The main one and the biggest influence of all in the history of the music group was Peter McGeary. In lots of ways Peter was the father figure of the music group. He gave so much and was so enthusiastic. He loved being in the music group. He and his wife Pat used to come along for years and years. Peter would look after and encourage all of the youngsters who played the fiddle. I remember my niece, Lucy, was very much under his wing and influence for a few years and she proudly possesses one of his violins now."

The role played by Peter over the years highlights another development in the music group, namely the involvement of very many young musicians. "Another development over the years has been the growing number of young musicians who have always come with the school groups," says David. "There were two exceptional communities of young people who have impressed me particularly over the years. One came in 1994 and 1996 and contained the Corbett and Barrett twins, Helen O'Connor, Kirsty McNaughton and many others. They were all very close friends and almost became a group within the music group. Their presence was very gentle and supportive. They really did make the music group better by being there. The same thing happened again with a different group of people in 1998 and 2000, Jimmy Perry, Tom Gorman and Sarah Kirkman and their friends."

The ever-growing number of musicians led to the development of music ministry during the Pilgrimage, as David points out. "Music in Lourdes has several roles as well as the liturgical. It is also social, which is very important indeed. Music is used socially for partying and entertaining, allowing people, especially sick people, to have a good time. The third element is more subtle and perhaps not very well known. Small groups of musicians or single players will provide music to help people who are very ill or suffering. I remember once seeing a youngster with learning difficulties who was part of the English National Pilgrimage. He was very distressed and would not be comforted. One of our musicians got his guitar and played and really calmed him down."

Over the years this growing band of musicians not only became more and more aware of their own strengths and weaknesses, but also of the sensitivity of the role that they had begun to play. The most important of all of the unwritten rules of the music group is that they do not take over or dominate any liturgy; they are there to enhance and accompany it. "I believe music has been at the forefront of renewing the way we celebrate the liturgies in Lourdes," says David. "Of course, we have had to learn how to do that. There was a time when we would simply slot any old song in at any old time and it wasn't really relevant to what was happening. We do have liturgical principles now that we try to stick to as much as possible."

In 1999, after a meeting between Mgr Ricardo Morgan, Canon Dan Spaight, Fr Brian Nicholson, Fr Paul Farrer and Mike Boyes, the Lourdes Liturgy Group was formed. This was in response to the changing liturgical demands of our modern day Pilgrimage. The days of Canon Rickaby choosing a few hymns before Mass were definitely over. The purpose of the group was to try to recognise and overcome some of the obstacles that got in the way of good liturgy during the Pilgrimage. Of course, as David points out, not all of them could be planned for.

"In Lourdes there are many challenges to providing good liturgy. We can often get into a church late if the previous group overrun. We may have to use a totally alien sound system or even play in the rain. Sometimes we may have equipment that refuses to work or have problems understanding the French-speaking sacristans. If we overcome those obstacles we can find ourselves in churches where there isn't enough room to have a music group. It usually all works out though, and the end result is usually something we think most pilgrims enjoy. Not everybody, but most."

The first group was a very small affair. David and Fr Paul joined the then Diocesan Master of

Ceremonies, Fr Michael Sellars, himself a very accomplished musician. Together they worked to produce the liturgies for both the 1999 and 2000 Pilgrimages. Of course, they did not simply pluck liturgies out of the air. Such is the level of organisation in Lourdes in the modern era that each year the Bishop of Tarbes and Lourdes publishes a spiritual theme for each year which every pilgrimage from all over the world is asked to adopt as they arrive at the shrine.

Working from the notes provided by the Lourdes authorities, the group managed to provide a more cohesive set of services which flowed through the week of the Pilgrimage following a common theme. In 2001 Fr Gerard Robinson succeeded Fr Michael as Diocesan MC. For the 2003 Pilgrimage, Laura Jeffers and Rory Connelly joined the group. The group now spends a great deal of time preparing before the Pilgrimage and works on each of the liturgies, providing readings, readers, bidding prayers and music.

This has been a very useful working group and we have become much better, as a Pilgrimage, at tying all the themes of the week in Lourdes together. For many years we never bothered with the suggested Lourdes theme, but now we are able to link it in with our own themes and agendas and give a much better shape to the Pilgrimage as a whole. The job of the group is to co-ordinate what happens liturgically and ensure that the heart and soul of the Pilgrimage is kept fresh and alive.

In everything they do it is the principles of good liturgy that guide them. These are well illustrated when David talks about the music group. "Whatever we sing should tie in to whatever else is happening at the time," he says. "It also has to be music that as many people as possible know or, if it is a new piece of music, it has to be very easy to learn. Really we strive to have liturgy that is practical, relevant and enjoyable. Perhaps musically the best example of this is the hymn *Sing It In The Valleys*, which has been done to death over the years, but very many people like it and so we always find a place for it. There are some wonderful new pieces of music around by some great composers such as Bernadette Farrell and Chris Walker and we do our best to use them. *Everyday God* is a great example of Bernadette's music. It is beautiful and very simple so everyone can join in."

Lourdes is an ideal place to introduce something a little out of the ordinary liturgically. Neither the music group nor the liturgy group have been afraid to experiment with new forms of worship in a sensitive and sensible manner. This has always been done in a way that highlights the talents of particular pilgrims in

Photo: David Boyes

Drumming up support: Mike Mackin shows John Paul Vaughan how it's done.

particular years.

"Another development, which has made a massive difference to the music group, was the introduction of a drummer," says David. "Michael Mackin was the first of our drummers and we have a lot to thank him for, not only because of his skill and sensitivity to the many liturgical situations he performed in, but also because he shared his playing with many beginners. Michael brought on and trained John Paul Vaughan, who eventually replaced Michael, and he also teaches Paddy, one of our current percussionists. In fact, for a few years we had percussionists who have taught each other and passed this new

Accomplished musician Norman Evans, one of our disabled pilgrims.

Photo: David Boyes

tradition on with great pride. They lend something very special to our larger celebrations."

However, it would be inaccurate to paint a picture of liturgical development over the years that simply abandoned the old and replaced it, lock, stock and barrel with more modern material. There has always been at least one of our Masses which has specifically been planned as a more traditional liturgy with music to suit. Again, this approach relies on the talents of many dedicated people.

"We've had just about every instrument possible over the years," says David. "We've never had a harp or a double bass, but I'm pretty sure that over the years we have had every other musical instrument. We are very proud that on occasion we have had people gifted enough to gain permission to play some of the three great organs of the shrine. I can think of three, Martin Richardson from Scarborough, Joe Nolan from Hull and Fr Bill Charlton, who is an absolutely brilliant organist. The organs in the Underground Basilica, the Rosary Basilica and the St Bernadette Basilica are such special instruments that you have to have written permission to play them. All three of those people gained that permission and brought wonderful music to the Pilgrimage."

Those who are not musically gifted will, perhaps, be unaware that many different instruments require whole sets of different music to fit both key and arrangement. Providing this from year to year, while being sensitive to international copyright laws, is no mean feat. David takes no credit for this part of the operation at all. "One person who springs to mind is David Warnock, a teacher from Newlands FCJ School in Middlesbrough," he says. "He has worked very hard behind the scenes over the years on some of the more technical stuff. He was very skilled at arrangement and composition and would make sure that parts were available for musical instruments of differing musical keys such as trumpets and horns. It always seemed to me to be quite a chore, but David could do it on the hoof and thanks to him we have been able to include very many people."

The role young people have played over recent years in providing music is of equal importance to the role they have played in helping care for the sick pilgrims. They could do neither without their teachers, David Warnock, Chris Whittle and John Turver, all from Newlands FCJ School, Leo McCormack, from St John's in Bishop Auckland, Jeremy McMurray, from St Michael's in Billingham, and Finola Barron, from St Richard's in Hull, to name but a few.

Interestingly, David recalls some young people who joined the music group during their early pilgrimages who have then returned either to the music group or to play another role. "Cath Capraro, from Hull, came as a musician for a few years and then went off to medical school and returned as one of the medical team for a short time. Paul Farrer went away and returned as a priest. And we are delighted that we will welcome back one of our most gifted musicians in 2003, as Olly Barron returns to the music group as Head of Music at St Augustine's School, Scarborough."

The heart and soul of the music group is teamwork. There are some people who have worked very hard over the years to make sure that a large number of people can join together and play good music. David works closely before the Pilgrimage with key musicians such as guitarist Brendan McGeary and flautist Nicola Collins. In 2002, David asked Nicola and trumpeter Mark McCauley to act as team leaders, making sure other musicians were welcomed and included as much as possible.

"I want people to feel that when they have helped the music group, they have participated and that they have given something to sick people," he says. "There are some people who attend these liturgies who will never do so again. They are given something very special. In doing what the music group does, I hope we help pilgrims engage in what's happening and experience something that is prayerful and good."

There have been lots of developments over the years and they are a tribute to all the people who have been involved. Perhaps their biggest achievement is that fact that they have always worked as a team. Involving people has always been the highest priority. Their efforts have helped us gather as a pilgrim people around the table of the Lord in a spirit of deep prayer. They help us offer prayers of praise, thanksgiving, and intercession. Without them our Pilgrimage would not be the same.

Chapter Ten

SHOUT IT FROM THE MOUNTAIN TOPS

THE Pilgrimage would not be what it is without the sick pilgrims. They are the focus of everything that happens and the reason we go to Lourdes. Next to them are the vast numbers of young people who travel in school groups or with their families and ensure that the Pilgrimage has a future. Executive Director, Mike Boyes, puts the contribution of the young people in context.

"Perhaps the biggest change in recent years that has made a vast difference to the Pilgrimage is the development of the youth section," he says. "The fact that it has grown to about 350 young people from all over the Diocese and beyond each year is a massive achievement. They are the biggest single grouping of pilgrims within the current set up. What is very impressive to me about them is that year on year they are more and more integrated with the whole Pilgrimage, rather that apart and doing their own thing. The Pilgrimage would not survive without them and as they grow into adulthood many of them come back.

"They give a tremendous amount, probably more than they realise. I never cease to be amazed at how easily the children form friendships across the barriers of age and illness. They are a great treasure. I know the sick pilgrims get so much from them. Many are lonely and do not see people at home and they value the time they get to spend with the young people. They are a breath of fresh air. Of course, it also has a massive effect on the children. You simply have to look at how many of them come back over the years to know that."

Young people were among the early pilgrims from our Diocese in the 1920s and 1930s. Indeed, Mike's mother, Barbara, was only 15 when she made her first trip. Tom Barbour, now organist at the Sacred Heart Church, is pictured on a very early group photo as a child standing next to Bishop Lacy. It was not to be very long before young people started travelling to Lourdes in larger numbers. In 1951 there was a youth pilgrimage a whole year before the Diocesan Pilgrimage took place. Fr

Walter O'Connor had taken groups of boys from the Marist College in Middlesbrough from 1939 whenever circumstances allowed. By 1950 this group was one that everyone wanted to be part of. There was even a competition in the College with the prize of a free place for the most studious boy. The Young Christian Workers also sent boys on this pilgrimage for the first time and so what had been simply the College group expanded

The year 1958 was an important year for all Lourdes pilgrims. It marked the centenary of the apparitions of Our Lady at the Grotto. Devoted people the world over made a special effort to ensure this landmark date was marked by large numbers of pilgrims walking in procession at the shrine. The people of the Diocese of Middlesbrough were no different. They travelled in greater

Lourdes 1958

"Easter Monday 1958 saw the start of Middlesbrough Diocese Pilgrimage to Lourdes for the centenary celebrations," says Rita Morris. "After Mass in the Cathedral the pilgrims walked over the road to the railway station to begin their journey. Among the pilgrims were many pupils from the schools of the area, including a large number from Newlands Convent. During the journey one of the pupils, who had come despite suffering from flu – after all, we'd been saving for nearly two years – developed pneumonia and had to be transferred to the ambulance section. She spent the rest of the week in the Accuile, the only visitors allowed being members of staff.

"Our accommodation in Lourdes was in a convent on the hill opposite the Grotto, there was a lovely view from our room, Rose Window North, if you stood on tiptoe. This elegant-sounding room contained eight beds – straw mattresses on the roof beams – and not much else. This made it difficult to hide the wherewithal for a midnight feast, the only place was under the bedcovers when Miss Kennedy came to ensure lights out. We took part, of course, in all the services, including both processions each day. As Children of Mary, the Newlands girls got the opportunity to lead the Blessed Sacrament Procession wearing their white veils. This looked very good with our thick winter coats and scarves! There was no problem about what to wear as the rule was school uniform at all times. But at least it was warm as the weather was cold and wet; the snow at Gavarnie meant there was no outing to the mountains.

"Mary Thompson used to take the sixth formers to the early morning Mass at the Grotto and was persuaded to let some of our group of fourth formers join them. The only problem was it was the morning after our midnight feast, but we struggled to appear awake. This was a memorable experience. However, that night we had Holy Hour followed by Mass at midnight, then a climb back up to the convent for a few hours' sleep. We had to be up at 6am for a speedy breakfast and an early departure. Despite checks, it was only as we were on the train that it became apparent two pupils were missing! Mary Thompson went back and found they had ignored the wake-up calls and so she had to follow on with them.

"The long journey home was made more tiring when we reached Calais to find a force eight gale was blowing. As good convent girls, we were instructed to remain below in the Ladies Saloon, but as many succumbed to seasickness, a couple of us escaped to the top of the stairway where the fresh air and gift of spearmint gum from the crew meant we stayed fit enough to help carry the cases of those who were too ill to do so when we landed in Dover. You can imagine the welcome given to the British Rail full English breakfast as we journeyed home!"

number than they had ever done before. Mgr Peter Storey, well remembered for his devotion to young people throughout his priestly ministry, took charge of a whole second train full of children. They came from far and wide, almost every school in the Diocese was represented and even schools from Leeds and Matlock joined the fray. Among the schools represented were St Alphonsus, Newlands, St Mary's College, St Philomena's and St Richard's from Middlesbrough; St Peter's from South Bank; Sacred Heart from Redcar; St Hilda's from Whitby; the Convent from Filey; St Joseph's, Keighley; St Joseph's, Stourbridge and the Presentation Convent from Matlock.

However, it would not be until the early 1980s that young people started to come regularly and in large numbers. Again, this was to be largely the initiative of Barney Connelly, whose efforts were mirrored by Fr Michael Coleman SM down in Hull. A report written by Theresa Dunne and Suzanne Stonehouse in 1983 sheds a little more light on the role young people play during the week in Lourdes. At the time of writing they were both 13-year-old pupils of St Paul's School in Middlesbrough describing their first experience of the Torchlight Procession.

"We couldn't see the faces of the people, only the thousands of candles slowly moving up towards the Basilica. Looking back we can remember lots of things; all the soldiers from different countries, the ants in our tents, the sunshine, Bernadette's house, the view from the castle, the friendly bus drivers, going swimming, the tent nearly falling down one night, the lovely sun, Sheila and Tom's wedding anniversary, the sick people, a picnic by the river, all of the new friends we made, Archie and his jokes, the drive up to Gavarnie, the silence at the Grotto, especially at night with all of the candles lit. We all want to go back!"

Rita Morris, who has devoted years of service to Catholic secondary schools on Teesside, became one of the first teachers of the current generation to bring young people to Lourdes. She did so at the request of Barney Connelly, who was keen to follow the mandate he received from Bishop Harris to get young people to join the Diocesan Pilgrimage. Hot on the heels of Families Camping came the Schools Service. Rita's recollections are slightly different to Barney's. "'You can do it, you speak French!' With these words I was persuaded to take over the leadership of a group of pupils going to Lourdes," says Rita. "Little did I think that 20 years later I would still be involved.

"In 1983 Barney had a brainwave. He realised the best way to introduce young people to the work of Lourdes would be to take them there with the

Photo: Rita Morris

A special moment: Cardinal Hume stops to greet his old friend Barney Connelly, much to the surprise of young pilgrims.

85

Diocesan Pilgrimage. This, he realised, would have to be done as cheaply as possible. From his experience of taking family, adults and students camping in Lourdes in the summertime, he conceived the idea of a youth camping group. The first school to respond to his invitation was St Paul's Comprehensive, recently formed from the amalgamation of St Thomas' and St Michael's. When the PE teacher who was to go left, I was drafted in as a replacement.

"For this first year the group travelled on a coach as part of a Marist group. The campers consisted of 12 girls and four friends and family groups, myself and Barney and his son, Kevin. In this first year it took a little while for the children to be accepted as helpers, but they were allowed to push chairs, join in the sing-songs and take a part in the Children's Mass in the Underground Basilica. In 1984 it was again St Paul's that responded to Barney's call to pilgrimage. This time we had a smaller number, four girls and five boys, two of them ex-pupils, now at the sixth form. So it was decided to borrow a minibus to be driven by Barney and Roland Connelly and myself. We were joined by my eight-year-old cousin and two other helpers. The journey took a little longer as we visited Lisieux and Rouen en route and camped overnight at Poitiers. The trip up and down to the Domain was easier in the minibus, especially as the weather was very, very hot. This year we were able to help in the hospital, serving meals and washing up, thanks to contacts with the Head Handmaid, Mildred Raw. The two older boys were also honoured to join Archie Coxhead in carrying the Middlesbrough banner in the Torchlight Procession. Archie always had a ready stock of jokes to keep the youngsters amused. The group was also impressed by the fact that Cardinal Hume knew Barney and stopped to talk to him."

The important thing to remember about the young people now joining the Pilgrimage in large numbers is that they did so specifically to help. They began to be allowed on to the ward in small numbers at various times of the day and they were also allowed to help push and pull people in wheelchairs to various services. It was certainly a case of a slow, one step at a time development which carried people along with these new ideas. Fr Brian Nicholson says: "You have to remember that the mentality of Lourdes, not just our people, was that young people were simply not allowed to do some of the things they now do. Someone in authority within the shrine would have stopped them helping with the transport of the sick. So I would say we have progressed alongside the Lourdes authorities in understanding pilgrimage and pilgrims a little bit better."

The years from 1982 to 1984 had also seen a large group of young people from Hull make the Pilgrimage. On a coach organised by Fr Michael Coleman, St Stephen's Pastoral Centre began to bring a group that was the forerunner of the present group, Hull Youth. Fr Tom O'Neill and Sister of Mercy, Jean Barker, led that first group. Despite Fr Tom moving on from St Stephen's, the group continued. Another significant group began in 1984. It was led by Fr Pat Day, from St Andrew's Youth Club in Middlesbrough. Fr Pat's contribution to the Pilgrimage in terms of involving and encouraging young people is immeasurable. It was the early days of the Hull Youth group under his leadership that developed the role of the young people in helping minister to the sick. He is a great champion of the Lourdes cause in the Hull area, following the example set by Fr Olly Plunkett in years gone by.

Fr Pat tells us there was a Lourdes tradition in his family even though he didn't know it. "I never went to Lourdes as a young person," he says. "I only discovered years later that my Dad had gone regularly as a brancardier, but as a child I had never known. Maybe something of his devotion got into me. Only recently I found photos of the 1958 Jubilee Pilgrimage from Derry and saw him in them. Amazing! Anyway, I never had any great desire to visit Lourdes, it seemed to be too holy for me.

"I first went with probably the first organised group of young people from the Diocese, back in around 1980. I was at St Bede's in Marske and chaplain to Sacred Heart School in Redcar. One of the RE teachers thought about taking a group of kids to Lourdes but making it a bit more interesting by visiting other places on the way. All I remember is that we travelled by coach, stopped in Tours and other French towns overnight, stayed only two days in Lourdes and then went on to San Sebastian in Spain for a couple of days. We did the same on the way home, this time missing out Lourdes. I can remember nothing of what I did but it must have had some impact as I've been almost every year since!"

Fr Pat soon found himself appointed as assistant priest to Fr Liam Carson at St Andrew's, Teesville. He worked in the hugely successful St Andrew's Youth Club alongside the likes of Jim and Liz Boyle, with hundreds of young people. It seemed only natural to Fr Pat to think of Lourdes. "I went to St Andrew's in Middlesbrough in 1982 and there they had an organised adult group going to Lourdes every year," he says. "I went with them on alternate years to Liam Carson - one of us would always stay at home and mind the shop. Then Liam had had enough and let me go each year. It was great fun but the average age would have been a lot older than me. We stayed, as they still do, in the St Catherine's Hotel.

"By this time the Andrew's Youth Club was thriving and we thought about taking them to Lourdes as well. Liam was very supportive. Most of the kids came from St Peter's School in South Bank." Having decided they would make the Pilgrimage, Fr Pat needed someone to get them there. There was only one place to turn. "Barney 'Mr Lourdes' Connelly did all the arranging for us," says Fr Pat. "He offered us a place on his Families Camping but I told him to get lost! By this stage I was too old for sleeping in tents, I was in my early 30s! So I asked him to suss out a cheap hotel we could use. He did and came up trumps. We used the Hotel Panoramique, a small family-run place with just enough beds for our group. This was great. It meant no sharing with others and no problem with disturbing other guests. It was only a short walk downhill to the Grotto, but a steep climb back up! The owner was Madame Suscapsauret, who did all the work. Her husband was an architect in Lourdes and only appeared in the evenings. They were a delightful couple with a lovely, friendly staff. After a few years, they moved on to a bigger place but we remained."

As fate would have it, Fr Pat found himself appointed to St Stephen's Pastoral Centre in Hull by 1987 and he took over their Lourdes Group. With the amalgamation of the Marist College and St Mary's School for Girls, Fr Pat discovered that all his young pilgrims attended the same school, the new St Mary's College on Cranbrook Avenue. Eventually the college rather than St Stephen's became the focus and the group was renamed Hull Youth.

"When I came to Hull and St Stephen's in 1987, I discovered that there was a group from Hull going to Lourdes for the past few years," he says. "They used to stay at the City of the Poor, which was a bit of a walk from the centre of town. I arrived in Hull not long before the 1987 Pilgrimage, having already organised a group from the Andrew's. So I decided to travel with the Boro group that year and then transferred my loyalties. We stayed in the hotel but the Hull group was up in the City of the Poor. I went up to see them a couple of times and it was a bit of a trek. They used to have to come up and down three or four times a day, good exercise but nothing else. Our group was within five minutes of the town centre. It didn't take me long to realise that the following year the Hull group would also be in a hotel. As it turned out, the Boro group didn't come any more for a few years so I was able to steal the hotel from them and use it myself. Good and cheap as the City of the Poor was, some of the hotels were offering good rates as well."

Gradually more of the school groups opted for hotels, although Newlands continue to camp. "A huge amount of credit must go to Barney Connelly for all his work in getting us all on the road in the first place," says Fr Pat. "If it hadn't been for him, God knows where we all would have stayed." Credit is also due to Fr Michael Coleman, who got the first St Stephen's groups there from Hull.

"These groups of young people were around at the time the Pilgrimage was undergoing renewal," says Fr Brian Nicholson. "They drove this renewal forward, in many ways becoming a focal point for it. They have continued to do that with greater effectiveness each year and they probably don't even know it." It is almost as though the young people came along just at the right time.

At this time Fr Pat Cope was the Diocesan Youth Officer. He managed to generate an atmosphere in which school and parish groups of young people were made to feel welcome. This was a stroke of genius. He took charge of no one but chose instead to make sure the young people could begin to play some small part in the Pilgrimage. He took on an organisational role, encouraging and enabling the young people to work with the sick pilgrims in harmony with the nurses, brancs and handmaids. This was only possible now. Before this era in the Pilgrimage hardly anyone, never mind a group of young people, was allowed anywhere near the hospital and extra help was not needed. The brancs, nurses and handmaids all worked all of the time.

The early 1980s were a definite milestone in the life of the Pilgrimage. Doors were opened, smiles were welcoming and sing-songs abounded. Attitudes had changed. Young people not only came to Lourdes and enjoyed it, they all wanted to come back.

Gilly France, of Hull, made her first Pilgrimage in 1989 and on July 9 that same year wrote to Fr Pat Day to thank him for the experience. "Being at Lourdes gave me such a strong, undoubtable belief in God and heaven and I think being there was the first time I enjoyed praying," she said. "Seeing all the sick people, being at the Grotto, lighting candles, going to the baths; all this seemed so right and good."

Another of Fr Pat's correspondents told him: "I'm really upset that I can't go next year. I would love to. I would still go even though I have my exams but Mum won't let me. I am definitely going the year after. It'll be awful to think of you all there next year and me studying at home. You'll have to pray for me while you are there, I'll definitely need it!"

From the earliest days, this new innovation of large, organised groups of young people was immensely popular. The young people enjoyed it and told all of their friends. Another young columnist for a school newsletter ended a report on Lourdes saying: "Trying to write about the way Lourdes can make a person feel is hard. You can never fully understand what it is like unless you have been there. So if you are ever presented with the opportunity to go, do. I promise you will enjoy it and never forget your time there."

With endorsements like this ringing in their ears, more and more young people each year filled the coaches from their schools and journeyed south. Rita Morris fills in a few more gaps. "By 1985 word of the success of the trips had spread and the first joint youth group was organised," she says. "By now St Paul's was part of St David's and was joined by Newlands, Sacred Heart Redcar, three pupils from St Patrick's, Thornaby, and students from St Mary's Sixth Form in their minibus, to make up a total of 68 in the group. The pupils were able to be more involved in helping with the sick, pushing and pulling, serving teas and entertaining the sick pilgrims.

"Over the next few years the number of schools and groups increased. All secondary schools from the Diocese are now involved, along with the Hull Youth group, St Michael's, Billingham and, for a number of years, Marling School, Stroud." The Marling group are unique in the youth section not because they come from outside the Diocese but because they come from a non-Catholic school. Their group leader, Janet Hogg, lived and worked in Middlesbrough for a while and saw the Pilgrimage close up. On taking her new appointment she decided a Lourdes pilgrimage would work well for the Stroud school too.

They have joined us for many of the recent Pilgrimages and are one of our largest groups combining both sixth formers and younger pilgrims also. They join many of the Pilgrimage services and provide crucial cover working very hard in the hospital on the day all the other youth groups

Flat out: A young pilgrim resting between shifts.

Photo: David Boyes

89

visit the mountains at Gavarnie and celebrate Mass there.

Once a branc and now a teacher, George Metcalfe found himself wishing he was back in Lourdes at just the right time. "My Dad had become a stalwart of the Pilgrimage and had assumed responsibility for looking after the luggage of the special pilgrims and their helpers," he says. "In 1984 I offered to take dad to the Cenotaph to meet the coaches taking the pilgrims to Dover for the first part of the journey to Lourdes. To say it didn't feel right not to be going would be an understatement and I was not a happy teacher that day or a happy husband that night. I decided that come hell or high water I would go in 1985.

"In October 1984 I was summoned to the Head's office to be asked if I would consider helping a colleague take a group of pupils to Lourdes by coach. My response was immediate and positive. I reacquainted myself with Barney and other members of the Connelly dynasty and experienced yet another intriguing and enjoyable aspect of Lourdes, seeing young adults cheerfully working their socks off so that people less energetic than themselves could have a memorable time. Knowing I was part of a team enabling this to occur brought its rewards."

By now the youth section of the Pilgrimage was the biggest single grouping of pilgrims. It dwarfed other groupings, such as parish groups or the sick pilgrims. Their involvement spread beyond helping with the sick and began to affect the liturgies of the Pilgrimage. Eventually Fr Pat Cope, in collaboration with Fr Pat Day and teachers such as Rita Morris and George Metcalfe, was able to put the first Youth Mass together. In its early days the Youth Mass was as much about recognising the large numbers of young pilgrims in Lourdes as anything else. The Mass itself was a clarion call to all other pilgrims to sit up and take notice of this significant group of people. It was also a liturgy which was prepared and presented by the young people in their own way. It was a fresh, colourful celebration.

The preparation for the first Youth Mass was all done on the hoof. Rita recalls that it was prepared the night before it happened up on the campsite. "We sat up until the early hours of the morning with Fr Pat Cope and some pupils preparing the Mass and then ringing home to get the words of *All You Need Is Love*," she says. Among those pupils were Michael McCauley and Julie Walton. Julie recalls: "Using *All You Need Is Love* was Michael's idea but we couldn't remember the words. We rang home to get them. It was very late but we decided it was an hour earlier in England so it would be okay!" Each school group took responsibility for a part of the Mass and did something creative with it. Whether it was the Sign of Peace or the bidding prayers, it was going to be different.

By 1995 Fr Pat Cope moved on and was replaced as Youth Officer by Sister Lorraine Millar FCJ. Lorraine, a Scot, came to the Diocese after working as part of a youth mission team in Salford. Sister Lorraine was a breath of fresh air in the youth set up. She was a great team player and was able to build on what Fr Pat had set up. She struck up great friendships in a very short period of time with many of the group leaders and was able to encourage them to work very closely together. Her years as Youth Officer laid the foundations for the close working relationship the youth groups enjoy today. But perhaps the biggest single development Sister Lorraine managed during her time in office involved the Youth Mass. By 1997 Fr Paul Farrer had been appointed Assistant Youth Officer and he recalls the dilemma Lorraine found herself in. "The Youth Mass had always been a spontaneous event," he says. "That was its great strength and also its great weakness. When things worked well it was fantastic but if things went wrong it could be awful. Because it was arranged on the hoof you never really knew what was going to happen."

Mgr Ricardo Morgan was Diocesan Master of Ceremonies at this time and he tried to persuade Lorraine to pull things together and organise them. Fr Paul says: "Unfortunately, it was too late to make any changes for the 1997 Pilgrimage, so Sister Lorraine and Mgr Ricardo came to a compromise. He had wanted a full text for the Mass before the Pilgrimage set off. Lorraine explained that many of the school groups actually used the journey to prepare their offering. So they agreed they would meet again in Lourdes in the Café Terasse the night before the Youth Mass and Mgr Ricardo would be told everything."

Sister Lorraine took Fr Paul and David Boyes to the meeting with her and sat waiting for Mgr Ricardo with some trepidation. "She was about to break her promise," says Fr Paul. "The reality was, she hadn't had any time to find out what exactly was going to happen in the Youth Mass. She couldn't even give Ricardo a general idea. We thought he would be furious."

But they were wrong. "He took it very well," says Fr Paul. "His face was a picture, I wish I'd had my camera with me! To his eternal credit, he just laughed it off. But it was a very useful meeting because it was the birth of the Master of Ceremonies and other people who were responsible for different liturgies working together. By the following year the Youth Mass was organised much better. The liturgy actually flowed. It was as it had always been but better."

As Director of Lourdes Music, David has a unique insight into the importance of the Youth Mass and why, since its conception by both Fr Pat Day and Fr Pat Cope, it has stood the test of time. "The most important thing for young people who join the Pilgrimage, even if it is for just one year, is that they leave Lourdes with the feeling that they have participated in the liturgy," he says. "I want them to believe they have been included. I feel very strongly that liturgy can be exclusive and I think it's great that in Lourdes they can feel they are putting something in; not performing but definitely participating. Kids, especially, may only come to Lourdes once. They may only experience that extraordinary liturgy that is the Youth Mass once. I hope it will stay with them forever. That's why I think the Youth Mass is the most important Mass of the Pilgrimage.

"Of all of the liturgies, the Youth Mass is unique. It is a huge Mass with great symbolism. It is full of participation and is often poignant and very moving. It can be very prayerful and reflective. We have gone beyond being simply spectacular and provide a liturgy that speaks to people. It doesn't happen anywhere else except perhaps for our Diocesan youth day at Ampleforth, Springboard, and that's very different anyway. The other Masses that happen in Lourdes happen in many parishes around the Diocese throughout the year."

These days the preparations for that Mass go on for weeks and weeks before we get there. Fr Paul says: "I am very aware that it is one of the great focal points of the week. Alongside the Mass of Anointing, it is the biggest celebration of our Pilgrimage. Others will say it's Mass at the Grotto or something else, but for the me the Youth Mass is special because it is always one of the largest gatherings of Middlesbrough pilgrims when we are actually on our own."

From 1999 the Youth Mass has also been the liturgy which has taken the Lourdes theme for the years as its central message. In that sense, it has been a very important event in terms of focusing our whole Pilgrimage. "It is very difficult trying to come up with something new and fresh each year, but we have a great team full of people with good ideas," Fr Paul says. "The popularity of the Mass goes beyond our Diocese. Each year I get phone calls from Liverpool and Manchester from small groups of pilgrims who are in Lourdes at the same time as us asking when the Youth Mass is. They tell me they wouldn't miss it for the world."

Each year since 1998 there have been more than 300 young people in Lourdes as part of the Pilgrimage. Most travel with school groups, some with their families. The normal routine has been for schools to offer places to young people in years nine and ten of comprehensive school. Year eleven pupils have usually been unable to make the trip as it takes place immediately before GCSE examinations. A growing number of sixth formers have returned to the Pilgrimage either as assistant leaders to their old school groups or with the Young Brancs and Handmaids group organised by Pat McBride.

These large numbers are wonderful to see. However, the pattern of youth group involvement in the Pilgrimage has had to change simply because of the size of the groups. In the early 1980s a small number of young people shared a simple timetable of involvement duties helping sick pilgrims in

Big finish: Paper fish float down on to pilgrims to illustrate the theme 'He fills the starving with good things' at the end of the Youth Mass.

the hospital. To cope with such large numbers things have had to change. While change has been inevitable, contact between the young people and the sick pilgrims remains the reason why they journey to Lourdes.

Young people now work in their school groups for a whole day during the week, following a rota. They are also available for an extra day's work if they are needed. They report to the hospital early in the morning and work with the sick pilgrims until after the Torchlight Procession in the evening. In addition to these responsibilities, there are plenty of opportunities to experience Lourdes. Tours of the places where Bernadette and her family lived and learning about the story are also high on the agenda. The youth groups all also follow the full pilgrimage programme, ensuring a packed timetable.

This direct work with the sick pilgrims is definitely viewed as Christianity in action by the young people. They are given the opportunity to work at something in the Church that they can see makes a huge difference to individuals who they come to know very well, very quickly. It matters very much to them and it has blossomed over the years. The youth section of the Pilgrimage is always a curious mix of old and new. Young people who visit Lourdes are able to come with their school group a maximum of three or four times and by then they have moved on, meaning each group has a healthy mixture of people who have been before and those who are experiencing things for the first time. It is always the time with the sick pilgrims they remember best of all. Hull Youth are the only group to travel to Lourdes a whole day before the Pilgrimage arrives. As a result, they have always worked first, simply because they are there while others are still on the road. Likewise, Newlands stay an extra day at the end of the Pilgrimage, so they are able to work the last day and see everyone else off. Only once in recent years has this happened any other way. Rita tells us how. "One of the highlights of the early years was bidding farewell to the main Pilgrimage group as they left by train, followed by a meal of chicken and chips in the station buffet – very welcome after surviving on the campsite all week. One year, thanks to altered travel plans because of a ferry strike, St Patrick's achieved a record. They were in Lourdes in time to welcome the train and also saw it off at the end of the week."

Over the years the youth groups have been identifiable in many ways. Scarves and hats have complimented banners and flags, all bearing school names and badges. But as the spirit of co-operation has grown so has the notion of togetherness between the groups. They all now wear a T-shirt emblazoned with the Diocesan Youth Service logo, announcing that they are there living Life To The Full. To say it is all work and no play for the young people would be very wrong. Traditional days out to Gavarnie and Pont d'Espagne are now complimented by afternoons out at the Lac de Lourdes or the newly discovered Green Lake, while some groups even manage a trip or two to the hypermarket. "An excursion to the Pyrenees became one of the highlights of the week," says Rita. "But in recent years concern for the safety of such large numbers has meant this has had to be relocated to Gavarnie, where a new highlight was Mass celebrated in a field with the backdrop of the glacier reflecting the grandeur of God's creation."

Of course, rain is never far away in Lourdes. Pilgrims have become used to the ever-present possibility of walking home soaked to the skin. Some will tell you it usually starts to rain just as we line up for a procession. In 2000 the heavens opened just as we reached the front of Rosary Square in the Torchlight Procession and we had to get everyone back to the hospital through the thunderstorm. Young people remained with other helpers to make sure the sick pilgrims were as comfortable as possible.

Until 2001 all youth groups had travelled by coach because of its relatively low cost. The first entire group to travel by air was a group of young singers from the Diocesan Choir. A group from Corpus Christi in Middlesbrough joined them on the Pilgrimage, but not on the plane. These groups became the first primary school children of the modern era to join the Pilgrimage. But coach continues to be the usual mode of transport for young people. Rita pays tribute to the drivers who have played their part over the years. "They are unsung heroes of our Pilgrimage," she says. "Their skill and inventiveness have kept us safely on the road. I can recall some of them replacing a coach gearbox on the campsite one year and another time they repaired the drive belt of the coach with a rubber band from George Metcalfe's tent."

David Boyes compares the effect of the young people on the Pilgrimage with the developments in other areas. "The involvement of the youngsters is even more important than the involvement of music," he says. "A lot of people say it is the music that makes Lourdes, but I think it is the young people who make it the experience it is. They have done an excellent job and their teachers have played a key role in that. Quite often they will proudly send very gifted young musicians along to me to be part of the music group. Last year, 2002, Newlands School had a disaster. One of the girls in the group contracted chicken pox and the medical team decided that they had to stay away from the hospital and anyone who may be going there. This meant the very large number of musicians they had with them could not be in the music group and they couldn't work in the hospital. It was terribly sad.

"Young people have a huge impact. They keep the Pilgrimage vibrant, noisy and enjoyable. It is a great experience for them, even if they only come once. It is a life changing experience that they will never forget."

Perhaps the main reason that Lourdes can have such a dramatic affect on young people is the fact that they spend a large amount of time working with the sick. Pushing and pulling wheelchairs and voitures and helping hand out drinks are great opportunities to serve, but they are not as important as the friendships that are formed. Gilly France was deeply affected by her time with the sick pilgrims. "The best thing really was making friends with Terry, who was a sick person," she says. "He was absolutely great. The atmosphere in the hospital was friendly, like one big, happy family. Terry, Helen, Annette, Alan, Richard, Simon and me all sat together and Terry was being really funny. He said he felt like we were all a family and he took our photo so he could show his own kids when he got home."

George Metcalfe has seen the youth section go from strength to strength in the 17 years he has been involved. "I now look forward to meeting colleagues and friends from other schools that share the same aspirations as myself," he says. "At a conservative estimate, I would say 5,000 young people have shared the experience of Lourdes through this initiative."

The benefits of the company the young people offer are invaluable. Each year the Medical Director Dr John O'Neill writes to the group leaders to thank them. Perhaps the last word should be left to him. "Would you convey my sincere appreciation to the young people from the various parts of the Diocese?" he writes. "They help the sick in many ways and were also a great help to us. I hope we continue to enjoy the company of the young people on the Diocesan Pilgrimage for many years to come."

Chapter Eleven

WORK, REST AND PLAY

FOR any good idea to become a reality someone has to put blood, sweat and tears into pulling it off. Although the inspiration for a Lourdes Pilgrimage came from a small group of people back in the 1950s, it only continues to be the success it is today because of the hard work of the hundreds of people who have volunteered their time and effort over the years.

For the most part they all come to work during the Pilgrimage as nurses, brancardiers or handmaids. They give hours and hours working in the hospital, nursing the sick pilgrims, helping them to wash and dress and serving meals. Their efforts often go unnoticed by most, yet without them the Pilgrimage would not work. Alongside them are the doctors, the Chaplains to the Sick and the Pilgrimage Committee.

Many of those helpers who return to Lourdes year after year have been inspired by the experiences and devotion of the previous generation. Margaret and Mary Stead were on that first Pilgrimage in 1952 and continued working as handmaids until they took a well earned rest in 1999 and were looked after by their fellow helpers in the hospital. The sisters' mother went to Lourdes in the 1920s and the postcard she sent home, which they still treasure, clearly had the desired effect.

"It said she would not rest until we two and Dad had visited Lourdes, 'For it was a little piece of heaven'," says Margaret. "We didn't discover the truth of this for ourselves until after her death, when we took Dad with us on the first Diocesan Pilgrimage." Fr Walter O'Connor then began the Lourdes Sick Fund and the Steads were among the ladies who baked and made toffee apples and other treats to raise money to help get sick pilgrims on the road.

Mary was asked by Fr Walter to design a handmaid's pocket badge incorporating the words *Ecce Ancilla Domini* – 'Behold the handmaid of the Lord'. Margaret and many friends joined in and embroidered hundreds of them over the years. Today they are machine-produced but are still

You've got the job! Head Handmaid Mildred Raw approves of Bishop McClean's technique.

proudly part of the uniform. Many years later the same group worked on Bishop John's Choose Life banner, the framework of which was made by brancardier Gerry McBride.

Ellen Metcalfe took a different approach to Mrs Stead when she persuaded her son George to go as a helper for his first time. It was 10pm on a Monday night in May 1973 when she simply asked George, then a 20-year-old shipping clerk, if he could get that Friday and all the following week off work.

"I replied that it was probably possible. She said, 'Good, because I've just booked you on this year's Pilgrimage to Lourdes! We'll leave on Friday afternoon and you will be a branc.' I knew I was going, but I tried to set some of my terms in place. I will push or pull chairs and fetch and carry equipment but I won't do any of the messy jobs that go on in hospitals. Mum assured me I would only have to do what I was capable of. At the brancs' meeting the next night I was more aware of my role, felt slightly more at ease and was conned into volunteering for a night duty.

"Our scheduled 3.30pm flight left Teesside at 4am on Saturday and I got to the hotel at 7.45am. After breakfast mum took me to the *Accueil* where I started to push and pull. The Head Branc, John Adams, joyfully welcomed me in his first breath, and asked me if I would work the night duty that night with his second. I pointed out the problems I'd experienced in getting to Lourdes and suggested I may be better served by getting a good night's sleep. The often-repeated phrase of, 'Don't worry about that' was invoked. 'The branc can get a stretcher and get some sleep.'

"I knew I'd be able to sleep on the proverbial clothesline and agreed to the duty. My shift

97

Middlesbrough pilgrims prepare for the Blessed Sacrament Procession in the 1950s.

was with two nursing Sisters of Mercy on their first pilgrimage, who elected to keep me plied with tea and conversation all night. They also co-opted me to help them perform all sorts of the messy nurse-type duties I'd said I wasn't going to do. Around 50 hours after getting up on the Friday I went to bed at 9am on the Sunday morning. At lunch that day someone enquired if I was enjoying myself. It only took a second to come up with the answer, an emphatic 'Yes'." George followed up his answer with deeds and now takes school groups from St Patrick's in Thornaby.

Everyone has their own story of how they came to join the Lourdes family. Brian McGowran's first visit was in 1978 when he went with Peter McGeary. It was a hot and exhausting week and Brian returned to Teesside in a sorry state. "It took me almost a week to get over it," he said. "I'd been over-enthusiastic, I thought I was the only person nobody could do without and it all caught up with me."

Brian knew very few people but remembers characters like ex-docker Jimmy McGurn, John and Dick McGee, and Bob Harrison and Eddie Lappin. "Ita Leahy was the Matron and Margaret Jackson was the Head Handmaid," he says. "But the Lourdes authorities in those days seemed to deal mainly with the Head Branc. Even though that was the case, I remember that the real boss was Ita. In those days, being a branc was a much more physically demanding job. On the train, particularly, more than double the amount of lifting needed to be done. We always had two Ambulance Cars and we would carry the sick on their chairs on to the train, then Ita would decide who would get which bunk. Obviously the lightest people would be put up at the top, as they were easy to manage."

Brian worked very closely with John Adams during much of his time as Head Brancardier and the time came for John to step aside from the demanding role, Brian was a ready-made replacement. In doing so, he was stepping proudly in the footsteps of former Head Brancs Harry Kelly, Leo

McLoughlin, Jimmy Coughlan and John Cassidy.

"John told me he wanted me to follow him, although it was the Bishop who asked me," says Brian. "I really got into Lourdes straight away and at the time I was in business for myself, so I could use company vehicles and time to get things ready before we set off. One time we lost some wheelchairs in Lourdes and I had to go up to Newcastle and borrow some from the Geordies. The Geordies were fantastic because when we used to pull into Lourdes there were always plenty of them there to do a *stage*. They used to make a point of being there to unload the train. Characters like Mick Davison and the late Eddie Woods used to make a great effort on our behalf."

Like Brian, another former Head Brancardier, Peter Dunne, is also grateful to Peter McGeary for first introducing him to Lourdes. But his story has an unusual twist. While several helpers have later been looked after in the hospital as sick pilgrims, he is one of a select band who have done things the other way round.

"I got a visit from my Parish Priest, Mgr Peter Storey, and he asked if I'd like to go to Lourdes," he says. "I was flabbergasted. I had a problem with my neck after an accident at work and Peter had put my name forward to go as walking wounded.

"The morning we left from Middlesbrough Station I could feel something special. At some point in the journey I went into the luggage compartment and met Brian McGowran and renewed an old friendship with him. From that point on, I wasn't a sick pilgrim, I was a brancardier. It rained all week, but it didn't bother me. I came home and cried my eyes out and I knew I would go again. From that point on I've been every year." Peter is also indebted to Brian, among others, for often helping financially to make sure he made it to Lourdes every year. No doubt Brian recognised Peter's value as a helper as well as appreciating his friendship. "I was a married man with three kids and each year I went financial assistance was always accepted," says Peter.

After Brian stepped down, Steve Holder was Head Brancardier for a year, before Peter Dunne was asked to fill the role. "It was a great honour but also a big responsibility and I had to give it a lot of consideration," he says. "It was one of the best decisions I've ever made, although people could see on the Wednesday of my first year when we led the Blessed Sacrament Procession there was a visible change in my demeanour!"

Peter helped shape the brancs' rota as it exists today by identifying times in the day when it was no longer necessary to ask all brancs to be on duty at the same time. "John Adams was a very astute man," says Peter. "One year someone told him the trouble with the brancs was there were too many indians and not enough chiefs. From that came team leaders and the rota as we know it.

"But no matter what the Head Branc did, there was always someone who reckoned it could be done better. My job was as a planner and I spent many hours thinking about it. Eventually it hit me that twice a day when we had all brancs on duty we didn't need them all. I did away with that and gave people quality time off. But the reason I could do that was because of the school groups getting more involved."

Current Head Brancardier Paul Griffiths traces his roots in the Pilgrimage back to 1982 – and he wasn't even there! Paul was working abroad and his wife Teresa, mother-in-law Doreen and his then young daughter Catherine went to Lourdes. The kindness helpers gave his young family on the long train journey made a lasting impression on him. "Their kindness was not forgotten," he says. In 1984 he agreed to join the family on Pilgrimage, but he had no intention of working as the train pulled out of Middlesbrough Station. Of course, he was soon in the thick of things, as has become his familiar role.

"Tom Waterson, my wife's uncle, had been a brancardier for many years, and after making sure we were settled in the correct coach he set off to do his

Three Head Brancardiers, (from left) Paul Griffiths, Peter Dunne and Brian McGowran, relax at the Hotel Solitude.

'luggage duties'," says Paul. "I couldn't sit around doing nothing, so I followed him. I finished up working with the luggage team of George Metcalfe Snr, Jim Rainey, Tommy Wright and Tom. The mickey-taking was unbelievable, but then so was the work that was carried out so efficiently and quickly."

This was what Paul describes as his first experience of helper camaraderie and he outlines three more along the way. "After the transfer from the British train, the ferry crossing and on board the French train for the long overnight journey, I found my second experience. The handmaids, having catered for all sick pilgrims, appeared smiling warmly with hot tea for everyone in the compartment. I wanted to know more and Tom showed me along the carriage to the guards van, and there I found my third experience - Brian McGowran's kitchen!"

Paul soon realised that this cheerful band of helpers doing such tough work with joviality and goodwill was something he needed to be part of. In 1985, he signed up as a brancardier proper. "In Lourdes, I learned of all the behind-the-scenes work, attending mainly to the men in the hospital and also the ladies as we were able, doing most of the lifting, carrying and general jobs around the hospital. If anyone is not sure of what to do, where to go or who should do it, they call on the brancs. During this first week I had my fourth experience of helper camaraderie – the nurses and doctors. I've never missed a year since then, and neither have many others. Our senior branc on this year's Pilgrimage will have served for a total of 42 years, mostly continuous since 1956. I'm proud to say it is Tom Waterson."

One year George Metcalfe, whose father George Snr was a brancardier for many years and whose sisters Maureen and Ellen and their families are also regular helpers, completed a two-week *stage* with another legendary branc, Derek Brough. "Derek was one of those helpers so smitten by Lourdes that he went back whenever he could," he says. "We worked all day every day at the station, helping disabled and able-bodied pilgrims from every part of Europe off and on to the trains. We mainly teamed up with three disparate groups of people; Scousers, Welshmen and a combined group of Geordies and Mackems. They all worked hard and, much against my wishes, forced me to socialise with them at that well-known alternative 'Shrine de Brickies' until all hours of the morning."

The Brickies is, of course, the popular café *Le Carrefour*, where the relaxation often begins after a hard shift in the hospital. One version of the story has it that the nickname was bestowed by a thirsty Middlesbrough branc many years ago. It's a home from home for many, where English is spoken and where inside and out on the *terrasse* English voices laugh and swap stories of the day's events.

Derek, who died a few years ago, was a much-loved brancardier whose dedication to the Lourdes cause was an inspiration to all. Brian McGowran remembers his immense contribution to the Pilgrimage beginning each year on the train journey.

"Derek had a photographic memory and could recall which sidings would be used at various stations," he says. "He knew exactly where the train would pull in. He also used to do his homework. He would have found out about the tide so that when we arrived at the port he knew if we would have to carry people up or down to the ferry. The tide made carrying a real problem and it was always great to be forewarned so that we could prepare.

"Derek was a big anchorman. He was the only man from the Diocese who was a member of the Lourdes *Hospitalité*. I used to go with him to London once a year to the *Hospitalité* meeting. We always promised we would get a larger membership involved from the Diocese but it never happened."

The Knights of St Columba Institute in Southfield Road, Middlesbrough, which played such a crucial role in the early years of our story, was a focus for year-round fundraising.

"We always showed Derek's famous cine films and then we used to organise a bus down to Hull and show it there during a social evening. The Lourdes social scene was buzzing then. The bus would pick up the York brancs on the way and we would all stay in Anchor House in Hull. It was great."

It was also Derek who refurbished the statues of Our Lady and St Bernadette in the 'Lourdes Corner' at the Knights, so called because of the Pilgrimage photographs displayed there. In this same corner Jack Wilson, a stalwart branc, collected 6d per week from all who frequented the club, whether of the Lourdes fraternity or not. These sixpences, collected over the year, paid for three or four

Brancs a lot! Legendary brancardier Derek Brough (far right), always happy in the company of fellow brancs.

Photo: David Boyes

101

sick pilgrims to go to Lourdes.

Of course, as costs climbed it was realised that more funds needed to be raised, so John Urch and Les Clark founded the KSC Lourdes Sick Fund and who could forget Charlie Roe barking out his wares selling 'blind cards'. "At the same time, Ita Leahy was always running fundraising events in the canteen at the General Hospital and getting new nurses," says Brian. Like Derek, Ita joined the *Hospitalité* and still works *stages* each year. Handmaid Pat McGeary also recalls Ita's tireless efforts. "Even before becoming Matron she did sterling work in recruiting young nurses," she says. "She helped with their fares if necessary by fundraising in various ways, like social evenings in the hospital canteen and selling baby clothes she'd knitted to new mums in the Maternity Ward – have you tried saying 'No' to Ita?

"She was also a founder member of the annual retreat for Lourdes helpers at Ampleforth more than 25 years ago. Initially for nurses, it now welcomes handmaids and brancs. This has proved so successful it has just changed by popular request to twice a year. Only in 2002 did Ita hand over the organisation of this event to someone younger, and it is now in the capable hands of Rachel Forgan."

Peter Dunne relied heavily on Ita during his time as Head Branc. "She always knew where to empty the bins and collect the laundry," he says. "She was so good, she was working to raise funds all year round - not like some of us! The nurses do a lot of work during the year that goes unseen."

Ita was nursing at Middlesbrough General Hospital in 1958 when she first went to Lourdes. She has missed just one year since, when she had her son, John. She served as Matron from 1971 to 1986 and has also been with the Faith and Light group, Across and has completed 15 *stages*. And she says every year she goes it gets better. "We'd begin fundraising for the next year as soon as we got

Head Brancardier Peter Dunne assists Bishop John during the Blessing of sick pilgrims.

Photo: Margaret Stewart

home, with a lot of social events," she says. "The preparations would begin shortly after Christmas. We'd sort out the blankets we used to use, airing and washing them. We had everything packed up down in the cellar at the Holy Name. We would beg, steal and borrow from various places to get hold of all the things we needed. Father Harrison would bring us tea and chocolate biscuits."

Another Lourdes stalwart, without whom the Middlesbrough Pilgrimage did not seem complete for many, was Archie Coxhead. Loved by all, especially young people, Archie was a huge character, both in physical stature and his contribution to our story. "Archie should have been knighted," says Tom Waterson. "He didn't have a relation in the world and he didn't even know his mother. But he couldn't do enough for the sick. He used to do all the nights on the train and it was hard work lifting people down from the top bunk. One year he couldn't go and it nearly broke my back! He used to get up and sing in the Brickies and Philipe, the gaffer, wouldn't let anyone talk until he was finished. Sometimes he would sleep in his shirt and tie, then he'd jump up and put his trousers on and he'd be first in the hospital."

Paul Griffiths learned about Archie's unusual sleep pattern the hard way. "I have an endearing memory of Archie which I later found out to be famous," he says. "In my early years as a branc I was asked if I would share a room with him. I readily agreed, only to find out that he could snore not only for England but also the Rest of the World! He was always last into bed after enjoying Lourdes for as much as his waking hours would allow, then first up and down to the hospital. It was always Archie who switched on the boilers for piping hot tea as soon as the first shift arrived at 6am."

Although the story of our transportation to Lourdes is recorded elsewhere in this book, those mammoth train journeys continue to dominate many helpers' Pilgrimage memories. Mary and Margaret Stead are no exception. "There were some difficult journeys in the early years," says Margaret. "In those days the sick travelled in the luggage van and then on the ship's deck. Fortunately, the sick bays on the French train did have bunks but they were very crowded and the facilities for the handmaids to make drinks were very limited.

"However, the joyful companionship and laughter permeated our work. Indeed we had fantastic results from our tea making and washing-up efforts made in an alcove of a few square feet, in a tiny space no bigger that a train toilet compartment. "We even managed to produce silver service for Bishop Brunner's compartment at Mildred Raw's suggestion. The helpers did get tired and were glad

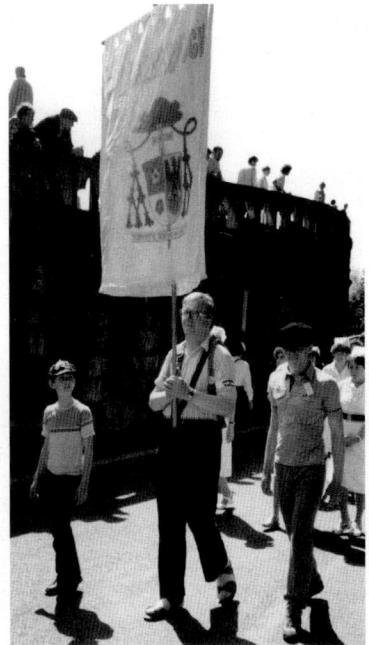

Photo: David Boyes

Flying the Flag: Archie Coxhead proudly carries the Middlesbrough Banner.

ARCHIE COXHEAD

Every year a group of people from the St John of God Hospital at Scorton, escorted by the Brothers, would join the Pilgrimage. These patients were often the most ill and infirm of all of the sick people we have ever taken to Lourdes. It was the Brothers who brought Archie with them as part of their contingent because he was living there.

When he first made the Pilgrimage, Archie was very inarticulate and struggled to communicate. But he was big and strong and well known to all the sick pilgrims from Scorton. As a newborn baby, Archie was left on the steps of an orphanage and never knew his family. He was brought up in institutions and worked at St John of God, Scorton, for many years assisting the Brothers there.

Ita Leahy discovered that Archie had a great potential and she, along with many others over the years, struck up a lifelong friendship with him. He was invaluable to the nursing staff. "Archie was the one person who knew exactly how to handle each one of the sick pilgrims from Scorton," says Fr Brian Nicholson. "If the Brothers weren't there he could lift them all like a feather. In those early days he could almost do it one-handed."

Ita found that despite Archie's own lack of words he possessed another great gift to equal his strength. "He could talk to all of those very sick people and understand them," she says. "If there was ever any kind of problem with any of the sick from Scorton, Archie would automatically sit with them and translate."

For a long time Archie made the Pilgrimage ostensibly as one of the sick pilgrims of Scorton but he became an invaluable brancardier. He was ever-present at the hospital and became the man everyone looked out for when we began to line up for the processions.

Present day Head Brancardier Paul Griffiths remembers Archie the branc well. "It was easy to see why he was nicknamed Big Archie," he says. "Once you got to know him it was also easy to understand that his heart and personality were as big as his frame. In the days of the long train journey, Archie was famous for a number of things. He worked endlessly on the long night shifts, tending the sick during those difficult and restless journeys. He always covered those shifts both outward and return, asking for help only when needed.

"A typical branc, Archie was never one to miss out on a little bonus either. A packed meal was provided each way, including a quarter bottle of French table wine, which was notorious for its poor quality and sour taste. Before leaving the train, Archie would go through the compartments collecting many of the still sealed quarter bottles of wine left by pilgrims. These he took to St John of God, Scorton, where I assume there was an impromptu party.

"Every year on the first Sunday back after his return from Lourdes, he would take a group of sick and disabled people from Scorton hospital and, with his helpers, they processed around the village green singing Lourdes hymns, Archie leading with his booming voice. Later, of course, he took them all to the village pub on the green! This was Archie bringing Lourdes home to those who could not go."

In 1965 John and Ita Leahy, who by now had struck up a lifelong friendship, gave him a key to their home in Berner Street so he always had a home in Middlesbrough. Consequently, he was often found there, and thankfully at the Knights' Club with his many Lourdes friends.

Archie moved from the North East to the North West to live with a community of religious sisters. He went to Lourdes for 32 years. He retired to Silverdale, where he worked in the kitchen until his death. His small cottage was full of Lourdes memorabilia, particularly photographs. After 25 years' service, the Lourdes nurses bought and presented him with a camera. This recognition was very important to Archie.

He will be remembered above all for his love and attention to children. In his day, all sick pilgrims used the hospital and this included the sick children. Any accompanying parents were accommodated in hotels since there was no accommodation in the old hospital and this may obviously have proved difficult if it were not for Archie. He looked after them and never failed to have them eating out of his hand. He would often be spotted hauling a voiture full of children behind him. Perhaps it was his own childhood background, but everywhere Archie went the children followed. And if you asked any of the children then or even now as adults what they remembered most of Lourdes, they would all say Archie.

He was perhaps best known for his love of the Middlesbrough banners. The job of carrying them in the processions he famously claimed as his own. Pilgrims walking into the Domain before a procession looked for the banner and gathered there. If anyone was unsure where to go, they were simply told to look for Archie. He is probably our most famous brancardier.

to stretch out in the French train in any vacant compartment while the occupants were having a meal in the Dining Car. In later years couchettes were available to us all. When we arrived in Lourdes on the first Pilgrimage, many helpers had to sleep on landings and corridors for the first night, owing to the lack of beds in some of the hotels. It all got sorted out in the end."

Once the journey was over and the Pilgrimage arrived in Lourdes, it was far from luxury all the way. The Steads remember the hospital in the early years being basic to say the least. "Facilities in the old *Accueil* were very limited but we managed to overcome many of the drawbacks with God's help and the initiative and good humour of all of the helpers," says Margaret. "We used to have a lovely little procession and ceremony when the very sick folk in the wards received Holy Communion. The handmaids were often invited to accompany the procession with candles and the singing of hymns. "This also happened for mini-torchlight processions which wound through the wards on certain evenings back in the days when the sick didn't join in the official torchlight procession."

Photo: Ita Leahy

Pilgrimage Doctor Bill Boyes with Bishop O'Brien and Matron Ita Leahy.

Photo: Eileen Kelly

Proud to serve: Middlesbrough brancs in the 1950s assist during the Blessed Sacrament Procession.

Ita says the Middlesbrough Diocese bought the first washing machine for use in the *Accueil* to try to make things more bearable for everyone. "Before that we used to go down to a trough in the laundry and scrub the clothes and there was a great big clothes horse they pulled out for drying them on," she says. "The nuns were very strict. The doors of the *Accueil* had to be locked at 10pm and nobody could get in after that. The nun responsible for making sure the door was locked was vicious! We used to call her 'The Witch' and if anyone saw her they would run a mile. But some of them were wonderful. One of our favourites was Sister Jo. I had John then and he was always a great support to me. He went for the first time in 1965, the year after we got married and he loved it."

So did Peter Dunne, who is still thankful for the unexpected knock on the door that changed his life. "I am one of those people who fell in love with Lourdes," he says. "I've had some of the most spiritual experiences of my life in Lourdes and made some wonderful acquaintances with really good people. I've met so many people I would never have met otherwise."

Paul Griffiths, who became a branc almost by accident, would now recommend the role of helper to anyone. "You can make more real friends in a week than some do in a lifetime, and have a fantastic and rewarding time too. Our sick pilgrims could not go without full teams of helpers. The hours are sometimes long but only as long as you can offer, the fun unending and the rewards immeasurable," he says. "It doesn't matter if you can't come every year or if you only do one, try it and see."

Chapter Twelve

THE MIRACLE OF LOVE

IN a place where mutual love and respect is the order of the day, it is no surprise that romances have blossomed when people meet in Lourdes. There are very many we may be unaware of, but in the Evening Gazette of July 17 2000, Julie and Martin Allinson told reporter Mike McGeary their story.

Martin's Story

"I did the Great North Run in October 1995 and knew something wasn't right. I put off going to the doctor until afterwards and went thinking I had a hernia. He referred me to North Tees Hospital where I was told I had cancer.

"Within a fortnight the tumour was removed and I was told I'd be going to Newcastle for chemotherapy. By the time they'd found the cancer it was in my legs and chest and everywhere. At the end of February I got a chest infection and I was put in an isolation unit.

"Our parish priest, Fr Tom Brophy, came and comforted me, saying that these were the dark days but there will be light days to come. He later died of cancer himself.

"When I came back I was as weak as a kitten. I'd never had anything to do with Lourdes, although I knew the story. One day out of the blue I said I wondered who was going to Lourdes from our parish. Mam said another priest, Canon Spaight, had asked if I would go. I had no hesitation, I just said, 'Yes'.

"My monthly check-up in March 1996 revealed things were starting to grow again in the lung. The bad news was I needed an operation. I came straight home with a cloud hanging over me. I was thinking to myself that at the end of the month I was due to go to Lourdes, should I go? Only four days before the trip I decided I would.

"When we arrived in Lourdes on the Friday it was absolutely throwing it down and the hospital was very austere. I didn't know what to expect from this Lourdes place at all. I didn't feel I was in a special place. But it was like a fuse had been lit and soon things started falling into place. The feeling developed as the week went on.

"I'd see Julie about in the hospital and the music group and I thought what a special girl, to come here and do this. I had my Boro towel on the bed, just so people knew it was my little space I suppose. Along came Julie one morning with a cup of tea and she started talking about football. Chauvinistically, I thought she'd think it was a Man United towel! Julie went on to describe where she sat in the East Stand Upper at the Riverside. It turned out that we were about 30 seats away from each other! That was an ice-breaker and we became friends.

"We got on very well for the rest of the week, and when Julie's coach left I felt the spirit of the Pilgrimage went with her. When I came home I bored everyone talking constantly about Julie and the Pilgrimage. My sister was a bit sceptical about the wonderful feeling I'd come back with. But I told her that if Julie was as nice at home as she was in Lourdes, I'd marry her!

"At home, the letter with the operation date had arrived. I thought about the lung biopsy and just said to myself, 'So What? I've been to Lourdes now and I'm going to be okay'. I don't know if it was just bravado. The operation was on the Monday and I don't remember anything until waking on the Tuesday. I remember my sister and Mam being around the bed. Then in came Julie Walton…"

Julie's Story

"I just bundled in and said 'Move over' and sat on the bed. I took his oxygen mask off, gave him a kiss and put it back on again. I'd promised I was going to bring some photos round to Martin's house but his Mam rang me to say he was going into hospital. I was thinking, 'If Martin had a wife, she would surely have said'.

"I asked if I could see Martin after the operation and she said yes. I visited again on the Thursday and then on the Sunday. Then Martin rang to say he was out. He sent me a huge bouquet of flowers in Lourdes blue and yellow with a beautiful message on the card. 'Thank you for bringing the spirit of Lourdes home and sharing it, Love Martin.' It was lovely.

"I still didn't really know what was wrong, I only knew it was cancer. I said to him, 'From now on we're in this together.' And that was it, from then on we were a couple.

Ten days later he proposed. He said, 'Us boys with cancer can't hang around, will you marry me?' I said yes straight away, we both knew. But we didn't tell anyone.

"It was a great relief when the lung biopsy result came and was clear of cancer. Then in the August we got news that there were cells growing in his stomach which they would need to investigate with surgery. We got engaged in November, while Martin was trying to get stronger to face the operation.

"He went into hospital in the April, the night Boro got to the FA Cup final. They'd decided to take the cells out and do another biopsy. He was in theatre for 11 hours altogether. We went to see him that night in intensive care but he wasn't really aware. I came back and he just held my hand and said, 'I'm frightened, don't leave me'. It turned out the cells were clear, they weren't cancer.

"Martin stayed in hospital for a week, then he came out and his aim was to get fit and well for our wedding on October 7 1997. People talk about that momentous season for Boro fans but for us it was two cup finals, a relegation, an operation and a wedding! Since then Martin has never looked back, he's gone from strength to strength and we can look forward to a future together."

Mike concluded his report with this postscript which ties the story together in a way that will delight but not surprise regular pilgrims.

Martin and Julie have just returned from Lourdes, this time travelling as helpers. They were determined to return as a way of giving something back. "We wanted to do our bit because of what had happened. Martin was an inspiration to everyone," says Julie. Martin's reason for going back was to offer his own experience to others.

"I wanted to be there in case someone needed pushing like I did. Hopefully there will always be people to push. Now we don't think anything can happen to us that we won't be able to handle. Every life has heartache and I don't expect not to face anymore just because we've been through so much."

Martin is certain a miracle happened in Lourdes. "Was the growth in my lungs cancerous before I went? We'll never know for sure. All I know is when I came back it wasn't. But I believe it was a miracle."

Chapter Thirteen

RISE AND SHINE

SOMETIME in the 1980s, IBVM sister Lucy Wilson organised a group of young disabled people who joined the massive numbers making up the Handicapped Children's Pilgrimage Trust. The pilgrimage was very different to the Diocesan Pilgrimage. A small 'family' group of pilgrims joined hundreds of other groups all doing the same thing at Easter, with the young disabled people receiving one-to-one care. Lourdes becomes a different place when so many pilgrims arrive making the same pilgrimage with the same organisation.

Sister Lucy was keen to give as many young disabled people as possible the chance to experience this special week. Being based at the Bar Convent in York, her efforts had a very different emphasis from the Diocesan Pilgrimage. This was definitely not part of the Diocesan set up. She was able to work with the legendary Sister Agnella and Sister Ursula, Sisters of Mercy who ran Eston House respite care home near Middlesbrough while they were attached to Crossbeck Convent.

With great support from the staff and pupils of All Saints' School in York, funds were provided to pay for all the disabled children. A nurse and a chaplain travelled with the group. Many of the carers themselves were young volunteers who managed to raise money for their own fares. Flying from Manchester with many other HCPT groups from the Yorkshire region, the groups set out on Easter Sunday each year until 1993.

From the very beginning Fr Pat Hartnett has been the group chaplain. They enjoyed years of stability and welcomed several new additions in the early 1990s. In 1989 Paul Farrer, who had travelled up with fellow seminarians from the English and Scots Colleges in Valladolid and Salamanca, Spain, joined the group. A year later fellow student Phil Evans, from Middlesbrough, also joined. Around this time the group was bolstered not only by the services of a nurse, but also a doctor, Kate Doherty of York, who was practising in Liverpool's Fazackerly Hospital at the time.

In 1990 seasoned Lourdes pilgrim, 14-year-old Louise Cornforth, joined the group. There was nothing remarkable about this, but what was significant was that her foster father joined her. He was Rev Ted Appleyard, vicar of Great Ayton, near Middlesbrough. In his retirement years, Ted wrote a book about his years in ministry called *Zest For Life*, devoting a whole chapter to his HCPT experience.

"Of course I had heard about Lourdes and I had fixed attitudes about it, deeply-seated from a Protestant past," he wrote. "One of my false assumptions was that every sick person going to that famous Grotto looked for a miraculous cure. I now know that sick folk do not have that thought uppermost at all. I found myself in Manchester Airport with Louise and the other members of the group. My initial feeling of being the odd man out in the group soon gave way to a sense of belonging to those who in the normal way could not give in return. The love shown by the children and their absence of self-pity was remarkable.

"There was a healthy interest in spiritual things. There was real joy in worshipping together and contributing each day, by struggling to read – without embarrassment – parts of the Mass and accompanying the hymns with tambourines, triangles and bells."

Anyone who sees an HCPT group come together in Lourdes is seeing something very special. It is a very different experience to a diocesan pilgrimage. The small group of 25 people spend an intense week together and really do have a family experience. Ted had begun to see that very early. But events were about to overtake him and challenge some of his preconceived ideas.

"Towards the end of an eventful week I walked the Stations of the Cross and disaster struck. My old knees could take no more, I had been pushing and pulling too much. I ended up seeing a doctor who confined me to a wheelchair for the rest of the trip. I was very angry with myself. One thing I had never done was visit the Grotto alone at night. I had been saving that experience for the last evening. Now it looked as though I would not get there. Then one of the helpers who had worked hard all week offered to take me there. I felt as though I was imposing myself on someone who had already done a hard week's work but she insisted and I accepted.

"We did not talk when we got to the shrine. Our silence was mutually understood. She just left me there a while. I do not know how long it was. Time was irrelevant. There came an unusual experience of peace. Words are so inadequate. I began to realise that people do not go to Lourdes to be cured but to be healed. And that is so much better. Learning to love God and to love and value one another and learning to accept oneself. It was remarkable. There is something about the place, something intangible, inexplicable, whatever your convictions, your religion, your reservations. Perhaps it is what the theologians call 'numinous'. I do not know. What I do know is that I would not change the feeling I had at the Grotto for all the physical fitness in the world."

Ted retired some years later and has since died. He never went back to Lourdes but Louise continues to be a regular pilgrim, travelling either with the Diocesan Pilgrimage or, as in the year 2003, with HCPT Group 122.

While in Lourdes in 1992, the group discovered that the period of stability they had enjoyed was about to end. "While we were all in Lourdes together that year, Sister Lucy told us that she was leaving her order and would not be around to run the group next year," says Fr Paul. "As luck would have it there was a great guy with us that year, travelling to Lourdes for the first time with his youngest son. Joe Stead and his son Paul had joined the group from York.

"Fr Pat, Joe and I would all meet at 6pm each evening on the balcony of the Café Jean d'Arc and have a pint before supper. Fr Pat and I had decided we couldn't let the group fold. It had to carry on. The problem was that neither of us could take on the responsibility. Joe was the ideal candidate. So during one of our evening drinks we put it to Joe that he could run the group if we helped him and that really it wouldn't be too much work for him. I think he knew he was being conned but didn't mind too much. He had seen enough to realise he would be doing something very important."

Joe took over and, thanks to the excellent work done by Sister Lucy over the years, Group 122 carried on unhindered. Due to illness, Joe was unable to make the 1996 pilgrimage and for the first time the group did not travel to Lourdes. However, by this time Group 122 was not the only group from the Diocese travelling with the HCPT.

Group 96 was born in the mid-1990s and based in Middlesbrough. It did not last long but had some key helpers in it. Margaret Brooks, of St Joseph's Parish in Middlesbrough, Fr John Paul Leonard and Fr William Massie and helpers who had made the trip with Group 122 in the past, such as Paul Thomson, of Yarm, and members of his family.

HCPT - The Pilgrimage Trust

The Handicapped Children's Pilgrimage Trust was formed in 1956 after a young doctor, Michael Strode, first took four children with disabilities on a pilgrimage holiday to Lourdes. In doing so, he revolutionised the way children with disabilities could experience a trip to the shrine. Not content with letting the children stay in the usual hospitals and hospices, Dr Michael wanted them to stay in hotels as honoured guests and to get as much out of their holiday as other children - trips to cafes, a donkey ride in the mountains and the warmth and affection of a holiday among caring friends.

Nearly 40 years later, HCPT takes to Lourdes almost 2000 children from the UK, Ireland and increasingly from other countries. The children have a wide range of physical and mental disabilities, or are physically and emotionally deprived or neglected.

Cared for by voluntary helpers, including doctors, nurses and chaplains, most of whom pay for themselves, the total size of the Easter Pilgrimage is now about 5,000, making it the largest pilgrimage from the UK and Ireland and probably the largest children's pilgrimage from any country. The holiday pilgrimage is naturally centred around the shrine and gives children aged seven to 18 with many types of disability or special needs the opportunity to experience a really stimulating and highly enjoyable group holiday with the reassurance of one-to-one help the whole time.

From HCPT grew the Hosanna House Trust, which was the response to a request from young adults for an opportunity to experience a similar holiday to that of the children. Today, Hosanna House, the Trust's residential centre just outside Lourdes in Bartres, takes nearly 2,000 pilgrims in groups of 40 to 50, many of whom have disabilities or special needs. These guests stay for a week between Easter and November.

Unfortunately, this group also folded and for a few years there was no Diocesan representation on the HCPT Pilgrimage. On January 1 1998 Fr Paul began an 18-month appointment as Chaplain to the Convent of Mercy at Crossbeck. This was so he would be free enough to meet the challenges of his new appointment as Diocesan Youth Officer. Crucially, it meant that for some short

HCPT Group 122, back in Lourdes in 1999 after a five-year break.

Photo: Lacaze

time he would be free of parish responsibilities and able to put commitment to young people first.

This commitment was challenged during the Diocesan Pilgrimage that May. Fr Terry Creech CSSR, who was at the time Chaplain to the HCPT, asked Fr Paul when a group from the Diocese would be coming back at Easter. "I remember thinking we should establish the tradition again but I didn't really know how to make it work," he recalls. "So many of the people I thought I could ask to help me get things off the ground again were already heavily involved in the Diocesan Pilgrimage. Anyway, I did ask Joe and Teresa Harrison and they both readily agreed to be involved. Fr Terry came to see us off at Lourdes Airport. As I went through the check-in, he said, 'See you next May.' And I said, 'No, see you at Easter – Group 122 is coming back.' The look on his face was great to see."

Fr Paul got home and started contacting some of the old helpers. They were all as keen as each other to see things start up again. Margaret Brooks agreed to act as Group Leader and, in 1999, Group 122 made a welcome return to the HCPT Easter Pilgrimage. Fr Pat Keogh joined Fr Paul, both working as group chaplains, and Teresa Harrison acted as nurse. Margaret ensured it was business as usual and everyone enjoyed a great week.

Margaret remembers Fr Paul contacting her. "He told me he wanted to talk about starting a HCPT group again," she says. "I was delighted as I had missed going and I could see there were so many children around the place who would benefit from experiencing the HCPT pilgrimage. We mentioned it to some of the old helpers and they all flooded back. There was great enthusiasm for it."

Claire Shanks and Amanda Rochester, both of York, rejoined the group along with Kathryn Walsh, of Normanby, Middlesbrough. Kathryn was a great boon to the group. She had been a dedicated volunteer helper at Eston House for years. She was well used to helping disabled children and could even use sign language. Sadly, Kathryn died far too young. She suffered a brain tumour,

Mayor Norman Swash gives a civic send-off to HCPT Group 96.

which took her from us very quickly, but her legacy lives on in Group 122. A wheelchair was bought in her memory and is used each year by our group and other pilgrims who use Hosanna House near Lourdes throughout the year.

The following year Fr John Paul Leonard took over as group chaplain and things have gone from strength to strength. Traditionally Group 122 had a York base and Group 96 hailed from Middlesbrough. However, the HCPT map in the Diocese now looks a little different. Group 122 was reformed as part of the Diocesan Youth Service efforts for the young people of our Diocese and although it still has a York and Middlesbrough base, the home is now very much Middlesbrough. For the year 2003, there is to be another HCPT Group based in York. In a twist of fate, that group has taken the name Group 96.

Group 122 takes an average of ten children and approximately 17 helpers. When they get to Lourdes they join about 6,000 other people who make up the other HCPT groups from all over the United Kingdom, Ireland and the rest of the world.

New helpers are never far away from the HCPT experience and they are always welcome. Since the re-establishment of Group 122, a new generation has taken it forward. Paddy Rutherford, Katie Dawson, Catherine Shannon, Julia Kirkman, Kirsty McNaughton, Helen Smurthwaite and Ann Marie McDonagh, along with Val and Bill Clarke and many others, ensure the HCPT light shines brightly in our Diocese.

Chapter Fourteen

THE MARIST WAY

THE Marist Fathers have been involved in the life of the Diocese of Middlesbrough in many ways and for many years. Lads from the Diocese are now in ministry as Marist priests all over the world.

The contribution of the Marists to the Lourdes Pilgrimage is unique. As members of the Society of Mary, their vocation is bound up in deep devotion to Our Lady. Characters like Fr Walter O'Connor SM turned that devotion into action in helping get the Diocesan Pilgrimage off the ground. For many years, Marists have led groups of pilgrims either as part of the actual Pilgrimage in May or at other times of the year. It was Middlesbrough priest Fr Michael Coleman SM, son of Johnny Coleman, who established the Marist Pilgrimage which is in Lourdes at the same time as the Diocesan Pilgrimage each year.

The Marist pilgrims have joined more and more in the programme of the Diocesan Pilgrimage. They have their own Opening Mass and some other ceremonies separately but join us for everything else. Marist pilgrims traditionally travel by coach, although some of the more elderly now take the flight only option from Teesside. However they get there, they are all easily identifiable by their blue hats.

Agnes McGrogan has a foot in both camps. She has travelled with both pilgrimages and, having retired as Matron, has returned to being a Marist Pilgrim. She recalls how Fr Coleman began to operate. "The year there wasn't a pilgrimage lay people made approaches to the Marists because they had been doing them before," she says. "That was how it began. Fr Coleman decided he would take a group and it grew from there. It was never a split with the Diocesan Pilgrimage, it was simply him filling a gap for a year and it just continued."

Fr Michael tells us how things got off the ground for him. It is a story which begins in Whitechapel, in the East End of London. "A Christmas dinner in February would, at first sight, appear to have nothing to do with pilgrimages to Lourdes, but it had. The parish sister, Collette, spoke to me in October 1975 and proposed that St Anne's parish, Underwood Road, London E1, should hold their Christmas dinner late in February 1976 when people could enjoy a good meal. This made sense, so we did.

"It was a great success and I was seated next to Mrs Kay Lester Cheyne. Kay was a forthright person and during the meal enquired: 'Father, do you take your people to Lourdes?' 'No,' I replied. 'And why not?' retorted Kay. 'Because it is too expensive to travel by air,' I volunteered. 'Travel by coach,' was Kay's exhortation. At this point I thought she had simply gone out of her head because I knew something about coaches and knew that such a journey was impossible. However, the proposed cost was very affordable and Kay assured me the impossible was possible. Next morning I phoned Kay and was surprised to learn that her quotation of the cost still stood. Things moved along rapidly and a Parish Pilgrimage came in to being.

"At the end of July, after a mid-morning Mass, our pilgrimage coach left from St Anne's and travelled to Dover, where we boarded the hovercraft – an interesting form of transport, somewhat like travelling inside a washing machine. In Calais we boarded a French coach, enjoyed a meal in Paris and headed south overnight, towards Lourdes. This was long before motorways. Refreshments and toilets were an immense problem. I could not believe that France was so big and we arrived in Lourdes shortly before 7pm. Kay knew the owner of the Hotel ND de Paradis, Mme Marie Cazenave, who in future years played an immensely important role in the development of Marist Pilgrimages, and we stayed in her hotel. This pilgrimage had all the excitement of a very first event and the wonder of Lourdes was experienced by 43 pilgrims. Such an experience simply had to be repeated and so plans were made for the end of May 1977.

"In 2003 it is very difficult to realise that in 1977 motorways in Europe were virtually non-existent. Fax machines and e-mails were things of the future. Communication was by letter or telephone, hence travel agents were kings in the land of the blind and would tell people anything that was convenient. This was both a bad thing and a good thing for future pilgrimages to Lourdes. We had decided to make the 1977 pilgrimage as simple as possible and would travel overnight on both the outward and return journeys. A travel agent swathed the detailed arrangements in such a fog of confusion that I actually sacked him three weeks before travelling and hired our own coach from an independent source. Marie Cazenave, now in the Hotel ND de Pietat, assured me she would honour our booking. Ten American Air Force people, including their chaplain, Fr Jack Meade SM, from Mildenhall, Suffolk, joined the pilgrimage. Not everything was straightforward. We were met in France by a coach with 45 seats, despite the clear instruction that we had 47 passengers and so my sister and myself travelled to Lourdes and back on 'dickie' seats, which occupied the middle aisle. The pilgrimage was a success and, since the costs had been reduced, a refund was provided to each pilgrim. The May Bank Holiday was a popular time and the weather was not too hot.

"By 1978 I was serving as Parish Priest in Hull. Early in October I announced in the parish bulletin that there would be a pilgrimage to Lourdes, by coach and ferry, for a week over the Spring Bank Holiday 1979 and the cost would be £105 including insurance. Some of the more knowledgeable parishioners shook their heads and informed me that it was impossible to go to Lourdes for that price. The next week I had to humbly bow to their superior knowledge and reduced the price by £5. Within weeks I was looking for an extra coach and accommodation in Lourdes. People wanted to go to Lourdes and the price was right. Pencil and paper were the main tools of organisation and booking forms were readily ignored by many of the pilgrims. Not only did they not complete a simple booking form, but many referred to each other by their maiden names and my list and their names did not coincide! I spent a whole afternoon with Maggie Frankland unravelling the mysteries of Catholic marriage in Hull and the surrounding areas.

"Two Halcyon Travel coaches left the Marist Church at 7am for the journey to Lourdes. The 'Bingo Coach', directed by Fr Peter Coleman, referred to the other coach, directed by myself, as the 'Telegraph Coach'. Among the great characters were Maggie Frankland, Marie Laverack, Ethel Jackson, Elsie O'Connor, Mary Pettman, Evelyn Garton, Nora Cusick, Kath Moody, Albert and Dorothy Cox, Bernard and Hilda Oldroyd, Jim and Teresa McAllister, Joe, Kath and Fiona McAllister and Des and Lindy Boothby, to name but a few. We stopped in Paris for a meal before our long journey down France to Lourdes where we arrived at the Hotel ND de Pietat in good spirits.

"The weather was perfect and we enjoyed some wonderfully sunny days. But everything has its cost. The previous winter had been very severe and there was lots of snow on the mountains. This melted rapidly and the river Gave started to rise on Wednesday. By Thursday evening we were concerned about the ever-increasing amount of water in the river. On Friday morning Lourdes was flooded. By 10am the top of the altar in the Grotto was under water. Whole areas of Lourdes were sealed off. One of the road bridges gave serious cause for concern. The kitchens of our hotel were flooded and the water was rising in the surrounding area. We decided to leave as soon as possible but we were three people short. We began ferrying people and all their belongings to the coaches and were delighted to see our three pilgrims crossing over the bridge. We left immediately and were probably the last people to get out of Lourdes that weekend.

"On the journey north, we stopped at the newly opened supermarket at Pau in order to sort ourselves out and to have some lunch. Once on the road, we made good time and crossed the Channel on the hovercraft. The windscreen of the Bingo Coach was shattered by a flying stone between Dover and London and this caused a considerable delay. All arrived home safely. Despite all the difficulties it was decided to make the pilgrimage an annual event.

"The Spring Bank Holiday was accepted as the time for the Marist Pilgrimage and arrangements were made from year to year with this in mind. Two coaches provided transport for 1980 and we were joined by Fr Chris Pattison, Mary Thompson and Eileen, Mary and Teresa Hayes, who became legends of the Marist Pilgrimage. Without any apparent effort the numbers increased. It all seemed to grow like Topsy. Suddenly there were three coaches in 1981, six in 1982, including St Mary's, Hull, and St Stephen's Youth Group, twelve in 1983, 1984, 1985, and 1986, by which time other people started to arrange their own coaches. By now, well over 1,000 pilgrims from the Middlesbrough area were in Lourdes during the Spring Bank Holiday.

"Two events took place in 1983, the launch of the Blue Hats and the arrival of The Middlesbrough

Catholic Handicapped Fellowship pilgrimage. Despite all rumours to the contrary, the Blue Hats were never a military uniform. The original inspiration came to me during the Blessed Sacrament Procession the previous year. It was an immensely hot afternoon and, from the steps of the Basilica, I observed the distress of many of the sick pilgrims lying in the baking heat of the Rosary Square. My mind passed over the need for sun cream and the benefit of a hat. Eureka! Fr Jack Meade SM, the American Air Force chaplain, had told me that it was an offence to go outside without your head covered in the military. In future, Marist pilgrims would always be able to cover their heads with the Blue Hats. They became the symbol of the Marist Pilgrimage and also helped in the everyday arrangements. People could not get lost too easily and then there was the rule, 'If you see a Blue Hat, speak to it'. Many lasting friendships have thus been formed.

"Moira Flaherty is a name to be conjured with. Moira was a person to know and appreciate. When God created Moira, He certainly broke the mould. Moira was… well, Moira. Originally, Moira asked if she could have some seats on the Marist Pilgrimage on the condition that she, and her helpers, would decide on the travelling arrangements. Moira filled a coach and the group stayed in the Hotel Ste Anne, where she became known as 'Madame Moira, No Problem'. Very early on I realised that the correct answer to any of Moira's requests was simply to say 'Yes, Moira' and everything was perfect. How she and her helpers achieved what they did is one of the greatest mysteries of Lourdes. Perhaps it is in simply saying 'Yes' that we are following the example of Mary and listening to possibilities. Within a year the Atkinson's drivers knew that their first pick-up on the way to Lourdes was at Moira's front door. After that there was tea at all times and 'No problems'. In Lourdes in February 2003, I met the former owner of the Hotel Ste Anne who asked after 'Madame Moira, No Problem'. I had to tell her Moira died a few years ago and that wherever she is in heaven, there will be 'No Problems'.

"Since 1976 many of our pilgrims have died and all of us have grown older. An increasing number ask to fly, others ask for overnight stops on the journeys, while still more continue the traditional route of travelling through the night and arriving in Lourdes before lunch on Sunday. We are fortunate to be able to offer such options. All of us are responding to Our Lady's request to Bernadette, 'Ask the people to come in prayer, penance and procession'. We look forward to another 25 years of pilgrimage to Lourdes."

Chapter Fifteen

HEALING WATERS

BERNADETTE'S whole life is the message of Lourdes. She was a sickly, underprivileged, uneducated girl from the humblest of backgrounds. In many ways she was like the Virgin Mary, which may help to explain why she was chosen. The apparitions are a very important part of the story but we can't really understand them unless we know something about Bernadette's origins and, crucially, what happened to her after the apparitions.

She left Lourdes and lived a very quiet life, with illness and suffering never far away. One story from her final days provides an invaluable lesson in our understanding of the place of the sick in Lourdes. On her deathbed in the town of Nevers, she was cared for by one of the sisters in the convent. In a vain attempt to encourage Bernadette, the sister said to her, "Never mind, we shall soon have you back at your job". Through her agony, Bernadette said: "But I am at my job. My job is being ill." If we do not understand what Bernadette meant, it is difficult for us to understand the place of the sick pilgrim in Lourdes.

For many years it has been

A special bond: Sick pilgrims share the sign of peace during Mass.

traditional for pilgrims to say a silent prayer at the Statue of the Crowned Virgin in Rosary Square. If you did that, it was said, Our Lady would make sure you came back to Lourdes. But on their return many pilgrims, including a large number of helpers, have had a role they could not have expected. In a deeply moving sermon at the Mass of Anointing two years ago, Bishop Kevin O'Brien preached on the challenges this shift from serving to being served brings. Other members of the clergy who have later been among our sick in the hospital include Mgr Tony Bickerstaffe, Fr Tony Barry and the late Fr Gerry Smyth.

Kath McRae, who is 90 this year, was just 11 when she was taken on the 1925 Pilgrimage as a sick pilgrim. Years later she returned and gave lengthy service as a handmaid, before her life came full circle and she reluctantly joined the ranks of the sick once more. Tom Hoy was returning to Lourdes that year for the first anniversary of his cure, while Kath also recalls a blind lady who could see more at every station the train stopped at on their way home to Middlesbrough.

"We lived at Port Clarence but when he was on night shift my dad used to go to Mass at the Cathedral, where Tom was the sacristan," she says. Although Kath's memories of that distant trip have been dimmed by the passage of time, some things remain clear. "I went with Jack Donovan and Margaret and Molly McArdle. I did the Stations of the Cross every day because you got a cup of tea if you did!" And the visit also made a deep and lasting impression on the little girl.

"I promised Mary that as soon as I started work I would come back," she says. "But I was the eldest of eight and the family needed the money, so it had to wait a little longer. I got married during the war and all my children had been to Lourdes with their schools before I got to go back. We had a business and it was difficult to get away from that as well. But when I went to teach at St Joseph's School, the head handmaid Eileen McElhatton also taught there, as well as Mildred Raw and Eileen Hardy."

Eileen McElhatton was our first Head Handmaid, leading the ladies who tend to the sick, serve meals and refreshments and do so much to make the Pilgrimage the experience it is for everyone in the hospital. Later Mildred Raw would follow in her footsteps in a role which has also been filled by Margaret Jackson, Pat Ling, Peg Dasey, Marlene McCarthy and now Helen Pennington during Kath McRae's association with the Pilgrimage. While she was in charge, Peg Dasey was ably assisted by her sister, Joan, her right-hand woman. When Peg arrived at the hospital first for duty every morning, Joan would also be there.

In about 1959 Kath joined the ranks of the handmaids. She has been back every year but one since, more recently staying in the hospital. "At first it was a big blow to my pride to have to go in a wheelchair," she admits. "But I'd fallen before we went, and Agnes McGrogan came to see me and said I would have to go in the hospital." It was one thing being looked after as a child, but after so many years of doing her duty it was harder for the dedicated helper to take a back seat. Soon she began to discover that being on the receiving end brought blessings of its own.

"When you're working you take everything for granted but when you're sick you appreciate what goes on," she says. "I didn't used to think we worked that hard, but people are so willing and nothing is too much trouble. You really feel like a VIP when you're sick in Lourdes. You have to be ready to accept it when you can't give any more and be grateful for the people who are there looking after you. The amazing thing is the youth and the effect their work has on the sick. Whenever I hear people talk about the awful things young people are doing I tell them to go to Lourdes, any time and with any pilgrimage, and you'll see the other side of the story. Every year I think the Youth Mass can't get any better and every year it does."

Watch out, the boss is here! Bishop O'Brien looks pleased to bump into Cardinal Hume outside the Brickies.

Current Head Handmaid Helen Pennington tells a story which also illustrates how blurred the line between sick and helper often becomes in Lourdes. "The year my brother went to Lourdes as a sick pilgrim for the first time, I was allocated to sit next to a young man who was on the flight with his mother," she says. "He told me he'd never flown before and was frightened. He held my hand for most of the time. We exchanged stories, mostly about Lourdes and why we decided to come. While we were talking we discovered we had all suffered at some time with cancer. But we had great faith in Our Lady and Bernadette. On the way home the young man told me how much he had loved Lourdes and would like to return as a helper. The week after arriving home I visited South Cleveland Hospital and happened to see him there. To my surprise, there was one of our young handmaids visiting him. They had met in Lourdes and now they are married and both are helpers."

It is the popular perception of an outside world that watches our Pilgrimage with some degree of bemusement that sick people go to Lourdes in the hope of being cured. While it would be unwise to dismiss this altogether, it certainly does not come close to telling the whole story. Kath McRae learned this very early on in life. As an 11-year-old setting off on a great adventure, Kath left Middlesbrough Station not simply in the hope of being cured, but in its certain expectation.

"I'd told them to have some ankle straps ready for me for when I came back because I was going to get better," she says. But her priorities were dramatically turned upside down when she had what pilgrims might recognise by the description, 'a Lourdes experience'. "I remember waiting in Rosary Square for the Blessing of the Sick and there were some terrible cases, much worse than we see today. As I was waiting for the procession I never once prayed to get cured. I said 'Our Lady, if you're going to cure anyone today, cure that little boy over there'. I saw how badly off some people were and thought there was nothing the matter with me. I suppose that's one of the graces of Lourdes."

So if sick pilgrims don't go in search of a cure, why do so many return to Lourdes as often as they are able to? Karole Robinson, of Saltburn, intends to work as a handmaid this year after previously staying in the hospital. "I can see why people go back again each year," she says. "It is very hard to describe Lourdes in just a few words and no amount of photos could ever capture it. The town is lovely, set with a backdrop of mountains, a castle to look over it, a river running through it, café-bars to sit back and soak up the atmosphere, and an abundance of spangly gift shops brimming over with treasures.

"But the place where everything really happens is way down town. Beyond the gates you find hundreds of people, all at the same party, and you are bowled over by the incredible calm and tranquil atmosphere. A sense of peace is everywhere. People from all over the world are all sharing the same faith. And that's the bit you bring home and keep close to you. I had a wonderful week in Lourdes; the services, the experiences, the sightseeing, and meeting the amazing kind and devoted team of people on the pilgrimage whose faith inspired me. Bishop John said at one service, 'He gives us everything we need to get through the day.' Some days the memories of Lourdes help."

Anne Carr, also of Saltburn, has been to Lourdes several times along with her son, Peter. She says he altered after his first Pilgrimage. "It was nothing I can put my finger on, but an overall improvement," she says. "People in their own ways tried to tell us what Lourdes was like, but nobody quite got it right. It's a wonderful feeling to be there, very uplifting, something you can't quite describe. There is an overwhelming feeling of peace among people from all walks of life, and at the same time a feeling of deep excitement. This is the place to come when you are not well. You get excited at what could be and your faith gets stronger.

"Your emotions run high and you cry lots of tears; happy ones too. In Lourdes it is as if the sick for once are the special people, and that they belong. Peter and I felt like part of a big family and joined in. I have never seen so many very happy sick people. Lourdes has restored our faith and given us the strength to get up and go for another year. We came home very, very tired but a nice tired, a happy tired. If there is a heaven on earth it's got to be Lourdes. Peter and I thank all those who made it possible for us to go."

As well as the services and processions, another integral part of every sick pilgrim's week in Lourdes is the visit to the Baths. Here they are immersed in the icy cold waters from the spring Bernadette unearthed at Mary's request. "I always think of Bernadette saying we must come here and bathe in the water," says Kath McRae. "The cold water's a shock but it's worth it when you come out and just glow, that's the only way I can describe it. It's the most wonderful feeling. Every time I've been I've gone in the Baths. I would go more than once if I could."

For Fr Michael O'Connor, who was Chaplain to the Sick before Fr Brian Nicholson, Lourdes is all about the people who go there. "One of the great periods of my life has been meeting so many hard-working, dedicated, loving people in Lourdes," he says. "Life would not have been the same without them. So many of them have become good friends."

But he did not always feel this way. When he first went he admits he spent the week confused, lost or not really knowing what he should be doing. He is not alone in having experienced this feeling. Sometimes Lourdes can be a lonely place. "As time went by I felt the need to be more actively involved in the work of the Pilgrimage because all the other staff never seemed to stop working and I felt guilty because I was doing so very little," he says. "Things were much more strictly organised and formal back then. Today's routine is much better. I remember the clergy always had to wear cassocks, which meant you got very hot very quickly. Mgr Peter Storey taught me the trick of wearing shorts underneath as a way of keeping cool.

"We always used the *Accueil Notre Dame* as a base for the sick. It was a vast place but somehow always seemed overcrowded. It had a certain charm but it was very basic and lacked privacy for the sick pilgrims. Just outside the

Making short work of it: Fr Michael O'Connor shows sick pilgrims why he's such a cool cleric!

Photo: David Boyes

Accueil, at the end nearest the Grotto, there stood a little stone hut with a red cross painted on it. An old nun sat in there and one could hand in donations for the *Accueil*. I can't remember her name but over the years she became a great friend of my mother and myself. We used to take our donations along each year and have a great reunion."

The Stead sisters' wealth of experience as both handmaids and sick pilgrims makes it all the more pleasing to hear them report that one thing has remained constant for half a century, as all around has been subject to upheaval. The loving care helpers showed sick pilgrims in those pioneering years is still the Pilgrimage's hallmark today.

"Much has changed over the years but certainly not the love and devotion of all the volunteer helpers who go so often to treat the sick pilgrims like royalty. We can vouch for this because we have seen both sides of the situation. We have made every Pilgrimage working as handmaids until 1999.

Lunchtime at the old Accueil.

That year and those that have followed we have been waited upon and cared for by so many of our fellow workers. We hope and pray that the next 50 years of the Middlesbrough Pilgrimage will be as happy and grace-filled for those that follow us as the first 50 years were for us."

While the sick pilgrims are grateful for the help they receive, anyone who has ever had the privilege of serving as a helper will testify it is a two-way process of giving.

Among those who came with us as sick pilgrims in recent years whose passing was mourned by the whole Middlesbrough Lourdes community this year are John Adams, Barbara Boyes, Benny McMahon, Mary Maloney, Mary Mendoza, Ken Rae and Charlie Roe.

Kath McRae's many pilgrimages are a great example to us. Perhaps the greatest insight is into the role of a sick pilgrim. Their job isn't simply to be looked after and pulled here, there and everywhere. Nor is it necessarily to be cured. Kath waited in Rosary Square in 1925 in the same place Tom Hoy sat the previous year as he was cured. Sitting there as a young sick pilgrim, having travelled hoping to be cured, she would have seen Tom, now fully fit, working hard as a branc. Hopes for her own cure must have been high. And yet on seeing the suffering of a fellow sick pilgrim she still managed to make her prayer, 'Our Lady, if you're going to cure anyone today, cure that little boy over there'. Perhaps the ability to say a prayer like this signals a healing of some sort.

Kath will be back in Lourdes again this year. "You can't go enough times," she says. "Everybody gets healing of some sort. I've been fortunate I've been all these years but I would hate to think I was taking the place of someone who had never been." Still, when the envelope arrived notifying her of the Committee's decision on whether she had been selected to go, Kath had her fingers crossed.

Chapter Sixteen

A CERTAIN SOMETHING

WHEN Mary first appeared to Bernadette she asked if she would be so good as to return to the Grotto. Bernadette was the first pilgrim and many others have followed. Her call and transformation were the means Mary used to call other pilgrims to the Grotto.

Abraham answered God's call and left his own people to go to the Promised Land. Jews have journeyed to Jerusalem and Christians have followed their example, going on pilgrimage to the Holy Land, to Rome and now to Lourdes where the Gospel is again proclaimed. There, the people come to Mary, the water is changed, the sick are healed, sins are forgiven and the poor have the Gospel preached to them. And there the crowds gather to greet Jesus of Nazareth.

One of the many famous things that Mary asked Bernadette was, "Tell the priests I want the people to come here in procession". Surely this is the reason people like us decided to go to Lourdes in the first place. But what is it that draws us back year after year? Why do others hear us speak of the place and decide that they themselves have to go and see?

There are as many answers to those questions as there are pilgrims who have ever been to the shrine. But there exists an interesting chain of events which is probably unknown to most Middlesbrough pilgrims and that gives us a certain something special in our relationship with Lourdes, Our Lady and St Bernadette.

After the apparitions and the beginning of devotion at the Grotto, there was a need to mark the area where Mary had spoken to Bernadette. A statue set into the stone of the Grotto seemed to be the obvious thing to erect. However, the journey from this decision to the production of the statue we now see set into the rock below the Rosary Basilica is far from straightforward. Bernadette was to prove to be a little awkward over the whole enterprise.

In general terms, many of the images of Mary the Mother of Jesus would seem to be far from an accurate attempt to depict her. In the New Testament era it was customary for women to be betrothed to their future husbands at a very young age by modern day standards. Some scholars speculate that Mary may have been as young as 12 years old when the Angel Gabriel appeared to her. It is more likely that she was a few years older, but that is all. Interestingly, many of the images of Our Lady we see are not of a teenage girl but of a woman in her 20s. While this does not make any difference to our devotion to Mary, it does perhaps influence the way we view her relationship with Bernadette.

The decision to place a statue at the Grotto meant Bernadette was questioned intensely about the appearance of the lady. When asked how old she was, Bernadette replied, "The same age as me." Bernadette was 15 years old at the time of the apparitions. This is a dramatic set of facts. While many visitors to the shrine may look at the statue there and imagine the relationship between Mary and Bernadette to be one of a mother to an adopted daughter, this clearly was not the case. Instead we have two young girls together. As if to confirm this, the lady identified herself by saying, "I am the Immaculate Conception." By using these words, Mary not only revealed herself but also pointed to a momentous event in her life which helps us pinpoint how old she would have seemed to Bernadette.

Of course, for people of faith this is more than something skin deep. At the time of the apparitions Bernadette had been a lowly girl

The Grotto at Lourdes where our prayers are answered.

Photo: Paul Farrer

from a poor family, chosen to give a wonderful message to the world. How fitting, then, that during this momentous event in her life she should be guided by Our Lady who appeared as the young girl she had been when her life was similarly changed by the message of an angel. This fact lends a new weight to Bernadette's testament that Mary spoke to her with great politeness and respect.

Essentially, Our Lady of Lourdes appears as our equal. She is our fellow pilgrim, journeying with us through life, not above or ahead of us, but by our side. This is crucial to our understanding of that extraordinary slogan above the altar in the Rosary Basilica, "Through Mary to Jesus."

The statue that we see at the Grotto is by the sculptor Fabisch. When he prepared his first mock up, Bernadette was asked to see it and give her opinion. "Is it a likeness?" she was asked. "Not a bit," she replied. Unbelievably, Fabisch seems to have taken little notice of Bernadette's comments. In order to complete the work he used a 31-year-old model, twice the age that Bernadette had indicated. When the statue was placed and unveiled, Bernadette was not there.

Sadly, the potential for disbelief among God's people that He would choose someone so young to carry His message to the world remained as great in the 1850s as when Mary was herself a child. It seems Bernadette struggled to accept any likeness of Mary that she saw. Yet it is the shepherdess herself who gives Middlesbrough pilgrims a unique focus for their devotion to Mary at Lourdes. While she was being questioned over Our Lady's description, Bernadette was shown hundreds of images of Mary. She dismissed all of them out of hand.

And then she was presented with a picture of the icon of Our Lady of Perpetual Help. Again she dismissed it and moved away. However, a little later she asked to see the image again and declared that, "It had a certain something." This was as close as Bernadette came to finding a picture of Mary that came close to living up to what she had seen.

For Middlesbrough pilgrims this is full circle. If pilgrimage is about deepening our understanding of ourselves, then we have a very important insight here. Surely it is not simply coincidence that the image of Mary venerated by the first Bishop of Middlesbrough while he was a sick student is the same image Bernadette found some affinity with. As a Diocese, our Marian devotion is hugely influenced by Bishop Lacy's personal dedication. Some 20 years after the apparitions at Lourdes, the new Diocese of Middlesbrough was placed under the patronage of Our Lady of Perpetual Help.

Perhaps it is the 'certain something' Bernadette identified when she saw the icon of Our Lady of Perpetual Help that drove us as a Diocese to make pilgrimage such an important part of our spiritual journey. We have wandered far and wide to many different Marian shrines. The Lady Chapel at Mount Grace and the Slipper Chapel at Walsingham, to name just two, play a part. But our central focus as pilgrims has long been the shrine at Lourdes.

As pilgrims, we share so much of the experience of Bernadette. At first she was perplexed by the apparition she saw. However, she kept going back at the request of the Lady. As word spread of the apparitions, people began to quiz Bernadette and challenge her not to go back to the Grotto, telling her either she had seen nothing or that whatever was going on was evil. When she refused to stay away, other people began to follow her there. Although none of them saw what she did, they did recognise that something very special was happening. Even though it was Lent, the local tax collector, sent by the Parish Priest to see what all the fuss was about, was moved to get special permission from the cleric to have a party in one of the cafes.

This is reflected in so much of our pilgrimage experience. We are often perplexed by what we experience at the Grotto. We always encourage others we know to try the same journey. We pray in that special place and celebrate together. Driven by a devotion to Mary that is as old as our Diocese, Middlesbrough pilgrims will always travel to Lourdes to venerate Our Lady there and in doing so, come to be closer to her Son.

MIDDLESBROUGH PILGRIMAGE DOCTORS

Medical Directors

Bill Boyes 1952-1986
John Doherty 1987-1989
Sarah Bottom 1990
Ian John 1991-1992
John O'Neill 1993-Date

Doctors

S Anthony
S Baxter
J Cahill
C Capraro (Now Cormie)
J Connolly
D Donovan
S Dunn
E Garcia
P Grainger
D Hewart-Jaboor
D Hickson
M Hinman
M Hollinrake
A Hollinrake
J MacCabe
K McLean (Now Anthony)
P O'Neill
S O'Neill (Now Goodfield)
H Peters
A Ribeiro
W Ryan
K Walsh
F Wood

PILGRIMAGE NURSES

The lists of nurses, handmaids and brancadiers on the following pages have been put together from the Pilgrimage records. They are not complete, but include many of those who have served the Pilgrimage.

Almack G	Coleman B	Gamblin L	Kett L
Almack J	Collins S	Gamblin K	Kilmartin J
Askins J	Collins M	Garbut E	King M
Askins F	Collins M	Gaughan A	Kirby A
Askins A M	Connerton M	Gerrad B	Kirham Mrs J
Atkinson S	Conway V	Gill C	Lambert M
Bailey C	Coppinger A	Gordon W	Larkin M
Barnfather C	Corr A	Gormley M	Leahy I
Barnfather K	Coughlan J	Grace E	Lester N
Barry E	Cowell P	Grainger M	Lidster J
Begley M	Craggs E	Grice M	Liesh L
Bivens M	Cuff A	Griffiths S	Listen N
Bonner Mrs M	Curtis R	Hannan M	Lovell S
Boyes E	Danis D	Hannan A	Lowthorpe D
Boyes A	Danis F	Hargan M	Lynn K
Boyes L	Deakin C	Harrison T	Mackie J
Boyle B	Deehan K	Harrison T	Magdelen Sr M
Bradley V	Dick K	Hart P	Marie A M
Brankley I	Doods D	Hart G	Maughan C
Bright A	Dooley N	Holder P	Maughan K
Bryan I	Doto A	Holmes M	McAllister B
Burns M	Durant E	Homer J	McCarthur E
Busby M	Eagen P	Houseman H	McClinchy T
Byrnes A	Elson M	Hughes A	McDougall A
Cairns R	Fahy M	Hurton C	McElhatton C
Carling J	Fearon M	Jane Sr	McFadden J
Carling A	Ferrari G	Johnson J	McGeary E
Carrey L	Fitzgerald D	Kearns R	McGee E
Choosey B	Flemming L	Keenan J	McGeever A
Christie B	Forgan R	Kelleher Mrs	McGeever A
Clark Mrs V	Fortune D	Kelly M	McGrath M
Clark N	Fox M	Kelly D	McGregor C
Clifford D	French P	Kelly J	McGrowther A
Codd E	Frith E	Kelsey B	McKenna Br M
Coglin J	Gallagher J	Kennedy M	McKenzie S

McKinder M

McMenamin M

McMenhemin M

McQuillan S

McReddie S

McReddie B

Metcalfe E

Miller R

Mueigh B

Mullholand M

Mulligan B

Murray A

Murry M

Naughton-Doe M

Nee E

Newman Br M

Nora Sr

Noteyoung L

O'Brien K

O'Brien W

O'Neil A

O'Riordan S

Ormesby Rose

Pardoe M

Pearson S

Phillip Br

Philomena Sr

Pierre A

Power-Jepson J

Rayner M

Rees-Davies T

Rees-Davies T

Richardson J

Robertson M

Robinson C

Robinson K

Robson M

Ross L

Rossi L

Rossi I

Rossi K

Rowe S

Rowell P

Rowell R

Ruse D

Sheridan M

Skilbeck R

Smith J

Smith A

Stephens C

Stevens C

Stewart M

Summers A

Summers C

Swift R

Tasker S

Teirman C

Turner L

Urch J

Victorie Sr

Walsh B

Walsh I

Walsh E

Walsh C

Walsh M

Warton T

Weatherall L

Wesson M

Wharton T

Whittle D

Willingham A

Willis M

Wilson M

Wilson M

Wilson F

Wood L

Wood E

Wood L

Woods A

Wright L

Wright J

Wright E

Wright J

Wrightson A

Stevie

Yates C

Dr Bill Boyes, Dr Katherine Anthony, Dr Sony Anthony, Bishop John, Canon Dan Spaight and Middlesbrough nurses.

HANDMAIDS

Adams M
Atkin A
Ackerman E
Ackerman S
Allen K
Allinson J
Atkinson E
Askins J
Askins C
Balmer M
Binks K
Boyes B
Brown M
Boyes R
Brady M
Bonner E
Brown C
Barnfather K
Bruton E
Brynolf-Trett C
Boyes A
Butler L
Bourne C
Bryan M
Burns C
Clarke M
Campbell S
Campbell B
Campbell J
Collinson C
Callan T
Clark A
Clark A
Clarke M T
Clarke L
Cliff M
Chidlow L
Christie E

Couhig S
Conway L
Coleman C
Cofinas C
Coyle C
Collins D
Collins N
Cowell C
Craggs E
Crossman S
Cuff A
Dasey M
Dasey J
Dahms C
Doherty F
Doherty M
Danowski C
Davidson E
Dent Sr M
Devlin A
Devlin B
Duffew C
Davey J
Elsey M
Evans R
Edwards J
Farrer S
Farrer T
Frank P
Finn J
Forgan R
Fox P
Ford P
Francis R
France E
Freeman C
Fleming D
Gamesby P

Gilligan M
Gillan B
Green K
Gallagher E
Grace Z
Grayson A
Hornby M
Highfield A
Hardgrave M
Hardwick K
Hackett R
Holtby M
Harrison M
Harrison H
Hoyland K
Hazard J
Heagney G
Herd C
Hall C
Harkin M
Hoggard R
Hodson H
Jackson M
Johnston N
Keech L
Kosina G
Kavanagh T
Lanny M
Leng G
Ling P
Leonard M
Lidster J
Longstaff S
McDonough A
McCarthy M
McGowran C
McGowran J
McRae K

McKenna N
Mawston S
McAllister J
McAllister N
McCullagh H
McCullagh I
Mulderrig A
Milburn B
McAllister P
McSorley M
Murray C
Murray M
McKeown D
Moxon M
Marsh M
McGeary P
Morgan B
McDonough K
McLean M
Moran F
McCall S
McLeary B
McBride P
McBride P
McAllister A
Murphy L
Mawdsley J
Mawdsley K
McDermott M
McElhatton E
Murray B
Martin B
Mackin P
Maughan V
Nestor M
Nestor L
Noble C
Oyston M

O'Donaghue R	Stead M	Warrener L
O'Brien B	Stead M	Watson G
O'Connor P	Shaw B	Walsh R
O'Neill V	Sutcliffe L	Wade A
O'Brien L	Smith M	Wilson I
Phillips L	Sandison M	Whittingham E
Pennington H	Stott P	Whittingham A
Pattinson M	Speight T	Wieczorek P
Parker M	Stonehouse S	Walker M
Pattison V	Summerhill E	Wilson B
Radford L	Smith M	Wilson S
Raw M	Taylor M	Wordsworth D
Riggs A	Taylor C	Walton C
Robinson J	Taylor S	Williams A
Robinson J	Tester B	
Robinson K	Tuthill K	
Robinson A J	Tillotson C	
Robinson K	Wright E	
Rowney S	Wright M	
Riley T	Warren A	
Rickard M T	Wood M	
Rudd P	Wood L	

Bishop John and Middlesbrough handmaids on the roof garden at the new hospital.

BRANCARDIERS

Ablett M	Clarke T	Flynn P	Kelly H	McCurney D
Adams J	Clarke L	Ford P	Kelly D	McDonough T
Adams A	Codd C	Ford A	Kelly G	McDonough C
Allen J	Coleman J	Fox A	Kelly T	McElhatton F
Allinson M	Coleman G	France B	Kenny R	McEwan S
Askins J	Collins J	France D	Kilgallon P	McGeary P
Askins K	Collinson R	Frith K	Kilmartin T	McGeary D
Atkinson T	Conley D	Gales A	Kinlan J	McGeary B
Bain C	Conway F	Gales P	Kitcheyan F	McGeary M
Bainbridge D	Cosina K	Gallagher P	Lally S	McGee P
Baker G	Coughlan J	Gallagher D	Lane L	McGee R
Barritt M	Coulthurst J	Gallon T	Leahy J	McGowan K
Bell L	Coxhead A	Gannon M	Lee J	McGowran P
Bice B	Cronin K	Gardiner T	Lee T	McGowran B
Booth A	Curtis J	Gardner G	Lloyd K	McGuire M
Boyes D	Dale T	Gillespie F	Lockey B	McGurn J
Boyes D	Darby R	Gilligan T	Lombard A	McIntyre G
Boyes M	Dasey T	Gilroy G	Lovell M	McIntyre W
Boyes T	Dasey P	Grace H	Lovell L	McKenna G
Boyes M	Davies M	Grace D	Lovell K	McKenna P
Boyes P	Davies P	Green T	Luke N	McLoughlin L
Brennan S	Dawkins S	Griffiths P	Lyons K	McNeil J
Broadbent A	Defoe M	Grimes J	Mackie A	McNicholas N
Broadhead K	Denetto R	Grindley T	Mackin B	Megson P
Brough D	Dewhurst A	Hannaway F	Maiden L	Merlinson R
Brough G	DiLorenzo F	Hardgrave L	Malloney L	Metcalfe G
Brown J	Dobson L	Harrison J	Mannix J	Metcalfe G
Brunton C	Doherty M	Harry J	Matthews K	Metcalfe T
Bryan A	Doherty S	Heagney M	Matthews G	Miller A
Bryan R	Donaghue T	Holcombe P	Maurice K	Molloney P
Bryce J	Donaghue W	Hold J	Mawdsley A	Moran K
Campbell M	Donovan P	Holder S	McAllister S	Morgan J
Campbell H	Donovan J	Horkan J	McBride G	Morroco M
Carel J	Duck R	Horsman M	McBride K	Mothershill D
Carey E	Dunne S	Hoyland V	McCabe L	Moxon G
Carr D	Dunne P	Hughes G	McCann G	Mulholland F
Carrick A	Dunne T	Hughes J	McCart J	Mulligan A
Carter D	Dunne C	Hunt R	McCarthy F	Murphy W
Carter N	Elliott M	Jackson S	McCartie C	Murphy J
Casey N	Ellison A	Jackson P	McClurey E	Nelson G
Cassidy J	Fairweather R	Johnson S	McCourt T	Nestor C
Christie P	Farrer L	Jones D	McCoy E	Nestor R
Clare H	Field D	Jones P	McCoy J	Nestor P
Clarke F	Flynn M	Jones V	McCoy R	Nicholson J
Clarke H	Flynn M	Kelleher S	McCullagh M	Nicholson W

O'Brien A
O'Connor N
O'Connor F
O'Donoghue M
Ord A
Ord B
Packer D
Pattison J
Pawson D
Pawson J
Peitson B
Pennington J
Pierre J
Porritt S
Potter J
Power F
Preddy R
Pridis C

Pybus F
Quinn A
Quinn S
Ragusa P
Rainey J
Ramsay B
Ramsay M
Raw J
Rawson P
Raynor M
Redchurch G
Reidy J
Reilly M
Retallick P
Ridsdale P
Roe N
Rollings P
Rossi D

Rossi B
Ruxton O
Savage L
Sergison J
Shaw R
Sherrington J
Short A
Smiles J
Smith H
Smith M
Stewart P
Stewart J
Stubbs I
Summerhill R
Swann D
Swash M
Sykes W
Tasker A

Taylor J
Tempest N
Thompson D
Thorpe M
Tillotson K
Trainor C
Treacy A
Urch J
Vallely F
Vevers C
Waites S
Wall B
Walton A
Ward T
Warwick V
Waters P
Waterson T
Waterson L

Welford J
Wharburton M
Whitfield T
Wildy B
Williams B
Willis L
Wilson M
Wilson J
Woods J
Woods A
Wordsworth P
Wrigglesworth P
Wright T
Young N

Middlesbrough brancadiers outside the Rosary Basilica around 1990.

MIDDLESBROUGH PILGRIMS, 1952-2003

The following list of pilgrims has been compiled from the official brochure for each Pilgrimage. The names are listed in the same order as found in these brochures. It has been impossible to include those pilgrims that have made their way to Lourdes by any other route, as there is no source for this information. Every endeavour has been made to ensure the accuracy of these lists.

1952

Bishop George Brunner
Mgr C Tindall
Canon W Brunner
Canon A Wood
Rev L Cornwall
Rev L Craig SM
Rev J Currie
Rev J Heslin SM
Rev J McGarrell
Rev C Mundy
Rev J Norton SM
Rev W O'Connor SM
Rev D O'Donnell
Rev J O' Mahoney
Rev A Pippet
Rev G T Rickaby
Rev P Rynn SM
Rev Bro Joseph
Sr Bernadette
Sr M Catherine
Sr M Christopher
Sr M Dorothy
Sr Gerarda
Sr Rosalie
Sr M Therese
Aspland Mr G
Aspland Mrs G
Atkin Mrs E
Atkin Mr B
Atkinson Miss M
Auksteritis Miss
Bainbridge Mrs J
Baker Mrs
Barnacle Miss M
Baugh Miss P
Bentall Mrs
Benson Mrs A
Benson Mrs L
Bird Mrs F
Black Mrs M
Boughan Mrs E
Borrett Mrs M
Bonner Mrs M
Brady Miss M
Bradbury Mrs
Breen Miss J
Brennan Miss M K
Brolley Miss M
Brunner Miss C
Boocock Mr J J
Boocock Mr J S
Boocock Miss M

Boyes Dr W
Brennan Mrs M
Butler Mrs M
Butler Miss S
Butler Miss C
Butler Mrs
Butler Mrs MA
Callan Miss M
Caherty Mrs A
Cameron Miss E
Carabine Mr V
Carey Miss A
Carey Mr J T
Carroll-Hair Miss C
Carter Mrs
Cartwright Miss A
Carlin Miss F
Carroll Mrs W
Cavanagh Mrs E
Chapman Mrs A
Clare Mr H
Clare Mrs H
Clynes Miss V
Coates Mr J
Coates Mrs J
Coleman Mr J
Coleman Mrs J
Coleman Miss R
Collins Miss K
Conway Mrs C
Conway Mrs M
Conway Mr T
Conway Mrs T
Connaughton Miss B
Corrigan Miss M
Cornforth Mrs S
Costello Mrs W
Coulthard Miss A
Coyle Mrs
Coyle Mr A
Coyle Miss M
Crawforth Mr J
Crawforth Mrs J
Crosskill Mrs K
Crow Miss G
Cuff Miss B
Cuthbert Mrs H
Daly Mrs A
Davies Miss M
Davies Mrs P
Davis Mrs R
Dawe Miss L
Dean Mrs A

Devine Mrs C
Dickerson Mrs M
Dobbs Miss M
Docherty Mr J
Donaghy Mrs M
Donnelly Miss V
Doonan Miss M
Duck Miss M
Dunne Mr T
Early Mrs M
Early Miss N
Egan Miss K
Eglington Miss I
Ellison Miss H
Ellison Miss I
Ellison Miss T
Fagan Mrs J
Feeney Mrs C
Feeney Miss M
Ferguson Miss N
Flanagan Miss B
Flanagan Miss C
Fleisch Miss C
Fleisch Miss M C
Ford Miss O
Fox Miss C
Fox Mrs S
Fulton Miss
Gaffney Miss M
Gallagher Miss C
Gardiner Mr T
Gaynor Mrs M
Gaynor Mrs O
Geary Mrs
Goodwin Mr H
Goodwin Mrs H
Goodwin Mstr J
Gowans Mrs M
Grace Mrs M
Grainger Mrs J
Gray Miss
Griffin Mrs M
Griffin Mstr R
Grogan Mrs D
Hall Mrs C
Harding Mrs A
Harrison Miss E
Harrison Mrs H
Harrison Mr J
Harte Miss T
Hawkins Mrs
Hearty Mr D
Hearty Mrs M

Hearty Miss W
Hennessey Miss M
Hewson Miss A
Higgins Mrs A
Higgins Mr J SM
Higgins Mrs J
Hinson Mrs T
Hogarth Miss D
Hodgson Miss K
Hogan Mrs
Hogan Miss M T
Hollingsworth Mrs M
Holbrook Miss M
Hoggard Mrs
Hooper Miss T
Horn Mr J R
Horn Mrs J R
Hoskisson Miss G
Hoyland Mr P
Hoyland Mrs P
Hudson Miss J M
Hughes Miss A J
Hunt Mrs A M
Ireland Miss M
Ireland Mrs M
Jackson Mrs C
Jackson Miss E
Jackson Mrs M
James Mrs M
James Miss S
Johnson Mrs G
Johnston N G
Jones Mrs M
Keane Mrs N
Kearns Miss E C
Kearns Mr J H
Keegan Miss C
Keegan Mrs S
Kegney Miss M
Kelly Mr A
Kelly Mrs M
Kelly Mr H
Kelly Mr J
Kelly Mrs J
Kelly Mrs M J
Kennedy Miss D E
Kennedy Mr J
Kennedy Mrs J
Kennedy Miss M
Kennedy Miss R
Kennington Mrs
Killgallon Mr P
Kirby Miss A

Kirby Miss E
Kirkbright Miss M
Laftley Miss H E
Laird Mrs
Lambert Mr H
Lambert Mrs H
Lancaster Mrs G
Lapsley Mrs A
Lavan Miss M
Lavery Mrs M
Lewis Mrs
Livingstone Miss N
Lockey Mr B
Lockey Miss M
Lyth Mrs H
Lynch Miss C
McBride Mrs A
McBride Miss C
McBride Miss H
McBride Miss J
McCarthy Miss M
McCoy Miss M
McClusky Mr J
McDermott Miss M
McDonald Miss K
McElhatton Miss E
McElhatton Miss M
McElhatton Mrs
McEvoy Mrs A E
McGoown Mrs
McGinty Miss K
McGarrity Mr P
McGrath Mrs H
McGrogan Mr J
McGrogan Mrs
McIntyre Mstr V
McKenna Miss M
McKiernan Mrs
McKlernan Miss A
McLoughlin Mr L
McLoughlin Mstr J
McLoughlin Mrs
McMenamin Miss M
McQueeny Mrs T
MacCabe Dr J E
MacCabe Mrs J E
Makam Mrs K E
Machin Miss S
March Miss C
Marsh Mr J
Marsh Mrs J
Marsh Mr V
Marsh Mrs V
Martin Mrs
Martin Miss A
Martin Mr T
Martin Miss V
Mason Mrs A
Malone Miss M
Mathers Miss M
Maudsley Miss M
Metcalfe Mrs

Mellon Miss A
Meeson Mrs
Merryweather Miss M
Miller Miss A
Monaghan Miss A
Monaghan Miss H
Monaghan Mrs E
Moore Mrs
Morley Mr T
Morley Mrs T
Mossey Miss A
Mudd Mrs
Muir Miss A
Muir Miss T
Muir Miss J
Mulholland Miss M
Mulholland Mr F
Mulligan Miss A
Mulligan Miss B
Mulligan Miss M
Mulligan Miss J
Mundy Miss C
Mundy Miss M
Murray Mr H
Murray Mrs H
Murray Mrs M
Mahon Mr P
Mahon Mrs P
Nesbitt Miss B
Newlove Mrs G
Nightingale Miss E
Nightingale Miss S
O'Brien Mrs
O'Brien Miss B
O'Brien Miss C
O'Connell Mrs A
O'Connor Mrs E
O'Connor Miss N
O'Donoghue Mrs D
O'Dowd Miss E
O'Dowd Miss M
O'Hagan Mr
O'Hagan Mrs
O'Hanlon Miss F
O'Hara Miss E
O'Key Mrs M
O'Mahoney Miss M
O'Mahoney Miss P
O'Neill Mr J
O'Neill Miss M
O'Shea Miss B
Parks Mrs
Parrott Mrs M
Perkins Mr P
Pilmoor Miss M
Popplewell Miss A
Postlethwaite Miss E
Posttethwaite Miss S
Potter Mr J
Pullen Mrs J
Prior Mrs M
Quinn Mrs E

Readman Miss J
Readman Miss H
Reardon Miss A
Reardon Miss W
Richardson Mrs A
Riley Mr S
Riley Miss J
Robertson Miss M
Robinson Mrs H
Roe Miss D
Roe Miss M J
Roe Miss M P
Ronchetti Mr A
Ryan Miss M C
Ross Miss A
Saywell Miss D
Scarth Miss E
Sheals Mrs
Sheals Miss H
Sherrington Mr J A
Shipley Mrs J
Shipley Miss M
Shorttle Miss E K
Sinnott Mrs J
Skilbeck Mr A
Skilbeck Mrs A
Slingsby Miss C
Sleightholme Mrs E
Smith Mr H
Smith Mrs H
Smith Mr D
Smith Miss R
Smith Miss V
Spayne Mrs J
Spink Miss B
Spink Miss I
Spink Miss J
Stacey Mr E
Stead Mr H
Stead Miss M
Stead Miss M
Steel Mrs E
Storey Miss L
Stow Miss M
Swales Miss E
Tate Mrs E
Taylor Mrs S
Thompson Mrs G
Thompson Mr L
Thompson Miss P
Throssall Mrs
Train Mr J
Trimble Mrs
Trimble Miss A
Vause Miss M
Walsh Miss E
Walsh Miss I
Walsh Miss N
Walsh Miss M
Walsh Mrs T
Watson Mrs M
Ward Mrs L

Welford Mr G
Welford Mr J
Welford' Miss H
West Mstr A
Whelan Mrs E
Whelan Miss M
White Miss P
Williamson Miss E
Wilson Mrs A
Wilson Mr
Winterburn Miss G
Winstone Miss E
Wood Miss M
Wright Mrs G
Wright Mrs M
Yoemans Miss E
York Mrs M

Sick Pilgrims

Askins Mrs M H
Boyle Mr J
Carter Mrs K
Caveney Mr T
Crabtree Mr G
Cochrane Miss E
Edghill Mrs M
Emerson Mrs M
Glogowski Mrs B
Gilleeney Mrs H
Hart Mrs J
Heaven Miss S
Kingston Mrs M
Laws Mrs B
Leahy Mrs M
McArdle Miss M
McCarrick Miss M
Marty Mr R
Molson Mr J
Monaghan Mrs M
Morrison Mr T
O'Hara Miss A
O'Neill Miss
Pearson Mr R
Read Mr C
Reynolds Miss M
Richards Mr W
Tinsley Mr J
Waters Mr J
White Miss W

1953
Bishop George Brunner
Tindall Mgr C
O'Sullivan Canon
Breen Rev T
Boyd Rev M
Donovan Rev D J OSB
Gibbons Rev J A OSB
Keating Rev C
Kinane Rev P
McAniff Rev P
O'Connor Rev A

O'Connor Rev W SM
O'Riorden Rev R
Power Rev G
Ryan Rev D
Rickaby Rev G T
Slattery Rev T
Toner Rev C
Brother Rev
Aspland Mrs
Aspland Mr
Allan Miss M
Baxter Mr J A
Blair Miss M A
Black Miss J P
Black Miss M B
Baxter Miss M
Brady Mrs M P
Boyes Dr W
Briggs Mrs H
Battle Mrs A E
Craig Miss R
Cranny Mrs E
Campbell Miss J
Campbell Miss M T
Copley Mrs R A
Caherty Mrs A
Carter Mrs M
Clark Mrs P
Clarke Mrs C
Chidzey Mrs E A
Cross Mrs R A
Curtis Mrs C
Dobson Mr L
Drew Miss F M
Dolan Miss R A
Dukes Mrs K
Dean Mrs A
Dunnakey Mrs S A
Darragh Mrs M
Donovan Mrs C
Donovan Miss K
Early Mstr V
Foley Miss H
Ferguson Miss N
Fox Mrs M J
Fitzgerald Mrs M A
Garbutt Mr T
Goodall Mr W J
Goodall Mstr R W
Grimes Miss S S
Gannon Mr M
Gibbons Mrs F
Gibbons F/Sgt M W
Gallon Mr F
Grant Miss P J
Hughes Mrs E
Hagan Miss M
Hodgson Mr P F
Headland Mrs M
Harrison Miss M
Hugill Miss T

Hodgson Miss L
Hollingsworth Mrs M
Higgins Mrs A
Humphrey Mr R D
Iggleden Mrs F
Johns Mrs L
Jackson Mrs G
Jameson Mr J R M
Jameson Mrs G E
Kelsey Miss E
Kilbride Mrs B
Kilbride Mr J F
Kirk Mrs W
Kidd Mrs R
Kenny Miss A T
Kegney Miss M
Killick Mrs S
Killick Miss P A
Leahy Miss M F
Lavey Mr T J
Luvey Mr A
Muir Miss A
Muir Mr T
Murphy Mrs T
Myers Mrs B
Maule Mrs
Mullholland Miss M
Mallen Mrs P
Martin Mr T P
Mulligan Miss M
Mulligan Mr A
Mulligan Mrs
Metcalfe Mrs W
Mnason Mrs C
Mason Miss M
Matthews Mrs L
Mackin Miss S
Melligan Miss J S
McGee Mrs J
McGee Miss M T
McHale Miss W
McDermott Miss C
McElhatton Miss E
McElhatton Miss M
McKeown Miss M E
McLoughlin Mr T L
McInnes Mrs M M
McInnes Miss J M
McInnes Miss M M L
McPartland Mrs P S
Nicholson Miss H
Nolan Mr E
O'Neill Miss M P
O'Brien Mrs K
O'Brien Mrs E M
Ord Miss E
O'Hara Mr J
O'Hara Miss J E
O'Hara Miss E
O'Mahony Mrs M
Plowman Mrs F
Poupard Mrs M

Rowland Miss M
Riley Miss J
Raw Miss M
Roe Miss e M
Stead Miss M E
Stead Miss M C
Stead Miss L
Stranger Miss J A
Sherlock Miss M
Simpson Mrs M
Storey Miss L
Smith Miss A M
Simpson Miss C J
Wilson Miss M J
Wilson Miss A C
Walker Mr A
Wilson Mr E
Wilson Miss H M
Walsh Miss E
Walsh Miss M
Winterburn Miss G M V
Walsh Miss E
Walsh Miss M
Whenray Miss K T
Wordsworth Mr J
White Mr J T

Sick Pilgrims

Ager Mr J
Addison Mr W A
Brown Mr F
Black Mrs M J
Calvert Miss A
Connell Mst J T
Connell Mrs J
Clarkson Mr W
Cross Mr A
Docherty Mrs C
Downing Mr M A
Dryden Miss A M
Durant Miss A
Ferguson Mrs M
Graham Mr J
Graham Miss N M
Hinson Mr T P
Jackson Mr J
Kimmet Mr T
Kingston Mr M
Laird Mrs S
Larkin Mr G T
Lee Mr J
Molloy Mrs N
Mullen Mr E
Murphy Mrs B
Martin Miss V
Molson Mr J
Marty Mr R
Maume Miss M
O'Berg Miss H
O'Brien Miss M P
Peacock Mrs A
Pearson Mr R

Shaw Miss F A
Swatman Miss E
Williams Miss K
Whitehead Miss S
Williams Mrs M A
Wynne Mr W

1954

Bishop George Brunner
Tindall Mgr C
McMullan Canon J
O'Sullivan Canon M
Breen V Rev T
Boyd Rev M
Bolger Rev M
Cahill Rev D
Crowley Rev M
Carroll Rev W
Joseph Brother
Keily Rev P
Kelly Rev P
Keating Rev C
Nolan Rev T A
O'Byrne Rev D
O'Connor Rev A
O'Connor Rev W
O'Mahony Rev J
Rickaby Rev G T
Rice Rev F
Shannhan Rev J
Storey Rev P A
Williams Rev H R OSB
Andrew Sr M
Flynn Sr M Mildred
Isidore Sr M
Thomas Sr M
Small Sr M Monica
Veronica Sr
Allen Miss M
Allen Mr H
Antoniewicz Mrs H
Adams Mr J A
Andrews Miss E M
Appleby Miss M A
Boocock Mr J J
Brannen Miss M
Boal Mrs A
Bentley-Hunt Miss M J
Blair Miss M A
Baxter Mr J A
Baxter Miss M
Bice Mr B
Beck Mr P
Bagnall Mrs C
Black Miss J
Black Miss M
Black Mr A
Breen Miss M
Barbara Mrs I
Baines Mr H P
Burns Mr J
Baker Mrs M

Brunton Mr C W
Banks Miss M
Baker Mrs G
Coughlan Mr J P
Conlon Miss M B
Carter Mrs M A
Chidzcy Mrs E A
Cameron Miss B
Conway Mr J
Conway Mrs M
Connaughton Mrs
Cavanagh Mrs E
Cassidy Miss M
Cottam Miss L P
Coxhead Mr A
Curran Mr A
Conway Mr P
Cadley Miss I A
Conley Mr J R
Cone Mrs M
Cox Miss M
Clynes Miss V N
Caulfield Mrs
Caulfield Mr E
Caster Mrs M A
Coakley Mrs
Dean Mrs A
Dobson Mr L
Drew Miss F M
Denston Mrs E
Dolan Miss R
Duffin Mrs M C
Duffy Miss G
Dukes Miss K
Dukes Miss M
Devine Mrs C
Dukes Miss P A
Doherty Miss B M
Doherty Mr
Doherty Mrs
Douglas Miss E
Empson Miss A
England Mr B
Flannagan Miss M M
Flanagan Mrs M F
Fitzgerald Mr M
Fitzgerald Mrs M
Ferguson Mrs M
Ferguson Miss N
Farrell Miss R A
Feetenby Miss A M
Gannon Mrs F P
Gordon Mrs W
Gallon Miss C
Grainger Miss M T
Garbutt Mr T
Gannon Mr M
Gillespie Mr F
Golden Miss E
Gargan Mr A
Grant Miss' P J
Gardiner Mr T

Gardiner Mrs W
Hollingsworth Mrs M
Hodgens Mrs E
Hodgson Mr P F
Horn Mr J: R
Horn Mrs E
Harrison Miss W
Harrison Miss B M
Hart Mrs M
Hatfield Mrs H
Harrison Miss V
Harding Mrs A
Harrison Miss M
Hoy Mr T
Hoy Mrs E
Hughes Mr B
Harrington Miss T
Harrison Mrs
Hearne Miss A
Caroll-Hair Miss C A
Higgins Mrs T
Horgan Mrs E
Hogg Mrs K C
Hurley Mrs M
Hurley Miss G M
Hurley Mr M
Heagney Mr A
Heagney Mrs A
Irwin Miss M
Jackson Mrs A
Jopling Miss M
Johnston Miss G L
Jackson Miss M W
Jackson Mr J
Jackson Mrs M
Jackson Miss M
Keane Mr J
Kilbride Mr J F
Kilbride Mrs B
Kelly Miss M
Kegney Miss M
Kilgallon Mr P
King Miss M
King Mr P
King Mrs W
Kingston Mr M
Locker Mrs A
Lawlor Miss M K
Loo Miss T
Lee Mrs M
Lee Miss A
Lee Miss T
Lee Miss J
Lee Mstr K
Lee Mstr P
Martin Mrs M
Martin Mr J
Martin Mrs M A
Murray Mr F J
Malone Miss M
Muir Miss A
Muir Miss T

Mossey Miss A
Marsh Mr J
Marsh Mrs
Mackin Mr B
Mackin Mrs S
Maule Mrs A
Maule Miss C
Maule Miss J
Mulligan Mr A
Murphy Mrs T
Muiholland Miss M
Mulligan Miss M
Mulligan Miss M M
Muir Miss J
Mendoza Mrs M
Mason Mrs J
Mason Miss M
Mulligan Mr J
McBean Mr E
McLoughlin Mr T
McGee Miss M T
McCabe Mr L
McElhatton Mrs E
McPartland Mrs P
McMenamin Miss M
McCreton Mr P
McLean Mrs J
McLean Mstr C
McElhatton Miss M
MacCabe Dr J E
McLoughlin Mr R
McElhatton Miss E
McElhatton Miss C
McCrory Miss M
McKillop Mrs M J
McKinstry Mrs M
McMahon Miss E
McKenna Miss M
McElhatton Mr F
Nolan Miss E
Nolan Miss A
Nesbitt Miss N
Nesbitt Miss B
Nolan Mrs
Nolan Mr E
O'Neill Miss M
O'Rourke Mr J
O'Byrne Mr D J
O'Byrne Mrs
O'Flynn Miss
O'Flynn Miss
O'Connell Mrs K
O'Hara Mr J
O'Hara Mrs A
O'Hara Mrs E
O'Neill Miss E
O'Neill Miss P
O'Connor Mrs A
O'Toole Mrs E
O'Toole Miss C
O'Toole Mstr M
O'Farrell Miss A

O'Hara Miss E
Perkins Mr C
Potter Mr J
Potter Miss J
Parks Miss H
Palairet Lady M
Passman Mrs
Riley Miss J
Readman Miss H M
Raw Mr J E
Raw Miss M M
Rafferty Mr H
Rafferty Mrs M
Raw Miss A
Raw Miss T
Randall Mrs
Reynolds Mrs A
Reynolds Mstr G
Royal Mrs S
Richards Mr W
Robertson Miss E
Storey Miss L
Shaw Mrs S
Shaw Miss F A
Stead Mr M
Stead Miss M E
Stead Miss M C
Shore Miss
Sherlock Miss M
Stead Miss L
Stranger MissJ A
Sleight Miss J
Shackleton Mrs R D
Shackleton Miss M V
Scaife Miss M
Sheveling Miss M S
Slingsby Miss C
Stonehouse Mrs M
Snailham Miss E
Stancer Mrs G
Sharp Mrs M M
Seaman Mrs E
Sayers Mr W
Shaw Sgt
Shaw Mrs
Terry Miss M
Tevlim Mrs P
Taylor Mrs S
Traynor Mr C A
Tasker Mrs E
Traynor Mrs K
Walsh Miss M
Walsh Miss M
Walsh Miss E
Wilkinson Mr J A
Whenray Miss K T
Wilson Mr J W
Walker Mrs C C
Walker Miss J C
Walsh Mrs M
Wilkinson Mrs V
Wood Mr A

Wood Mrs G
Wood Miss P M
Wentworth Mrs K
Wadsworth Mrs A
Wadsworth Miss M
Ward Mr M
Young Miss M
Barry Miss E
Barry Miss M
Barrett Mr J
Bartley Mr J P
Calvert Miss A
Cochrane Mrs M I
Doherty Mrs C
Durant Mr J N
Early Miss T
Foley Mr T
Fox Mstr Fred J
Haxby Mr F
Joel Mrs M
Kimmett Mr T
Lee Mr J
Mahon Mr B J
Maloney Mrs M
Martine Mr J
Martin Miss V
Marston Miss K D
Molson Mr J A
McBean Mrs C
McIntyre Mr M
McCurley Mrs D
Norman Mrs A
O'Donnell Mrs M
Pearson Mr R
Pitcairn Miss M
Rafter Mr J J
Read Mr C
Sharp Miss P
Smith Mr F
Smith Mr P
Smith Mrs R
Solt Mr P
Stead Miss M
Tinsley Mr J
Twyford Miss V
Whitehead Miss S
Williams Miss K

Juvenile Section
Cassidy Miss H
Cassidy Miss M
Kennedy Miss E M
Afford Miss P P
Anderson Miss E
Delmar Miss R
Gartland Miss G
Hughes Miss M
Kelly Miss E
Kirkpatrick Miss J
Lymas Miss B G
Mitchell Miss M P
McDermott Miss D

McNally Miss S
Rea Miss M
Smith Miss A M
Summerfield Miss M
Tevlin Miss P

Boy Scouts
Brown P
Davies W
Murray B
Murray P
McDonagh A
Robinson R
Stanley G
Woodhouse M

Air Pilgrims
Brunner Canon W
Wood Canon A
Anderson Mother T
O'Connor Mother J
Brunner Miss M J
Carey Mr J T
Carey Miss A
Coleman Mr J
Duck Mrs E
Everingham Miss I
Gardiner Miss V
Goodall Mr W J
Goodall Mstr R W
Hardy Miss E
Horwell Mrs E T
Horwell Miss M T
Horwell Mr R
Hughes Miss M
Hunt Mrs E
Hunt Mr J R
Kelly Mrs J B
Kelly Mr J E
Merryweather Miss I M
Morrison Mr T
Morrison Mr R
Mullen Mr E
Mullen Mrs E
McGurk Miss A E
Porton Mrs A
Reardon Miss A
Rosenbrock Miss H I
Shortle Miss K M
Spayne Mrs B
Spayne Miss M
Walsh Mrs M
Walsh Miss M
Collins Mr J M
Hadley Mr W
McLean Mr J B

1955
Bishop George Brunner
Tindall Mgr V
McMullan Canon J
O'Sullivan Canon M

Dennett Rev L
Hughes Rev J
O'Callaghan Rev
O'Mahoney Rev J
Pippet Rev A
Rickaby Rev G T
Paulinus Rev Bro
Andrew Rev Mother
Agnes Sr
Mary Denis Sr
Ablett Mrs K
Allen Miss C
Allen Mrs J
Allison Mrs M
Andrews Miss E
Barrett Mrs H
Baxter Mr A
Beck Mr P
Bice Mr B
Black Mrs
Black Mr G
Black Miss J
Black Miss M
Boocock Mr J
Brady Mrs M
Brannigan Mr P
Bridgeman Mr
Bridgeman Mrs
Burke Mrs E
Burke Mr G
Burke Mstr P
Burns Mrs M
Caherty Mrs A
Cameron Miss E
Carney Miss J
Case Mrs C
Cave Mrs A
Cave Mstr K
Chidzey Mrs
Clifton Mrs F T
Clynes Miss V
Condon Dr J
Condon Mrs M
Conway Mr J
Conway Mrs
Conway Miss M
Coughlan Mr J
Couhig Mr
Couhig Mrs
Couhig Miss
Coxhead Mr A
Culkin Mrs
Culkin Miss M E
Curran Mr A
Dean Mrs
Dobson Mr L
Donovan Mr J
Doonan Miss J
Doonan Miss J
Duck Miss M
Dunne Mr T
Fish Mrs E

Fitzgibbon Mr P
Fitzpatrick Mrs W
Flanigan Miss R
Fox Mr F
Fox Mstr F
Franklin Mrs H
Franklin Mrs H
Gardiner Mr T
Gillespie Mr F
Golden Mrs E
Golden Miss J
Greenhough Mrs I
Hair Miss C
Hagney Miss
Harrison Mrs I
Harrison Mr R
Harrison Mstr J
Harrison Mstr R
Henry Mr D
Hogan Miss
Hooper Miss T
Hughes Mr J
Hughes Mrs L
Hughes Miss S
Hunter Mr
Huntington Miss E
Jackson Mrs M
Jackson Miss M
Jennings Miss M R
Jinks Miss V
Jones Miss E
Kirkbright Mrs
Kirkbright Miss M
Lawson Mrs D
Mackin Mr
Mackin Miss
March Mrs M
March Mstr K
Maher Miss S
Martin Mr P
Martin Mrs M
Mason Miss H
Mason Miss M
Mondoza Mrs M
Moran Mr R
Murphy Mr C
Murray Mrs E
Murray Mrs E
MacCabe Miss F
MacCabe Dr J B
MacCabe Mrs P C
McAlger Miss
McCullagh Miss M
McCullough Mrs
McElhatton Miss
McElhatton Mr F
McKenna Miss A
McKenna Miss A
McKenna Miss S
McLoughlin Mr T
McMenamin Miss M
Nolan Mr E

O'Callaghan Mrs
O'Connell Mrs
O'Connor Mr
O'Flyn Miss
O'Neill Mrs A
O'Rourke Mrs A
Pattison Mr C
Pattison Mrs M
Pearson Mrs M
Perkins Mr C
Potter Mr J
Potter Miss J
Quinn Mrs M
Raw Mr J E
Raw Miss M M
Raw Miss T
Riley Miss J
Rodgers Mrs
Scully Miss E
Scully Mrs
Shaw Mrs F C
Shaw Miss M E
Shields Mrs C
Smith Mrs E H
Smith Mr P P
Staines Mrs
Stead Miss M C
Stead Miss M e
Traynor Mr C
Wade Miss J
Waldron Miss E
Walsh Miss I
Walsh Miss M
Walsh Miss M
Walsh Mrs A
Walsh Miss M
Walsh Miss S
Whelan Mrs
Whelan Miss M

Sick Pilgrims
Barrett Mr P
Brett Mr J
Cain Mrs A
Callaghan Miss R
Calvert Miss A
Conway Mr V
Coughlan Mrs G
Coughlan Miss S
Docherty Mrs C
Donnelly Mrs B
Eals Mr S
Golloghly Miss D
Hartley Mr B
Havelock Mr T
Hemblade Mr L
Hird Mrs E
Hunter Mrs B
Joy Mr N
Kennedy Miss M
Kingston Mr M
Lee Mr P

Mahon Mr B
Molson Mr J
Mullen Mr E
McGuiness Mr A
O'Callaghan Mr J A
O'Donnell Miss
Pearson Mr J
Power Miss M
Quinn Mr T
Richards Mr W
Smith Mr P
Varey Mrs M
Walker Mr H
Walsh Mr J
Ward Miss C
Whelan Mr A
Wilcox Miss M

Air Section
Wood Canon A
Brennan Rev J
Currie Rev J D
Noonan Rev L
O'Connor Rev W
Bagnall Mrs C
Black Mrs
Black Miss
Cameron Miss E
Chidzey Mrs E A
Coleman Miss D
Coleman Mr J
Connelly Mr B
Cox Miss E M
Dolan Miss R A
Goodreid Miss L
Hart Mrs
Jackson Miss C M
Jackson Mr J
Kilbride Mr J F
Kilbride Mrs J F
Maley Miss W
Maule Mrs A
Maule Miss C M
Maule Miss J
Mulligan Mr J
McDonald Miss R
McLoughlin Mr R
Pickering Mrs I
Plowman Mrs F
Porton Mrs
Rea Mrs
Rhodes Mrs E
Roe Miss E M
Roe Miss W
Roberts Mrs M
Scarth Miss B
Stead Mr M H
Urry Mrs P A
Walsh Dr D K
Walsh Mr P
Walsh Mrs P

CTA REPS
Mr M J Collins
Miss J Connell
Mr V Major
Mr G Perombelon

1956
Bishop George Brunner
Tindall Mgr C
McMullan Canon J
Nolan Canon TA
O'Sullivan Canon M
Coughlan Rev K
Keogan Rev P
McAniff Rev P
Pippet Rev C A
Plunket Rev O
Rickaby Rev G T
Flynn Rev Bro D
Dominic Sr Mary
Bridget Sr Mary
Adams Mr J A
Addyman Miss L
Allison Mrs M
Barrett Mr M
Barry Mr J
Bickerstaff Miss M
Bice Mr B
Bell Mrs M A
Black Mr G
Black Miss M
Boocock Mr J J
Boyes Dr W
Boyes Mrs B
Brown Mr R
Brunner Miss M C
Brunton Mr C W
Buckton Miss K
Burke Mr W
Caffrey Mrs
Caherty Mrs A
Cameron Miss B
Carroll-Hair Miss C
Carter Mr J
Chidzey Mrs B A
Clare Mr H
Clarke Mr R J
Cole Miss
Coleman Mr J
Conlon Miss M B
Cox Mrs E M
Coxhead Mr A
Dean Mrs A
Dobson Mr L
Donovan Mr J
Donovan Miss M
Doocey Mrs C
Dougherty Mrs
Duck Mr R
Ferguson Mr J J
Fitzgibbon Mr G P

Flannagan Mr P
Frankish Mrs A
Gallagher Mr J
Gallon Miss C
Gannon Mr M
Gardiner Miss A
Gillespie Mr F
Golding Mrs M
Goodall Mr W J'
Goodall Mrs W J
Goodall Mstr W J
Gordon Mr W
Grainger Mrs
Henderson Miss M
Henderson Mrs N
Henderson Miss E
Herrington Miss E
Higham Mrs
Holmes Miss M
Hooper Miss T
Hughes Miss M:
Jinks Miss V
Jones Miss E
Kegney Miss M
Kelly Mr J
Kelly Miss K:
Kilbride Mr J
Kilbride Mrs B
Kilgallon Mr F
Kress Ivhs
Loughran Mr F
Loughran Mrs K
Mackin Miss S
Madden Miss E
Mailey Miss A
Manderville Miss M
Maule Mrs A;
Miller Miss W
Moss Miss D
Mulligan Mr A
McElhatton Miss M
McElhatton Miss B
McKenna Mrs A
McKenna Miss S
McLoughlin Mr T L
McMenamin Mr J
McMenamin Mrs G
McMenamin Miss M
Nicholson Mr W
O'Rourke Mrs A
O'Rourke Miss N
Perkins Mr C
Piasecki Mr M
Piasecki Mr C
Potter Mr J
Potter Miss J
Rafferty Mrs H
Raw Mr J E
Raw Miss M M
Reid Dr F
Reid Mstr M
Reynolds Mrs S

Reynolds Mr T
Richards Mr J
Riley Miss J
Shackleton Mrs R D
Sherrington Mr J A
Slingsby Miss C
Smith Miss M D
Storey Miss L
Stranger Miss J A
Taylor Miss M
Taylor Miss S
Templeman Mrs C
Terry Miss M
Thompson Miss M
Thompson Miss T
Traynor Mr C
Tumber Miss M
Twohig Mr B
Vause Miss M
Waldron Miss M
Walsh Dr D K
Walsh Miss E
Walsh Miss I
Walsh Miss M
Whelan Miss M
Wilson Mr J
Wilson Mrs E
Wilson Miss H M
Wilson Miss M
Wise Miss E Ashford
Wood Mr A

Sick Pilgrims
Xavier Sr Mary
Batchelor Mr J
Bickerstaffe Mr J
Burrows Mr J
Cochrane Mrs M
Cosgrove Miss E
Coward Mr A
Devlin Mrs M
Downing Mr W
Duggan Miss M
Eastwood Miss M
Eeles Mr S
Gilfinnan Mrs M
Gilkerson Mrs C
Hallett Mrs W
Hanlon Mr L
Hargan Mr M
Henry Mr D
Henry Mr J
Hollingsworth Mrs M
Joel Mrs M
Kingston Mr M
Lacey Mr M
Langan Mrs L
Langan Miss V
Langan Miss M
Lee Mr J
Matthews Mr E
Molson Mr J

Mullen Mr E
Murray Mr J
McGarrity Miss P
McWilliams Mr T
Nicholson Mrs I
Reynolds Miss M
Taylor Miss A
Turner Mrs M
Walker Mr H
Juvenile Section
Catherine Sr
Germaine Sr
Flanigan Miss R
Lowe Mrs M
Bradley Joyce
Corrigan Margaret
Crook Margaret
Devonshire Christine
Flanigan Margaret
Hallett Winefred
Hawkeswell Angela
Kelly Patricia
Lockey Gillian
Moor Elisabeth
Murray Mary
Nicholls Elisabeth

Air Section
Brunner Canon W
Currie Rev J D
Duffy Rev F M
O'Connor Rev A
O'Mahoney Rev J
Ryan Rev J J
Armstrong Mrs M
Carroll Mr L M
Carroll Miss M E
Cole Mrs C
Cole Miss D
Copeland Mrs W
Daly Mr J
Daly Mrs E M
Daly Mr V
Dowson Mrs W E
Dowson Miss A
Hall Mrs T
Jackson Miss M W
Kane Miss R
Langton Mrs W
Malia Mrs J M
Mecrow Miss D
Monaghan Mrs E
McLeary Mrs J
McLeary Mstr D
McGrogan Mrs M
McGrogan Miss B M
McGrogan Miss M G
Scarth Miss E
Stead Mr M
Stead Mr C
Turner Mrs M
Turner Mstr J

Unwin Mrs N
Walsh Mr P
Walsh Mrs W
Walsh Miss M
Wheatley Mr J

CTA REPS
Collins Mr J M
McDermott Mr J
Major Mr V
Perombelon Mr G

1957
Bishop George Brunner
O'Sullivan Canon M
Tindall Mgr C
McMullan Canon J
Collingwood Rev L J
Knowles Rev J
Muffins OP Rev G A
McAniff Rev P
O'Callaghan Rev C G
O'Mahoney Rev J
Pippet Rev C A
Plunkett Rev O
Rickaby Rev G T
Ryan Rev M J
Toner Rev C M
Basil Rev Bro
Bede Rev Bro
Helen Sr
Veronica Sr
Addyman Miss L
Allison Mrs M
Allon Mrs E
Almond Mrs M
Amos Mrs M
Badenhorst 'Mrs B V
Baker Miss B
Barringer Miss M
Barry Mrs
Beck Mr P
Bell Mrs M A
Blair Miss M A
Bonner Mrs
Boocock Mr J J
Boughan Mrs E
Boyes Mrs B
Boyes Dr W
Bradley Mr G
Brannick Mr H
Brown Mrs
Brunner Miss M C
Burke Mr W
Burns Mrs M
Byrne Mrs E
Callaghan Mr P
Cameron Miss B
Carter Mr
Chidzey Mrs E A
Clare Mr H A
Cole Miss M

Coleman Mr G
Coleman Mr J
Collingwood Mr B J
Costigan Mr
Costigan Mrs
Coughlan Mr J P
Coupland Miss S
Coward Mr A
Coward Mrs M
Cox Mrs B M
Cox Mr F
Coxhead Mr A
Craig Mrs B
Crawford Mrs F E
Curran Mr A
Curran Mrs M
Dean Mrs A
Devine Mrs C A
Dixon Mrs E
Dobson Mr L
Dodson Miss D
Dolan Miss R
Donovan Mr J
Donovan Miss
Downey Mrs M
Dowson Mr B
Draper Mrs V
Duck Mr P
Dullaghan Mr P
Dunne Mrs G M
Dunne Mrs R
Dunne Mr T
Earley Mr J'B
Flanagan Mr P
Flanigan Mrs
Flanigan Miss R M
Frankland Mrs E
Frankland Miss E
Frankland Mrs M
Gallagher Mrs B E
Gannon Mr M
Gannon Mr T
Gardiner Mr T
Gibbons Miss B
Gibbons Mstr C
Gibbons Mr T
Gibbons Mrs T
Gibbons Mrs D
Gibbons Mr M
Gillespie Mr F
Golding Mrs M
Gordon Mr W
Gordon Mrs W
Grainger Mrs F
Green Mrs J
Hanafin Miss C
Harrison Mrs E
Harrison Miss M
Head Miss B
Heslehurst Mrs J
Hewitson Miss M
Hindley Mrs M

Hindley Mrs M
Hogarth Miss A M
Hogarth Miss M M
Hollingsworth Mrs M
Huggins Mrs S
Hunt Mrs A
Hunt Mr R
Igo Mr E
Jackson Mrs E
Jarratt Mr G
Johnson Mrs L
Jones Mr D P
Jones Mrs V N
Jones Miss M C
Jordan Mrs M
Kelly Mrs M
Kilbride Mrs B
Kilbride Mr JF
King Mrs E
Leddy Miss M
Lighton Miss M
Little Miss E
Loughran Mr F
Loughran Mrs
Lowe Mrs M
Lyons Mr A
Lyons Mrs A
Mackin Miss S
Mallinson Mrs V
March Mrs M
March Mr N
Marsden Mr B
Marsden Mr P
Marsey Miss S I
Marsh Mr
Marsh Mrs
Marty Mr
Mason Miss M
Maule Mrs A
Maule Miss A
Maule Miss C
Maule Miss J
Mendoza Mrs M
Mett Mr A
Mossey Miss A
Muir Miss A
Muir Mrs E
Muir Miss J
Mullen Mrs M J
Mulligan Miss A M
Mulligan Miss M B
Murphy Miss C
Murphy Miss P
Murray Mrs M
McAllister Mr J A
McCartin Mr C
McDonagh Miss M
McElhatton Miss E
McElhatton Mr F
McGeown Mrs E
McGrother Miss M
McKenna Mrs A

McKenna Mrs M
McKenna Miss S
McLoughlin Mrs A
McLoughlin Mr L
McMahon Miss E
McMenamin Miss M
McShea Miss A E
Newlove Mrs F A
Nichol Mrs M
Nicholson Mr B A
Nicholson Miss V M
Nicholson Mr W
Olivier Mrs E
O'Mahoney Mrs M
O'Rourke Mrs A
Pearson Mrs M
Pearson Miss M
Perkins Mr C
Pickup Miss H M
Pippet Miss M
Pippet Miss M G
Potter Mr J
Poupard Mrs M
Poupard Mstr M
Rafferty Mr E
Rafferty Miss F
Rafferty Mr H
Rafferty Mrs K
Rafferty Mrs M
Raw Mr J E
Raw Miss M M
Reynolds Mr T F
Richards Mr W
Riley Miss J
Roper Mrs E
Scanlan Miss M
Sciberras Mrs M
Shackleton Miss' M
Shaw Miss J
Shimmin Miss 'B M
Short Mrs A
Smith Mrs M
Smith Miss M D
Stead Miss M C
Storey Miss L
Taylor Miss M
Thompson Mrs M
Thwaites Miss A
Titterton Mr B
Titterton Miss M
Traynor Mr C
Twohig Mr B
Twohig Mstr E
Twohig Mr L
Twohig Mrs T
Van Eck-Lyons Mrs T
Wade Mrs Y
Waldron Miss E
Walsh Miss E
Walsh Miss M
Walsh Miss M
Walsh Miss P A

Warwick Mr V C
Whatlin Mrs L
Whelan Miss M
Whelan Mrs S
White Miss C M
Wilson Miss H M
Wilson Mr J

Sick Pilgrims

Barrett Mr J M
Barrett Mr P
Burns Mr T
Campbell Mr A
Chamberlain Mrs
Clark Mrs M
Curley Mrs A
Donaghy Mr L
Doran Mr J
Durrant Mr J N
Durkin Mr J N
Fallon Mr T
Gallagher Mr E
Graham Mrs N
Griffin Mrs L
Hargreaves Mrs E
Kelly Mr D
Kimmett Mr J
Kingston Mr M
Lazzarini Mrs M
Livingstone Mr J
Lockhart Mrs E
Lucas Miss K
Martin Mrs C
Molson Mr J
Moran Mr K
Morris Mr R
McCaffrey Miss J
McCarthy Miss J
McGee Mr J
McGrother Miss E
Ogden Mr E H
O'Sullivan Miss C
Smith Mr F
Solt Mr P
Treacy Mrs F
Whelan Mr J C
Whelan Mstr M
Whelan Mrs R
Williams Mr C \V

Air Section

Brunner Canon w
Carson Rev L
Currie Rev J D
Ryan Rev J
Bowman Miss R
Clarke Mrs S
Elwick Mrs M A
Flannaghan Miss B
McAuliffe Mr J
McAuliffe Mrs A
McGrogan Mrs M

McGrogan Miss B
McLoughlan Mrs A
O'Neill Miss J
Scarth Miss E
Smith Mrs M
Taylor Mrs E
Thompson Mrs M N
Williams Miss K J
Woodwark Mrs

1958

Bishop George Brunner
O'Sullivan Mgr M
Lannen Mgr P
McMullan Canon J
Nolan Canon T
Bluett Rev P
Boyd Rev M
Breen Rev D
Breen Rev T
Culkin Rev G
Dewar Rev J A
Donlon Rev B M
Dooley Rev V
Doyle Rev M CM
Dunne Rev M CM
Kielty Rev J N
Kitchen Rev S F
Mortell Rev J
O'Callaghan Rev C G
O'Mahony Rev J
Pippet Rev A
Plunkett Rev O
Purcell Rev J
Purcell Rev P
Rickaby Rev G T
Ryan Rev M J
Storey Rev A J
Storey Rev P L
Walsh Rev J
Aloysius Sr
Bridget Sr
Christine Mother M
Conway Sr M C
Dominica Sr
Flynn Sr
Gregory Sr
Helene Sr M
Louise Mother M
Marguerite-Marie Sr
Paul Mother
Philomena Sr
Scott-Allen Sr M J
St Edouard Sr M
Vincent Sr M
Adams Mr A J
Allen Miss J E
Allsopp Miss M J
Armes Mrs M
Aukstinatis Miss J
Ayres Mrs K
Baikie Miss S

Baker Mrs G
Baker Mrs M A
Batchelor Mrs C
Baxter Miss M
Bearpark Mrs V
Bell Mrs M A
Benneworth Mrs T
Bennett Mrs K
Bennison Mr H
Bilton Mrs E
Brand Miss E
Brady Miss M
Briggs Miss M
Brooks Mrs G
Brown Miss B
Brown Mr George
Brown Miss M C
Browne Miss Y T
Boocock Mr J J
Booth Mrs M
Borzumato Mrs M
Botley Miss F
Bourke Miss P
Bowler Mr M
Boyes Dr W
Burnes Miss E
Byrne Mr J
Byrne Mrs O
Byrnes Mr W
Caherty Mrs A
Cahill Dr J
Cahill Mrs
Callaghan Mr P
Callaghan Mrs D H
Cambell Mrs A
Canty Mrs R
Carter Mrs M
Casey Miss
Caulfield Miss
Cajany Miss
Cavany Mrs
Caveney Mrs M
Caveney Miss M
Caveney Miss M
Cellopah Miss C
Chapman Miss G
Clark Mr J
Clark Mrs J
Clark Mrs
Clark Mrs P
Clarke Miss J
Cleary Miss E
Clinton Mr H
Clinton Mrs E
Coakley Miss P
Cockett Miss M T
Coleman Mr J
Collier Mrs S
Collingwood Miss E M
Collins Mrs P M
Collins Miss A
Conlon Miss M

Conway Mrs M
Conway Miss
Cooper MissJ M
Costello Mrs A
Coughian Mr J P
Coult Mrs M
Coxhead Mr A
Crowley Miss N
Dagleish Miss T
Dagleish Miss K
Dasey Miss M
Davison Miss M
Dean Mrs A
Denston Mrs
Devine Mr J
Devine Miss
Dipassio Mrs E
Dobson Mr Lawrence
Dolan Miss R A
Dobson Mrs A
Donoghue Mr M J
Dooley Miss M
Downey Mrs J
Duffy Miss E M
Dunlavey Miss A
Dunn Mr J
Dunn Mrs M
Earl Mrs A
Edwards Miss M L
Elders Mrs T
Etheridge Miss J F
Farley Miss E F
Farley Miss W H
Farrell Miss B
Ferguson Mrs E
Fewster Mrs
Finn Miss C
Finn Miss M
Fishwick Mrs R E
Flanigan Miss R
Fleisch Miss C
Fleming Miss A
Fletcher Mr B
Flynn Miss B
Foley Miss P
Fox Mrs B
Frankland Mrs C
Fry Miss B
Ganley Miss M
Gannon Mr M
Gannon Mr T
Garvey Mrs
Garvey Mrs T
Gaukroger Miss
Gillespie Mr F
Goodson Miss E R
Goonan Miss M
Gordon Mr W
Grass Miss V
Griffin Miss M K
Hainsworth Mrs W
Hair Miss C

Hall Miss J
Hall Miss P
Hall Miss M
Halidron Miss S M
Hardiman Miss J M
Hardy Miss J
Hargan Mr M
Hargan Mstr J
Harrison Mr R
Harrison Mrs R
Harrison Miss F
Harrison Miss
Hart Mrs
Hart Miss M
Hemblade Mr L
Hemblade Mrs L
Heslhurst Mr E E
Hewitt Miss J M
Hewson Miss M A
Hickman Miss A
Higgins Mrs T
Hildyard Mrs L A
Hill Mrs K
Hill Miss S C
Holden Miss A
Hollingsworth Mrs M
Holton Miss K
Holton Miss A
Hooper Miss T
Hopkins Miss C A
Horwell Miss A
Houghton Mrs T
Howlett Mrs A
Hoyland Mr R V
Hoyland Mrs M P
Hoyle Mrs M
Hunt Mrs M
Hunt Miss T
Hunter Miss I
Hurl Mrs A
Hutchins Mstr D
Jackson Mr A
Jackson Mrs M E
Jackson Mr J
Jackson Mrs G
Jackson Miss M
James Mrs M
Jefferson Mrs
Jefferson Mrs S A
Jenkinson Mrs T
Jevons Mrs R
Jevons Mr S F
Johnson Miss K
Jones Miss E
Jones Mr D P
Jordan Miss P T
Kaberry Mr J
Kane Mrs C
Kilgallon Mr P
Kilmartin Mr T
Kirby Mrs T
Kirby Miss R

Kirkbright Mr J
Keany Mr J L
Keany Mrs K
Keany Mr D
Keenan Miss
Kegney Miss M
Kelly Mrs E:
Kelly Mrs M
Kuehn Mrs R
Lanigan Mrs E
Langham Miss A
Langdon Miss B
Langham Mrs H
Laws Miss F
Leahy Mrs M
Leeming Mrs M
Liddane Miss J
Liddane Miss C
Livingstone Miss M
Livingstone Miss K
Loo Miss T
Lowe Mrs M
Lumb Mrs C
Lynch Miss C
Madden Miss K
Maccabe Dr J E
Mackin Mr P
Mackin Mr L
Mackin Miss S
Malone Miss M
May Miss S A
Meaney Mrs E
Mendoza Mrs M
Mitchell Mrs B
Morrison Mr T
Moss Miss D
Moran Mr K
Mortimer Miss H
Mortimer Mrs M
Mullee Mr J P
Mullee Mrs A C
Mulvey Mr L
Mulvey Mrs A N
Murphy Mrs T
Murphy Mrs B
Murphy Miss B
Murphy Miss J
Murray Mrs N
McCart Mrs M
McCartin Mr C
McDonald Mrs K
McElhatton Miss E
McElhatton Miss M
McFarlane Mrs C M
McGrother Miss M
McKenna Mrs A
McKenna Miss S
McKillop Mrs M J
McKillion Miss M
McLoughlin Mr L J
McManus Miss E
McMenamin Mrs G

McMenamin Miss M
McNally Miss R
McNally Mrs M
McNally Mr J
McNulty Miss M
McGee Miss A
McGeown Mrs E
McGough Miss C
Natter Mrs M
Neasham Mrs M
Newlove Miss
Newlove Mrs G
Newcome Miss A I
Nicholson Mrs
Nicholson Miss V
Norton Mr K:
Northcott Mrs
Nugent Mrs N
O'Brien Miss K
O'Callaghan Miss A
O'Callaghan MissN
O'Connor Miss E
O'Connor Miss M
O'Connor Miss C G
O'Connor Mrs J L
O'Connor Mr J L
Oldroyd Mrs B
Oliver Miss P
O'Mahony Mrs M
O'Malley Miss B
O'Neill Miss I
Palmer Miss M C
C Parkinson Mrs A
Parsons Miss I
Pearson Miss H M
Peckston Mr J G
Pickup Miss H M
Plater Miss M B
Potter Mr J
Prior Miss R
Prior Mrs A
Prunty Mr M I
Pybus Miss E
Quinn Mrs M
Raw Miss T
Raw Mr J E
Raw Miss M M
Readman Mr E J
Reeson Mrs D
Richardson Mr P
Riley Miss J
Robinson Mrs E
Robinson Miss N
Rodman Mr
Rodman Mrs M
Roe Mrs N
Russell Miss H M
Rouardi Mrs H
Ryan Miss
Ryan Miss M C
Sanderson Mrs H
Sanderson Mstr A

Sanderson Mr A
Sanderson Mrs M H
Searle Miss P
Sherman Mrs E
Sherwood Mrs
Shipley Miss
Shirlaw Miss E L
Slatery Miss B
Slingsby Miss Caroline
Slyth Miss E
Smith Miss M
Smith Miss D
Smyth Dr J
Spink Miss J
Starr Miss V
Starford Mrs C
Stanislaus Sr
Stead Miss M E
Stead Miss M C
Seavers Mrs H;
Steedman Mrs M
Stokeld Mrs B
Storey Miss L
Stun Miss R
Stutt Mrs D
Styles Miss C
Sweetman Mrs F M
Taggart Mrs Louisa
Taylor Mrs
Taylor Miss H
Taylor Miss B
Taylor Miss M
Tevlin Miss M
Tevlin Mrs P
Thompson Mrs E
Thompson Mrs W
Thompson Mr J
Tomlinson Mrs
Toms Mrs M
Toms Mstr F G
Tongue Miss Patricia
Traynor Mr Charles
Trimble Mrs C
Trodden Miss W
Twohig Mr V
Wainwright Mr
Wainwright Mrs
Waidron Mr B
Walker Mrs C C
Walker Miss J
Walsh Miss E
Walsh Miss I
Walsh Dr K
Walsh Miss M
Walsh Miss M
Ward Miss Teresa
Warwick Mr V C
Warwick Mrs R
Watson Mrs M L
Watts Miss Doreen
Webb Mrs E
Welford Mr J

Welford Miss M T
Welford Miss M
Welford Miss M E
Wells Mrs I
Wentworth Mrs K
Westcough Mrs Eva
Westwood Miss P
Whelan Miss M
White Miss L
Widdowson Mrs M
Wilde Mrs J
Willan Miss Gaye
Williams Miss K
Williams Mrs M
Wilson Mrs
Wilson Miss D
Wilson Mrs H
Wilson Mr J
Wilson Mrs J
Wilson Miss M
Wilson Miss ME
Wilson Mrs M
Wood Mrs M:
Woodhouse Mrs R
Worswick Mrs I
Wright Miss E
Wright Miss V

Sick Pilgrims

Abbott Mr J
Anderson Mrs I
Askins Mrs H
Barker Miss R
Barrett Mr P
Batchelor Mr J
Beisty Mrs H
Bielby Mrs A E
Burrows Mr J
Byrne Mr M
Calvert Miss A
Carter Mrs K
Cochrane Mrs I
Cross Mr A
Davies Mrs V
Dixon Mr W
Earl Mrs M
Etherington Mrs
Harris Mr J
Hartley Mr E
Hodgson Mr E
Holden Miss B
Jacques Mr W
Jones Mr W
Kingston Mr M
Lacey Mr M
Laws Mrs B
Le Milliere Mr C
Mahon Mr B
McCamley Mr M
McLoughlin Mr B
Molson Mr J
Morris Mrs M

Mullen Mr E
Murray Yvonne
O'Brien Mrs V
Pitcarn Mrs E
Pybus Mrs C
Rigg Mrs K N
Rooke Mr J
Savage Mr F
Siddle Mrs R
Smith Miss G
Smith Mrs R
Studdard Anthony
Telford Peter
Thampson Mr T
Tutney Mr P
Whelan Mrs
Whelan Peter
Wiencek Mrs N
Wood Mr M
Wright Mrs E

St Alphonsus School

Sr Mary Campion
Sr Mary Vincent
Mrs M McKenna
Mrs Evans
Bullock Geraldine
Butcher Patricia
Dearlove Cecilia
Evans Robert
Griffin Christine
Groom Christine
Hill Rosemary
Irvine Shirley
King Terence
Kirk Michael
Liddle June
Liddle Patricia
Maguire Bernadette
Maguire Maureen
McGaskill James
McKenna Mary
Norman Josephine
Parks Joan
Sturdee Maureen
Van Vliet Pamela

St Mary's College

Mr H Kelly
Mr D McNicholl
Afford Peter
Blackwell Arthur
Carroll Raymond
Clarke Ian
Durkin Paul
Gorman John
Grainger Ian
Hanlon Paul
Harrison Joseph
Harrison Robert
Hawley Herbert
Herdman Michael

Jeffrey Brian
Kelland Bruce
Kelland David
Kellett Michael
Kelly Denis
Kennedy Paul
Langhan James
Mohan Anthony
Moran Anthony
McCoy Thomas
McNicholl Desmond
McTigue John
Newcombe John
Orchel Jacek
Preston James
Sherrington Philip
Smallwood John
Thompson Michael
Walshaw John
Wilson Anthony

St Mary's Convent
The Newlands
Miss E M Kennedy
Miss P Boylan
Miss J Broomfield
Mrs L Butler
Miss C Carolan
Miss D Carr
Miss E Harris
Miss K Jevons
Miss C Kennedy
Miss E Madden
Mrs E Middleton
Miss M Thompson
Alexander Sheila
Allain Elizabeth
Anderson Christine
Anderson Mary
Baister Patricia
Barras Pauline
Batch Dorothy
Bell Doreen
Bell Jean
Boyle Patricia
Caddy Cecilia
Campbell Patricia
Carey Pauline
Carney Maureen
Clark Margaret
Clark Patricia
Cleary Eileen
Coleman Marie
Connolly Anne
Crawford Anita
Cresswell Anne
Cresswell Veronica
Cuff Rosemary
Daniels Margaret
Davies Alexandra
Davies Philomena
Davies Sandra

Dickens Maureen
Doherty Kathleen
Doherty Margaret
Dolan Susan
Dooley Sheelagh
Durkin Joan
Flintoff Anne
Flynn Mary
Forrestal Mary
Fox Pauline
Gibson Leonie
Gillespie Joan
Gray Margaret
Grieve Rosemary
Hadwin Patricia
Hall Audrey
Hartley Teresa
Healey Lesley
Henry Caroline
Heslin Maureen
Highfields Brenda
Hogan Edith
Hopkins Brigid
Hughes Patricia
Hunter Joan
Kelly Eileen
Kelly Frances
Kelly Jean
King Patricia
Kok Geraldine
Laverick Madeleine
Legg Margaret
Lockey Eileen
Loo Patricia
Lowes Anne
Lynas Barbara
Mageean Stella
Mahan Kathleen
Marsay Barbara
Martin Judith
Martin Judith
Mitchell Patricia
Moore Maureen
Moran Pauline
Morris Rita
Munro Alexandra
Murray Elizabeth
McBretty Anne
McBretty Carole
McCutcheon Lynda
McDonnell Maureen
McGloin Sheila
McGrath Patricia
McGravey Eileen
McLoughlin Rita
McNicholl Margaret
McPartland Marie
McWilliams Rita
Nesbitt Carol
Nesbitt Victoria
Newcombe Valerie
O'Sullivan Patricia

Parker Irene
Payne Barbara
Pettler Margaret
Priest Joyce
Rafferty Veronica
Routh Patricia
Sanderson Marian
Sanderson Rosalyn
Scott Pamela
Seaman Susan
Shaw Janet
Shaw Pauline
Smith Angela
Spellman Kathleen
Stoddart Patricia
Storman Madeleine
Sullivan Patricia
Terry Mary
Tevlin Josephine
Tevlin Pauline
Thompson Anne
Thornhill Barbara
Thorpe Eileen
Thwaites Anne
Trainor Elaine
Turley Clare
Tyzack Patricia
Vernails Anne
Vickers Carol
Wall Rosemary
Walsh Anne
Walsh Elizabeth
Walsh Sheila
Watson Veronica
Weldrake Jacqueline
White Patricia
Wood Patricia
Wright Elizabeth

St Peter's School
South Bank
Mr F Mageean
Miss A Mossey
Miss T McGowan
Ainsworth Patricia
Bartley Catherine
Conway Kathleen
Corrigan Kathleen
Evans John
Fitzsimmons Patricia
Gardiner R
Grieve Maura
Mohan Kathleen
Mohan Patricia
Murphy Josephine
McCormack Edward
O'Neill Margaret
Quinn; Mary
Shaw Terence
Walsh Damien
Wilcox Sharron

St Philomena's School
Middlesbrough
Sr Mary
Sr Augustine
Rev R Liddane
Mr J Ferguson
Mrs Ferguson
Miss R E Hughes
Armes Ann
Bate Carolyn
Berrie Maureen
Chapman Patricia
Crissell Barbara
Dasey Gerard
Dodd Ann
Drumm Dorothy
Duggan Catherine
Farrington Diane
Fulton Jennifer
Heslin Frances
Knott Anne
Marron Jenifer
Maxwell Pauline
Mulvaney Rita
Murphy Agnes
McCann Ann
McCulloch Margaret
McKenna Sheila
McMahon Anne
Neale Maureen
O'Brien Mary
O'Leary Moira
Partridge Margaret
Richardson William
Rodgers Valerie
Urquhart Caroline
Sargeant Christine
Sheilds Barbara
Simpson David
Smales Rita
Walton Michael
Walton Veronica
Whatmore Patricia
Wilson Susan

St Joseph's School
Keighley
Sr St Paschal
Sr Emmanuel
Sr Marie Reparatrice
Mrs E Hodgkiss
Miss E O'Connor
Bailey Jean
Ballard Patricia
Bradley Sandra
Calpin Lawrence
Czerniawski Teresa
Driver John
Fowler Robert
Gavins Donald
Hudson Janet

Inman John
McKie Christine
McNultyy Geraldine
Paton Joan
Quinn Monica
Sheridan Francis
Stack Anthony
Ulanowski Zigmunt

Presentation Convent
Matlock
Alexander Ruth
Beck Margaret
Blackburn Carole
Brittain Patricia
Byrne Patricia
Curtis Judith
Edwards Judith
Pinney Margaret
Hargan Alison
Hargan Brigid
Higgs Susan
Howell Josie
Keogh Patricia
Massarella Diane
Mimes Anne
Morton Andrea
Newson Anna
Pearce Mary
Pernyes Magda
Ross Jean
Shapeero Judith
Sinclair Margaret
Stiegler Margaret
Worsick Penelope

St Joseph's School
Stourbridge
Sr Agnes
Miss E S Doherty
Miss Thompson
Bicknell Terence
Bradford Ann
Cartwright Cynthia
Fletcher Muriel
Hyman Kathleen
Kelly Anne
Ives Maureen
Jones Christine
Powell Marion
Smith Margaret
Stead John
Steele Margaret
Stubbins Patricia
Talbot Marilyn
Thomas Barbara
Timmins Mary

CTA REPS
Mr J M Collins
Mr R Daniel
Miss McLoughlin

Mr R Doherty
Mr Angold
Mr Coleman
Mr A Yellup
Mr A Watts

St Richard's School
Middlesbrough
Mr M R Doherty
Mrs M Doherty
Mr A Brown
Brown Peter
Burgess Anthony
Donaghue Terence
Fitzsimmons Joseph
Gardiner William
Gibson James
Grainger Michael
Hickman Derek
Hide Ronald
Honeyman Peter
Murphy Joseph
McGrother Ann
McLoughin Peter
O'Brien William
Pearce Leslie
Ralph Cuthbert
Richardson David
Shutt Denis
Tonge David

Sacred Heart School
Redcar
Mr H Crossan
Mr R Utteridge
Miss E Nelson
Miss M King
Atkinson Christine
Bell Maureen
Bottomley Joan
Brooke Joan
Brown John
Carroll Anthony
Claydon Patricia
Dennis Dianne
Dunn Margaret
Feldman Vivienne
Flanigan Marie
Flanigan Theresa
Forsythe Barbara
Forsythe James
Gibson Margaret
Hainsworth Carmel
Hammill Ann
Harker Patricia
Horrocks Ann
Hudson Joan
Hunt Bernard
Jones Peter
Kelly Elizabeth
Lannon Jean
Lythe Patricia

McCue Carol
McGarrel Sheila
Paul Anthony
Roberts Barbara
Thompson Alan
Wood Winifred
Woodwark Rosalind
Young Damien

St Hilda's Bagdale
Whitby
Rev P Storey
Mr K Jackson
Collis Norman
Gallon Mark
Hoggarth William
Locker Reginald
Lowis David
Straw Geofrey
Trillo Michael
Walker Michael
Wilson Michael
Witt James

The Convent
Filey
Miss J Albin
Miss E Pybus
Miss C Crook
Miss M Flanigan
Miss J Wright

1959
Bishop George Brunner
O'Sullivan Canon M
Tindall Mgr C M A
Brunner Mgr W
Lannen Mgr P
McMullen Canon J
Pippet V Rev C A
Bluett V Rev P
Boyd Rev M
Dodds Rev A W
Higgins Rev J L S M
Kielty Rev J
O'Brien Rev J
O'Callaghan Rev C G
O'Mahoney Rev J
Rickaby Rev G T
Riordan Rev Bro E
Anne Marie Sr
Gerard Sr
Germaine Sr
Mary Magdalene Sr
Veronique Sr
Adams Mr J A
Adams Mrs
Addyman Miss L
Addyman Miss M
Bennett Mr J
Bice Mr H
Bickerstaffe Mrs M

Boocock Mr J J
Boyes Dr W
Boyes Mrs
Brunton Mr C W
Byrnes Mr J
Byrnes Mrs
Carany Mrs
Carany Miss M
Carter Mr J
Catto Mstr D
Chidzey Mrs E A
Clifton Miss P
Cochrane Mrs M
Coltman Mrs N
Coughlan Mr J
Coulton Mrs B
Coxhead Mr A
Crabtree Miss L P
Crossfield Miss M
Crowley Miss C
Curran Mr A
Curry Mrs M E
Dean Mrs
Dobson Mr L
Donaghy Mstr F
Dunne Mr T
Elliot Mrs L
Flanigan Miss R
Gannon Mr J
Gannon Mr M
Gillespie Mr F
Gordon Mr W
Hair Miss C
Hawkswell Mrs M
Hibbert Mrs F M
Hickman Miss A
Hoyle Mr R
Jackson Mr: J
Jackson Miss M
Jaeger Mr A W
Jaeger M rs
Kegney Miss M
Kielty Mrs J
Laville Mrs
Lockwood Miss J
Loo Miss T
Mackin Miss S
Marty Mr R
Mendoza Mrs M
Moran Mr K
Morrison Mr T
Moss Miss D
Mossey Miss A
McDonald Mrs
McDonnell Miss I
McElhatton Miss E
McElhatton Miss M
McGrother Miss M
McKenna Mrs A
McKenna Miss S
McLoughlin Mr L
McMahon Mrs M

McMahon Miss E
Nevison Mstr J
Nicholls Miss A
Nicholson Mrs M
Nicholson Mr W
Nicholson Miss V M
O'Brien Mr J
O'Brien Mrs
O'Brien Miss M
O'Neill Miss
O'Rourke Mr J G
O'Rourke Miss N
Parker Mrs D
Pegden Mrs E
Pickup Miss H M
Potter Miss K
Prunty Mrs M J
Prunty Mr E
Raw Mr
Raw Miss M
Richards Mr W
Riley Miss J
Ritchie Mr J
Robinson Miss A
Rudd Mr R
Rudd Mrs
Salvatore Mrs M P
Savage Mr L
Scarr Miss T
Shane Mrs A
Shipley Mr W J
Slingsby Miss C
Stead Miss M C
Sullivan Miss M
Taylor Mr A
Taylor Miss M
Taylor Miss S
Thompson Mr B
Traynor Mr C
Tunney Mrs M
Usher Miss I
Waldron Mr J
Walsh Miss A M
Walsh Miss E
Walsh Miss I
Walsh Mr J
Walsh Dr K
Walsh Miss M
Walsh Miss Mary
Warrior Miss M
Warwick Mr V C
Watson Mrs J A
Watson Mrs M W
Welford Mr F O
Welford Mrs
Welford Mr J
Welford Miss M
Welford Miss M M
Whelan Miss M
White Miss E
Wilson Mr J
Wilson Miss K

Wilson Miss Marie
Wilson Miss Mary

Sick Pilgrims

Almond Mrs I
Barrett Mr P
Batchelor Mr J
Burrows Mr J
Coyle Mrs M
Cross Mr J A
Dell Mstr M
Devlin Mr J
Dixon Mr W
Donkin Miss S
Downey Mr E
Eeles Mr S
Garncarek Mr W
Gee Mrs F
Gee Miss P
Gormanly Miss
Hodgson Mr E J
Horkan Miss M
Howes Miss M
Hutchinson Mrs A
Jones Mr W
Kingston Mr M
Loret Mrs A
Loughran Miss B M
Lyons Miss H
McGarrity Miss P
McLaughlin Mr B
McLean Mrs B
Magee Miss A
Molson Mr J
Mullen Mr E
Myers Mr A C
Pippet Miss J
Pybus Mrs C
Smith Mr H
Spencer Miss C E
Tyreman Mrs I M
Whelan Mr J
Whelan Mrs
Whelan Mstr Paul
Wyatt Mrs M E
Young Miss T

CTA REPS
Mr R Daniel
Mr T J Daly
Miss F McLoughlan

1960
Bishop George Brunner
O'Sullivan Canon M
Brunner Canon W
Lannen Mgr P
Wood Canon A
O'Connor V Rev W
Pippett V Rev A
McAniff Rev P
O'Connor Rev M J

Rickaby Rev G T
Storey Rev A J
Spence Rev Bro
Bonaventure
Adams Mr J A
Addis Mrs P
Addyman Miss L M
Addyman Miss M W
Amar Mrs A E
Askins Mr K
Bachelor Mrs
Barner Miss K M
Battle Mrs A
Bice Mr B
Bice Mrs
Bickerstaffe Mrs M
Blair Miss M
Boyes Dr W
Brunton Mr C W
Colton Mr J
Cleary Miss EM
Cockerill Mrs J
Connolly Mrs E M
Connolly Miss A
Coughlan Mr J
Coxhead Mr A
Crawford Mr J E
Crawford Mrs
Curry Mrs M E
Dics Mr A
Dics Mrs
Dimech Mrs M
Dobson Mr L
Dodd Mrs D
Dodd Miss M F
Dodson Mrs D C
Donoghue Mr
Donoghue Mrs
Donoghue Miss M
Duck Miss M B
Earley Mrs M
Farrell Miss M P
Flanigan Miss R M
Fleisch Miss C
Fox Miss I P
Ganley Miss M
Gannon Mr M
Gillespie Mr F
Gordon Mr W
Gormanley Miss M
Gray Miss E
Greaves Mrs N
Gregory Miss P
Hamilton Mrs L
Harrison Mr J
Harrison Mrs
Harrison Miss M
Hart Mr G
Hawkeswell Mrs M E
Hill Mr D
Hogarth Mr G W
Hogarth Mrs

Jackson Miss M W
Kilbride Mr J F
Kilbride Mrs
Kilmartin Mr T
Kilmartin Mrs
King Mrs D
Knott Miss A
Lambert Miss M
Langan Mrs L
Lawton Mrs M
Mackin Mr L
Mahoney Mrs I
Mallett Mr J
Mangion Mrs M
Maule Mrs A
Maule Miss A G
Maule Miss C
Maule Miss J
Middleton Mrs
Moon Mr K
Moran Mr K
Morley Miss O
Mossey Miss A
Murray Miss K
McCart Mrs M
McCartin Mr C
McDonnell Miss J
McElhatton Miss E
McGowan Miss T
McGrother Miss M
McLoughlin Mr L J
McShane Miss R
Newton Mrs D
O'Connor Mrs A
O'Riordan Miss N M
Pearson Miss H M
Pearson Miss M
Peters Miss E A
Pickup Miss H M
Power Mrs
Quinn Miss D E
Raw Mr J E
Raw Miss M M
Raw Miss T
Reeson Mrs D
Richards Mr W
Riley Miss J
Ritchie Mr J
Savage Mr L
Shane Mrs A
Sherlock Miss M
Simpson Mrs M
Simson Mstr A
Slack Mrs S A
Smith Miss J
Smyth Mrs M
Stokeld Mr A
Suddaby Mr E
Thompson Mr B
Thompson Mr F
Thompson Mrs
Thompson Mr J P

Thompson Mrs
Toole Miss E M
Traynor Mr C
Vallely Mr F R
Vaz Mrs M
Wadrop Mrs C
Wadrop Miss C
Walker Mrs A
Walsh Miss I
Walsh Dr K
Walsh Miss M
Walsh Mr T
Warwick Mr C C
Warwick Mrs
Warwick Mr V
Welford Mr J
Welford Miss M
Welsh Mr P
Welsh Mrs
Whelan Miss M
Wilkinson Miss M
Williams Mrs M
Williams Miss M
Wilson Miss H M
Wilson Mr J W
Wood Mrs M
Young Mrs F

Sick Pilgrims
Askins Mrs T
Batchelor Mr J
Batt Mr B
Burrows Mr J F
Crammon Mr J T
Cockerill Miss S
Das Mr M
Donkin Miss S
Donnelly Mrs T A
Flanagan Miss R
Frew Mrs M A
Foster Miss M
Fox Mrs M
Galloway Mrs S
Graham Miss N M
Green Mr J
Gormanly Miss C M
Johnson Mrs M
Jones Mr W
Hall Mstr C
Hamilton Mr E J
Kingdom Mrs L
Kingston Mr M
Kirby Mr R R
Langan Miss V T
Lyons Miss H
Lukaszewicz Miss C
Mahoney Miss L S
Mallen Mr M H
Moxon Mr E
Ralph Miss K M
Smith Mr H
Taylor Mrs L M

Teece Mrs C
Varey Mrs M
Walsh Mrs A
Whelan Mr J C
Whelan Mstr M P
Whelan Mrs R
Williams Miss C V

CTA REPS
Mr J Collins
Mr T J Daly
Mr J McLoughlin

1961
Bishop George Brunner
Brunner Mgr W
R Lannen Mgr P
Nolan Canon T A
Wood Canon A
O'Connor V Rev W
Pippett V Rev A
Knowles Rev J
Loughran Rev P J
Rickaby Rev G T
Ryan Rev J J
Spaight Rev D
Storey Rev A J
Gould Rev Bro Xavier
Wilson Rev Bro Sylvester
Angela Sr
Mother Mary Annuntiata
Aquinas Mother
Glare Sr
Gerard Sr
Adams Mr J A
Arnold Mrs M
Bailey Mrs C M
Barrett Mr M
Baxter Mrs M
Berry Mrs M K
Bickerstaffe Mrs M
Bicknell Miss E
Boocock Mr J J
Boyes Dr W
Boyes Mrs
Brannick Mr H
Brown Mrs A
Brown Mr H
Brown Mrs
Bryant Mrs
Bryant Miss I
Burke Mr W
Burns Mrs M
Burrows Mr J
Cunniff Mr T J
Carroll Miss M
Carroll-Hair Miss C
Clarke Mr F
Colton Mr J
Coughlan Mr J P
Coyle Mrs S V
Coxhead Mr A

Craddock Miss C
Crane Mrs V M
Curry Mrs M E
Dean Mrs A
Dixon Mrs E
Dobson Mr L
Dodson Miss D C
Duncan Mrs C V
Duncan Miss P A
Dunne Mrs G M
Dunne Mr T
Dunne Mrs T
Durrant Mrs M J
Durrant Miss E S
Earley Mr J B
Eaton Miss J
Featherstone Mrs M
Ferisy Mrs B
Finlayson Mrs V
Fishwick Mrs
Flanigan Miss R
Found Mrs D
Fox Miss I
Gallon Miss C
Game Mrs N
Game Mstr J
Gillespie Mr F
Gollogly Mrs T
Gordon Miss E M
Gordon Mr W
Graystone Mr J W
Hager Mr T
Hager Mrs
Hannon Mr P
Hawkeswell Mrs M E
Hayes Miss E
Hayes Miss T
Hewitt Miss W
Higharn Mrs S
Hogarth Mrs E
Hollingsworth Mrs M
Hudson Mrs W
Jackson Mrs E C
Jackson Miss M W
Kilmartin Mr
Lambert Miss M
Large Mrs K
Lee Mr W
Leonard Mrs G
Lynch Mr G
Manson Mrs R
Masters Miss
Molloy Miss N
Moloney Mrs M
Moloney Mstr E
Mossey Miss A
Moon Mr K
Muldowney Mrs R
Muiholland Mrs O
Mulligan Miss B
McCart Mrs M
McDonnell Miss

McGeown Mrs E M
McGeown Mr H E
McGlade Mrs A
McGowan Mrs M A
McGowan Miss T
McGrother Mrs E
McGrother Miss M
McGrother Miss S
McGuire Miss F
McIntyre Mr W H
McIntyre Mrs
McKenna Mr G V
McKenna Mrs
McKenna Mr J F
McKenna Mrs
McKenna Mstr K A
McKenna Miss S
McLoughlin Mr L
McPartland Mr T
McPartland Mrs
Nicholson Mr B
Nicholson Mr W
O'Donoghue Mrs D
O'Hara Miss M
O'Leary Miss M
Pattison Mr W A
Pearson Miss M I
Peckston Col J
Penna Miss G
Peters Miss E A
Phillips Miss I K
Pickering Mrs O
Pickup Miss H M
Porter Mrs E
Raw Miss M
Readman Mrs H M
Richards Mr W
Riley Miss J
Rudd Mr R
Rudd Mrs
Scanlan Mrs M
Sewell Mr R E
Shane Mrs A
Skilbeck Miss R
Smith Miss D
Smith Miss J
Snee Mr L
Smith Miss E
Smith Miss J
Smith Miss M
Spence Mrs C
Squire Mrs M
Squire Miss E
Stead Miss M C
Storey Miss L
Sumner Mrs M
Suddaby Mr E
Tarpey Dr R
Tarpey Mrs
Thompson Mrs M C
Thompson Miss M
Thompson Miss G

Thwaites Miss A
Todd Mrs W
Traynor Mr C
Vincent Miss S M
Wallis Mrs H
Walsh Dr K
Ward Mrs M A
Warwick Mrs K
Warwick Miss M
Warwick Mr V
Watterson Mr T
Welford Mr G
Welford Mr J
Welford Miss M
Whelan Miss M
Whelan Mrs R
White Mrs W
Wilson Mr J W
Young Mrs J

Sick Pilgrims
Anderson Mrs M
Ayres Mrs K
Bailey Mr J
Brown Miss S
Burns Mr S
Carroll Mr R
Colligan Mr G
Colligan Miss M
Collinson Mrs R
Cummings Mstr J
Dean Miss C
Donkin Miss S
Donovan Miss M
Farrington Miss R
Gormanly Miss C M
Graham Miss N
Greaves Mrs N
Harper Mstr T
Harrison Mr P
Jacobs Mr F
Kingston Mr M
McCaffrey Miss J
McCormick Mr J
Muldowney Mr J
Neary Mr J
O'Donnell Mr F
O'Donnell Mrs S
Ralph Miss K
Rutherford Miss S
Whelan Mr J
Wright Mrs M E
Young Mstr R

Juvenile Section
Doherty Mr M R
Brown Miss P
Grainger Miss
Joseph Allen
Florence Bonner
Peter Brown
John Bunn

Mary Chaney
Kathleen Clifford
Martine Cuff
Linda Dawson
Eileen Donnelly
Jane Donnelly
Pat Downing
Jane Ewing
Peter Gettings
Pat Hand
Joan Hoar
Peter Marron
Myra Middlemoss
Angela McCartie
Pat McCrae
Phil McCrae
Catherine O'Neil
Pat Smith
Marie Stockill
Christopher Whelan

CTA REPS
Mr J M Collins
Mr T J Daly
Mr J McLoughlin

Air Section
Currie Rev J
Harney Rev P A
O'Brien Rev S
O'Connor Rev M
Addis Mrs P
Addis Miss S
Bouttell Mrs T
Clark Mrs M M
Copeland Mr
Copeland Miss B
Curran Mr A
Curran Miss M
Ganley Miss M C
Hughes Mr A
Hughes Mr J
Hughes Mrs
Hughes Miss M
Hughes Miss M A
Jenkins Miss R
Kirby Mrs T
Love Mrs M
Mageean Mr
Mageean Mrs
Minchela Mrs
Murphy Mrs A
McGulkin Mr J
Payne Mrs H
Reeson Mr G
Reeson Mrs
Robinson Miss
Taylor Mrs M
Tortalano Mrs
Wade Miss
Wood Mrs G

1962
Bishop George Brunner
Brunner Mgr W
O'Sullivan Mgr M
Tindall Mgr C
Wood Canon A
Pippett V Rev A
Boyd Rev M
Charlton Rev R
Harney Rev P A
Loughran Rev P J
O'Byrne Rev P
O'Connor Rev W SM
Rickaby Rev G T
Ryan Rev P
Storey Rev A J
Storey Rev P L
White Rev M
Linane Rev Bro Canice
Fegen Rev Bro Casimir
Elizabeth Sr M
Stanislaus Sr M
Adams Mr J
Addyman Miss K
Addyman Miss L
Allison Mrs M
Bailey Miss E
Barrett Mr M
Beale Mr B
Bean Miss H
Beavers Mrs L
Bickerstaffe Mrs M
Bland Mrs J
Boyes Dr W
Boyes Mrs
Brannick Mr H
Brunton Mr C
Bryan Mr R
Bryan Mrs M
Bryan Miss I
Burke Mr W
Burns Dr M
Burrows Mr J
Byrne Mr J
Byrne Mrs
Callaghan Mr P
Carey Mrs E
Carey Miss G
Carroll Mrs N
Carter Mr J
Cassidy Mr J
Cavanagh Miss P
Clarke Mr F
Colligan Mrs M
Collins Mrs E
Collins Miss M
Coughlan Mr J
Coughlan Mrs J
Cuff Mrs D
Cuff Mstr J
Daan Mrs A

Dilks Mrs E
Doherty Miss C
Donnelly Mr T
Donnelly Mrs
Duffy Mrs M
Duke Miss M
Dunn Mr J
Dunn Mrs M
Durant Mrs M
Durant Miss E
Early Miss N
Edwards Mr H
Edwards Mrs A
Edwards Mr J
Elliott Mrs L
Fleish Mrs M
Fletcher Mr B
Gallagher Miss I
Gannon Mr M
Gardiner Mr T
Gavanagh Mrs E
Giblin Miss T
Gillespie Mr F
Golding Mrs M
Gordon Mr W
Gormanly Miss M
Harrison Mr W
Higgins Mrs
Holder Mrs D
Hoyland Mr R
Hoyland Mrs
Jackson Miss M
Jones Mrs N
Jones Mr W
Kennedy Mrs M
Kilmartin Mr T
Kilmartin Miss C
Kochanowski Mrs J
Lighton Mrs U
Lighton Mstr S
Lee Miss E
Lee Miss G
Lynch Mr G
Lynd Miss V
Maplesden Mrs A
Maplesden Miss M
Moody Mrs S
Moody Miss E
Moody Mstr M
Morren Mrs J
Mossey Miss A
Mulligan Miss A
Mulligan Miss B
Murphy Mr W
McCann Mr G
McCart Mrs M
McCaskill Mrs J
McClure Mrs V
McDonnell Miss I
McGeary Mr P
McGeown Mr H
McGowan Mrs M

McGowan Miss T
McGrogan Mr J
McGrogan Mrs L
McGrogan Miss M
McGrother Mrs E
McGrother Miss M
McGrother Miss S
McIntyre Mr W
McIntyre Mrs T
McLoughlin Mr L
Nertney Mr B
Newton Mrs M
O'Connor Mrs A
O'Rourke Mrs A
Patterson Mrs M
Pattison Mr W
Pippet Miss J
Powe Mrs M
Raw Miss M
Roberts Mr E
Roland Mrs M
Shane Mrs A
Shane Miss M
Skilbeck Miss R
Smiles Mr J
Smith Mrs C
Smith Miss J
Stead Mrs
Stead Miss A
Stead Miss M
Suddaby Mr E
Traynor Mr C
Tyzack Mr V
Tyzack Mrs
Tyzack Miss
Varey Miss E
Walsh Miss I
Walsh Dr K
Walsh Miss M
Walton Mr A
Walton Mrs N
Ward Miss F
Warwick Mrs C
Watson Mrs M
Waterson Mr L
Waterson Mr T
Webster Mrs A
Welford Mr J
Welford Miss M
Whelan Miss M
Whelan Mrs R
Whelan Mstr C
Whelan Mstr P
White Mrs M
Wieczorek Mrs A
Wilson Mr J
Wilson Mrs E
Wood Mstr J

Sick Pilgrims
Barrett Mr P
Brown Mstr A

Bryan Mr S
Burnell Mr C
Byrne Miss S
Cochrane Mrs I
Cronesbury Mrs C
Cronesbury Mstr P
Cross Mr A
Dapkus Mr M
Dean Miss C
Durant Mr E
Gregan Mr T
Ketteringham Mrs B
Kingston Mr M
Kirby Mr R
Kirk Mr K
Lacey Mrs
Lannon Mrs
Moxon Mr E
Mullen Mr E
McNicholas Mr T
McPartland Mr J
Nelson Miss A
Nelson Mr J
Nelson Mrs
Nelson Mstr M
Parr Miss A
Pearce Mstr M
Redfern Mr M
Robinson Mrs E
Rushton Mrs P
Skilbeck Mr J
Tarling Miss A
Tinsley Mr J
Varey Mrs M
Walsh Mrs
Walsh Miss E
Whelan Mr J
Wicks Mstr P

CTA REPS
Mr J M Collins
Mr F Cuss
Mr T J Daly
Mr R de Peyrecave

Air Section
Currie Rev J
O'Brien Rev M
O'Connor Rev S
Catherine Sr
Manness Sr
Peter Sr
Addis Mrs
Beddard Mrs
Birtley Mrs
Bradley Miss
Brennan Mrs
Brennan Miss
Brown Mrs
Cain Mrs
Corby Mrs
Dorgan Mrs

Dankin Mrs
Fee Miss
Flannagan Miss
Fleming Mrs
Foley Mrs
Fox Mrs
Goodman Mrs
Harris Mrs
Holwell Mr
Hughes Miss
Hutchinson Miss
Jarvis Mrs
Jenkins Miss
Joyce Mrs
Kearney Miss
Kelly Mrs
Mann Mrs
Mulcahy Mrs
Murkin Mrs
Murray Mrs
McAuliffe Mrs
McElhatton
McGrogan Mrs
Power Mrs
Richardson Mrs
Riley Mr
Slingsby Miss
Smith
Smith Mrs
Smith Miss
Smith Mrs
Smith Miss
Sweeney Miss
Sweetman Mrs
Ward Miss
Wilie Mrs

1963
O'Sullivan Mgr M
Tindall Mgr C
Pippett V Rev A
Harney Rev P
Harrison Rev G
Kielty Rev J
Loughran Rev P
O'Connor Rev M
O'Connor Rev W
Rickaby Rev G T
Ryan Rev D
Sacco Rev A
Alfred Rev Bro
Francis Mother M
Clare Sr M
Josephine Sr M
Philomena Sr M
Adams Mr J
Ashworth Mr A
Baker Mr A
Baker Miss P
Bean Miss H
Bickerstaffe Mrs M
Blake Miss N

Boyes Dr W
Brankley Miss I
Brock Mr J
Bryan Miss I
Bryan Mr R
Burrows Mr J
Carter Mr J
Cassidy Mr J
Chidzey Mrs M
Clarke Mr F
Cone Mrs M
Cone Miss G
Cone Miss S
Corrigan Mrs E
Coughlan Mr J
Coughlan Mrs J
Couhig Mrs C
Coxhead Mr A
Daniels Miss M
Davison Mrs
Davison Mstr
Dean Mrs A
Dobson Mr L
Dodd Mrs D
Donnelly Miss M
Dunne Miss F
Dunne Miss R
Durant Mrs M
Durant Miss E
Edwards Mr H
Edwards Mrs
Edwards Mr J
Ferguson Miss N
Gannon Mr M
Gillespie Mr F
Gordon Mr W
Harrison Mr B
Harrison Mrs
Harry Mr J
Hodgson Mr G
Hogan Mr M
Hogan Mrs
Howdle Mrs A
Howdle Miss M
Hudson Miss M
Jackson Miss M
Jones Mr W
Keane Mrs V
Keenan Mr E
Kelly Mr J
Large Mrs K
Lyth Mrs M
Mallon Mrs M
Maughan Mrs M
Miller Miss A
Miller Mstr F
Mitchell Mrs M
Mossey Miss A
Mulligan Miss B
Murphy Mrs A
Murphy Miss B
McAllister Miss B

McCann Mr G
McDonald Miss I
McGee Mr
McGeown Mrs E
McGeown Mr H
McGowan Miss T
McGrother Mrs E
McGrother Miss S
McIntyre Mr W
McKenna Miss S
McLoughlin Mr L
McMahon Miss E
McNulty Miss M
Nicholson Miss V
O'Connor Mrs A
O'Hara Mr J
O'Hara Mrs
O'Neill Miss M
Pattinson Mrs M
Pattinson Miss J
Pattinson Miss P
Pearsall Miss A
Pippet Miss J
Raw Miss M
Reardon Mrs M
Redchurch Mr G
Richards Mr J
Rodgers Miss E
Rodgers Mrs R
Rudd Mr R
Rudd Mrs
Ruddy Miss E
Sacco Mrs C
Salvatore Mrs M
Shane Mrs A
Shane Miss M
Shearer Miss C
Smiles Mr J
Smith Mrs E
Smith Mr H
Smith Miss J
Squire Miss E
Stubbs Mrs L
Suddaby Mrs M
Suddaby Mr E
Sweeney Miss E
Tempest Mr H
Tempest Miss K
Thompson Mrs G
Tyzack Mr C
Walsh Miss E
Walsh Dr K
Walsh Miss M
Ward Mr N
Ward Mrs
Warwick Mrs K
Waterson Mr T
Welford Mr G
Welford Mr J
Welford Miss M
Whelan Mrs R
Whelan Mstr D

Wood Mr A
Wood Mrs N
Woods Mr J
Woods Mrs
Woodward Mrs
Woolfard Miss J

Juvenile Section
St Peter's & St Anne's
School South Bank
Mageean Mr F
Biesterfield Mrs P
Fell Miss E
Kosina Mrs K
Anthony Barry
Teresa Calvert
Christine Evans
Carol French
Maureen Gallagher
Kathleen Harding
Margaret Hayes
Kathleen McPhillips
Anthony Meskill
Michael Mohan
Kathleen O'Brien
Josephine O'Neill
Paul O'Neill
Joseph Ord
Anthony O'Sullivan
Gerard Pearson
Patricia Robinson
Susan Robinson
Ann Skinn

St Thomas School
Doherty Mr M R
Brown Miss P
Anne Costello
James Dearlove
Philomena McDonagh
Kevin McGlade
Kathleen McGuire
Philomena McRae
Patricia McRae
Catherine O'Neil
Peter Rowcliffe
John Rowney
Vanessa Skyrme
Lynn Tomlinson
Mary Whittle
Bernard Williams
Joan Wood

Sick Pilgrims
Barry Miss E
Batchelor Mr J
Battison Mrs
Battison Mstr P
Burliston Miss D
Burns Mr W
Byrne Mrs M
Coleman Miss R

Cross Mr A
Cummings Mr J
Dale Mrs A
Das Mr M
Donkin Miss S
Dowson Miss A
Flynn Mrs M
Graham Miss N
Hartley Mr E
Henderson Mrs C
Hood Mrs M
Hudson Mrs J
Jordan Mrs P
Keane Mr P
Lamb Mrs A
Langan Miss V
Manning Mr J
Morgan Mrs E
Murphy Mrs E
McGee Mstr S
McGlynn Mr P
Nicholson Miss A
Oates Mr J
Quinn Mr M
Roberts Mr R
Sherwood Miss M
Trejonis Mrs E
Wesley Mr J
Whelan Mr J
Winter Miss L
Woodward Miss C

CTA REP
Collins Mr J
Daly Mr T
Daniel Mr R

Air Section
O'Brien V Rev S
Coleman Rev P
Currie Rev J D
O'Neill Rev J
Arblaster Mrs M
Beacy Mrs M
Boagey Mrs A
Chidzey Mrs E
Crossan Mrs J
DeGroor Mrs W
Forsyth Mrs B
Forsyth Mrs C
Gilfayle Mrs P
Green Mr B
Harding Mrs A
Hogan Mrs
Holwell Mr H
Horn Mrs K
Hutchinson Miss A
Kearney Miss E
Larvin Mr J
Mrs Larvin
Livingstone Miss M
Marsden Mrs C

McAninly Mrs
McCarron Mrs E
McGuire Mrs M
Newby Mrs A
O'Brien Mrs S
O'Neill Mr J
O'Neill Mrs
O'Neill Miss C
O'Neill Miss M
Rafferty Mr H
Rafferty Miss F
Rafferty Mrs M
Richardson Mrs A
Robson Mrs T
Russell Mrs
Salvidge Mr
Smyth Mr D
Smyth Mrs
Tiernan Mr S
Tiernan Mrs
Urry Mrs P
Urry Miss P
Venue Mrs E
Walker Mrs M
Woods Mrs F

Hughes Mr J
Hughes Mrs
Hughes Miss A
Hughes Miss K
Rush Mrs E
Shaw Miss L

1964
Bishop George Brunner
Provost Mgr W
O'Sullivan Mgr M
Tindall Mgr C
Pippett V Rev A
Burke Rev M SM
Charlton Rev J R
Harrison Rev G
Hawksworth Rev B
McKeever Rev J
O'Brien Rev S
O'Connor Rev M
O'Connor Rev W
O'Mahoney Rev J
Rickaby Rev G T
Riley Rev R SM
Ryan Rev D
Sebastian Rev Bro
Gabriel Sr Mary
Gertrude Sr Mary
Loreto Sr Mary
Abbs Mrs C
Arnold Mrs M
Bailey Mrs C
Barrett Mrs F
Barry Miss E
Barry Mr J
Barry Mrs

Basford Mr J
Bavey Mrs D
Bavey Miss D
Bickerstaffe Mrs M
Blake Miss N
Boyes Dr W
Boyes Mrs
Brankley Miss I
Brodrick Miss C
Brown Mrs M
Bryan Miss I
Burrows Mr J
Carey Miss E
Cassidy Mr J
Clarke Mr F
Conning Mrs M
Coughlin Mr J
Coughlin Mrs
Coyle Mrs S
Dean Mrs A
Dinsdale Miss A
Dodd Mr R
Dodd Mrs
Dobson Mr L
Downey Mrs E
Driscoll Mrs M
Drummond Mr F
Duck Miss M
Duggan Mr J
Duggan Mrs
Edmond Miss J
Edwards Mr J
Fell Mrs M
Ferguson Miss N
Fitzgibbon Miss S
Flanigan Miss R
Fleisch Miss C
Fleisch Miss G
Fleisch Mr G
Foy Miss B
Gallogly Mrs E
Gannon Mr M
Gordon Mr W
Hancock Mrs B
Harris Mr A
Harris Mstr A
Harrison Miss F
Harrison Mr J
Heatley Mrs M
Hodges Mr H
Hodges Mrs
Hogan Mr M
Hogan Mrs
Holwell Mr H
Hughes Mrs C
Hughes Mstr S
Hunt Mrs M
Hunt Miss T
Jackson Miss M
Johns Miss R
Jones Mr W
Kearney Miss E

Kelly Mr J
Kershaw Mrs M
Large Mrs K
Leahy Mrs I
Lupton Miss P
McGuire Mrs M
Metcalfe Miss M
Moon Mr K
Mossey Miss A
Murray Mrs E
McCann Mr G
McGeown Mrs E
McGeown Mr H
McGough Mrs C
McGough Miss C
McGowan Miss T
McGrother Mrs E
McGrother Miss S
McHale Mrs E
McIntyre Mrs A
McIntyre Mr W
McLoughlin Mr L
O'Neill Miss E
O'Neill Miss K
O'Neill Miss P
O'Rourke Mrs P
Pattinson Mrs M
Pattinson Miss P
Pearsall Miss A
Peart Mrs H
Peckston Col J
Pippet Miss J
Popplewell Mrs L
Priest Mr W
Raw Miss M
Redchurch Mr G
Rudd Mrs I
Rush Mr G
Rush Mrs
Salvatore Mrs M
Shane Mrs A
Smiles Mr J
Smith Mr H
Smith Mrs N
Smith Miss J
Squire Miss E
Stead Miss M
Stocks Miss S
Swainson Miss J
Tempest Mr H
Trainor Mrs K
Traynor Mr C
Turton Mr T
Waldron Mrs S
Walker Mstr J
Walsh Miss E
Walsh Dr K
Warwick Miss K
Warwick Miss M
Warwick Mr V
Waterson Mr T
Welford Mr J

Welford Miss M
Welsh Mrs M
White Mrs M
White Mrs M
Wilson Mrs C
Wilson Mr J
Woods Mr J

St Mary's College

Byrne Rev F SM
Brendan Boyle
Michael Churms
John Doherty
Vincent Haynes
John Hughes
Paul King
Thomas Kirtley
Kevin Martin
John McIntosh
Peter McNulty
Paul Rowney
John Wright

Sick Pilgrims

Bailey Mr J F
Barrett Mr P
Bielby Mrs A E
Burgess Mrs W
Burke Mstr K
Carroll Mr J
Conlon Miss M
Connelly Miss R
Fell Mr A
Hatfield Mr J
Horner Mrs L
Keenan Mr E
Kingston Mr M
Langan Miss V
Lavelle Miss N
Martin Miss P
Melton Mr H
McIntyre Mr F
McIntyre Mrs T
Oates Mr J
Quinn Mr M
Shillock Mrs J
Smith Mr D
Smyth Mr D
Starzewska Mrs H
Starzewska Mstrr P
Thraves Mstr P
Treacy Mrs F
Williams Mr E K
Wood Mr A
Wood Mr A

Catholic Ass Reps

Collins Mr J M
Daly Mr T J
Bassadone Mr R

1965

Brown Miss M A
Brunner Miss M J
Cane Mrs
Collins Miss B
Collins Miss T
Cluderay Mrs
Crosskill Mrs K
Culkin Mrs E
Culkin Miss M E
Das Mr M
Dorsey Mr A
Edmund Miss J
Everingham Miss I
Farrington Mr G R
Fortune Mr J
Garton Mrs E
Garvey Mrs T
Garwell Miss S
Goonan Miss E
Haswell Mrs M
Haswell Mstr M
Holwell Mr H
Jackson Mrs E
Kearney Miss E
Kent Miss U
Gilmartin Miss C
Kirkbride Mr H
McAlister Miss M
McConnerty Mrs M
McGeown Mrs E
McMackin Miss A
McManemy Miss C
Nelson Mrs M
Noble Mrs T
O'Connor Mrs A M
Palmer Mrs D
Parsons Mrs M
Pickering Mrs A
Pickup Mrs H M
Pieper Mrs M
Richardson Mrs A
Scanlon Mrs M
Scanlon Miss C
Shearer Miss C
Smith Mr E
Smith Mrs
Smith Mrs N
Smith Miss J
Stocks Miss S
Tiernan Mrs K M
Warwick Mrs K M
Warwick Mr V C
Waterson Mrs M
Wellford Mrs H
Welford Mr J
Welford Miss M
Woods Mr J
Wright Mrs J G

CTA REP
Collins Mr J

Air Section
Bishop Wheeler
Tindall Mgr C
Nolan Canon T A
Aelred Rev O F M
Harrison Rev G SM
Columba Sr
Almond Mrs J A
Anderson Miss N
Arbon Miss N
Aukstinaitis Miss J
Barry Mr J
Barry Mrs
Bateman Mrs I
Bateman Miss M
Beavers Mrs C
Bolton Mrs E
Boyes Mrs B
Breward Mr T A
Brown Mr G
Brown Mrs E
Brunton Mr C
Burrows Mr J
Cassidy Mr J
Clark Mr
Cockerill Mr A
Cockerill Mr M
Coleman Miss A
Crelly Miss M
Crossen Miss K
Curran Mr A
Daniels Mrs A F
Dasey Miss J F
Dooley Miss N
Doyle Mrs E
Duck Miss M B
Duggan Mrs I
Fascia Mr F
Ferguson Miss N
Flanigan Mrs A
Gannon Mr M
Green Mr R
Hancock Mrs B
Harrington Mr D
Harris Mr A G
Harris Matr A
Harris Mrs M
Hemblade Mrs M
Hemblade C
Hemblade Miss E
Johnson Mrs E
Jones Mr W
Keelan Mr F
Kelly Mr H
Kelly Mrs
Lyth Mrs M V
Mackin Miss S
Metcalfe Miss M

Miller Mr A
Miller Mrs
Miller Miss E
Moreland Miss A T
Murphy Mr W
Murray Mrs E
McCann Mr G
McIntyre Mrs A
O'Brien Mrs K
O'Neill Miss S
Quinn Mr P
Reevell Miss D
Rush Mr G M
Rush Mrs
Stanley Mrs M
Swinburne Mrs E
Vaughan Miss J
Warwick Miss R A
Whelan Mr J
Whelan Mstr P
Whitley Mr J
Whitley Mrs
Wilson Miss

Air Section
Bishop George Brunner
Provost Mgr W
O'Connor Rev M
Ashton Miss I
Barry Mrs A
Barry Miss E M
Boyes Dr W
Bryan Miss I M
Chidzey Mrs E
Coleman Mr J
Coleman Mr G
Coughlan Mr J
Coughlan Mrs J
Dean Mrs A
Dodd Mrs D C
Durant Miss E
Flanigan Miss R M
Gordon Mr W
Jackson Miss M
Lambe Mr S F
Leahy Mr J
Leahy Mrs J
Liversedge Mr
McCart Mrs M
McGahey Mrs W
McGowan Miss T
McIntyre Mr W H
McLoughlin Mr L
McReddie Miss B M
McReddie Miss S
Mossey Miss A
Payne Mrs M
Raw Miss M M
Shane Mrs A
Shane Miss M
Smiles Mr J
Stead Miss M C

Tempest Mr H N
Waldron Mrs S
Walsh Dr K
Waterson Mr T W
Wilson Mr J W

CTA REP
Daly T Mr J T

Sick Pilgrims
O'Connor Rev W
Barry Mr J
Barry Mrs C
Boddy Miss E
Byrne Mr J
Byrne Mrs M
Costello Miss M
Daly Mrs J
Farrington Miss R
Ferris Miss P
Flanagan Miss R
Goult Mr B
Hatfield Mr M
Horner Mrs E
Kingston Mr M
Langan Miss V
Liversidge Mstr P
McCaffrey Miss J
McGlone Mstr S
McGurk Mr P
McIntyre Mrs T
Moore Mr C
Murray Miss M
Murray Mrs
Oates Mr J
O'Brien Miss M
Payne Mstr C
Smith Mr T
Sugden Mstr J
Swatman Mrs E
Vallely Mrs E
Varey Mrs M

Rail Section
Allen Mrs F M
Allen Miss A M
Fitzsimmons Mrs E
Fitzsimmons Mstr P
Fitzsimmons Miss R
Kelly Mr J
McQuade Mrs A M
McQuade Miss M C
Moore Mrs E M

Marist College Hull
Riley Rev R
Derek Dawson
Sean Fugill
David Gray
Michael Gutowski
Andrew Hall
Christopher Howlett

Peter Jackson
Patrick McGlone
John Peterson
Peter Qualey
Anthony Reading
Stephen Reed
David Sadler
Patrick Taylor
Leonard Whiting

St Mary's Convent Middlesbrough
Thompson Miss M
Keilly Mr P
Keilly Mrs P
Madden Miss E
Thompson Miss G
Patricia Clark
Carmel Ferguson
Maureen Green
Vivien Green
Angela Langham
Patricia Manging
Maureen Metcalfe
Patricia McElhatton
Ann Smith
Rosalind Smith

St Mary's College Middlesbrough
Byrne Rev F M
Michael Atkin
Brendan Boyle
Michael Doherty
Edward Dolan
John Green
Peter Harris
Michael Kirkbright
Brian McNulty
Peter McNulty
John Sullivan
Kevin Tsyman

St Joseph's Scouts Stokesley
Storey Rev P
Philip Coates
David Crossen-Brett
John Morley
Richard Roe
Francis Tait
Philip Tait
Michael Thompson
Roderick Westbrook

CTA REP
Brennan Mr J

1966
Bishop George Brunner
Lannen Mgr P
Tindall Mgr C

Fitzgerald Rev P
Harrison Rev S M
Lovelady Rev B R
Ryan Rev J
Rickaby Rev GT
Benedict Sr M
Dolores Sr M
Sr Emmanuel
Sr Helen
Loyola Sr M
Philomena Sr M
Allinson Mrs E
Allison Mrs M
Appleton Mrs M
Ashworth Mr A
Barrett Mr M
Barry Mrs
Barry Mr J
Beddard Mrs L
Borg Mrs A
Boyes Mrs
Connelly Mrs E M
Convey Mrs A
Darrell Mrs D
Duffy Mr D
Duffy Mrs M
Flannagan Miss B
Fortune Mr J
Fortune Mrs M
Hunt Mrs M
Hunt Miss T
Igo Mr
Jackson Miss M
Kaberry Mrs M
Laird Mr C
Miller Mr A
Miller Mrs
Moody Mrs S
Morley Mrs A
Murphy Mrs I
Murphy Mr W
Murray Mrs E
McCann Mr G
McGrother Mrs E
McGurn Mrs M
McHale Mrs E
McMahon Miss M
McMahon Miss E
Nicklin Miss C
O'Connor Mrs W
O'Rourke Mrs A
Rush Mrs E
Shaw Mrs L
Sidgwick Mr B
Sidgwick Mrs S
Thomas Mrs E
Thomas Mrs M
Walker Mrs M
Ward Mrs J
Warwick Mrs R
Whitley Mrs C
Williams Miss M

Catholic Ass Reps
Collins Mr J

St Mary's College Middlesbrough
Byrne Rev F SM
Cassidy Rev P SM
Michael Atkin
Michael Boanas
Peter Callaghan
Michael Close
David Collier
Kenneth Devereux
Philip Edwards
Graham Frank
Steven Geraghty
Edwin Mack
Anthony Rhatigan
John Stinton
Ian Storman
Peter Taylor
Kevin Twyman

Air Section
Wood Canon A
Pippet V Rev C
Currie Rev J D
O'Brien Rev S
O'Connor Rev M
Hilda Sr
Atkinson Mrs A
Atkinson Mstr P
Addis Mrs P
Baker Mrs M
Bancroft Mrs J
Beardsell Mstr M
Boyes Dr W
Boyle Miss V
Bryan Miss I M
Collins Miss M
Cosgrove Miss S
Cramer Mrs M
Cramer Mstr A
Culkin Mrs E
Culkin Miss M
Coughlan Mr J
Coughlan Mrs J
Cassidy Mr J
Cullen Mrs S
Davies Miss M
Dooley Miss M
Duffy Miss A
Durant Miss E S
Gallon Miss C
Garvey Mrs T
George Dr L
Geraghty Mrs V
Graham Miss R
Grainger Miss J
Hart Mrs E
Holwell Mr H

Kearney Miss E
Kelly Miss C
Kelly Mrs M
Kelly Miss M
Kent Miss U M
Kershaw Mrs M
Kilmartin Mr T
Kilmartin Mrs
Kilmartin Mstr C
Kilmartin Mstr M
Kinlan Mrs
Langan Mrs L
Leahy Mrs J V
Marsey Miss R
Mason Mr M
Mason Mrs
Mossey Miss A
Murphy Miss E M
McCart Mrs M
McGeown Mrs E
McIntyre Mr W H
McMackin Miss A
McManemy Miss C
McReddie Miss B M
McReddie Miss S M
Nevin Miss J
O'Connor Mr N
O'Neill Miss M
Perry Mrs A
Pickup Miss H M
Poupard Mrs M
Raw Miss M
Redchurch Mr G
Richardson Mrs A
Shane Mrs A
Smiles Mr J
Smith Miss J
Smith Mrs N
Sprigge Mrs E
Stead Miss M C
Tempest Mr N H
Tiernan Mrs K
Walsh Miss I
Walsh Dr K
Waterson Mr T
Welford Mr J
Welford Miss M M
Welford Mrs R
Whelan Mr D
Whelan Miss M
Whelan Mrs R
Whitfield Mrs A W
Wilkinson Mrs B

CTA REP
Daly Mr T J

Sick Pilgrims
O'Connor Rev W SM
Anderson Mr F
Barry Mrs C
Burrows Mr J

Cullen Mr M
Devlin Miss E
Dixon Mr J D
Duggan Mr F
Ferris Miss P
Graham Miss N
Gunstead Mrs H N
Hartley Mr E G
Hatfield Mr M J
Hooley Miss M
Horton Mr G
Jackland Miss S
Kinlan Miss L A
Kingdom Mr J
Kingdom Mrs L A
Kingston Mr M
Langhan Miss V
Lappin Miss C T
McGowan Mrs M B
McIntyre Mrs T
McParland Mr M
O'Connor Miss M
O'Neill Miss L
Poole Mr L
Weston Mrs M
Whelan Mr J

Rail Section
Josephine Mother M
Antonia Sr M
Colette Sr M
Dominic Sr M
Monica Sr M
Sylvester Sr M
Adams Mr J
Adams Mr S
Brennan Mrs E
Busfield Mrs A
Carroll_Hair Miss C A
Devereux Miss B
Harry Mr J
Hempenstall Mr J
Lazarou Mrs
Mills Mrs
O'Sullivan Mrs M
O'Sullivan Miss B
Thompson Mrs R
Thompson Mstr P

Catholic Ass Reps
De Peyrecave Mr R

1967
Air Section
Bishop George Brunner
Currie Rev J
Harrison Rev G SM
Hughes Rev W L
Lannen Mgr P L
O'Brien Rev S
O'Sullivan Mgr M
Pippet Rev A

Rickaby Rev G T
Ferguson Sr M Delores
Liddane Sr M Joanne
Addis Mrs P M
Addis Miss S
Allen Mrs A
Anderson Mrs B
Anderson Mstr V
Ashworth Mr
Baker Mrs M
Barry Mr J
Barry Mrs E
Bateman Miss M
Blazier Mrs M
Bilton Mrs E
Birkett Mrs C
Boyes Dr W
Burrows Mr J
Cassidy Mr J B
Connaughton Miss D
Cooke Mrs M
Cookson Mrs M
Coughlan Mr J B
Donnelly Mr B
Dooley Miss N
Edon Mstr E
Ferguson Mrs E
Fox Mrs A
Grant Miss M M
Gordon Mr W
Heagney Mrs E
Holwell Mr H
Howlett Mrs M
Hughes Miss A
Hutchinson Miss D M
Jackson Miss M W
Jones Mrs M C
Kairis Mrs J
Kearney Miss E
Kelly Mrs E M
Kent Miss U M
Kershaw Mrs M
Lambert Miss M
Leahy Mr J V
Lumb Mrs C
Maplesden Mrs A M
Miller Mr P
Miller Mr A
Murphy Mr W
Murther Miss M
Murray Miss C
Murray Mrs G
Murray Mstr P
McAuliffe Mrs A
McCart Mrs M
McGeown Mrs E M
McGowan Miss T
McGrogan Mrs M
McGrother Mrs E
McGrother Miss S
McHale Mrs E
McIntyre Mr W

McManemy Miss C
McManus Mrs M
Orr Mrs H
O'Brien Mrs E
Paddison Mrs S
Palmer Mrs D
Palmer Mr H
Pickering Mrs A
Raw Miss M M
Reay Mrs E
Redchurch Mr G
Richards Mrs E C
Richardson Mrs A
Rodgers Mr V J
Rush Mrs E
Shame Mrs A
Swan Mr J
Swan Mrs M
Shaw Miss L
Stead Miss M C
Stephenson Miss M S
Smiles Mr J
Smyth Mrs M E
Taylor Mrs S J
Tiernan Mrs K M
Tinkler Mrs M E
Wake Miss C
Wake Mr T
Walker Mrs H
Walker Mrs M R
Warwick Mrs K M
Waters Mrs M E
Waters Mr P
Welford Mr J
Welford Miss M M
Whitley Mrs C
Whitley Mr J W
Wilkinson Mrs K
Williamson Mrs M
Wilson Mr J W
Wright Mrs M J
Woods Miss A
Woods Mr J

CTA REP
Gavin Mr J

Sick Pilgrims
Arksey Mrs R
Borzumato Mrs M
Borzumato Miss M
Chapman Mr H E
Finn Mrs J
Finn Miss M C
Harbinson Mrs
Kingston M
Langan Miss V
Lewandowski Mr M
Lillford Mrs
Lillford Miss S
McCormack Mr E
Ripley Mrs N

Rodgers Mrs A W
Telford Mr J R
Telford Mstr V A
Williamson Miss R

RAIL SECTION
O'Connor Rev M
Sr Francis OSC
Pauline Sr Mary
Adams Mr J
Adams Mrs M
Brady Miss M
Beardsell Mstr M
Burdett Miss J
Clarke Mrs P
Dahl Mrs M
Daniels Mrs A F
Dooley Mrs B
Dooley Mr J
Harbinson Mr P F
Harding Mrs E
Loughran Miss B
Maunsell Mr E H
McCann Mr G
McCarthy Miss M
McLean Mrs P
McReddie Miss B
McReddie Miss S
Mrs McReddie
Slingsby Miss C
Smyth Mr D
Smyth Mrs D
Wentworth Mrs K
Williams Mrs M

*St Mary's College
Middlesbrough*
Riley Rev R SM
Hugh Appleton
Paul Brennan
Thomas Clarke
Patrick Doherty
David Duffy
Michael Gosney
Michael Greenup
Jeffrey McCann
Michael Orchel
John Robinson

*St James School
South Bank*
Rosario Sr M
Mrs Allen
Auskstinaitis Miss J
Mackin Miss S
Ellen Garbutt
Dorothy Hardwicke
Gerald Hegarty
Karen Wilson

1968
Bishop John

Gerard McClean
Allen Rev B
Bury Rev J
Carson Rev R
Currie Rev J
Lannen Mgr P
O'Connor Rev M
Pippet V Rev
Rickaby Rev G T
Sullivan Mgr M
Fitzgibbon Sr Aquin
Flynn Sr Mildred
Gillen Sr M Gertrude
Jones Sr M Stanislaus
Kelly Sr M Peter
Kennedy Sr M Elizabeth
Abbot Mr J
Bainbridge Mrs M
Barry Mr J
Mrs Barry
Baldock Mrs B
Boyes Dr W
Bradbury Miss A
Bradley Mrs M
Bradley Miss A
Brittain Mrs E
Burrows Mr J
Carolan Miss C
Cassidy Mr J
Clarke Mr F
Collier Mrs N
Collier Miss P
Connolly Mrs E
Conroy Mrs J
Cordes Miss M
Cordes Mrs F
Coughlan Mr J
Curran Mr A
Curtis Mrs N
Dearlove Mrs M
Docherty Miss M
Dooley Miss M
Duffy Mrs C
Eccles Miss M
Fox Mrs A
Francis Mrs N
Francis Mstr T
Garrigan Miss V
Golden Miss J
Gordon Mr E
Green Mr G
Green Mr R
Gunn Miss J
Jackson Miss M
Kennedy Mrs M
Kennedy Mrs M
Kilbride Mr E
Lambert Miss M
Leahy Mr J
Livingstone Miss M
Malone Mrs E
Mackin Mr M

March Mrs M
Miller Mr A
Miller Mrs E
Mossey Miss A
Murphy Mr W
McAuliffe Mrs A
McCart Mrs M
McCartin Miss M
McGrath Mr D
Mrs McGrath
McGrogan Mrs M
McHale Mrs E
McIntyre Mr W
O'Connor Mr H
O'Connor Mrs A
O'Connor Mrs T
O'Sullivan Mrs C
Raw Miss M
Richardson Miss M
Roberts Mrs C
Robinson Mrs N
Robinson Mrs W
Rush Mrs E
Salmon Mrs S
Sayer Mrs E
Shane Mrs A
Smiles Mr J
Smith Mrs J
Smith Miss J
Smith Mrs N
Stead Miss M
Stephenson Miss R
Stott Mrs W
Tempest Mr H
Tiernan Mrs K
Tunley Miss J
Wadrop Mrs C
Walker Mrs H
Walker Mrs M
Whelan Miss M
Whitley Mr J
Mrs Whitley
Wilson Mr J

CTA REP
Gavin Mr J

Sick Pilgrims
Baxter Mr D
Boughton Miss F
Burlison Mrs D
Cairns Mrs
Conlon Miss M
Crossen Mr T
Das Mr M
Derbyshire Mrs S
Duggan Mr F
Jackson Mrs E
Langan Miss V
Martin Mstr J
Martin Mstr S
McCaffrey Miss J

McCluskey Mrs
McCluskey Mstr
Murphy Mr A
O'Sullivan Miss J
Roberts Mr A
Savage Mrs M
Treacy Mrs S
Wadrop Miss C
Weston Mrs M
Wilson Miss J

Air Section
O'Brien Canon S
Rommens Sr F
Cottrell Sr K
Beasty Mrs E
Charlton Mrs J
Clifton Mrs F
Clarke Mrs P
Gilmartin Mr J
Gilmartin Mrs J
Gilmartin Miss
Harrison Mrs B
Harry Mr J
Hinkins Miss A
Hinkins Miss J
Holwell Mr H
Kearney Miss E
Kershaw Mrs M
McGeown Mrs E
Richardson Mrs A
Warvill Mrs O
Warvill Miss D
Welford Mr J
Welford Miss D
Wilson Mrs A
Woods Mr J

Rail Section
Adams Mr J
Adams Mrs
Dooley Mr J
Dooley Mr S
Dooley Miss A
Dooley Miss E
Fitzsimmons Mrs E
Gardiner Miss A
Gourdel Miss E
Kiely Mrs A
Levi Miss E
McGeary Mr P
McGeary Mr S
Pickup Miss H
Rowsome Mrs E
Rudd Mr R
Rudd Mrs
Thompson Mrs D
Walker Mstr M
Winter Mrs B
Wood Mr T

St Mary's College

Middlesbrough
Riley Rev R
Martin Cunningham
Michael Greenup
Michael Hegarty
David Jennings
Peter Kennedy
Ronald Lynch

1969
Bishop John
  Gerard McClean
O'Sullivan Mgr
Lannen Mgr
Pippet Canon C A
Wood Canon A
Carson V Rev R L
O'Callaghan Rev C G
O'Connor Rev M J
Rickaby Rev G T
Ryan Rev J J
Scanlon Rev Bro A
Agatha Sr M
Brady Sr Patricia
Cottrell Sr Vincent
Cottrell Sr Dorothy
Elwell Sr Celine
Fenton Sr Euphemia
Fitzgerald Sr Bridget
Magdalen Sr M
Stanislaus Sr M
McCleod Sr Colette
Stacey Sr Imelda
Wroe Sr Catherine
Wroe Sr Teresa
Adams Mr J
Adams Mrs M P
Allen Mrs P
Alexander Mr N W
Alexander Mrs
Andy Mrs C
Barry Mr J
Barry Mrs J
Beardsell Ms A
Beardsell Mstr M A
Bean Ms H
Biesterfield Mrs P
Boyes Dr W
Bryan Ms I M
Burrows Mr J F
Butler Ms J
Camley Mrs J
Carberry Ms M M
Carberry Mr J B
Chaunce Mrs D
Cleasby Ms A
Collins Mr J
Connolly Mrs E M
Costello Ms M
Coughlan Mr J P
Coughlan Mrs

Coughlan Mast P
Coxhead Mr A
Curran Mr P
Curran Mrs
Daniels Mrs A
Davidson Mrs S
Dean Mrs A
Dixon Mrs T M
Douglas Mrs R
Douglas Mr F
Drinkell Mrs M
Duck Mr R
Duggan Mr J
Dugan Mrs
Duncan Mrs E
Durant Mrs M
Durant Ms E S
Eccles Ms M
Farrell Ms G
Fendall Mrs E M
Franklin Mrs W
Furnell Mrs B
Furnell Mrs E
Gardiner Ms A
Garnett Mrs W
Gawthorpe Mrs G
Gawthorpe Ms S
Gell Ms J
Gell Mrs M
Grennan Mstr M
Hackett Ms C
Hackett Mr J A
Harry Mr J
Hinkins Ms A J
Hinkins Ms H
Hinkins Ms J
Hoare Mrs M
Holwell Mr H
Hughes Mr J
Hughes Mrs J
Jackson Ms M
Jackson Mr R A
Johnson Ms J M
Jones Mrs M E
Jones Mrs V N
Jones Mstr D
Kelly Ms M M
Kelly Mrs M
Kennedy Mrs M
Kerrigan Ms P
Kivosinski Mr
Kivosinski Mrs
Langan Mrs L
Laverick Mrs E
Leahy Ms I
Leahy Mstr J
Leahy Mr J V
Lee Mrs I
Lynch Mr G A
Lynch Mrs
Mackin Mr M
Maynard Ms M

Miller Mr A
Miller Mrs E M
Metcalfe Mrs M
Monaghan Mr J
Morris Mr J
Mossey Ms A
Mulligan Mrs A
Murray Mrs E
McAndrew Mr W
McAuliffe Mrs A
McCart Mrs N
McGeown Mrs E M
McGowan Mrs T
McGeary Mr P
Grogan Mrs M
McGrother Mrs E
McGrother Ms S
McIntyre Mr W H
McNicholas Mr N
McReddie Ms B M
McReddie Ms S M
McLoughlin Mr L
O'Callaghan Mr M
O'Connor Mrs A M
Pipe Mr B
Postgate Mrs E
Pullen Mrs I
Quinn Mrs
Raw Mrs M M
Readman Ms H M
Redchurch Ms M
Rodrigues Mstr G
Rodrigues Mr L
Robinson Mrs S
Robinson Mrs W
Rowell Mrs B
Rudge Mrs C
Rush Mrs E M
Rush Ms E F
Ruxton Ms I
Salvatore Mrs M P
Shane Mrs A
Shields Mrs E
Short Mr C A
Simpson Mrs M
Smith Mr H
Smith Ms J
Smith Mrs N
Smythe Mr D
Snook Mr T H
Snook Mrs
Southgate Mrs J
Starford Mrs C
Stead Ms M C
Sterricker Mrs P
Tempest Mr H N
Thompson Mr A
Tiernan Mrs K M
Tierney Ms C
Tunley Ms J N
Treacey Ms P A
Walsh Ms E

Walsh Dr D K
Walsh Mr P T
Waterson Mr T
Waterfield Mrs C
Warvill Mrs D M
Warvill Ms D
Watson Mr J V
Welford Ms M M
Welford Mr J
Whelan Ms M
Whittingham Mrs C
Wilkinson Mrs B J
Wilkinson Ms M J
Wilkinson Mr D J
Wilkinson Mrs A
Wilkinson Ms H
Wilkinson Mstr T
Wilkinson Mr J W
Wood Mrs D
Woods Mr J

Juvenile Section

St Thomas' School
Middlesbrough
Horkan Mr J W
Metcalf Ms M
White Mr J
McGrath Mrs
Barwick Rosemary
Butcher Jacqueline
Clarke Paul
Deacy Mary
Howard John
Lanny Marisa
McGrath Sean
McNicolas John
McPhilips Doreen
O'Neill Maureen
Pearsall Anne
Skinn Jayne

Sick Pilgrims
O'Connor Rev W
Arskey Mrs R
Beck Mr P
Clarke Mrs P A
Duggan Mr F
Graham Ms N M
Gunn Mr B
Hackett Mrs M
Hayes Mrs E
Hewitt Mrs D
Jackson Mrs E
Johnson Mrs A
Johnson Ms A M
Kane Mrs P
Kane Ms S
Martin Ms M B
Marty Mr R
McKeown Mrs M
Metcalfe Mr M

Odell Mr P
Passmore Mrs R A
Ralph Ms K M
Trainor Mrs D
Varey Mrs M
Yates Mstr N

CTA REPS
Gormley Mr A J
Gavin Mr J
Bouchier Mr M

1970
Bishop John
    Gerard McClean
O'Sullivan Mgr M
Bickerstaffe Mgr A
Lannen Mgr P
Nolan Mgr T T A
Carson V Rev R
Pippett Canon C A
Marsden Rev
O'Connor Rev M
Rickaby Rev G T
Storey Rev P L
Blakey Sr Catherine
Larkin Sr M Finbarr
Meynell Sr M Angela
Murray Sr Helen
Abel Mrs J
Ablett Mrs C
Adams Mr J A
Adams Mrs M P
Albin Mrs A M
Allon Mrs E
Appleby Mrs D M
Arkle Ms K P
Bailey Mrs C M
Bailey Mr J
Barker Mrs D
Baker Mr G A
Batty Mr T P
Bean Ms H
Beavers Mrs C
Bell Mrs M
Bell Ms M A
Bennington Mrs M
Booth Mr G
Booth Mrs S
Boyes Dr W
Boyes Mrs M B
Brown Mrs R
Brown Mrs R T
Burnham Mrs D
Burrows Mr J F
Captain Mrs A
Carolan Ms C A
Cassidy Mr J B
Clarke Ms C
Clarke Mrs K
Clarke Mstr P A
Collins Mr J

Connors Ms M
Cooper Ms E
Coughlan Mr J P
Coughlan Mrs J
Coughlan Mstr P D
Coward Mrs M
Cox Ms L
Cox Mrs M
Cox Ms V
Coxhead Mr A
Crane Ms H
Cunningham Mrs E M
Cunningham Ms G
Dakin Ms M
Desbruslais Mr B J
Desbruslais Mrs
Desbruslais Ms M E
Donoghue Mrs
Dougan Mrs S
Drayton Mr W H
Drinkell Ms M
Duck Ms M B
Duggan Mr J
Duggan Mrs M W
Dunne Mr T
Dunne Mrs M
Dunne Ms A
Dunne Mass S
Dunne Mstr T
Durant Ms E S
Durant Mrs M J
Durant Mrs P
Durkin Mstr J
Dyson Mrs M
Fawcett Ms R
Flanagan Ms
Flintoff Mstr J
Flowerdew Mrs
Gair Ms C A
Galpine Ms M
Gannaway Mrs R
Gannon Mr M
Gardner Mrs B M
Gardner Mr S H
Gell Mrs M
Gorman Mr W
Gorman Mrs C
Grant Ms E M
Gribben Ms L M
Halifax Mrs J
Hamilton Mr E J
Hancock Mrs A M
Handy Mrs K
Hanrott Mr E G
Harcourt Ms D
Harrop Ms M
Harry Mr J
Henderson Ms J
Henry Mrs C
Holder Mrs P A
Horkan Mrs C
Horkan Mr J W

Huggans Mr J
Jackson Ms M W
Johnston Ms G I
Joshua Ms D
Kaberrry Mrs M
Kelly Mstr A M
Kelly Mstr D W
Kelly Mr J
Kelly Mrs E
Kelly Ms M
Kennedy Mrs M
Kirkbright Mrs W
Knisz Mrs M
Leahy Mr J V
Leahy Mrs I G
Leay Mstr J
Leahy Ms M
Lee Ms C
Lummas Mstr J B
March Mrs M M
Martin Ms A
McAndrew Mr W
McAuliffe Mrs A
McCamley Mrs J
McCart Mrs M
McClelland Mstr K P
McCormick Mrs A
McDonald Mrs E
McDonnell Ms K
McGarrell Mrs M P
Geary Mr P
Geary Mrs
McGee Mr R
McGowan Ms T
McGrath Mrs M
McGrogan Mrs M
McGuire Mr J
McGuire Mrs K
McIntyre Mr W H
McKeown Mrs M
McManus Mrs P
McNicholas Mr N
McReddie Ms B M
McReddie Ms S M
Metcalfe Mrs E
Metcalfe Ms M
Miller Mr A
Miller Mrs E M
Monaghan Mr J
Norris Mr J
Mossey Ms A
Mothersill Mrs M M
Murphy Mr W
Newton Mrs D
O'Connor Mrs A M
Parkinson Mrs P A
Passmore Mrs R
Peachey Mrs H M
Pearson Mrs M I
Peckston Mr J G
Peters Dr H J
Peters Mrs M G

Pieper Mrs E
Pippet Ms M P
Raw Ms M
Readman Mr A J
Readman Mrs K
Redchurch Mr G
Redchurch Ms M
Rees Mrs
Rhea Mrs M
Rush Mrs E M
Rush Ms E F
Slater Mrs V
Savage Ms T
Seymour Mstr N A
Shane Mrs A
Shane Ms C M
Short Mr A
Smith Ms J B
Smith Mrs N
Smith Mr H
Snook Mr T H
Snook Mrs
Stead Mrs J
Stead Ms T
Stead Ms M C
Storey Mrs E T
Suddes Mr J
Sullivan Ms C L
Tempest Mr H
Tiernan Mrs K M
Tierney Ms C
Tracey Ms P A
Treacy Mr A J
Trowsdale Ms D M
Tsakarisianos Ms A
Tuplin Mrs N
Vallely Mr F
Walsh Dr D K
Walsh Mrs B F
Walsh Mr P T
Warvill Mrs D M
Warvill Ms D
Waterson Mr T
Watts Mrs J
Watts Ms P
Welford Mr J
Welford Ms M M
Welsh Ms A
Whelan Ms M
White Mrs M
Wilkinson Mstr T
Wilson Mrs T
Wilson Mrs J W
Woods Mr J J

Sick Pilgrims

Abel Mrs J
Barry Mr E
Batchelor Mr J
Brown Mr D
Brown Mrs V I
Carroll Mrs M A

Carter Mrs K
Coulthard Ms M A
Cox Mr J A
Cushley Mr J P
Dougan Mr G J
Drayton Mrs M A
Gales Mr P
Graham Miss N
Griffin Miss S
Gunn Mr B
Gunn Mr G
Hamilton Mr E J
Holmes Mr A
Martin Ms M B
McGurk Mr J P
O'Conner Rev W S
Passmore R
Saunders Mrs J E
Treacy Mrs S A
Whitaker Mr L

CTA REPS
Gormley Mr A J
Bass Mr R
Bass Mrs H

1971
Bishop John
   Gerard McClean
O'Sullivan Mgr M
Pippet Mgr C A
Bickerstaffe Mgr A
Carson V Rev R
Bury Rev J
Carson Rev E
Collingwood Rev L J
Crowley Rev M
Gilligan Rev J
Marsden Rev M K
McGrath Rev J
O'Connor Rev M
Rickaby Rev G T
Ryan Rev T
Spaight Rev D
Celine Sr M
Collingwood Sr M Monica
Doherty Sr M Evangelist
Doherty Sr M Luke
Finbarr Sr M Dowling
Francoise Sr M
Stonehouse Sr M Ethelreda
McDonnell Sr M Magdalen
Sweeney Sr M Bridget
Twomey Sr M Josephine
Adams Mr J A
Adams Mr M P
Allen Mrs P A
Allinson Ms J A
Allon Mrs E
Andrews Mrs M
Atkin Mrs
Atkinson Mr G

Atkinson Ms S
Ayres Mr S
Ayres Mrs P
Bailey Ms M C
Baker Mr G A
Barker Ms A
Barry Ms E
Basford Mr J
Bean Ms H
Beardsall Mstr M
Boland Mrs W
Boland Ms K
Boyes Dr W
Boyes Mrs M
Boyes Mr D W
Brannen Ms M
Brodie Mrs H
Brodie Ms S
Brodie Ms J
Brodie Mrs R
Brough Mr J
Brough Mr D J
Brown Mrs R
Brown Mstr M
Burrows Mr J F
Caddy Mrs C M
Carberry Ms M
Carroll-Hair Ms C A
Carter Mr J
Cassidy Mr J B
Caulfield Mr W
Caulfield Mrs B
Chambers Mrs A
Chapman Mrs H E
Clarke Mr F
Clifford Mr T
Collingwood Ms M
Collingwood Ms N
Collins Mr J
Connorton Mrs M M
Conroy Mr J
Conroy Mrs A
Costello Mstr P
Coxhead Mr A J
Cuminskey Mrs
Daley Mrs I
Daley Mstr J
Dasey Ms J
Dasey Ms M
Davison Mrs S
Dobson Mr L
Dodd Mrs D C
Donaghy Mr L
Donaghy Mr F
Dooley Ms E
Douglas Ms E
Dring Ms A
Duck Mr R
Duck Ms M B
Duggan Mr J
Duggan Mrs M M
Duncan Mrs E

Dunne Mr S D
Durant Ms E S
Durant Mrs H J
Durkin Ms D
Fair Mrs W
Ferguson Mrs E
Fieldhouse Mrs H
Finn Mrs J
Finn Ms P A
Flanigan Ms R M
Fletcher Mrs
Fletcher Ms C
Flowerdew Mrs H
Gales Mr P
Gallagher Mr T
Gallagher Mrs M
Galpine Ms M
Gell Mrs
Gell Ms J
Gibbin Mrs M I
Gibbins Mrs D
Goodall Mrs D
Goonan Mrs E
Goonan Ms M
Gorman Mr W
Gormley Mrs E
Greaves Mrs M
Hall Mr R E
Hall Ms L M
Handy Mrs
Harker Ms E G
Harrop Ms M
Harry Mr J
Hirst Ms B
Hoare Mrs
Holder Mrs D M
Holder Mrs P A
Holder Ms M A
Hollwell Mr H
Horkan Mr J W
Huggans Mr J
Husband Ms J
Jackson Ms M
Jefferson Mrs M
Johnson Mrs M
Kearney Ms E
Kerrigan Ms P
Kilmartin Mr T
Kilmartin Mstr M
Kilmartin Mstr C
King Mrs M
Knight Ms D
Langan Mrs L
Leahy Mrs I
Leahy Mr J V
Leahy Mstr J
Lee Mrs I
Lee Mrs J
Lockhart Mrs E
Manning Mrs M A
March Mr K T
March Mrs M M

Maxwell Mrs M
Metcalfe Mrs E
Miller Mr A
Miller Mrs E
Mills Mrs M
Mitchell Ms J M
Monaghan Mr J
Morris Mr J
Mossey Ms A
Murphy Mrs M
Murphy Mrs H
Murphy Ms A
Murphy Ms E M
Murphy Mrs M
Murphy Mr W
McAndrew Mr
McCallen Mr J W
McCallen Mrs M W
McDonnell Ms B
McGee Mr R
McGowan Ms T
McGuire Mr J
McGuire Mrs M
McGuirk Mrs J
McGurry Ms A
McGurry Mrs A
McReddie Ms S
McReddie Ms B
Nicholson Mr R P
Nicholson Mrs B W
Noble Mrs T
O'Connor Mrs A M
O'Donnell Mrs E
Parker Mrs
Passmore Mrs R
Pearson Ms S M
Peckston Col J G
Peters Dr H J
Peters Mrs M G
Pieper Mrs M
Qualter Ms A
Redchurch Mr G
Redchurch Ms M
Rhea Mrs M
Robertson Ms S M
Robinson Mrs W
Rossi Mrs E
Rossi Ms P
Rossi Mr B
Shane Mrs A
Shane Ms A M
Sharples Mrs K J
Shaw Mrs G M
Shaw Mrs S M
Sherlock Ms M E
Short Mr C A
Slater Mr H
Smiles Mr J
Smith Mr H
Smith Ms J B
Smith Mrs N
Smith Mr N

Smith Mrs S
Smith Mrs M E
Southgate Mrs J
Squire Ms E
Starford Mrs
Stead Ms M C
Stephenson Ms R M
Storcy Mrs
Storcy Ms G
Thompson Ms D
Tierney Ms C
Treacy Msr A J
Trowsdale Ms D
Tubridy Mstr M
Villa Ms R M
Walker Mrs I V
Warvill Mrs D M
Warvill Ms D M
Waterson Mr T
Watson Mrs A T
Watts Mrs J
Welford Mr J
Welford Ms M M
Whelan Ms M
White Mrs M
White Ms E
Whittingham Mrs C
Wilkins Mrs M
Wilson Mr J W
Wilson Mrs M I
Woods Mr J J
Woods Ms A
Yates Mstr N

Sick Pilgrims

Ayres Mr E
Brown Mrs V
Bryan Mr S
Burnett Mr E
Bywater Mr A
Carroll Mrs M
Cave Mrs E
Cross Mr A
Cushley Mr J
Daly Mr T
Doyle Ms C
Drewery Ms J
Fish Mr J
Gallagher Ms A
Harrison Mr R
Hartley Mr J
Johnson Ms I
Kilmartin Mrs J
Leonard Mr E
Matson Mrs J
Matthews Mr J
Maxwell Mr P
McGee Mr J
McGee Mr T
McGlade Mrs E
O'Connor Rev W
O'Dell Mr P

Parker Ms S
Rafton Mrs M
Whelan Mr P
Wrigglesworth Mr P

CTA REPS

Gormley Mr A J
Perombelon Mr G
Bassadone Mr R

Lannen Mgr P
Bryan Ms I
Hughes Mr J
Hughes Mrs J
Kennedy Mrs M
McCart Mrs M
McGrowther Mrs
McIntyre Mr I
Rush Mrs E
Tiernan Mrs K
Walsh Dr K
Walsh Mrs M

1972

Bishop John
    Gerard McClean
O'Sullivan Mgr M
Pippet Canon C A
Barry Rev J A
Canon V Rev A
Carson Rev E
Marsden Rev M
O'Connor Rev M
Rickaby Rev G T
Ryan Rev D
Ryan Rev M
Spaight Rev D
Storey Rev P L
Bebb Sr Eleanor
Bernadette Sr M
Catherine Sr
Hawes Sr Josephine
Linnane Sr Mary
Murray Sr Helen
McDonnell Sr M Magdalen
Phillipa Sr M
Slade Sr D A
Adams Mr J A
Adams Mrs
Bailey Mrs E
Bailey Ms M C
Baker Mr G A
Bean Ms H
Beverley Ms S
Black Mrs M
Boyes Dr W
Boylan Mr I
Bradley Mr A M
Bradley Mrs
Brady Mrs M A
Brankley Ms I
Bright Ms A

Brough Mr D J
Brough Mr G P
Brough Mr J
Browne Mrs M A
Burrows Mr J
Cadman Mrs B
Cassidy Mr J B
Caton Mrs B
Clarke Mr F M
Clifford Mr T
Colley Mr C V
Colley Mrs
Coxhead Mr A J
Crawford Ms R M
Cregan Mr M
Davies Mrs P
Dixon Ms L
Dixon Mrs N
Dobson Mr L
Donoghue Mr M
Donovan Mrs Z
Dooley Mrs B
Dooley Mrs E
D'Souza Ms S S
Ellwood Mrs M
Ferguson Ms N
Fionda Mr F A
Fitzgerald Mr
Fitzgerald Mrs
Fleisch Mrs C
Flowerdew Mrs H
Flynn Ms S
Foley Mr M P
Foley Mrs A
Francis Mr W T
Francis Mrs
Freeman Ms M
Gales Mr P
Gannon Mr M
Gilmartin Mr J P
Gilmartin Mrs J P
Gilmartin Mrs N
Gilmartin Mrs K
Gollogly Mrs E
Hall Mr P
Hannon Ms A
Hanson Mr H E
Hanson Mrs
Hargan Mrs M
Hargan Mrs M T
Harrison Mrs F
Harrop Mrs M
Henderson Ms E
Higham Ms H
Hughes Mrs A
Jackson Ms M
Johnson Mr F
Johnson Mrs
Johnson Mrs S
Keegan Mrs J
Lane Mrs M
Lane Mstr M

Leahy Mr J V
Leahy Mrs
Leahy Mstr J J
Lyth Mrs W
March Mrs C
Martin Mrs A
Metcalf Mrs E
Miller Mrs A
Miller Mrs
Mimmery Mrs K
Mothersill Mrs M M
Moverley Mr A
Moverley Ms O
Moxon Ms S
Murphy Mr W
McCarthy Ms V
McDonald Mr G E
McDonald Mrs
McGreary Mr P
McGreary Mrs
McGreary Ms A
McGee Mr R
McGee Mr T
McGowan Ms T
McGuire Mr J
McGuire Mrs
McGuire Ms P
McGurry Ms A
McNally Ms P
McManus Mrs P
Nevison Mrs H
Noble Mrs T
Norris Mrs T
Norris Mrs G
O'Connor Mrs A M
O'Drisoll Mrs M
O'Neill Mrs W
Parkinson Mrs A
Pearson Mrs S M
Peters Dr H J
Peters Mrs
Pieper Mrs M
Rafton Mr C
Rees Mrs C
Reidy Mr J
Robertson Ms S M
Robinson Mrs P
Robinson Mstr M
Rollings Mr P
Rowan Mrs C
Rylands Ms M J
Salvatore Mrs M P
Scanlon Ms C
Scanlon Ms H
Shane Mrs A
Short Mr C A
Slattery Mrs H
Smiles Mr J J
Smith Mrs E
Stonehouse Mrs B A
Stonehouse Ms S M
Studwick Ms A

Sullivan Ms M M
Sullivan Ms S H
Swalwell Mrs P
Tait Mr D
Tait Mrs M
Tait Ms V
Tiernam Mrs K M
Tierney Ms C
Traynor Ms R
Treacey Mrs K
Treacey Ms M
Treacy Mr A J
Vallely Mr F
Wake Mr T
Wake Mrs D K
Wake Ms J L
Waterson Mr T
Welford Mr J
Wentworth Ms K E
Whelan Ms M
White Mrs M
Wilde Mrs J D
Wilson Mr J W
Woods Mr J J
Woods Ms A

Sick Pilgrims
Armstrong Ms K
Armstrong Ms M
Bassett Ms F
Burns Ms F
Cox Mr J
Connelly Ms G
Das Mr M
Devlin Ms J
Devlin Mrs
Drewery Ms J
Fionda Mstr V
Flynn Ms A
Hand Mr P F
Hancock Mrs B
Hargan Ms M
HarnessWilliamson Mrs
Harry Mr J
Johnson Ms M I
Kilmartin Mrs J
Kirby Mr R
Loughran Mstr N
Loughran Mrs S M
Loy Mrs M
Manders Mrs C
Morris Mrs M
Murtha Mr J L
McGurn Mr J
O'Henly Mrs E
O'Brien Mrs E
Pearce Mstr G
Pearce Mrs
Pederson Mrs R
Pidgeon Mrs R
Penna Mr F
Rafton Mrs M

Ralph Ms K M
Rowe Mr J
Sellars Mrs D
Swalwell Mstr D
Tait Ms Y
Whittington Ms J
Whittington Mrs M
Yates Mstr N J

CTA REPS
Perombelon Mr G
Bassadone Mr R

By Air
Nolan Canon T A
Davern Canon M
Agnew Rev P
Bickerstaffe Rev J A
Currie Rev J D
Plunkett Rev O
Shanahan Rev J
Allum Mrs M E
Adams Mrs F L
Atkinson Mr A C
Atkinson Mrs
Atkinson Mr A F
Atkinson Mr B E
Atkinson Mr J A
Atkinson Mr P J
Atkinson Mr T P
Allon Mrs E
Bailey Mr C G
Bailey Mr W
Bailey Mrs
Barnes Mrs D
Barrett Dr T
Barrett Mrs
Bateson Mrs O
Bateson Ms M
Beavers Mrs C
Carvill Ms L
Carvill Ms J
Carvill Ms M
Carvill Mr O
Collins Mrs D
Cosgrove Mr J D
Cosgrove Ms
Cousins Mr J
Cousins Mrs
Coward Mrs M
Cox Mr A
Cox Mrs
Coyle Mrs A
Dixon Mrs M
Dixon Mstr A
Downey Mrs M
Duck Ms M B
Duffy Ms A
Dunne Ms M
Farrell Mr P V
Fletcher Mrs K
Foster Mrs A

Foy Ms B
Frankland Mrs M
Frankland Ms C
Gallagher Ms C
Gibson Mr E
Hare Mrs G
Hall Mr L
Hall Mrs
Harding Mrs A
Hayes Ms E
Hayes Ms T
Hayes Ms M
Heaney Ms E
Heaney Ms M
Heard Ms L
Hearne Mrs M L
Houlton Mrs A
Hunt Mrs M E
Hurst Mrs A
Jackson Mr T
Jackson Mrs
Kearney Ms E
Lodge Ms M
Mason Mrs M J
Moore Ms M I
McAllister Mrs T
McConnerty Ms M
McGrother Mrs E
McGrother Ms S
McKeown Ms N V
McNally Mr P T
McNally Mrs
McNally Mr C
McTigue Mrs M F
O'Kane Mr C
O'Kane Mrs
Pamplin Mr S
Pincri Mrs M
Readman Mrs H M
Sant Mrs E
Shaw Ms L M
Shearer Ms C
Spencer Mrs H
Stitt Mrs L
Stitt Ms P G
Swindell Mrs E
Taylor Mrs S J
Trowsdale Ms D M
Vincent Ms S
Wainwright Mrs E M
Walsh Ms A M
Waterson Mrs M
Wells Mrs I
West Mrs M
Wright Mrs M
Young Mrs M
Young Ms S

1973
Bishop John
  Gerard McLean
O'Sullivan Canon M

Bickerstaffe Mgr A E
Carson Canon R
Hughes Canon W L
Pippet Canon A
Bickerstaffe Rev J A
Bury Rev J
Byrne Rev F J
Carson Rev E
Charlton Rev J R
Gannon Rev J
Gannon Rev J
Gould Rev T
Marsden Rev M K
O'Connor Rev M
Plunkett Rev O
Rickaby Rev G T
Ryan Rev C M
Spaight Rev D
Storey Rev P L
Trehy Rev K F
Bailey Sr Gabriel
Bebb Sr M E
Carabine Sr S M
Egan Sr Anne
Hoolahan Sr F
Jones Sr M E
Carabine Sr M E
Kelly Sr S M
McLaughlin Sr V
Marnell Sr A
Stacey Sr Imelda
Tobin Sr S M E
Adams Mr J A
Adams Mrs M P
Afford Mrs M
Allew Mrs P
Allon Mrs E
Anderson Ms N
Andrews Mrs M
Bagshawe Mr K R
Bailey Mrs E
Bailey Ms M C
Bainbridge Mrs M
Baker Mr G A
Baldock Ms M K
Barrett Mr J M
Barry Mr J
Barry Mrs E
Breadle Mrs C
Bean Ms H
Bell Mrs P V
Bell Ms P
Bennett Mrs A
Bennett Ms G
Biott Mrs W B
Blythe Mr J
Blythe Mrs M
Boyes Dr W
Boyes Mrs M B
Bradley Mr D G
Bradley Mrs E
Brankley Ms I

Brannen Ms M
Brereton Ms J E
Bright Ms B A
Bright Ms E
Brough Mr D J
Brough Mr B
Brown Mrs C
Brown Mr H
Brown Mrs V I
Brown Ms E M
Brown Ms C B
Brown Mrs M
Brown Mstr M
Bryan Ms I
Burke Ms M
Burns Mrs R
Burrows Mr F F
Calum Mrs E
Calum Ms S
Cameron Ms E
Cantwell Ms A
Carolan Ms C A
Carpenter Mrs A
Carroll-Hair Ms C A
Carter Mrs M E
Cassidy Mr J
Charles Mrs E
Charlton Mr A
Charlton Mrs S C
Cheesbrough Mrs P M
Clifford Mr T
Close Mr J
Connelly Ms J
Connors Ms E A
Connors Ms E M
Connors Mr J A
Connors Mrs E
Connorton Mrs M M
Cooper Mrs L A
Cooper Mstr L
Cousins Mrs C
Coward Mrs M
Cox Mrs E
Coxhead Mr A
Cregan Mr M
Cronin Mr K
Crosby Mrs E
Crummay Mr J B
Crummay Mrs M
Cumiskey Mrs A
Curran Mr A
Dasey Ms J F
Davies Mrs P
Devereux Mr M
Devine Ms C
Dickens Mr A
Dickens Mrs M
Dixon Mr G
Dixon Ms L
Dixon Mrs N
Doherty Ms M
Donaghue Ms G

Donaghy Mr L
Donaghy Mr F
Donaghy Mr A
Donnelly Ms V
Dooley Mrs B
Dooley Ms E
Dougan Mr G
Dougan Mrs S
Doyle Ms R
Duck Ms M B
Duck Mr R
Duffy Mrs C
Duffy Mrs E
Duggan Mr J
Duggan Mrs M M
Durkin Ms S
Elliott Mrs A
Farrell Mr P V
Fawcett Mrs A
Fieldhouse Mrs H
Flay Mrs M
Flowerdew Mrs H
Flynn Mr F J
Flynn Mrs C
Forkin Mr S P
Forkin Mrs M A
Giblin Mrs
Gibson Mr H
Godfrey Mrs A
Golden Mrs E
Golden Ms J
Golighlty Ms W
Gorman Mr W
Gray Ms R
Graves Ms M
Hall Mr W R
Hall Mrs J M
Hall Mstr R
Hall Mstr P
Hall Mr T P
Hammill Ms R
Hammill Mr J R
Hannon Ms A G
Hanson Mr H E
Hanson Mrs I
Hargan Ms M
Harker Mr J
Harker Mrs S
Harker Ms J
Harrison Mrs B M
Harrison Mrs E M
Harrison Mr R
Harrison Mrs M
Harrop Ms M
Harry Mr J
Haughey Mrs N
Haughey Mrs F
Heaney Ms M
Hirst Mrs A
Hodge Mrs M
Holder Mrs P A
Hollier Mrs D

Horwell Mr M
Horwell Mrs M
Houlton Mrs A
I'Anson Mrs E
Jackson Ms M
Johnson Mrs M
Jones Mrs M
Kearney Ms E
Kelly Mr J
Kennedy Mr F
Kennedy Mrs M
Keogan Mrs S L
Kerrigan Ms P R
Kershaw Mrs M
King Mr J
King Mrs M
Kinlan Mr J
Kirby Ms A
Kirk Mrs F
Knox Mr P
Knox Mrs D
Langan Mrs L
Lannon Mr T
Lannon Mrs F
Laverick Mrs E
Leahy Mr J V
Leahy Mstr J J
Leddy Ms M
Leonard Mrs H D
Leonard Ms M J
Lindup Mrs L
Lynn Mr B
Lynn Mstr J
McAndrew Mrs M
McCabe Mr P
McCabe Mrs A
McCart Mrs M
McCarthy Ms N
McCormick Mrs M A
McCourt Mrs M E
McCrainor Mrs K D
McCullagh Mrs E
McDermott Ms P
McGeary Mr P
McGeary Mrs P
McGeary Ms M
McGee Mrs A
McGee Mr R
McGowan Mrs M
McGowan Ms T
McGrath Mrs M G
McGrother Mrs E
McGrother Ms S
McIntyre Mr F
McIntyre Mr W H
McLean Mr P
McPartland Mrs M A
McRae Mrs C
McReddie Ms S M
McReddie Ms B M
Mackin Ms S
Maguire Mrs W

Maidment Ms A J
Mallon Ms A
Manning Mrs M A
March Mr K T
March Mrs M M
Matson Mrs E W
Metcalfe Mrs E
Metcalfe Mrs S
Miller Mr A
Miller Mrs E M
Moffatt Mrs A M
Moloney Mr P J
Monoghan Mr J
Morris Mr J
Moss Mrs F J
Mulholland Mrs M
Mulholland Mr S
Mulholland Mr F
Mullender Mrs M
Murphy Mr W
Nicholson Mr P
Nicholson Mrs P
Noble Mrs T
Norton Ms A
O'Brien Ms M
O'Connell Mrs T
O'Connor Mrs M
O'Driscoll Ms M
O'Hara Mrs
O'Hara Ms B M
O'Neill Mr J
O'Neill Mrs M M
O'Neill Mrs W
Osborne Mrs G
Osborne Mrs J
Osborne Mstr P
Osborne Ms S
O'Sullivan Mr T
Pamplin Mr S
Parkinson Mrs P A
Pearson Ms S M
Peckston Col J G
Pennock Mrs E
Peters Dr H J
Peters Mrs M G
Phillips Mrs W M
Pieper Mrs M
Plumpton Mrs M J
Plumpton Ms E J
Plunkett Mrs M A
Quinn Ms K
Quinn Ms
Radford Mrs D M
Ramsay Mr B T
Ramsay Mr M P
Readman Mr J C
Readman Mrs J C
Redchurch Mr G
Redchurch Ms M
Reed Ms G
Reidy Mr J
Ritchie Mr J

Robertson Ms S M
Robinson Mrs P
Robinson Mrs W
Robinson Mr W
Rodgers Ms E M
Rodgers Ms A R
Roe Mr S
Roe Mr C
Rossi Mrs E
Rutt Mr A E
Ruxton Mr O F
Ruxton Mrs Y
Sanderson Mrs A
Sanderson Mr J
Scanlan Mrs E
Scott Mrs T
Sexton Mrs E
Shane Mrs A
Shannon Mr T
Sharp Mrs E
Shaw Mrs
Shearer Ms C
Short Mr A
Sloan Mr J
Sloan Mrs A
Smiles Mr J
Smith Mstr D
Smythe Mrs D
Squire Ms E
Stonehouse Mrs B A
Stonehouse Ms S M
Swash Mr M
Sweeney Mrs M A
Tait Mr D
Tait Mrs M
Tait Ms Y
Tait Ms V
Tasker Mrs E
Tasker Mr M
Taylor Mrs D
Tebbs Mrs E
Tebbs Ms B
Telford Mr J R
Tempest Mr H M
Tiernan Mrs K M
Tierney Ms C
Topliss Mrs V
Trainor Mrs K
Trehy Mrs M
Trowsdale Ms D M
Vallely Mr F
Walsh Dr D K
Walsh Mrs B F
Ward Mrs G
Warvill Mrs D M
Waterson Mrs M
Waterson Mr T
Welford Mrs F
Welford Mr J
Warvill Mr W E
Warvill Mrs M A
Wells Mrs I

Whelan Ms M
Warvill Mrs J A
Whittingham Mrs
Wilkinson Ms H
Wilkinson Ms A
Wilson Mr J W
Woods Mr J J

Sick Pilgrims
Atkinson Mrs M
Austin Mr D
Banks Mrs C
Bassett Ms F
Brown Mrs M
Cobby Mrs M
Cox Mr J
Das Mr M
Donnelly-Goulding Mrs T
Ferguson Mstr P
Ferguson Mrs M
Gillespie Mr T
Harrison Mr P
Johnson Ms W
King Ms D
Kirby Mr R
McCann Mr G M
McGaskill Mrs J
McGlade Mrs E
McGurk Mr P
Mallon Baby J
Mallon Mrs M
Manders Mrs C
Martin Mrs J
Martin Mr J
Morris Mrs N
Murphy Ms L
Murphy Mrs M
O'Connor Mr M
O'Dell Mr P
O'Sullivan Mr T
Perren Mrs D
Shaw Mr R
Spiteri Mr P
Telford Mr V
Todd Ms I
Todd Ms I
Varey Mrs M
Walker Mrs J
Yates Mr N
Yates Mrs J
McGoune Mr P
McGoune Mrs F
McGurn Mr J
Rowe Mr J

CTA REPS
Daley Mr T
Connelly Mr B A
Daly Mrs N
Barrere Mr P
Gastmans Ms G

1974
Flight A
Bishop John
   Gerard McClean
O'Sullivan Mgr M
Rickaby Canon G T
Byrne Rev F J
Carroll Rev W
Martin Rev C S
O'Neill Rev J
Spaight Rev D
Holwell Br H
Davitt Sr J
Jordan Sr A J
Lanigan Sr V
McCarthy Sr A
O'Connor Sr Noreen
Adams Mr J A
Adams Mrs M P
Allinson Ms J A
Allinson Mrs E
Bailey Ms M C
Bailey Mrs E B
Barnes Mrs D
Bennington Mrs J
Blamires Mrs
Boyes Dr W
Boyes Mr D W J
Boyes Mrs M
Bright Ms B A
Bright Mrs E
Burrows Mr J F
Cameron Ms E
Carroll-Hair Ms C A
Collins Mr J
Cosgrove Mrs J
Cosgrove Ms P M
Coxhead Mr A
Craggs Mrs E
Cunningham Mrs M
Cuthbert Mrs H
Devlin Mrs M
Devlin Mrs M J
Dewhurst Mr A C
Dickons Mr A H
Dickons Mrs M
Doherty Ms M
Duncan Mr A V
Duncan Mrs M R
Gibbons Mrs D
Giblin Mr J
Giblin Mrs A
Harkin Mr J M
Harrison Ms F
Heatley Mrs M C
Hebron Mrs W
Hodge Mrs M M
Jackson Ms M
Jackson Mr T
Jackson Mrs D
Jackson Mrs T

Langley Ms C
Langley Mrs C
Leahy Mr J V
Leahy Mrs I
Leahy Mstr J J
McDaid Mrs K
McGeary Ms A
McGeary Ms B
McGeary Mr P
McGee Mr R
McGouran Mr H P
McGouran Mrs M
McGrath Mrs M G
MGurn Mr J M
McNulty Ms M
McRae Mrs C
Manning Mrs M A
Matthew Mrs O
Miller Mr A
Miller Mrs E M
Milner Mrs N
Moloney Mr P J
Moody Mrs A
Mothersill Mrs M M
Murphy Mrs A
Nolan Ms W
O'Hara Mrs A
Ormesby Mstr G
Ormesby Mrs M R
Pacy Mrs I
Ramsay Mr B T
Ramsay Mr M P
Rodgers Mrs E
Roulston Mrs M E
Rowland Mr P
Ryan Mrs M J
Short Mr A
Smiles Mr J T
Smith Ms F O
Smith Ms R M
Smith Mrs M
Smyth Mrs D
Swash Mrs C
Taylor Mrs M E
Tempest Mr H N
Thorpe Ms M I
Turner Mr P T
Turner Mrs P T
Tyerman Ms J
Vallely Mr F R
Walsh Dr D K
Walsh Mrs D F
Waterson Mr T
Wilson Mr V P
Wilson Mrs M C
Wright Mrs M

Sick Pilgrims
Arnold Mrs M
Baldwin Mrs C
Bassett Ms F
Blamires John

Cushley Joseph
Dale Mrs
Harkin Mrs M
Harrison Mstr
Harrison Mr
Higgins Margaret
Honeyman Mrs M
Manders Mrs C
McGarvey Mrs C
Morris Mrs N
Murtha James
Murphy Mrs M G
O'Callaghan Mrs E
Ramsay Mrs S
Ryan Mr J
Smart Mrs S
Smith Paul
Todd Imelda
Todd Isabella
Tye Mr R E

CTA REPS
Daly Mrs N
Perombelon Mr G

Flight B
Davern Rev M
Pippet Canon C A
Bickerstaffe Rev J A
Dutton Rev A
Murphy Rev D
Plunkett Rev O
Ryan Rev C
Ryan Rev D
Trehy Rev K F
Ferguson Sr M D
Agnes Sr G
Hoolahan Sr F
Afford Mrs M F
Allon Mrs E
Atkin Mrs E
Austin Mr D
Barrett Ms J
Bean Ms H
Bell Mrs E M
Bennett Mrs M
Bennett Mstr A
Buckel Mrs E
Byrne Mrs D
Coleman Ms J M
Cox Mrs C C
Coward Mrs M
Dasey Ms J F
Dasey Ms M M
Davies Mrs P
Davies Mrs P
Davis Mr P J
Donnelly Ms V
Donovan Mrs J
Doyle Mrs A
Farrell Mrs M
Ferguson Ms N

Ferguson Mrs E
Fieldhouse Mrs H
Flannagan Ms B
Forester Ms D M
Gallon Mrs C A
Gallon Mr J T
Gaskin Ms S L
Gaskin Mrs M B
Gilmour Mrs N
Grant Ms E M
Greenheld Mrs K
Greenheld Mstr D
Goonan Mr T F
Goonan Mrs E
Hampson Mrs L M
Hanson Mr H E
Hanson Mr P E
Hanson Mr S J
Hanson Mrs I
Harker Ms E
Harry Mr J
Hart Ms G M
Hart Ms P E
Hart Mrs E O
Henry Mrs C
Henry Mstr P
Hodgson Mrs A M
Ibbotson Mrs E
Johnson Mrs M
Jones Mrs E
Keane Mrs A
Keane Mrs M B
Kearney Ms E
Kirby Ms A
Lyons Ms C
Lyons Mrs A
Lyons Mrs C
Lyons Mstr R
McGarry Mrs A B
Maidment Ms A
Marron Ms G A
Martin Mrs A
Megson Mrs J
Megson Mrs M
Metcalfe Mrs E
Miller Mrs E
Morgan Mr K
Morkos Dr P
Murphy Mr W
Murray Mrs H
Murray Mrs N
Murray Mstr S L
Newton Mrs D
Nottingham Ms J A
Nottingham Mrs A
O'Connor Mrs A M
O'Donnell Mstr A
Owen Mrs M S
Pace Mrs G
Pank Ms A
Pank Mrs J
Pank Mr R

Pank Mrs J
Pearson Mrs H E
Penrose Mrs D
Pieper Mrs E
Popplewell Mrs L A
Renwick Mrs M
Rhodes Mrs M S
Robertson Ms S M
Rourke Ms M
Ryan Ms K N
Selkirk Mr D J
Sellars Mrs M
Sellars Mstr J
Shaw Mrs G M
Squire Ms E
Starr Mrs N
Standbridge Ms A
Suggitt Mrs N I
Taylor Mrs S J
Tierney Ms C
Treacy Mrs K
Trehy Mrs M
Trowsdale Ms M D
Welford Mr J
White Mr P
White Mrs E
Wilkinson Ms A
Wilkinson Ms H
Wilkinson Ms J
Wilkinson Mrs N
Wood Dr F B
Woods Mr J J
Wray Mrs M
Young Mr G M
Young Mrs M M
Young Mrs N

Sick Pilgrims
Carter Mrs K
Dwerery Joan
Everitt Mrs A
Moxon Ernest
O'Brien Mary
Perren Mrs D
Telford Vincent
Woodward Anthony
Woodward Mrs

Jumbulance Pilgrims
O'Connor Rev M
O'Donnell Sr M M
Baker Mr G A
Barker Mr
Barker Mrs A
Boyes Mr D
Brankley Ms I
Gillespie Thomas
Hatfield Martin
Kelly Ms M M
Lee James
Matson Mrs G
Metcalfe Mr G

Murray Stephen
McGlade Joseph
Pace George
Peters Dr H J
Peters Mrs M G
Priest Mrs C
Shane Mrs A
Vamplew Raymond
Whelan Ms M

1976
Flight A
Bishop John
   Gerard McClean
Rickaby V Rev G T
Adams Mr J A
Adams Mrs M P
Allinson Mrs E
Allinson Ms J A
Bailey Mrs E
Barbour Mrs M H
Barbour Mrs T
Bebb Sr E
Boyes Dr W
Boyes Mrs M B
Brown Mrs C
Bright Ms B A
Bryan Ms I M
Cameron Ms E
Campbell Ms W
Carson Canon R
Coxhead Ms A
Craggs Ms E
Curran Mr A
Dasey Ms J F
Dasey Ms M M
Davies Ms P
Duck Ms B
Duck Mr R
Dyer Mrs A
Eglington Ms M J
Evans Mrs M M
Finn Mrs J
Finn Mrs P A
Gallagher Dr J B
Gallagher Mrs J F
Gallagher Mr P
Gallagher Mrs M
Gannon Rev J
Giblin Mrs A
Hainsworth Mrs W
Hume Mrs M
Jackson Ms M
Kennedy Mrs M
Kenny Mr R
Kershaw Ms A E
Kinlin Mrs M
Kyle Mrs K M
Lanny Mr P
Leahy Mrs I
Lovell Mr M G
McArthur Mrs W

McBride Mrs A
McBride Mr J
McCart Mrs M
McClean Mrs E M
McDermott Sr E
McDermott Ms G
McElhatton Ms E
McElwee Mrs M
McGurn Mr J
McMahon Mrs A
Maughan Ms C
Metcalfe Ms E
Metcalfe Mr G V
Monoghan Mr J
Murray Ms B A
Murray Mrs M M
Noonan Sr A
Pass Mrs D
Raw Ms M M
Reed Ms G
Rosa Sr
Ryan Mrs M J
Shane Mrs A
Sykes Mrs S
Smiles Mr J
Spain Mr J
Spain Mrs M
Sullivan Mr T P
Swales Ms M A
Tiernan Mrs K M
Trehy Rev K F
Trehy Mrs M
Van Geffen Mrs G B
Waterson Mr T
Watson Mrs M I
Weir Mrs W
Whellan Mrs M
Wotton Mrs L
Wotton Ms M

Sick Pilgrims
Castle Mrs W
Chapman Mrs G
Conlon Mrs M
Giblin Mr J
Hodgson Ms H
Jenkins Mrs M
Jenkins Mstr I
Kenny Mrs A
Long Mrs J
Loughlin Mr J
Murray Mr J J
Murtha Mstr C
McDonald Mrs E
McGreevy Mstr M
Nolan Mr J P
Noonan Rev L
Parker Mrs M
Patterson Mrs N
Ralph Ms K
Robinson Ms L
Rodgers Mstr D

Rodgers Mrs N
Rodgers Mr W A
Rolands Mr P
Ryan Mr J
Sullivan Mrs M
Todd Mrs I C
Todd Ms I
Wood Mrs P

CTA REP
Daly Mrs M

Flight B
Armstrong Mrs L
Baldock Ms M K
Baldwin Mrs S
Bankes Rev G Y
Bankes Ms M T
Baker Mr G A
Barnett Mrs J A
Barrett Rev N
Barrett Ms E
Bean Ms H
Bentley Ms J
Bickerstaffe Mgr A E
Booth Mrs A
Borg Mrs N T
Boyes Mr D M
Bryan Mr A
Bryan Mrs A
Burrage Mrs M S
Burtwhistle Mrs N
Carey Mrs E
Carey Mr J F
Carroll Rev W
Clarke Mr F
Clifton Mrs F
Coady Mrs E J
Cole Mrs M
Conroy Ms E
Cooper Rev G T
Cooper Mrs A M
Cornforth Mrs K
Crowley Rev M
Devlin Mrs J
Devlin Mrs M
Dix Mrs F
Dixon Mrs N
Donnelly Ms V
Farrell Mr P V
Frankland Mrs M
Gilmartin Mr J P
Gilmartin Mrs N
Gilmartin Ms K
Gilmour Mrs N
Graham Mrs E M
Greaves Ms M
Hall Mrs R
Handley Ms A
Harry Mstr J
Hawksworth Rev B
Henry Mrs C

Howe Ms L
Keegan Mrs E A
Kelly Mrs J
Kerins Mrs J
Keirney Ms E
Kirby Ms A
Larkin Ms A L
Leahy Mstr J J
Leahy Mr J V
McFarthing Mrs L
McKeown Mrs C
McManus Mrs M
Martin Mrs A
Moody Mrs A
Moss Mrs F J
Murphy Mr W
Noble Mrs T
Norton Ms A
Norton Rev J
O'Connor Mrs M
O'Connor Rev M
O'Dowd Ms E
Ormesby Mrs M R
Phillipson Mrs A
Pinnegar Mrs R
Pippet Canon C A
Plunkett Rev O
Reeson Mr G H
Reeson Mrs G H
Roberts Mrs R
Rotherham Mrs A
Sands Mrs H
Sands Mr S L
Short Mr C
Spaight Rev D
Swales Ms E
Tempest Mr H N
Thompson Mrs E
Vause Ms M
Walsh Mrs B F
Walsh Dr D K
Ward Mrs M
Welsh Ms B
Williams Ms K
Woods Mrs M D
Woods Mrs C
Woods Mr J
Woolin Mrs M E
Wright Mrs A
Wright Ms R

Sick Pilgrims

Austin Mr D
Carter Mrs E
Das Mr M
Jackson Mrs M
Jackson Baby Andrew
Kirkman Mr C
Langan Mrs L
McCauley Mrs E
McCauley Ms B
Pidd Mrs M

Quinn Mstr M
Roberts Mrs R
Rudderforth Mr H
Spouncer Mrs M
Sykes Mrs L
Varey Mrs E
Wiles Mrs B

CTA REP

Daly Mr T

Hotel Only

Mulholland Mstr J
Mulholland Mrs M
Peters Dr H J
Peters Mrs M G

1978

Bishop John
    Gerard McClean
Carson Canon R
Davern Canon M
Pippet Canon C A
Plunkett V Rev O
Rickaby Canon G T
Barrett Rev N
Cannon Rev J
Carroll Rev W
Coughlan Rev T
Murray Rev M
O'Connor Rev M
Spaight Rev D
Stewart Rev J
Abbs Mrs C
Abbett Mrs K
Adams Mrs M
Adams Mr J
Allinson Ms J
Allinson Mrs E
Austin Mr D
Barry Mr J
Barry Mrs E
Bean Ms H
Bebb Sr E
Black Mrs H
Burnton Mrs A
Bryan Mrs M
Bryan Ms I
Burns Mr J
Burrage Mrs M
Byrne Mrs D
Byrne Mr P T
Byrne Mr M W
Byrne Mrs E
Boyes Dr
Caley Mrs M
Carter Mrs J
Casey Mrs B
Cavaney Ms B
Cavaney Mr J
Cavaney Ms M
Chapman Ms M

Christon Ms M J
Clarke Sr N
Codd Mrs C A
Colligan Mr G
Colligan Mrs E
Cornforth Ms J
Costello Mr T
Costello Ms C
Coxhead Mr A
Craggs Mrs E
Croft Mr T C
Cryer Mrs M
Cullen Ms M
Cuthbert Mrs A
Curran Mrs M
Curran Mr A
Daley Ms M
Dasey Ms J
Dasey Ms M
Davies Mrs P
Dearlove Mrs M
Devlin Mrs J
Devlin Mrs M
Donnelly Ms V
Donnelly Mrs M
Donovan Mrs Z
Duck Mr R
Duck Ms M
Duckney Ms M
Dunne Mr S T
Farrel Mr P V
Frankland Mrs M
Furber Mrs D
Gardner Mrs M
Gerundini Mstr A
Gerundini Mrs
Gilmour Mrs R
George Mrs M
Goodwin Mrs M
Goodwin Mrs B
Gray Mrs M
Greaves Mr J
Greaves Mrs M
Greenwood Mrs M
Greenwood Mrs M
Harrison Mr R
Harrison Mrs I
Harry Mr J
Healey Mrs C
Healey Mr J D
Healy Mrs M
Healy Mr J
Heatley Mrs M
Heelan Sr A
Higgins Ms M
Hodgson Mr C
Hopkins Mrs M
Hornby Mrs M
Hornby Ms C
Hough Ms B M
Hough Mrs M T
Hough Mr W

Housemann Mr G
Jackson Ms
Jackson Ms E
Jamison Mrs B
Jayamanne Dr F
Jayamanne Dr I
Jewitt Mrs H C
Johnston Ms M
Kearney Ms M
Kennedy Mrs M
Kerrins Sr M B
Kerwin Mr W P
Kirland Ms M
Lambert Ms V
Lanny Mrs M
Larry Mrs J
Leahy Mrs I
Leonard Mrs H
Lloyd Mrs M
Lohan Mr E J
Lovell Mr M
Maughan Ms C
Magor Sr R
Mallon Mr T
Mallon Mstr J
Mallon Mrs M
Melling Mrs C
Miller Mrs M
Moody Mrs A
Moran Mrs M V
Moran Mstr P J
Moran Ms H M
Morris Mrs W
Mothersill Mrs M
Moverley Ms O
Mulroy Mstr M
Mulroy Mrs J
Murphy Mr W
Murray Mrs
McAllister Ms C
McAllister Mstr P
McBride Mr G J
McClury Mrs R
McElhatton Ms
McGeary Mr P
McGee Mr R
McGeown Mr J
McGeown Mrs G
McGowran Mr
McGrother Ms S
McGrother Mrs E
McGurn Mr J
McNeill Mrs M
McNeill Mrs M J
McPartland Mr F
McQuade Mrs N
McRae Mrs C
Newham Mr G
Nicholson Mr J
Noble Mrs T
O'Connor Mrs V
O'Connor Mrs

Patrick Mr
Paul Ms J
Phillipson Mrs A
Pieper Mrs M
Prior Mrs A
Prior Mrs R
Prior Sr M
Pritchard Mrs F
Proudler Mrs R
Raw Ms M
Rose Mrs M
Sellers Mr J
Sellers Mrs L
Smiles Mr J
Smith Mrs D
Squire Ms E
Stead Ms M C
Steels Mrs B
Stephenson Mrs A
Stewart Mrs C
Suddaby Mrs P A
Swaine Mr
Taylor Mrs W
Taylor Ms E
Taylor Mstr R
Tempest Mr H
Tiernann Mrs K
Tierney Mrs T
Tierney Mr J
Traynor Mrs K
Tucker Mrs J
Wadsworth Ms S
Walsh Dr D
Walsh Mrs B
Ward Mr T
Ward Mrs M
Warwick Mrs R
Warren Ms A
Waterson Mr T
Wenes Ms E E
Whelan Ms M
Wilkinson Mr J
Wilkinson Mrs T
Williams Mrs T
Wilson Mrs
Wilson Mr
Wood Ms E
Wray Mrs M
Wright Ms E
Young Mrs E
Zuk Mrs M

Sick Pilgrims
Benbow Mrs Y L
Cannell Mrs V
Cassidy Ms F
Connor Mstr A D
Coupland Mrs M
Craig Mr T
Cummins Mrs E
Cummins Ms J E
Davidson Ms J A

Dearlove Mr J G
Drayton Mrs A M
Drayton Mr H
Finn Mrs N
Gray Mr A F
Hartley Mr E
Hartley Mrs B
Hodgson Mrs M B
Jackson Mrs M
Jackson Mstr A
Kenny Mrs A
Kirby Mr R
Kirkham Mr C F
Larry Ms A
Lohan Mrs M
Loughlin Mr J
Loughrane Mstr A
Loughrane Mrs E
Manders Mrs C
Marshall Mstr S
Marshall Mrs T
Martin Mr J
Norris Mrs N
McAvoy Mr F
McBridge Mrs M
McDonagh Mstr M
McDonagh Mr J
O'Brien Mrs E
O'Brien Ms M
McGowan Mstr S
McGowan Mr K
Patterson Mrs N
Rhoden Mr D
Shepherd Mstr M
Shepherd Mrs F
Swaine Mrs L
Sykes Mrs L
Symonds Mstr L
Symonds Mrs D

1979
Bishop Augustine Harris
Pippet Canon C A
Plunkett Canon O
Rickaby Canon G T
Ryan Canon D
Barratt Rev N
Bickerstaffe Rev A E
Kerwick Rev P J
Murray Rev M
Nicholson Rev B
O'Donnell Rev S I
Rice Rev
Speight Rev D
Allen Mrs R
Allen Mrs P
Anderson Ms N
Atkinson Mstr J J
Atkinson Mrs L
Barry Mrs E
Barry Mr J
Bean Ms H

Bell Mrs D
Bielby Mrs J
Bird Mrs E
Booth Ms F
Booth Mrs A
Borzumato Mrs
Borzuamto Ms M
Boyes Mr D M
Boyes Mr D W
Brannen Ms M
Bright Ms B
Broadbent Mrs M
Brough Ms H
Brough Mr D J
Bryan Mr A
Bryan Ms T M
Carey Mrs M
Casimer Sr M
Clarke Mr T
Close Mrs M
Colligan Mr G
Colligan Mrs E
Cornerford Sr E
Cope Mrs
Coxhead Mr A J
Cunleen Ms A
Cunleen Ms H
Cunleen Mrs J
Daly Mr
Darling Mrs A
Dasey Ms J F
Dasey Ms M M
Doherty Mrs M
Dolby Mrs I
Donnelly Sr C
Donohoe Ms M
Duell Ms A
Duggan Mrs I
Durkin Ms C
Durkin Mrs G
Durkin Mr J
Edwards Ms P
Edwards Mrs W
Edwards Mr A
Ferguson Ms N
Flanigan Mrs M
Flannigan Mrs M
Flynn Mrs G
Gilmour Mrs N
Gray Mrs M
Grindley Mr T
Guy Ms L
Hainsworth Mrs W
Harrison Mrs I
Harrison Mr R
Harrison Mrs E
Harry Mr
Hawksworth Mrs W
Hawksworth Mr J
Hetherington Mrs F C
Hodgson Mrs D E
Hornby Mrs M

Hornby Ms C
Housemann Mr G
Johansson Mr C A
Johnson Mrs J
Jones Mrs A
Jones Mrs U N
Jordan Mr F
Jordan Mrs E
Kaiser Ms E A
Kearney Ms M
Keeley Mrs M
Kelly Mrs P
Kelly Mrs M
Kennedy Mrs M
Kerby Ms A
Kosina Mrs K
Lake Mrs K
Langham Mrs S M
Langley Mr C
Lanny Mrs M
Loftus Mrs K
Lovell Mr G
Maher Sr J
Matthews Mrs A
Matthews Mrs B
Matthews Mstr K
Maughan Ms C
Maughan Mrs M
Maughan Ms V N
Metcalfe Mrs E
Metcalfe Mr G V
Miller Mrs M
Murphy Mr W
Murray Mrs E
McCabe Sr A N
McDonald Mrs M
McDonnell Mrs K
McDonnell Mrs A
McDonough Mrs E
McDonough Mrs A
McElhatton Ms E
McElhatton Ms C
McGee Ms E
McGowan Ms T
McGowan Mr B
McGrath Mrs M
McKenna Ms B
McKenna Ms S
McLean Mr P
McRae Mrs C
Nendick Mrs M
Noble Mrs T
O'Brien Mrs F
O'Donnell Mrs A
O'Neill Mrs J
Pascua Mrs M M
Pattison Mrs M
Plunkett Ms M
Plunkett Mrs M A
Prior Ms R
Proffitt Mrs M
Proffitt Ms T

Proffitt Mrs E
Proffitt Ms E
Proudler Mrs R
Raw Ms P
Readman Mrs K
Readman Mr A
Readman Mrs H
Reed Mrs E
Rice Ms M
Rice Ms J
Ritchardson Mrs A
Robertson Ms E
Rowcliffe Mrs M
Rowcliffe Mr L
Rumak Mrs M
Scarth Mrs A
Shane Mrs A
Sherlock Ms M E
Sherrington Mr J A
Shillito Mrs T
Smiles Mr T
Smyth Mrs M
Stead Ms M C
Sullivan Ms C
Summers Ms C
Tarren Mrs V
Taylor Mrs K
Tempest Mr H N
Tiernan Mrs K M
Tooley Mr G W
Tooley Mrs S
Traecy Mr D
Traecy Ms M
Traecy Mrs K
Trees Mrs D
Villa Ms M D
Villa Mrs M
Walsh Mrs B
Warren Ms A
Warwick Mrs R
Waterson Mr T
Watts Mr J r
Watts Mrs S
Welsh Mrs M
Westwater Mrs M
Whelan Ms M
Wood Ms E A
Wright Ms E M
Young Ms R C

Sick Pilgrims
Allum Mrs M E
Austin Mr D
Benbow Mrs Y
Bielby Mrs J
Bielby Ms P
Bird Ms S
Conway Mr A A
Craig Mr T
Chambers Mrs B V
Cummins Mrs E
Cummins Ms J

Dewse Mrs P A
Everitt Mrs A V
Gaines Mr J
Gaines Mrs M
Gaines Ms L
Grindley Mr C
Guy Mrs E
Hanratty Mr J
Harkin Mrs K
Jones Ms M M
Jones Mr A
Kelly Mr G
Lake Mr B
Lavin Mr J P
Lawrie Ms I
McGill Mrs D
Moore Mrs C
Morris Mrs N
Murphy Mr J
Murphy Mstr J
Nicholson Mr G
O'Connor Mrs E
O'Neill Mr P
Oliver Mrs K
Parker Mrs O
Patterson Mrs N
Peterson Mrs G
Relph Mrs H
Tate Mrs D
Toker Ms B
Vaughan Ms J
Welsh Mrs W
Wilde Rev C
Wilkinson Ms M B
Wren Mrs A
Wyatt Mr E

1980
Bishop Augustine Harris
Rickaby Canon G T
Abbs Mrs C
Adams Mr J A
Adams Mrs M A
Akeroyd Mrs I
Arbuckle Mrs M
Atkinson Mrs A
Atkinson Mr J D
Atkinson Mrs O
Avery Miss M H
Baker Mrs I
Barker Mrs C L
Barker Mr R L
Barron Mrs M S
Baxter Miss M
Bean Miss H
Boyes Mr D M
Boyes Mr D W
Boyes Miss E M
Boyes Mstr M
Boyes Mrs H B
Boyes Mr M G
Boyes Mrs R C

Boyes Dr W
Bright Miss B A
Brough Mr D J
Brown Mrs R
Bryan Mr A
Bryan Miss I M
Burns Mr G A
Burns Mrs M
Burrage Mrs M S P
Busby Miss M E
Byrnes Miss A N
Cameron Miss E
Chaplin Mrs P
Clark Mrs V
Coombe Mrs H
Conley Mrs D
Conley Mr D
Connors Miss M M
Conway Mrs A
Coxhead Mr A J
Craggs Mrs E
Cronin Mrs A E
Cronin Mr G
Dasey Miss J F
Dasey Miss M
Dawson Mrs M
Duggan Mr J
Duggan Mrs M M
Duke Miss M C
Dunne Mr J
Donoghue Mr W
Douglas Miss E
Dowling Mrs H
Elgey Mrs M
Elwell Sr C
Fenwick Mrs M
Flaherty Mrs M
Finn Mrs J
Finn Mr J T
Gibson Mrs M T
Gibson Miss T A
Gilligan Mrs M
Gilligan Mr T
Gilmour Mrs M
Ginty Mrs B
Greaves Mr J
Creaves Mrs M
Green Mrs R M
Hanton Mrs S M
Harrison Mrs C H
Harrison Mrs I
Harrison Mr R
Harry Mr J
Higgins Mrs T
Hilton Mr S
Hobson Mr M C
Hodgson Mr G C
Holmes Mrs E M
Hoolahan Sr E
Hornby Miss K
Hornby Mrs M
Horn Mr J R

Hutchinson Mrs E
Hutchinson Miss J
Hunt Mrs M
Hunt Mrs V
Jackson Miss M
Jones Hr D
Jones Mr D P
Jones Mrs V N
Kane Mrs P M
Kane Miss S M
Kilmartin Mrs J F
Langan Mrs L
Langan Mrs L
Laird Mrs J M
Lanny Mrs M
Leahy Mrs I
Lee Mrs G L
Leedham Mrs E M
Lester Mstr J
Lloyd Hr K
Lloyd Mrs M
Lovell Mrs G
Lovell Mr L
Lovell Mr M G
Lynch Mrs F E
Macdonald Mrs N M
Martin Mrs E
Maughan
Mcallister Miss M B
McDermott Mrs M
McDonald Mrs H M
McDonnell Miss E
McCory Miss M
McElhatton Miss C
McElhatton Miss E
McGee Mr R
McGouch Miss C M
McGowran Mr B
McGowran
McKenna Mrs A
McKlenna Mr G
McMahon
McMahon Miss M
McNeil Mrs K
McCrae Mrs C
Murphy Hr W
Mcveich Miss B
Mellinc Mrs C
Metcalfe Mr G V
Murray Rev M
Nicholson Rev B A
Noble Mrs T
Norman Mrs E
Noman Miss E M
Norton Miss A
Norman Mr T P
O'Brien Mrs L
O'Brien Mstr M
O'Brien Mrs W
Organ Mr. D H
Payne Mr J
Payne Mrs T

Pawson Mr D
Pawson Mr J
Peters Dr H J
Peters Mrs M G
Pieper Mrs M
Pieper Mrs S
Pippet Canon C A
Plunkett Canon E
Raw Miss M M
Rawcliffe Mrs E
Rawe Mrs M C
Rawson Mr P
Redican Sr E M
Ruddick Miss E A
Ruddick Mr M E
Ruddick Mrs W K
Richardson Mrs E M
Shakesby Mrs J
Shane Mrs A
Shaw Mr T W
Sloan Miss M E
Singleton Miss M
Smiles Mr J J
Spaight Rev D
Stead Miss M C
Squire Miss E
Tempest Mr N
Thompson Mrs G
Tiernan Mrs K M
Tray Miss C
Troupe Mrs M
Turner Mr P
Urch Mr J
Van Der Heijden Miss B
Waland Mrs A E
Ward Mr T
Warren Miss A
Waterson Mr T
Weir Miss J F M
Welch Mrs R
White Mr M W
White Mrs M
White Mrs P M
Wilson Mrs A
Woodworth Mrs M
Wright Miss E M
Wyatt Mrs E
Young Mrs M E
Young Mr J N

Sick Pilgrims
Aaron Mr J
Bennet Miss J
Boddy Miss E
Cail Mrs K
Christie Mrs B
Christie Miss L M
Dargue Mrs E
Das Mr M
Davies Mrs K
Dodsworth Mrs C
Donoghue Mstr S

Flynn Mrs J
Fullerton Mrs O M
Fullerton Mr T H
Hancock Mrs B
Hanratty Mr J
Hutchfield Miss S
Jones Miss M
Joyce Mr P
Keegan Mrs F

1981
Bishop Augustine Harris
Adams Mr J A
Adams Mrs M P
Adams Mr A F
Alexander Mrs M
Anthony Mrs A
Atkin-Train Mrs T
Austin Mr D
Barker Mrs M
Barry Mrs A
Bassett Miss F
Bean Miss H
Bebb Sr E.
Beevers Mrs L
Bell Mr R S
Bell Mrs M
Bennett Mrs A
Bickerstaff Mgr A
Boyes Mr D M
Boyes Mrs R C
Boyes Dr W
Boyes Mrs M B
Boyes Mr D W
Boyes Mr N
Boyes Mstr M J
Boyes Mrs M
Bradford Mrs J
Bright Mrs F
Brine Mrs A P
Brough Mr D J
Bryan Miss I M
Brennan Rev J
Brown Mrs R
Bryan Mr A
Burns Mrs P
Burns Mrs M
Burns Mr G
Burns Mrs M
Burdon Miss R M
Byrnes Miss A
Byrne Mrs O
Byrne Miss S
Callow Mrs I
Casey Mr H G
Casey Mrs C
Christie Mrs B
Christie Miss L
Clark Mr A
Clark Mrs M
Clark Mr L
Clark Mrs V

Cockerill Mr A
Conley Mr D
Conley Mrs J
Conway Mrs A
Coughlan Mrs J
Coyle Miss V
Coxhead Mr A J
Craggs Mrs B
Crotty Miss M R
Crinion Mr C
Dalby Mrs E
Daniels Miss M
Das Mr M
Dasey Miss M
Dasey Miss J
Delafosse Sr J
Dean Mrs A
Denny Mrs M
Denny Miss E
Dodd Mrs D C
Donoghue Mr T
Donoghue Mr W.
Donovan Mrs Z
Douglas Miss E
Doyle Mr P
Doyle Miss M
Doyle Miss M
Durkin Miss D
Dunne Mr P
Falvey Miss M M
Fawcett Mrs M
Fitzgerald Mrs M J
Finn Mrs J
Finn Mr J T
Forgan Miss R
Fox Mrs P A
Fox Mstr F A
Frost Mrs F
Gallagher Miss B
Gallagher Mrs M
Gallagher Miss E
Gerundini Mstr A
Gilligan Mr T
Gilligan Mrs M
Gilmour Mrs N
Gormer Mrs V
Graham Mrs S B
Grant Mr P
Green Mrs M
Hall Mrs J.
Harding Miss P
Harry Mr J
Hammill Miss. R
Hanson Mr S. J
Harrison Mrs M M
Heward Miss F D
Hewison Miss A M
Higgins Mrs T
Hill Mrs S A
Hinds Miss S B
Hickney Mrs P
Holmes Mrs E M

Horn Mrs J
Horn Mr J R
Hornby Mrs M
Houseman Mr G E
Hudson Mr L E
Hunt Mr J R
Hurry Mrs J
Jackson Miss N
Jones Mrs M
Jones Mr D P
Jones Mrs V N
Jones Mr P G
Jones Mr D
Kilkelly Sr P
Kilmartin Mrs J
Laden Mr G
Langan Mrs L
Lanny Mrs M
Langham Mrs S M
Laville Mr T
Laville Mrs K
Leahy Mrs I
Leahy Mr J
Lickiss Mrs M A
Livesey Mrs K
Lloyd Mrs M
Lloyd Mr K
Lovell Mr K S
Lovell Mr L
Lovell Mrs G
Lydon Miss D
Lyth Mrs F
Maidment Mrs S D
Mann Miss B
Marlow Mrs C L
Metcalfe Mr G
Metcalfe Mrs E
Moon Mrs E
Mothersill Mrs M
Murral Mrs K
Murrall Mstr K
Murphy Mr J F
Murphy Mstr J
Murphy Mrs A
Murphy Mrs N
Myres Mrs G
McCart Mrs M
McDermott Mrs M C
McDermott Mr W
McDermott Mrs .E
McDonough Mrs
McDonald Miss K
McElvaney Mr D
McElvaney Mrs E
McGeary Mrs P
McGeary Mr D J
McGee Miss E
McGee Mrs M
McGee Mr R T
McGowan Miss T
McGowran Mr B
McGurn Mrs M

McKenna Mr G
McKenna Mstr S
McMorris Mrs M
McRae Mrs C
McVeigh Miss M
Naughton-Doe Mrs M
Newlove Mr L A
Newsam Mrs H
Nicholson Rev B
Noble Mrs T
Nutbrown Mr A
Nutbrown Mrs J
Nutbrown Mstr S
Owen Mrs M W
Oysten Mrs M
O'Brien Mrs W
O' Connor Rev M
O'Driscoll Mrs M
O'Mahony Rev J
Paul Miss J M
Pentland Mrs G E
Peters Dr H
Peters Mrs M
Pickering Mrs A
Pieper Mrs M
Pippett Canon C
Proctor Mrs M
Raw Miss M M
Raw Miss S
Rawson Mr P
Regan Miss S
Rhea Mrs M H
Ribeiro Dr A
Rossi Mrs I
Rowlands Mr W
Rowlands Mrs V
Rowlands Mrs C
Scarth Mrs A
Shane Mrs A
Shea Mrs M
Smith Miss C
Smiles Mr J
Southall Mrs A
Spaight Rev D
Squire Miss E
Stead Miss M C.
Stonehouse Mrs B A
Stonehouse Miss S M
Sykes Mr W
Tasker Mr A J
Tasker Mrs M
Tattersfield Mrs M
Taylor Mrs K
Tobim Sr M
Topliss Mrs V
Toth Mrs N
Toth Miss J
Tims Mrs R A
Turner Mr P
Urch Mr J
Vallely Mr F
Wallace Mrs M I

Walsh Miss M
Ward Mr T
Warren Miss A M
Waterson Mr T
Weir Miss J
Wharton Mr F W
Wharton Mrs R
Williams Mrs M
Wimpress Mrs M
Wray Mrs E
Wright Mrs A M
Wright Miss E M
Wright Mrs E
Wright Mrs M
Wright Miss S
Wrightson Mrs B A
Young Mrs M E

Sick Pilgrims

Barry Mr E
Bennett Mr G
Bryan Mr S
Cockerill Mr G
Donaghue Mstr S
Echlin Mr J
Echlin Mr T
Fawcett Mstr A
Glynn Rev E
Hanratty Mr J
Hewitt Mr J
Hurry Mr C
Kennedy Mr M
Mann Mr M
Moffatte Mr E
Myers Mr S
Smyth Mr W
Southall Mr P
Wright Mr J
Gillyon Mr E
Ashton Mrs E
Baron Mrs M
Doyle Miss E
Callo Miss E
Chandler Mrs C
Davies Mrs K
Davis Miss J
Fawcett Mrs P
Fisher Miss W
Hudson Mrs M
Hughes Mrs A
Jenkinson Mrs M
Jones Ms M
Miller Mrs A
Mullholland Mrs F
McGuiness Mrs A
Newsam Miss C
O'Connor Mrs M
Smyth Mrs K
Sterricker Miss P
Spence Miss P

1982

Bishop Augustine Harris
Adams Mr A E
Adams Mr J A
Adams Mrs M P
Agius Miss M R
Askins Miss A
Austin Mr D
Barker Mrs M T
Barry Mr J
Barry Mrs E
Bates Mrs M
Boyes Mrs E
Boyes Mr D W
Boyes Mr D
Boyes Mrs
Boyes Mr M G
Boyes Mstr M J
Boyes Dr W
Boyes Mrs M B
Bradford Mrs J
Brennan Rev J A
Bright Miss B A
Brough D
Burke Miss M
Burrage Mrs M S P
Burns Mr A
Busby Miss M E
Burns Miss A M
Cannon Mrs N D
Carroll Rt Rev W
Clark Mr L
Clark Mrs V S
Clark Miss A M
Clarke Mr F
Christie Mrs B
Christie Miss L
Charlton Rt Rev J R
Codd Mrs E A
Coles Miss B A
Collins Mrs D
Coltman Mrs D
Compton-Allenby Mrs
Conley Mr D
Conley Mrs J
Corr Miss A
Coxhead Mr A J
Curtis Mr J P
Dasey Miss M M
Dasey Miss J F
Davis Mrs A E
Dawkins Mr S
De Groot Mrs A
Dillon Mrs E
Dixon Mrs D
Dixon Mstr P
Dixon Miss M
Dodd Mrs D C
Dodds Mr W H
Donoghue Mr T
Donoghue Mr W
Dowling Mrs M
Dunne Mr P

Field Mr D W
Firth Mrs M
Fiske Mr E
Fiske Mrs E
Flanagan Miss R M
Gallagher Miss B
Gamesby Mrs P
Gardner Mr G
Gardner Mrs L
Gibson Mrs J M
Gilligan Mr T
Gilligan Mrs
Giurbrelli Miss J
Grange Mrs J T
Griffiths Mrs T
Griffiths Miss C
Gunn Mr F
Hackett Mrs W Hardgrave
Mr L S
Hardgrave Miss M E
Harkin Mr T
Harkin Mrs C
Heward Miss F D
Hewait-Jaboor Dr E
Hewait-Jaboor Mrs S
Hornby Mrs M
Horne Mr R
Hughes Mrs A
Hurry Mrs J A
Igoe Mrs C
Jackson Miss M W
Jamison Mrs T
Killgallon Mrs P M
Kilmartin Mrs J F
Kosina Miss G M
Laird Mrs J
Lane Mr L
Lane Mrs D
Langan Mrs L
Lanny Mrs M
Lawrence Mrs E
Loughlin Miss C A
Lovell M
Lovell Mr L
Lovell Mrs G
Leahy Mr J
Leahy Mrs I
Lloyd Mr K
Lloyd Mrs M
O'Brien Mrs M
O'Brien Mr W J
O'Brien Mrs M
O'Brien Miss W
Olencewicz Mr R
Oliver Mrs W
Oyston Mrs M
Machin Mr C
Mackie Mrs J
Madden Rev W C
Mannix Mr J K
Mannix Mr T B
Mannix Mrs A

Mannix Miss S
Marshall Mrs E M
Martin Miss N
Maughan Mr H
Maughan Miss C
McCarthy Mrs M E
McCarthy Mrs M M
McDonnell Sr M
McDonough Mrs A
McElavaney Mr D
McElvaney Mrs K
McGee Mr A
McGee Miss E
McGee Mrs M
McGee Mr R
McGee Mr S
McGlade Mrs M
McGowran Mr B K
McGowran Miss J
McKenna Mrs N
McKenna Miss S
McRae Mrs C
McVeigh Miss R M
Melling Mrs C
Metcalfe Mr G V
Moran Mr K
Mulligan Miss M
Murray Rev N
Narey Miss C B
Nicholson Rev B
Pearson Mrs L
Pease Mrs M
Petrie Mrs P
Phillips Mrs L
Power Mr F M
Power Miss C C
Power Miss R M
Power-Jepson Mrs J
Raw Miss M M
Raw Miss S M
Rawson Mr P
Reilly Mrs B
Reilly Mr J
Reilly Mr P
Robinson Mrs A
Rossi Mrs T
Rushworth Mrs L
Searson Mrs M
Shea Mrs M
Spaight Rev D
Speirs Miss H M S
Squire Miss E
Stead Miss M C
Stevenson Mrs M
Stevenson Miss G
Sykes Mr W
Thomas Mr R
Thomas Mrs K
Tourney Mrs V
Urch Miss B M
Urch J
Yale Mrs L

Young Miss E
Wallace Mrs M I
Walkers Mrs E A
Ward Mr T
Warren Miss A
Waterson T
Weir Miss J F M
Willingham Miss A M
Wood Mr A W
Wood Mrs V
Wood Mstr A
Wood Mstr P
Woods Miss P
Wooton Mr I H W
Wright Miss B
Wright Miss E M
Wright Mr T
Wright Miss E
Wright Miss C
Wrightson Mrs A

CTA REP

Bassadone Mr R

Sick Pilgrims

Allison Miss J
Askham Mrs M
Askam Mrs M
Avery Mr R
Barrow Mrs M
Cannon Miss A
Capraro Mrs N
Caparo Mrs P
Casey Miss P
Cockerline Mrs L
Crisp Miss H
Dale Mrs A
Daley Mrs K
Davies Mrs K
Davis Mr J
Dean Mrs V
Donaghue Mstr S
Echlin Mr T
Echlin Mr J
Fearon Mrs M
Gleeson Miss E
Glew Mrs C
Grace Mstr D
Hewitt Mr T
Hornsby Mrs M
Horton Mr G
Hughes Mrs A
Hurry Mr C
Jackson Miss A
Jowers Miss D
Knight Miss G
Mann Mr M
Martin Mr J
Meighan Mr G
Melton Mrs E
Moylett Mrs C

Murphy Mr P
McBain Mrs V
McCullough Mrs
McGarrity Mr J
McIntyre Mr J
Olecewicz Mrs M
Padgett Mr H
Rodgers Mstr D
Rogers Mr A B
Russell Mrs T
Southall Mr P
Speirs Miss D
Speirs Mrs S
Sykes Mrs L

1983

Bishop Kevin O'Brien
Adams Mr A E
Adams Mr J A
Adams Mrs M P
Asquith Mrs P
Atkinson Mr W R
Bainbridge Mrs P
Ballie Mrs P
Baker Mr J
Barnes Ms M
Barry Mrs E
Barry Mr J
Bickerstaffe Mgr A
Boland Miss M
Booth Mr A R
Booth Mrs H
Boyes Mrs E M
Boyes Mr D M
Boyes Mr D W
Boyes Mrs M B
Boyes Mr M G
Boyes Mstr M J
Boyes Mrs R C
Boyes Dr W
Busby Miss M E M
Brennan Miss D
Brennan Mrs P
Bradford Mrs J
Bradford Miss N
Brankley Miss I
Brough Mr D J
Bryan Mr A
Christie Mrs B
Christie Miss L
Clark Miss A M
Clark Mr L
Clark Mrs V S
Codd Mrs E
Conley Mr D
Conley Mrs J
Connorton Mrs M M
Cooper Miss L E
Cooper Miss S E
Coulton Sr A
Coxhead Mr A J
Coyle Miss W

Crotty Miss M R
Cuff Mrs B
Daniels Miss M
Danis Mrs F D
Dasey Miss J F
Dasey Miss M M
Deehan Miss C T
Delaney Mstr J
Delaney Mrs V
Dent Miss L
Dewhurst Mr A C
Dick Mrs I
Docherty Rev V
Doherty Dr J C
Doherty Mstr S
Donnelly Mrs M
Doto Miss A M
Dunne Mr P
Dunn Mrs M M
Durnan Miss C
Fawcett Mrs E
Fawgon Miss R
Fidler Mrs S
Finn Mrs J
Flint Mstr M
Flint Mrs R
Ford Mr A E
Ford Mrs P M
Fox Mr M V
Gallagher Miss J M
Gamesby Mrs P
Gaynor Mr E
Gaynor Mrs M
Gilligan Miss C T
Gillican Mrs M B
Gilligan Mr T
Goggins Ms W
Golding Mrs J A
Grace Mstr D
Grace Mr H
Hardgrave Mr L S
Hardgrave Miss M E
Harrison Mrs M M
Harry Mr J
Hatfield Miss C
Hemminoway Sr A
Heward Miss D
Hewat-Jaboor Mrs S
Hornby Mrs M
Howes Mrs A
Hudson Mr L E
Hutchinson Miss S
Igoe Mr M
Jackson Mrs F M
Jackson Miss M W
James Miss S C
Kendall Miss A M
Kilmartin Mrs J F
Kosina Miss G M
Labonte Mr G S
Larry Mrs M
Leahy Mrs I

Leahy Mr J V
Leo Mrs M E
Leonard Sr J
Lonsdale Mrs M E
Lovell Mrs G
Lovell Mr L
Lovell Mr M G
Maher Sr C
Mallinson Mr H W
Mallinson Mrs M K
Martin Miss S
Matthews Mrs B
Matthews Mr K
Maycock Miss P
Metcalfe Mr G V
Molloy Mrs D
Moyle Mrs M H
Murphy Mr W
Murray Mrs D
Murray Rev M
McCarthy Mrs M
McDonald Mrs E
McDonald Mr G E
McDonald Mrs P
McDonough Mrs A
McGee Miss S E
McGowran Mr B K
McGowran Miss J L
McGuinness Mrs R
McGuinness Miss R
McKenna Mrs A
McKenna Miss S
McMahon Mrs K
McMahon Mr R
McRae Mrs C
NcVeigh Miss B
Neilan Miss M T
Nelson Mr F G
Nicol Mrs A E
Nicol Mr D A
Nicholson Rev B N
Oyston Mrs M
O'Brien Miss W
O'Connor Mrs B
Park Mstr A
Park Mrs H
Petford Mrs M
Phillips Mrs L
Pierre Miss A M
Power-Jepson Mrs J
Power Mr F M
Quinn Sr L
Raw Miss M M
Raw Miss S M
Ridgeway Mr A
Rhodes Mrs T R
Roe Mrs J
Rossi Mrs T
Rudge Mrs N
Ryan Dr W M J
Simpson Miss S E
Smiles Mr J

Smith Miss C A
Smith Mrs J
Spaight Rev D
Speirs Miss H
Speirs Mrs S
Squire Miss E
Stead Miss M C
Stead Miss M E
Stewart Mrs M
Swallow Mrs 0
Swallow Mr W
Sykes Mr W
Sullivan Mrs J
Thompson Mrs B
Urch Miss B U
Urch Mr J
Vallely Mr F R
Ward Mr T
Warren Miss A M
Waterson Mr T
Weir Miss J
Westerman Mr A
Westerman Mrs M
Whitehurst Mrs M
Wilson Miss M
Wood Mstr A
Wood Mr A W
Wood Mstr P
Wood Mrs V
Wright Miss E
Wright Miss E M
Wright Mr T
Yale Mrs L

CTA Reps
Bassadoni Mr R
Bassadoni Miss J

Sick Pilgrims
Auko Mrs W
Bilton Mrs B
Booth Mrs K S
Brown Mrs C
Cassidy Mr J F
Cawthraw Mrs F
Cochrane Mrs E
Crutchley Mr R
Dixon Mrs D S
Donnelly Mr J
Donohue Mrs N
Drury Mrs M C
Echlin Mr J
Echlin Mr T
Fawcett Mstr A
Fawcett Mrs P
Gibson Mrs M
Golding Mstrer J P
Golding Miss P
Goldner Mrs W
Gowland Mr F
Hanson Mrs S
Hall Mr A

Hartley Mrs B A
Hartley Mr E
Hodgson Mr C A
Honeyman Mrs M
Horton Mr G
Hudson Mrs M B
HughesMstr A
Hughes Mrs J
Hutchinson Mrs R
Hutchinson Miss S R
Mann Mr M
Martin Mr J
Mee Mstr P M
Meehan Mr B
Metcalf Mrs G
Murphy Mr C P
McGuinness Mrs A
Osborne Mstr B
Osborne Mrs C
O'Neill Mrs E
Parnell Mrs H
Petford Mr J C
Raynor Mrs M A
Ralph Miss K
Shell Mrs S
Smith Mr B
Smith Mr D J
Swales Mrs B
Swales Mstr E
Swales Mstr J
Swalwell Mrs A
Swalwell Mstr W
Speirs Miss D
Stephenson Mr G
Symonds Mrs M E
Todd Miss I C
Usmar Mr N P
Voase Mrs J A
Whalley Mrs P
Whalley Mstr G P
Young Miss C A
Young Mrs L

1984
Bishop Kevin O'Brien
Adams Mr A E
Adams Mr J A
Adams Mrs M P
Addyman Mrs E J
Armitage Mr H
Armitage Mrs S
Arnold Mrs I
Askins Mr J
Askins Mr P J
Asquith Miss P
Atkinson Mrs B
Bain Mr C
Bainbridge Mrs P
Banks Mrs R
Barnes Ms M
Bartley Ms C
Bartley Ms N

Bluett Rev P A
Boland Miss M
Bollands Mrs M C
Booth Mr A R
Booth Mrs H
Booth Mrs K S
Boyes Dr W
Boyes Mr D M
Boyes Mr D W
Boyes Mr M G
Boyes Mrs E M
Boyes Mrs M B
Boyes Mstr M J
Bradbury Miss A T
Bradford Miss S
Bradford Mr G
Bradford Mrs J
Braithwaite Mrs M
Brankley Miss I
Broadbent Mrs A
Brough Mr D J
Brown Mrs R
Bruton Mrs P
Bryan Mr A
Bryan Mrs A
Burns Mr A
Burns Mrs A
Burrage Mrs M S P
Carmichael Mrs K
Carroll Mrs O M
Christie Miss E
Christie Miss L
Christie Mrs B
Clark Mr L
Clark Mrs L
Clayton Mrs A
Clutton Mrs J
Codd Mr C
Codd Mrs E
Collins Mrs P M
Coning Mr C
Conley Mr D
Conley Mrs J
Conway Mrs A
Cooper Mrs E
Cornforth Mr J
Cornforth Mrs M
Coxhead Mr A J
Crotty Miss M R
Cuthbert Miss J
Daley Mr F
Daley Mrs F
Danis Mrs F D D
Dasey Miss J F
Dasey Miss M M
Deehan Miss C T
Deehan Mrs H M
Dewhurst Mr A
Dillon Mrs M P
Dingwall Mrs F M
Dodd Mrs D C
Doherty Dr J C

Doherty Mstr S M
Donnelly Mrs M
Donoghue Mr M
Donoghue Mr T
Douglas Miss E
Dowling Mrs M
Dunne Mr P
Dunne Mr S
Dunne Mr T
Fake Mr G H
Fake Mrs E T
Fawcett Mrs E
Finn Mrs J
Fitzgerald Mrs D
Flannighan Miss R M
Flynn Mr M
Ford Mr A F.
Ford Mrs P M
Forsyth Miss J M
Fox Mr M V
France Mrs E M
French Mrs J S
Gamesby Mrs P
Gibson Mrs S
Gilhooley Mrs M M
Gilligan Mr T
Gilligan Mrs M B
Gilmour Mrs M B
Gilmour Mrs N
Goggins Ms W
Grace Mr H
Grace Mst D
Gray Mrs J
Greenan Miss M
Greenan Mrs W
Greenheld Mrs K
Griffths C
Griffths Mr D
Griffths Mrs T
Hardgrave Miss M
Hardgrave Mr L S
Henderson Mrs D M
Heward Miss F D
Higgins Mrs T
Hold Mr J E
Horn Mr J R
Horn Mrs K A
Hornby Mrs M
Hunt Mrs J
Hunter Mrs M
Jackson Miss W M
James Ms S C
Johnson Miss K
Jones Mrs P
Kearney Miss M E
Kearns Sr J
Keenan Mr W J
Kelly Mrs M
Kilmartin Mrs J
Kirby Miss A
Kosina Mrs K
Lacey Mrs M

Lane Mr L
Lanny Mrs M
Larkin Mrs M
Leahy Mr J V
Leahy Mrs I
Leonard Sr J
Little Mr K
Loveell Mr L
Lovell Mr M G
Lovell Mrs G
Lyth Mr W J
Machin Mrs C
Madden Rev N
Marlow Mrs C L
Marriott Mr A
Matthews Mr K
Maughan Miss C
McCallister Miss N
McCann Mr J
McCann Mrs J
McCarthy Mrs M
McDonald Mr G E
McDonald Mrs E
McDonald Mrs P
McDonough Mrs A
McGeary Mr P
McGeary Mrs P
McGee Mr R
McGee Mrs S
McGowran Mr B K
McIntyre Mrs A
McKenna Miss S
McKenna Mrs A
McNamara Mr T W
McNamara Mrs B A
McRae Mrs C
McVeigh Miss S
Mennrell Mr F
Mennell Mrs A
Metcalf Mr G V
Mitchell Mrs M T
Morgan Miss T A
Moxon Mr E
Moxon Mrs M
Murphy Mr C P
Murphy Mrs B M
Murphy Mstr P J
Murray Mrs H
Nelson Miss L C
Nelson Mr F G
Nicholson Rev B
O'Brien Miss W
O'Conner Miss A P
O'Conner Mrs E
O'Connor Mr N P
O'Connor Rev M
O'Dowd Miss M
Overfield Mrs I
Oyston Mrs M
Peaker Mrs M
Petford Mr J C
Phillips Mrs L

Pierre Miss A M
Pierre Mr J
Pierre Mrs M C
Power Mr F M
Power-Jepson Mrs J
Preston Mrs A
Proctor Mr M J
Proctor Mrs G
Rainey Mr J F
Rathbone Mrs L
Raw Miss M M
Raw Miss S M
Rayner Mrs M
Reddy Mrs S
Retallick Mr P E
Retallick Mrs N E
Richardson Mrs A
Riggs Mrs A E
Rodgers Mstr D
Rodgers Mr A B
Roe Miss M J
Roe Mr N F
Roe Mrs T
Russell Mr D
Russell Mrs E L
Ryan Dr W M J
Shakesby Mr M J C
Shakesby Mrs J M
Smith Mrs J
Smith Mstr G
Smith Sr M C
Spaight Rev D
Squire Miss S
Stead Miss M C
Stead Miss M E
Stewart Miss L M
Stewart Mrs M F
Sykes Mr W
Tasker Mr A J
Tasker Mrs M B
Tempest Mr H N
Temple Mrs P
Thompson Mstr M A
Tilly Mrs J
Trodden Mrs M
Tucker Mr D P
Tucker Mr G P
Turnbull Miss N
Turnbull Mrs B
Turnbull Mstr J G
Turner Mrs S E
Urch Miss B M
Urch Mr J
Wade Rev A
Walsh Mrs E S
Ward Mr T
Warren Miss A M
Waterson Mr T
Wears Mrs E
White Mrs M
Williams Mr G H
Williams Mrs K

Willingham Mrs A M
Wilson Miss N
Wood Mr A
Wood Mrs M
Wood Mrs V
Wood Mstr A
Wood Mstr P
Wright Miss A
Wright Miss C
Wright Miss E
Wright Miss E M
Wright Mr T
Wright Mrs E

CTA Reps
Bassadone Mr R
Bassadone Miss J
McNulty Mr B

Ascott Sr M
Bartaby Miss A
Bartaby Mrs M
Bell Miss L J
Bell Mrs G
Bilton Mrs B
Bradley Mrs M
Bride Mr P J
Bryan Mr S
Brynn Mrs M
Bullock Mrs S
Capraro Mrs N
Capraro Mrs P
Cassidy Mr J
Cavanagh Mrs F
Cooper Miss S
Crutchley Mr R
Daly Mrs C
Daniels Mr D
Dent Mrs A
Donnelly Mr J
Gouldner Mrs W
Hagestadt Mrs M
Hanratty Mrs P
Hanson Mr Sean
Hewitt Mr F
Hodgson Mrs M
Hold Mrs M
Horton Mr G
Jennison Mrs K
Jones Mrs B
Knight Miss G
Labonte Mr G
Lacey Mstr S
Lawlor Mrs Y
Little Mrs G
MacFarlane Miss M
Mackinder Mr J
Mann Mr M
Maplethorpe Mr T
Martin Mr J
McCarrick Mrs T
McDonnell Mr W

Mckay Mr J
Nutiall Mrs J
O'Brien Miss M
O'Dea Sr D
O'Dowd Miss E
Palotta Mr D
Pieper Mrs M
Ralph Miss K
Reilly Mr T
Rhoden Mr T
Russell Mrs M
Scanlon Miss H
Shakesby Mstr P
Shakesby Mstr P
Shell Mrs S
Short Mrs E
Siddaway Mrs S
Sired Mrs A
Smith Mr B
Taylor Mr E

1985
Bishop Augustine Harris
Adams Mr A E
Adams Mr J A
Adamsmrs M P
Allen Mrs E
Atkin Miss J
Atkin Mrs G
Banks Mrs R
Barker Mrs D
Barry Mr J
Barry Mrs E
Batcholor Mr J
Bavim Mrs M
Booth Mr A R
Booth Mrs H
Booth K S
Boyes Dr W
Boyes Mstr M
Boyes Miss L C
Boye S Mr D M
Boyes Mr D W
Boyes Mrs M G
Boyes Mrs E
Boyes Mr M B
Boyes Mrs R C
Bracken Mrs A B
Bradford Miss S
Branwood Mrs A M
Broadbent Mrs A
Brough Mr D J
Brown Mrs R
Bryan Miss I
Bryan Mr T
Bryan Mrs A
Buck Mr A H
Burns Mr A
Callaghan Mr J W
Carroll Mgr W
Clutton Mrs J
Christie Miss L

Christie Mrs B
Christie Mstr P
Clark Mr L
Clark Mrs V C
Cliff Mrs M
Clutton Mr J
Collette Sr
Connorton Mrs M M
Cooper Mrs V
Cornforth Mr J
Cornforth Mrs M
Corr Miss A P
Coxhead Mr A J
Coyle Miss W
Crallan Mrs M
Crotty Miss M R
Curtis Mrs V E
Danis Mrs F D
Dasey Miss J F
Dasey Miss M M
Dewhurst Mr A C
Dibb Mrs I C
Doherty Dr J C
Doherty Miss F M
Doherty Miss K S
Doherty Mrs M
Doherty Mstr S
Donnelly Mrs M
Donoghue Mr M
Doto Miss A M
Dunne Mr P
Dunnett Mrs W T
Eggermont Mrs M
Ellerton Mr A G
Finn Mrs J
Fox Mr M
Gallagher Miss C
Gallagher Mr S J
Gallagher Mrs J
Gallagher Mstr J
Gallagher Msir J
Gamesby Mrs P
Gibson Mrs S
Gilligan Mr I
Gilligan Mrs M B
Grace Mr D
Grace Mr H
Griffiths Mr P
Hardgrave Miss M
Hardgrave Mr L S
Hartnett Mr J
Hayes Mr J
Hayes Mrs M
Henri Mr P
Holder Mr S R
Hornby Mrs M
Howard Sr D
Hughieson Mr J
Hughieson Mrs P
Huntingdon Miss E
Jackets Mrs S M
Jackson Miss M

James Ms S C
Johnson Miss K
John J
Jones Mrs C
Kavanagh Mrs M T
Kearney Miss E
Kilmartin Mrs J F
Kirby Miss A
Kirby Mrs M K
Kirwan Rev N
Kohut Mr A
Lawson Mrs A
Leahy Mr J V
Leahy Mrs I
Lockham Mrs J
Lovell Mr M G
Lovely Mrs I D
Lower Mrs A
Machin Mrs C
Major Mr J
Major Mrs M
Marlow Mstr D
Marlow Msstr D G
Marlow Mr P M
Marlow Mrs M
Marriott Mr G
McAllister Mrs P
McBride Mr G
McCarthy Miss V
McCarthy Mrs M
McDonnell Sr M
McDonough Mrs A
McGee Miss E
McGee Mr R
McGowran Mr B K
McMahon Mr R
McMahon Mrs K
McPhillips Mrs M E
McRae Mrs C
McVeigh Miss B
Metcalfe Mrs E
Metcalfe Mr G V
Millar Mrs R
Mimmery Mrs K
Morgan Miss T A M
Moxon Mr E
Mulligan Sr V
Murphy Mrs A
Newman Mr C
Newman Mrs D
Nicholson Rev B
O'Brien Miss W
O'Connor Rev M J
O'Donnell Mr A
O'Donnell Mr A
O'Dowd Miss M
O'Neill Mr A
O'Neill Mr C
O'Neill Mrs W M
Oyston Mrs M
Pennincton Mrs H
Phillips Mrs L

Pierre Mr G J
Pierre Mrs M C
Pink Mrs C
Power Miss R M
Power Mr F M
Power-Jepson Mrs J
Prescott Mr J
Prescott Mrs R
Prior Miss P
Rainey Mr J F
Rathbone Mrs L
Raw Miss S M
Raynor Mrs M
Retallick-Mr P E
Reyes Mr G A
Riggs Mrs A E
Robinson Mrs M
Scales Rev E
Schofield Mrs A
Smith Mrs O
Smith Mrs S E
Spaight Rev D
Squire Miss E
Sreenan Miss M
Stead Miss M C
Stead Miss M E
Stevenson Mrs F
Stewart Miss L
Stewart Mrs M
Sykes Mr W
Tasker Miss M A
Tasker Mr A J
Tasker Mrs M B
Taylor Mr A
Tempest Mr H N
Tindall Mrs K
Tucker Mr D P
Tucker Mr G P
Turnball Mstr J
Turnbull Mrs B
Urch Mr J
Venton Mrs M L
Wade Rev A
Walker Mrs M
Walton Mr G A
Walton Mrs S
Walton Mstr S
Ward Mr T
Warren Miss A M
Waters Mr P F
Waterson Mr T
Welford Mrs M M
Westerman Mr A
Westerman Mrs M A
White Mr E
White Mrs N
Wilson Miss M
Wilson Mr M
Windle Mrs V M
Wood Mr A
Wood Mrs V
Wood Mstr A

Wood Mstr P
Wright Miss E
Wright Miss E M
Wright Mr T
CTA Reps
Bassadone Mr R
Bassadone Mrs H

Sick Pilgrims
Barugh Mrs M
Bell Miss J
Bell Miss P
Bemrose Mr M
Bibby Mrs L
Bilton Mrs B
Boddy Miss E
Bride Mr P J
Bryan Mr S
Bugg Mrs M
Cassidy Mr J
Cavangh Mrs F
Chetham Mrs A D
Cosgrove Mrs S M
Crutchley Mr R
Dale Mrs A
Dodds Mr N
Donnelly Mr J
Dyson-Taylor Mr S F
Farnhill Miss H
Flannagan Mrs J
Golden Mstr G
Golden Mrs J
Hanson Mr S G
Hewitt Mr F
Hindley Mr W
Honeyman Mrs M E
Horton Mr G
Hurton Mstr M
Hurton Mrs C
King B
Knight Miss G
MacLinder Mr J
Mangan Mr P
Maplethorpe Mr T G
Marritt Miss A
Marron Mr J
Marshall Mr T H
Martin Mr J
Martin Mrs M
McKenna Mrs M
Melton Miss M
Mitchell Mrs M
Murphy Mrs M
O'Brien Miss M
Outhart Mrs M
Ralph Miss K
Reynaro Mrs H
Smith Mr T
Spanoler Mrs A
Symonds Mrs M
Walker Mstr M
Watson Mrs M

Welford Mrs E
Welsh Mrs W
Willis Mr P
Youth Pilgrimage
Newlands
Sykes Sr Claire FCJ
Aitkin Sr Jane FCJ
McBride Mrs P
Tolliday Michael
Swalwell Heather
Christie E
Robinson Toby
McGurk Stephen
Hall Colin
Cammish Winifred
Noon Colleen
McLoughlin Paul
Currie Stephen
Bailey Amelia
McAdam Paul
Gough Nicola
Savage Andrew
McBride Kieron

St David's
Morris Miss R
Doat Catherina
McMahon Deborah
McVeigh Nuala
Coleman Anthony
Matthews Jason
Stephenson Gary

Sacred Heart
Corey Mr D
Pattinson Mrs M
McCullagh Mr B J
O'Brien Fiona
Dinsdale Helen
Bowens Louise
Couhig Joanne
Limon Esther
Walton Lisa
Pattison Marie
Moore Grace
Moscrop Stephen
Graham Alex
Johnston Robert
Murphy John

St Patrick's
O'Donnell Mrs L
O'Donnell Marie
Frew Geraldine
Corrigan Sharon

Connelly B A
Connelly Mr R
Morgan Mr K
Fletcher Mr A

St Mary's 6th

Form College
McGowran Julie
Dent Lynne
Wilson Elaine
Vallely Avril
Tate Mary Joan
Martin Louise

Connelly Rory
Connelly Kevin
Luke Nick
Corr David

1986
Bishop Kevin O'Brien
Adams Mr A E
Adams Mr J A
Adams Mrs I
Adams Mrs M P
Almack Mrs G
Barry Mr J
Barry Mrs E
Benjamin Mr M
Biott Miss C
Black Miss J P
Blair Mrs E M
Blake-James Mrs M
Booth Mr A
Booth Mrs K S
Boyes Dr W
Boyes Mr D M
Boyes Mr D W
Boyes Mr M G
Boyes Mrs E M
Boyes Mrs M B
Boyes Mstr M J
Brankley Miss I
Breeze Miss S
Breeze Mr B W
Breeze Mrs J
Broadbent Mr A
Broadbent Mrs A
Brough Mr D J
Bryan Miss I
Bryan Mr A
Bryce Mr J A
Burns Mr A
Burrage Mrs M S P
Burtt Mr W J
Cahill Mrs W M
Carrigan Mrs M
Christie Miss L
Christie Mrs B
Clark Miss A M
Clark Mr L
Clark Mr N
Clark Mrs V S
Clement Sr M
Collette Sr
Connelly Miss J R
Cornforth Mr J

Cornforth Mrs M
Corr Miss A P
Coxhead Mr A J
Dadd Mrs J
Daley Rev J
Dasey Miss J F
Dasey Miss M M
Dawkins Mrs E
Dewhurst Mr AC
Dineen Sr M
Doherty Dr JC
Doherty Miss F M
Doherty Miss K S
Doherty Mr J
Doherty Mrs M
Doherty Mstr S M
Doto Miss A M
Dove Mrs F
Downey Mr P J
Downey Mrs J
Dunn Mr J
Dunn Mrs J
Dunne Mr P
Eggermont Mrs M
Ellerton Mr A G
Fawcett Mr J W
Finn Mrs J
Foster Mr B
Foster Mrs M K
Fox Mr M
Gallagher Miss C
Gallagher Mr S
Gallagher Mrs J
Gallagher Mstr J
Gallagher Mstr J
Gamesby Mrs P
Gaughan Miss A C
Gilligan Mrs M B
Grace Mr D
Grace Mr H
Griffin Mr B
Griffin Mr T
Griffiths Mr P
Gubbins Rev E J
Hardgrave Miss M
Hardgrave Mr L S
Hawkins Sr R
Henderson Mr S
Henderson Mrs M D
Hornby Miss C
Hornby Mrs M
Hurton Mrs C A
Hurton Mstr M
Jackson Miss M
John Dr I
Kavanagh Mrs M T
Kearney Miss E
Kelsey Mrs B
Kilmartin Mrs J F
Kirby Miss A
Kitcheyan Mr F
Kohut Mr A

Lamb Mr AG
Lanny Mrs M
Laville Mrs K L K
Layton Mrs W
Leahy Mrs I
Lord Mr M
Lord Mrs C
Lorigan Mrs M
Low Mrs C
Lyth Mr S B
Lyth Mrs M E
Machin Mrs C
McAllister Miss J
McArthy Miss V
McAvoy Mr F J
McAvoy Mrs F P
McBride Miss R
McCarthy Mrs M
McDonough Mrs A
McGeary Mr P B
McGee Miss E
McGee Mr R
McGowran Mr B K
McKenna Mr L B
McKenna Mrs C
McKenna Mrs N
McLellan Mr J
McMahon Mrs A
McNamara Mrs
McRae Mrs C
McVeigh Miss B
Metcalf Mr G V
Metcalf Mrs E
Micalleff Mrs M
Minnery Mrs K
Mordue Miss A
Mordue Mrs J W
Morris Mrs H
Morrison Mr A
Morrison Mrs M
Moxon Mr E
Murphy Mr C P
Murphy Mrs B M
Murphy Mstr P J
Needham Mrs E
Nelson Mr F G
Nicholson Rev B N
O'Conmor Mrs C
O'Connor Rev M
O'Donoghue Mr M
O'Donoghue Mrs R
Organ Mr T
Organ Mrs M
Overfield Mrs I
Oyston Mrs M
Pearson Mrs B
Phillips Mrs L
Porter Miss L M
Quigley Mrs V
Rainey Mr J F
Rawson Mr P
Rayner Mrs M

Reyes Mr G A
Riggs Mrs A E
Riley Mrs J
Riley Mr M
Roe Mr C W
Ruddy Miss E
Ruddy Mr B
Ruddy Mrs C
Ruddy Mstr D
Russel Mrs L
Shakesby Mr M J C
Shaw Miss M J
Shaw Mrs B
Shaw Mrs M
Spaight Rev D
Stephenson Mrs R
Stewart Mrs M F
Stokes Mr H
Sullivan Mrs A
Sykes Mr W
Tasker Mr A J
Tasker Mrs M B
Taylor Mr E
Taylor Mr H
Trowsdale Mr J K
Trowsdale Mr W A
Tucker Mr D P
Tucker Mr G P
Turner Mrs A
Turner Mrs S E
Urch Mr J
Vallely Mr F R
Wade Rev A
Walker Mrs M
Ward Mr T
Warren Miss A M
Waterson Mr T
Wesson Miss M C
Wilkinson Miss C
Willis Mr P E
Wilson Miss M
Wilson Mr M
Wood Mr A
Wood Mr A W
Wood Mr P
Wood Mrs V
Wright Miss E M
Wright Mr J
Wright Mrs J

CTA Reps
Bassadone Mr R
Bassadone Mrs H

Sick Pilgrims
Allen Mr D
Askins Mr M
Boyle Mr P
Bride Mr P
Bryan Mr S
Carrigan Mr J
Cassidy Mr J

Crutchley Mr R
Ding Mr S
Dodds Mr N
Ecklin Mr J
Echlin Mr T
Flynn Mr J
Giblin Mr P
Horton Mr G
Knapp Mr F
Marshall Mr T
Martin Mr J
McGough Mr S
Shakesby Mstr P
Shakesby Mstr P
Solan Mr A
Solan Mr M
Wilcox Mr S
Woolley Mr J
Barugh Mrs M
Beisty Miss H
Benjamin Mrs A
Bilton Mrs B
Blackburn Mrs A
Brennan Mrs M
Carlyle Mrs M
Cavanagh Mrs F
Clutterbrook Miss J
Coleman Mrs T
Considine Mrs B
Cooper Mrs S
Doherty Miss K
Evans Mrs T
Gaffney Mrs M
Girvan Mrs R
Hartley Mrs B
Higham Miss H
Holyoake Mrs P
Honeyman Mrs M
Huntingdon Miss E
Jackson Mrs J
Knight Miss G
MacFarlane Miss M
Martin Mrs M
Matthews Mrs A
Mennell Mrs M
Metcalfe Mrs C
Micalleff Mrs M
Mitchell Mrs M
Parkinson Mrs D
Paranaby Miss M
Peachy Mrs M
Ralph Miss K
Reynard Mrs H
Senior Mrs D
Shell Mrs S
Symonds Mrs M
Trowsdale Mrs W
Van Der Jonckheyd Mrs C
Wombell Mrs G
Wright Miss M

1987

Bishop Augustine Harris
Abbs Mrs M C
Adams Miss D
Adams Mr A E
Adams Mr J A
Adams Mrs C
Adams Mrs M P
Askins Miss A M
Asquith Mrs P
Atkin Mrs A
Bainbridge Mrs P
Baxter Miss M
Benjamin Mr M
Benjamin Mrs A O
Best Mrs E
Bickerstaffe Mr J
Bickerstaffe Mgr A
Black Mrs G
Blake James Mrs M H
Boland Miss M
Booth Mr A R
Booth Mrs E S
Bottom Dr S F E
Boustead Mrs D A
Boyes Dr H
Boyes Mr D M
Boyes Mr D W
Boyes Mr M G
Boyes Mrs E M
Boyes Mrs M B
Boyes Mstr M J
Brankley Miss I
Broadbent Mrs A
Broogh Mr D J
Brown Mrs E R
Burtt Mr W J
Callan Miss T
Carroll Rt Rev W
Christie Miss E L
Christie Miss L M
Christie Mrs B
Clark Mr L
Clark Mrs V S
Clarke Mrs A
Coltman Mrs D
Conway Dr M
Conway Mrs V
Cornforth Mr J
Cornforth Mrs M
Corr Miss A P
Cosgrove Mr T
Coxhead Mr A J
Coyle Miss W
Daley Mr F
Daley Mrs K
Danis Mrs F D
Dasey Miss J F
Dasey Mrs M M
Davies Miss A W
Davies Mrs J A
Devlin Miss J
Devlin Mrs M

Dewhurst Mr A
Doherty Dr J C
Doherty Miss F M
Dowson Mrs S
Dunn Mrs M
Dunne Mr P
Ellison Mr A
Fallon Miss A
Fawcett Mrs P
Fawcett Mstr A
Feeney Mr J L
Feney Mrs H
Finn Mrs J
Fisher Miss R J
Fisher Mrs I J
Fisher Mstr L
Fox Mr M
Gallagher Miss C
Gallagher Mr S J
Gallagher Mrs J
Gallagher Mstr J
Gallagher Mstr J S
Gerrard Dr A
Gerrard Mrs B
Gillen Mrs E
Gilmour Mrs N
Glenton Mr G D
Grace Mr D
Grace Mr H
Grace Mrs E
Griffiths Mr P
Hall Mrs M
Hannah Mrs A
Hay Mr C G
Heagney Mr M
Hitchings Mrs M J
Holder Mr S R
Hornby Mrs M
Houghton Mr C
Houghton Mrs J E
Hunter Miss C F
Hutchinson Mrs J M
Jackson Miss M
John Dr I
Kearns Sr J
Keenan Mrs J
Kilmartin Mrs J F
Kohut Mr A
Layton Mrs M A
Lester Mr J E
Lorigan Mrs M
Lowery Mrs E
Maher Sr M C
Mason Miss E
Mason Mrs J
Maycock Miss P
Maziak Mrs D
Metcalfe Mr G V
Metcalfe Mrs E
Morley Mrs N
Moxon Mr E
Mulderrig Miss A M

McAllister
McAvoy Sr M
McBride Mr G
McBride Mrs M
McCullagh Miss H
McCullagh Mr M
McCullagh Mrs I
McDonagh Mr T J
McDonagh Mrs A
McDonough Mrs A
McGee Miss E
McGowran Mr B K
McGowran Mrs B K
McGrogan Mrs A M
McQuillan Mrs S
McRae Mrs C
Newman Br E
Newton Mr H
Newton Mrs R
Nicholson Rev Fr B
Northend Miss C
Noteyoung Mrs J L
O'Connor Rev Fr M
O'Donnell Rev S I
O'Donoghue Mr M
O'Donoghue Mrs R
O'Shea Miss H
Ord Mr B
Ord Mrs J
Owens Mr P
Owens Mstr O P
Oyston Mrs M
Pearson Mrs B
Peirson Mr H B
Phillips Mrs C R
Phillips Mrs L
Pinder Mrs B A
Podgorski Mrs J
Rainey Mr J F
Raynor Mrs M
Rees-Davies Mrs T M
Reyes Mr G A
Roe Mr C W
Ruddy Miss E
Ruddy Mr B
Ruddy Mrs C
Ruddy Mstr D
Russell Mrs L
Ruxton Mr O F
Siddle Mr F A
Siddle Mrs M
Simmons Mrs M
Sizeland Mrs E M
Slater Mrs M J
Slater Miss M L
Smith Mrs M
Smith Mrs M I
Spaight Rev D
Stead Miss M C
Stephenson Mrs L M
Stewart Mrs M F
Stockman Miss J

Summerfield Mrs M
Swalwell Mrs A
Swift Mrs R
Sykes Mr W
Tasker Mr A J
Tasker Mrs M B
Tye Mr B
Upton Miss J A
Usmar Miss K A
Usmar Mr N P
Usmar Mr P J
Usmar Mrs S
Wade Rev Fr A
Walsh Mrs M
Walton Mr G A
Walton Mrs S
Walton Mstr S L
Ward Mr T
Warren Miss A M
Westerman Mr A
Westerman Mrs M
Wilkinson Miss C
Wilson Mr M
Wood Mr E G
Wood Mrs E
Wood Mrs E F
Wood Mrs J
Wright Miss M G
Wright Mr T
Wright Mrs J

Sick Pilgrims
Batchelor Mr J
Bavey D
Beddoes Mr D
Bennett M
Best Mr M
Bilton B
Bride Mr P
Brunton Mr N
Bugg M
Burns Mr A
Carlyle M
Cavanagh F
Clarke E
Cone-Sheffield M
Cosgrove D
Dodds Mr N
Duffy L
Fleming Mr J
Floyd Edna
Hall Mr D
Hopper M
Huntington E
Johnson M
Joyce Mr N
Joyce Mr P
Jude Mr P
Knight G
Langan L
Long Mr N
Marrit P

Martin Mr J
Martin M
Matthews A
Melton E
Mennell M
Metcalfe C
Milner M
Mitchell M
Mooney K
Mulholland Mr T
McCann T
Nelson M
Norris A
O'Connor A
Power Mr F
Preston E
Rae Mr K
Ralph K
Reynard H
Rommell Mr J
Rutherford J
Shell S
Sheridan C
Simpson P
Spandler A
Sparkes E
Turner M
Varey M
Waites P
Wolley Mr J
Wright M

CTA Reps
Bassadone Mr R
Lamarque Mr R

1988
Bishop Augustine Harris
Argent Mrs M R
Bailey Mrs M
Banks Miss E
Barker Mrs A M
Baron Mr W
Beddoes Mr D
Bickerstaffe Mr J
Black Miss J P
Bond Mrs C
Booth Mr A R
Booth Mrs K S
Boothby Mrs P
Boyes Mr D W
Boyes Mr M G
Boyes Mrs E M
Boyes Mstr M J
Boyes Mstr P G
Bradford Mrs J
Brady Mrs M
Brankley Miss I
Broadbent Mrs A
Brough Mr D J
Brown Mrs J
Brown Mstr D J

Bryan Mr A
Bryan Mrs A
Cadley Mrs B
Callan Miss T
Capraro Dr C M
Carter Mr N H
Christie Mrs B
Christie Mstr P
Clark Miss A M
Clark Mr L
Clark Mrs V S
Clarke Mrs E
Clarke Mr W
Clerk Mr N J
Collins Mrs C
Cone-Sheffield Miss P
Cornforth Mr J
Cornforth Mrs M
Corr Miss A P
Crotty Miss M R
Curry Mr E
Curry Mstr A
Danis Mrs F D
Danowski Mrs C
Dasey Miss J F
Dasey Miss M M
Davies Miss A
Davies Mrs T M
Dewhurst Mr A
Dick Miss K A
Doherty Dr J
Doherty Miss F
Doherty Miss M M
Doherty Mr S
Dunne Mr P
Ellison Mr A
Farrell Mrs R
Ferrari Mrs G A
Finn Mrs J
Forgan Miss R M
Gamesby Mrs P
Gibson Miss H
Gilligan Mrs M B
Glenton Mr G
Glenton Mrs S
Grace Mr D
Grace Mr E
Grace Mrs E M
Gray Mrs E
Green Miss B M L
Green Mrs A
Greene Mr T P
Griffiths Mr P
Hall Mrs M
Hanson Mr S
Hay Mr C G
Heagney Mr M
Henry Mrs C
Heward Miss F D
Hines Ms S
Hitchins Mrs M J
Holder Mr S R

Hood Mrs F
Hornby Mrs M
Hunter Miss C F
Hunter Mrs K
Hunter Mrs S
Hyrst Mrs C
Jackson Miss M
John Dr I
Johnson Mrs L M
Johnson Mrs G
Joyce Mr P
Kane Mrs M
Kearney Mrs M E
Keenan Mrs J
Kelly Miss M
Kilmartin Mr T
Kilmartin Mrs J
Kohut Mr A
Lane Miss C
Lane Mr L
Lane Mrs M
Lanny Mrs M
Lee Mr P J
Lobo Mrs I
Long Mr N
Long Mrs M
Maher Sr C
Matthews Mrs B
Metcalfe Mr G B
Milburn Mrs F B
Morrison Mr R
Morrison Mrs M R
Morrison Mstr A
Morrocco Mr M
Mount Miss A
Mount Miss C
Mount Mrs G
Mulderrig Miss A
McAllister Miss J
McAllister Miss N L
McAndrew Mr J
McBride Mr G
McBride Mrs P
McCarthy Miss J C
McCarthy Mrs M
McCormack Miss E
McCoy Mr E
McCullagh Mr M
McDonough Mr A
McDonough Mr C
McDonough Mrs A
McGee Miss E
McGowan Mr J
McGowan Mstr P
McGowran Miss J L
McGowran Mr B K
McGowran Mrs C
McGrogan Mrs A M
McKenna Mr M P
McMenamin Miss Y
McMinn Mrs J
McRae Mrs C

McVeigh Miss M B
Newman Br M
Nicholson Rev B
Noble Mrs E
Northend Miss C
O'Connor Rev V M J
O'Donoghue Mr M
O'Donoghue Mrs R
Ord Mr A
Ord Mr B
Oyston Mrs M
Parks Mrs I
Parks Mstr R
Peirson Mr H B
Perrins Mrs A M A
Phillips Mrs L
Pierre Miss A M
Pierre Mr J
Pierre Mrs M C
Podgorski Mrs J
Quinn Sr L
Rae Mr K
Rae Mrs I
Rainey Mr J F
Rayner Mrs M
Redman Miss S F
Redman Mr A
Redman Mrs E
Roberts Mr B
Roberts Mrs R
Roberts Mstr B
Roe Mr C W
Roe Mr J
Roe Mrs K
Shakesby Mr M
Shakesby Mrs J
Sherlock Miss K J
Sizeland Mrs E M
Smiles Mr J J
Smith Mr F
Smith Mrs I
Solan Mr M
Solan Mrs A
Spaight Rev D
Stead Miss M C
Stead Miss M E
Stewart Mrs M F
Sykes Mr W
Tasker Miss M A
Tasker Mr A J
Tasker Mrs M B
Tournay Mrs V
Urch Mr J
Urmston Mr T
Walton Mr G A
Walton Mrs S
Ward Mr T
Warren Miss A M
Warrener Miss L M
Waterson Mr T
Wharton Mrs T
Willingham Ms A M

Wilson Mr M
Wood Mrs M
Wright Miss E M
Wright Miss M G
Wright Mr T
Wright Mrs J
Yoward Mrs N

CTA Reps
Bassadone Mr R
Bassadone Miss J

Sick Pilgrims
Allen D
Batchlor J
Blissenden E
Boyes E
Boyle C
Brady J
Brunton E
Bryan S
Butler C
Capraro N
Capraro P
Casey M
Cassidy J
Clutterbrook J
Crutchley R
Dodds N
Donnelly M
Everitt A
Farrell E
Floyd Mrs E
Gallagher B
Griffith P
Gunn D
Hall D
Hall T
Harrison J
Holmes E
Hopper M
Huntington E
Johnson Mrs M
Johnson P
Labonte G
Mark M
Metcalfe C
McDonough C
McQuade E
Nelson M
O'Hara A
Power F
Rafferty C
Raynor M
Rea M
Revill R
Robinson J
Robson A
Robson F
Rooney B
Rutherford S
Saunders J E

Symonds M
Walsh S
Wordingham E
Wheatley H
Whelan S
Wilkinson I
Wombwell G
Wright M
Young J

Joined At Lourdes
Adams Mr J A
Adams Mrs M P
Boyes Dr W
Boyes Mrs M B
Doherty Miss K
Doherty Mrs M
Doherty Mrs M
Donnelly Mrs M
McCullagh Miss H
McCullagh Mrs I
Ord Mrs J
Somerville Mrs S

1989
Bishop Kevin O'Brien
Adams Mr A E
Adams Mrs F P
Allen Miss K
Arnold Miss B M
Askins Miss A M
Bainbridge Mrs P
Beeston Miss L
Beeston Mrs P
Bickerstaffe Mr J
Bisby Mrs C
Boland Miss M
Booth Mr A R
Booth Mrs K S
Boyes Dr W
Boyes Mstr M J
Boyes Mr D M
Boyes Mr D W
Boyes Mr M G
Boyes Mrs E M
Boyes Mrs M B
Bradley Miss A M M
Brady Mrs D
Brady Mrs M
Brankley Miss I
Brennan Rev Fr J A
Broadbent Mrs A
Brough Mr D J
Brown Mstr D
Brown Mrs E R
Brown Mrs J
Browne Mrs G
Callan Miss A T
Campbell Mrs G
Campbell Mrs P V
Carroll Rt Rev Mgr W
Carter Mr N H

Christie Miss E
Christie Miss L
Christie Mrs B
Clark Miss S L
Clark Mr L
Clark Mrs V S
Collins Mrs L
Cone-Sheffield Miss M P
Connor Mr J
Connor Mrs C
Cornforth Mr J
Cornforth Mrs M
Corr Miss A P
Cowell Mrs P
Coyle Miss W
Crawford Mrs M C
Creaton Mrs D
Dasey Miss J F
Dasey Miss M M
Delaney Mstr A J
Delaney Miss R E
Delaney Mr A J
Delaney Mrs V R
Dick Miss K A
Doherty Dr J C
Donowski Mrs C
Downey P J
Downey Mrs J
Dunn Mrs M
Dunne Mr P
Ellison Miss C
Ellison Miss K
Ellison Mr A
Ellison Mrs V
Evans Mr F
Evans Mrs E
Fairweather Mr J R
Ferrari Mrs G A
Finn Mrs J
Ford Mr A R
Ford Mrs P M
Fowler Mrs J
Francis Mrs R M
French Mrs J S
Frith Mr K
Frith Mrs E
Gamesby Mrs P
Gaynor Mrs M
Gell Mrs M
Gilfoyle Mrs M
Gillen Mrs E H
Gilmour Mrs N
Golden Mstr G
Golden Mrs J
Grace Mr D
Grace Mr H
Gray Mrs S
Green Miss B
Greene Mr T
Greenfield Miss R
Greenfield Mrs C
Grice Mrs M

Griffiths Mr P
Hall Mrs M
Hargan Miss M
Harrison Miss M
Hay Mr C G
Heagney Mr M
Heslop Mrs K
Hodgson Mr J B
Hodgson Mrs A M
Holder Mr S R
Hornby Mrs N
Hughff Mrs A V
John Dr I F
Johnson Miss E
Jones Mr D
Jones Mr D P
Jones Mr J C
Jones Mrs M T
Jones Mrs V N
Jowers Miss M
Jowers Mrs M
Keenan Mrs J
Kendrick Mr P
Kendrick Mrs L M
Kohut Mr A
Lane Mr L
Lee Mr J
Mackenzie Mr L
Mackenzie Mrs D J
Maher Sr Colette
Maxwell Mrs F
Metcalfe Mr G V
McCart Mr C
McCart Mr J
McCarthy Mrs M
McCoy Mr J
McCullagh Miss H
McCullagh Mr M
McCullagh Mrs I
McDonough Mr C
McDonough Mrs A
McGee Miss E
McGowran Mr B K
McGowran Mr P
McGowran Mrs C
McGrogan Mrs A M
McRae Mrs C
McSorley Miss M
Nicholson Rev Fr B
O'Connor Rev Fr M
O'Donoghue Mr M
O'Donoghue Mrs R
Ord Mr B J
Oyston Mrs M
Parker Mrs M
Phillips Mrs L
Pitts Mrs L
Podgorski Mrs J
Pounder Miss C
Pounder Mrs V
Purvis Mstr M
Purvis Mrs J

Quinn Sr Laurence
Ragusa Mr P
Rainey Mr J F
Rawson Mr P
Rayner Mrs M
Reed Mrs J
Rees-Davies Mrs T M
Roe Mr C W
Rossi Mstr D
Rossi Mrs E M
Russell Mrs L
Ruxton Mr O F
Sharma Mrs M S
Sheridan Miss M E
Smiles Mr J
Smith Mr R
Smith Mrs M
Smith Mrs W
Smith Mrs M
Spaight Rev Fr D
Stead Miss M C
Stead Miss M E
Stephens Miss C
Stephenson Mrs N
Storey Mrs E
Stubbs Mr I J N
Sykes Mr W
Tasker Mr A J
Thompson Mrs I
Urch Mr J
Vevers Mr C
Wake Mrs D K
Walsh Mrs M
Walsh Mrs M J
Ward Mr T
Warren Miss A M
Waters Mr P F
Whiley Mrs M
Williams Mrs P A
Wilson Mr M
Wood Mrs E
Wood Mrs M
Wordsworth Mr M
Worth Mrs C
Worth Mrs K
Wrignt Miss E
Wright Miss E M
Wright Mr T

CTA Reps
Bassadone Mr R P
Bassadone Mrs H

Sick Pilgrims
Barwick A
Beeston G
Bisby W
Brady M
Bryan s
Corcoran F
Craig B
Cassidy J

Davies J
Gomes H
Gunn D G
Hall D
Johnston P
Marsh B
Martin J
Mulholland J
McCreton D
Tinney L
Urmston T
Young J
Bibby L
Brady C
Brown K
Cavanagh F
Chattterje I
Clarke E
Darrell S
Dent P
Dowding E
Doyle M
Earl P
Elwick W
Gomes P
Grant F
Hall T
Hill F
Holyoake E
Hopps E
Huntington E
Jackson M
Knight G
McCrainor K
McDonald E
McGhee M
McNeill M
Neylon A
Overend M
Pridgeon D
Profitt E
Rea M
Ripley N
Shaw O
Spashett C
Symonds M
Wales N
Walsh S
White O
Wright M

1990
Bishop Augustine Harris
Adams Mr A
Allen Mr J
Ansell Mrs J
Appleton Mrs E
Askins Miss A
Atkinson Mrs S
Ayres Mr S
Ayres Mr E

Banks Miss J
Baker Mr G
Bainbridge Mrs P
Beaumont Mrs C
Bickerstaffe Mgr A
Bickerstaffe Mr J
Bickerstaffe Mrs R
Biesterfield Mrs P
Boland Miss M
Booth Mr A
Booth Mrs K
Bowan Mr D
Boyes Dr W
Boyes Mrs B
Boyes Mr M
Boyes Mstr M J
Boyes Mstr P
Boyes Mr D
Boyes Mr D W
Boyes Mrs E
Brady Mr M
Bray Mr J
Bray Mrs J
Brennan Rev Fr J
Broadbent Mrs A
Broder Mrs J
Broderick Mr B
Broderick Mrs C
Brook Miss H
Brown Mrs J
Brown Mstr D
Bryan Miss I
Bryan Mr A
Bryan Mrs A
Burrage Mrs M
Butcher Mrs T
Butler Mrs K
Cairns Mrs P
Callan Miss T
Carey Miss L
Clafton Mrs A
Capraro Mrs P
Capraro Mrs N
Christie Mrs B
Christie Miss E
Clark Mr L
Clark Mr V
Clark Miss L
Clarke Mr W
Coleman Mrs B
Collins Mrs D
Coltman Mrs E
Connor Mrs M
Connor Mrs V
Corker Mrs J
Corker Mstr P
Cormie Dr C
Cornforth Mrs M
Corr Miss A
Couhig Miss S
Cowell Mrs P
Coxhead Mr A

Curtis Mrs R
Dale Mr T
Daniels Miss M
Daniels Miss G
Daniels Miss A
Danis Mrs F
Dasey Miss M
Dasey Miss J
Davidson Miss E
Dewhurst Mr A
Dick Miss K
Doherty Dr J
Doherty Miss F
Downey Mr P
Downey Mrs J
Duffy Miss E
Dunn Mr J
Dunn Mrs M
Dunn Mr J
Dunn Mr P
Durant Mrs M
Dyer Miss J
Fairweather Mr R
Fearon Miss M
Feeney Mrs M
Feeney Mrs M
Ferrari Mrs G
Fiske Mrs S
Flemming Mrs L
Flounders Mrs A
Flynn Mrs C
Flynn Mrs E
Forgan Mrs R
Fortune Mrs D
Fountain Mrs P
Francis Mrs R
Freeman Mrs C
French Bro P
Gallagher Mr E
Gamblin Mrs K
Garbutt Miss E
Gavin Mr J
Gaynor Miss E
Gibbins Mrs V
Gilmour Mrs N
Ginty Mrs B
Glenton Mr G
Glenton Mrs S
Golding Mrs J
Golding Mstr J
Grace Mr H
Grace Mrs E
Grace Mr D
Grainger Mrs T
Gredington Mr D
Gredington Mrs A
Greene Mr T
Grice Mrs M
Griffiths Mr P
Griffiths Mrs P
Griffiths Mrs T
Grindley Mr T

Halligan Mrs M
Hardin Mrs A
Harrison Miss T
Hardwick Mr A
Hardwick Mrs C
Hardwick Mr C
Hargan Miss M
Haw Mr H
Haw Mrs M
Hay Mr C
Hayward Mrs A
Heagney Mr M
Henderson Mrs E
Hendry Mrs P
Herety Mr E
Herety Mrs D
Heward Miss F
Hickson Dr D
Hitchens Mrs M
Hodgson Mr J
Hodgson Mrs A
Holder Mr S
Hornby Mrs M
Horsman Mr M
Houlden Mr R
Houlden Mrs J
Hutchinson Mrs B
Jackson Mrs R
Jackson Mrs J
Jackson Mstr A
John Dr I
Johnson Miss L
Johnston Mrs F
Johnston Mstr W D
Jones Mr D P
Jones Mrs V
Jones Mr D
Jones Miss K
Jowett Mr W
Jowett Mrs D
Keenan Mrs J
Kenning Mrs M
Killington Mr H
Killington Mrs E
Kilmartin Mrs J
Kirby Mrs A
Kirby Sr M B
Knox Mrs D
Knox Mr P
Knox Miss M
Kohut Mr A
Laird Mrs K
Lanny Mrs M
Layton Mrs M
Leahy Mr J
Lee Mr J
Lee Mrs M
Leng Mrs G
Lewis Mrs P
Lincoln Mrs M
Lincoln Mstr J
Ling Mrs P

Lovell Mr L
Lovell Mr K
Luck Mrs S
Macdonald Miss H
Mackenzie Mrs S
Magson Mr P
Maher Sr C
Maloney Mrs M
Marron Mr A
Marron Mrs L
Marron Miss E
Maxwell Mrs M
McCart Mr J
McCauley Mrs E
McCoy Mr E
McCoy Mr J
McCullagh Mr M
McCullagh Mrs I
McCullagh Miss H
McDonough Mrs A
McDonough Mr C
McElhatton Miss C
McGee Miss E
McGowran Mr B
McGowran Miss J
McGrogan Mrs A
McGrother Miss S
McKeown Mrs B
McMahon Mr B
McMahon Miss E
McNaney Mrs J
McQuade Mrs B
McRae Mrs C
McSorley Miss M
Metcalfe Mr G
Mills Mr W
Mills Mrs H
Mills Mr G
Mills Mrs G
Mockler Mrs E
Mockler Mr J
Moffat Mrs M
Mountain Mrs C
Mohan Miss C
Moon Mrs E
Moorcroft Mrs J
Morgan Mrs B
Morgan Mrs P
Morris Miss M
Murphy Mrs E
Murray Mrs T
Nicholson Rev Fr B
Noteyoung Mr J
Noteyoung Mrs L
O'Brien Rev Fr J
O'Byrne Canon D
O'Neill Mrs A M
Ord Mr B
Ord Mr A J
Oyston Mrs M
Padley Mrs A
Parker Mrs M

Pattinson Miss M
Pawson Mr J
Payne Mr E
Payne Mrs M
Peacock Mrs P
Petty Mrs S
Phillips Mrs L
Pierre Mr J
Pierre Mrs M
Purcell Rev Fr J
Pybus Mr F
Rainey Mr J
Rathbone Mr T
Rathbone Mrs L
Ray Miss M
Rayner Mrs M
Rawson Mr P
Riggs Mrs A
Riley Mr M
Ritchie Mrs S
Ritchie Mrs S
Robson Mrs V
Robson Mstr T
Roe Mr C
Rourke Mr T
Rourke Mrs M
Ross Mr F
Rossi Mr D
Rossi Mrs E
Ruddy Mr B
Ruddy Mstr D
Ruxton Mr O
Savin Mrs E
Saywell Miss D
Scanlan Miss C
Seeney Mrs
Sharma Mrs R
Sheridan Miss M
Smailes Mrs H
Smiles Mr J
Smith Mr J
Smith Mrs I
Snaith Mrs R
Sobey Miss B
Southall Mrs J
Spaight Rev Fr D
Stead Miss M
Stead Miss M
Stephens Miss C
Stewart Mrs M
Swales Mr L
Swales Mrs A
Sykes Mr W
Tasker Mr A
Tasker Mrs B
Tasker Mrs L
Tempest Mr H
Tiernan Mrs K
Tristram Mrs A
Urch Mr:J
Vevers Mr C
Vickers Mrs J

Wake Mrs P
Ward Mr T
Warren Miss A
Waters Mr J
Waters Mr T
Waterson Mr T
Watson Miss G
Wesson Mrs A
Westerman Mr A
Westerman Mrs M
Whittle Mr N
Whittle Mrs D
Wilkinson Mr P
Wilkinson Mrs P
Wilkinson Miss C
Wilson Miss J
Wilson Miss M
Wilson Mrs P
Wilson Mr M
Wood Mrs M
Wood Mr A
Wood Mrs V
Wood Mstr P
Woods Mr I
Woods Mrs L
Wright Mr T
Wright Mrs B

Sick Pilgrims

Batchelor Mr J
Blackadder Mstr R
Brady Mr
Bryan Mr S
Carr Mr J
Gunn Mr D
Horseman Mr J
Maloney Mr W
Martin Mr J
Murray Mr J
O'Donnell Mr A
Robson Mr F
Urmston Mr T
Wakefield Mr S
Walker Mr A
Whelan Mr C
Allen Mrs E
Ayres Mrs P
Boddy Miss N
Bohdanowicz Mrs C
Boyes Miss E
Bugg Mrs M
Clarke Mrs E
Ditchburn Mrs J
Dobbin Mrs H
Dover J
Egan Miss G
Elwick Mrs W
Floyd Mrs E
Foggin Miss A
Frawley M
Garbutt Mrs T
Hamblett Mrs A

Hill Mrs F
Hodgson Mrs A
Huntington Miss E
Johnson Mrs M
McCauley Miss B
McDonough Mrs C
McKeown M
Maloney Mrs M
Murray Mrs E
O'Brien Miss M
O'Connell Miss L
O'Connell L
O'Malley S
Openshaw Mrs R
Patterson Mrs M
Perry Mrs B
Rafferty Mrs C
Robson Mrs A
Smith Mrs L
Stephenson Mrs B
Stokes Miss P
Symonds Mrs M
Thompson Mrs A M
Thompson Miss J
Thompson Mrs W
Varey Mrs A
Weatherel C

1991

Bishop Augustine Harris
Bishop Kevin O'Brien
Adams Mr A
Allen Mr J
Amicucci Mrs K
Appleyard Miss T
Appleyard Mrs M
Appleyard Miss L
Baker Mr G
Baker Mrs J
Barker Mrs M
Barker Mrs P
Barker Mrs P
Bickerstaffe Mr J
Bickerstaffe Mrs R
Bickerstaffe Miss R
Bisby Mrs C
Bivens Mrs W
Blakston Miss K
Bland Mrs M
Booth Mr A
Booth Mrs K
Bottom Dr S
Boyes Mr M G
Boyes Mr D
Boyes Mr M J
Boyes Mr P
Boyes Mr D
Boyes Dr W
Boyes Mrs B
Boyes Mrs E
Brady Mr M
Bright Miss B

Brennan Rev Fr J
Brennan Mr J
Brennan Mrs A
Briggs Mrs V
Broadbent Mrs A
Brook Mrs H
Brough Mrs J
Bryan Miss I
Buckworth Mr B
Campbell Mrs P
Carney Mrs D
Cassidy Mrs K
Chilton Mrs E
Christie Mrs B
Clafton Mrs A
Clark Mr L
Clark Mrs V
Clark Mrs L
Clark Miss L
Codling Miss S
Collins Mrs D
Collins Mrs E
Cormie Dr C
Cornforth Mrs M
Cone-Sheffield Miss P
Corr Mrs P
Corr Miss A
Coyle Miss W
Cronin Mstr P
Cronin Mrs V
Crotty Miss M
Curran Mrs E
Cusworth Mrs A
Daniels Mrs W
Dasey Miss J
Dasey Miss M
Deakin Mrs C
Deacon Mrs N
Dennis Mrs D
Dent Mrs K
Dineen Sr M
Donnelly Mr J
Donoghue Mr W
Donovan Mrs Z
Drumm Miss J
Dryden Mrs M
Dufot Mr P
Dunn Mr J
Dunn Mrs M
Dunne Mr J
Dunne Mr P
Durent Mrs M
Eastwood Mrs S
Eastwood Mstr J
Eastwood Mstr P
Ebbs Mrs F
Egan Mrs P
Endrodi Mrs B
Fearon Miss M
Feeney Mr J
Feeney Mrs M
Ferguson Baby J

Finn Mrs J
Ford Mrs A
Forgan Miss R
Fowler Mrs H
Fowler Miss P
Frawley Miss M
French Bro P
Gallagher Mr E
Gamesby Mrs P
Gibbins Mrs V
Gibbon Mrs A
Gilmour Mrs N
Glenton Mr G
Glenton Mrs S
Grace Mr H
Grace Mrs E
Grainger Mrs T
Greaves Mr J
Greaves Mrs M
Greene Mr T
Griffiths Mr P
Harding Mrs A
Hardwick Mrs C
Harrison Mrs K
Heagney Miss G
Hemblade Mr V
Hemblade Mrs M
Hemblade Miss C
Hitchens Mrs M
Hodgson Mr J
Hodgson Mrs M
Holder Mrs S
Holmes Mrs M
Holmes Miss S
Hornby Mrs M
Hughes Mrs A
Hutchinson Mrs D
Hutchinson Sr A
Jagger Mrs H
Jagger Miss S
Jameson Mrs P
Jewitt Mrs H
Johnson Mrs C
Jones Mr D
Jones Mrs V
Jones Mr D
Jowtt Mr W
Jowett Mrs D
Kearney Miss E
Keenan Ms J
Keenan Mrs M
Kelleher Mrs M
Kelly Mr J
Kelly Mrs R
Kelly Mstr M
Keogh Rev Fr P
Kilmartin Mrs J
Kipling Mrs J
Knowles Mr M
Knox Mr P
Kosina Mrs K
Kosina Miss G

Leader Mrs M
Leahy Mr J
Leary Mrs T
Lee Mr P
Lee Mr T
Liddle Mrs I
Lingins Mrs P
Lovell Mr L
Lovell Mr M
Lovell Mrs M
Madden Rev Fr W
Maher Sr C
Maloney Mrs J
Marsh Mrs S
Marsh Mstr P
McAllister Mrs M
McAllister Miss A
McCart Mr J
McCarthy Mrs M
McCauley Mrs E
McCourt Mr T
McCrae Mrs C
McCullagh Mr M
McCullagh Mrs I
McCullagh Miss H
McDermott Mrs M
McDonough Mrs A
McFaddon Mrs J
McGee Mr R
McGee Mr J
McGee Miss E
McGowan Mr J
McGowran Mr B
McGowran Mrs C
McGrogan Mrs A
McHugh Miss M
McKenna Rev Fr W
McMahon Mrs D
McManus Mr E
McManus Mrs M
McMenamin Miss M
McMillan Mrs M
Metcalfe Mr G
Mitchell Mr E
Mitchell Mrs B
Moffit Mrs M
Moore Miss E
Morgan Mrs B
Morgan Mrs N
Mungham Mrs A
Mungham Mstr J
Nicholson Rev Fr B
O'Connell Rev Fr T
O'Connor Mr N
O'Connor Fr
O'Donoghue Mr M
O'Donoghue Mrs R
O'Hare Sr C
O'Hare Mrs S
O'Neal Mr L
O'Neal Mrs R
O'Sullivan Sr C

O'Toole Rev Fr E
Oyston Mrs M
Parker Mrs M
Pattinson Mrs M
Penn Mrs C
Pettman Mrs M
Phillips Mrs L
Pierre Mr J
Pierre Mrs M
Podgorski Mrs
Power Mrs D
Preece Mrs P
Prescott Mr J
Prescott Mrs R
Purvis Mrs E
Quinn Sr L
Rainey Mr I
Rayner Mrs M
Robinson Mrs C
Robinson Mrs
Roe Mr C
Roe Mrs K
Rose Mrs D
Rossi Mrs E
Rossi Mrs K
Rossi Mr R
Ruxton Mr O
Sandison Mrs M
Savin Mrs E
Scales Mrs E
Sharma Mrs M
Smiles Mr J
Southall Mr A
Southall Mrs J
Spaight Rev Fr D
Spark Mr F
Spark Mrs M
Spark Mrs M
Speight Mrs T
Speight Mstr C
Stead Miss M E
Stead Miss M C
Stephens Mr A
Stephens Mrs C
Stobbs Mrs R
Stubbings Mr C
Sullivan Mrs K
Sykes Mr W
Tasker Mr A
Tiernan Miss I
Taylor Mrs
Temple Mrs P
Thomas Mr K
Tillen Mr K
Tillen Mrs P
Toogood Mrs N
Urch Mr J
Varley Mrs P
Vevers Mrs
Wall Miss R
Ward Mrs A
Ward Mr T

Waters Mr P
Waters Mr J
Waterson Mr T
Waterson Mr J
Watson Miss G
Watson Mrs P
Watts Mr J
Watts Mrs J
Welford Mrs M
Welsh Sr U
White Mr T
Whittle Mrs D
Wilkins Mrs A
Wilkins Mr I
Wilkins Mrs O
Willerton Mr J
Willerton Mrs J
Wilson Miss M
Wilson Mr J
Wilson Mr M
Worth Miss E
Wrigglesworth Mrs V
Yarker Mrs C

Sick Pilgrims
Austin D
Bisby W
Connolly T
Coxhead A
Dodds N
Donoghue S
Dunne J J
Fewster E
Gunn D
Johnson J
McCreton D
McMahon B
McSorley M
Martin T
Miller J
Murphy V
Murray J
O'Donnell A
Padgett H
Robinson J
Smith Mr S
Trainor J
Allan B
Andrew Sr
Atkins T
Brogden R H
Carney P
Cass V
Connolly P
Connor J
Ditchburn J
Doherty C
Foy P
Garbutt T
Gibbons M
Graham S
Gregory E

Hartley B
Hudson W
Huntingdon E
Lee E
McAndrews M
McCauley B
McGeown M
McMahon E
McSorley V
Martin M
Pearson M
Peterson Betty
Scott Mary
Sewell Dora
Smith Mrs M
Walsh Sheila
Weatherall Carol
White Nancy

Flight Only
Abell Miss K
Arthur Miss L
Birkett Mrs C
Box Mrs J
Brough Mr D
Capraro Mrs P
Capraro Mrs N
Christie Miss E
Cowell Mr B
Davidson Miss E
Farnhill Miss H
Larvin Mr J
Ling Miss J
Maddison Mrs C
McGeary Mr P
McGowran Miss J
Nozedar Mrs J
Owen Mr T
Riordan Mr D
Riordan Mrs M
Thompson Mstr M
Woods Mr E
Wright Miss L

1992
By Coach
Austin Mr D
Bell Mr L
Boyes Mr M J
Burrage Mrs M
Capraro Mrs N
Carey Mr E
Chapman Mrs M
Christie Mr A P
France Mr B
Jackson Mr S
Mays Mr D
Mays Mrs I
Moxon Mr G H
O'Donoghue Mr M
O'Donoghue Mrs R M
Rawson Mr P

Rayner Mr M

First Aircraft
Bishop Augustine Harris
Spaight Rev Fr D
Allen Mr J
Amos Mrs C M
Ashe Miss G M
Baker Mr G A
Bisby Mrs C
Bivens Mrs W M
Booth Mr A R
Booth Mrs K S
Bottom Dr S F E
Boyes Dr W
Boyes Mrs M B
Boyes Mr D M
Boyes Mr D W
Boyes Mstr J
Boyes Mr M G
Boyes Mrs E M
Brady Mrs F
Brewster Mr A
Broadbent Mrs A
Brough Mr D J
Brown Mrs J
Brown Mstr D
Bryan Mr A
Buckworth Miss L M
Byrne Mrs B
Byrne Mr M
Caley Mrs M
Campbell Mrs P
Christie Mrs B
Clark Mr L
Clark Mrs V S
Codling Miss S M
Cowell Mrs P
Curtis Mrs R
Dasey Miss J F
Dasey Miss M M
Deakin Mrs C M
De Placido Mr A P
De Placido Mrs P
Ditchburn Mrs S
Dowling Mr J
Drury Mrs J
Dunn Mr P
Ferguson Mstr J
Gamblin Mrs K
Gillen Mrs E H
Gilmour Mrs N
Glenton Mr G
Grace Mr H
Grace Mrs E
Grace Mr D
Griffiths Mr P
Hargan Miss M
Heagney Mr M A
Holder Mr S R
Hughes Mrs A J
John Dr I

Keenan Miss J
Kilmartin Mrs J F
Knox Miss M
Labonte Mrs A
Labonte Mr T
Lax Mrs S M
Lee Mr T
Leonard Mrs H D
Lowthorpe Ms D M
MacDougal Ms A
Mitchell Mr E
Mitchell Mrs B
Moore Miss E
Moy Mrs A
Moy Miss R
Murphy Mrs E A
Murray Mrs E A
McCauley Ms E W
McCullagh Mr M
McCullagh Mrs I M
McGee Miss E
McGowran Mr B K
McGrogan Mrs A
McMenamin Miss M
McRae Mrs C
Nelson Mr B H
Nicholson Rev B
O'Connor Rev M J
Parker Mrs M C
Pileger Rev Fr J A
Phillips Mrs L
Rainey Mr J F
Rayner Mrs M
Ribee Miss M K
Robinson Mrs C E
Roe Mrs K
Rossi Mrs E M
Sharpe Mrs K
Sheekey Mr P
Sheekey Mrs P
Sheekey Mstr R
Smith Mrs R
Southall Miss N
Squire Miss E
Squire Mrs M M
Stewart Mr J
Sullivan Mrs C
Sykes Mr W
Tate Mrs D
Thorpe Mr M
Thorpe Mrs S
Tiernan Ms K M
Tolliday Mrs J
Tolliday Miss J
Tolliday Miss M
Wall Mr R W
Warburton Mr M
Watson Miss G M
Whitfield Mrs C
Whitfield Mstr C
Whitfield Mstr N
Whiting Miss J

Wilson Miss M
Wilson Mr M

Sick Pilgrims
Bisby Mr W
Boote Mr B
Bryan Mr S
Burns Mr J
Drury Mr C
Hunt Mr J
Jackson Mr T
Johnson Mr J
Labonte Mr G
Little Mr R
McMahon Mr B
Shakesby Mr P
Ward Mr T
White Mr T
Ascott Sr M
Atkins Ms T
Boote Mrs H
Boyes Mrs N
Bryan Mrs A
Cass Ms V
Cavanagh Ms F
Clarke Ms E
Dr Placido Ms C
Dover Ms J
Dowling Ms V
Endrodi Ms B
Floyd Ms E
Freeman Ms M
Gee Ms P
Hilberink Ms A
Johnson Ms M
Jowers Ms J
Keating Ms M
Lappin Ms M
Lee Ms E
Little Ms D
Lowes Ms A
McCauley Ms B
McCrainor Ms K
McMahon Ms E
Milner Ms M
Nelson Ms K
Norris Ms T
Sewell Ms D
Sharpe Ms M
Smart Ms V
Southall Ms J
Thompson Ms A
Walsh Ms S
White Ms N
Wilkinson Ms E
Windle Ms M

Second Aircraft
Alderson Mrs V I
Amicucci Mrs K
Appleyard Miss L M
Appleyard Mrs M

Appleyard Miss T M
Ashford Mrs A
Ashford Mr D
Ashford Miss M
Ashford Mrs M E
Ashford Mr T
Askins Miss J
Banks Mrs H
Barnes Mrs D F
Barwick Mr R
Baxter Miss D
Bickerstaffe Mr J
Bickerstaffe Mrs J
Bickerstaff Miss R
Bowden Mr G
Brady Mr T
Branch Mrs A
Branch Miss S
Brennan Rev J A
Brown Mrs C
Bryan Miss I M
Buchanan Mrs M M
Callan Miss A T
Cann Mr J
Carney Mrs D
Carney Mr L
Carroll Mgr W
Cockerill Mr A
Collins Mrs D
Cone-Shiefield Miss M
Conlon Mrs W
Cornforth Mrs M
Coxhead Mr A
Daley Fr J
Daniels Miss M
Deacon Mrs N
Donnelly Mr J
Duffy Mr D
Duffy Mr J
Duffy Mrs M
Duggan Mrs M M
Dunhill Mr S J
Dunhill Mrs V M
Dunn Mr J
Dunn Mrs M
Dunne Mr J
Durant Mrs M C
Durkin Mrs E
Durkin Mr J
Eastwood Mrs S
Eyles Mrs E J
Feeney Mr J L
Feeney Mrs M
Fenelly Mrs M
Fernandes Mr D
Finn Mrs J
Finn Mrs M E
Finn Mr M P
Fowler Mrs H J
Fox Mr G
Fox Mrs G
Gallagher Mr E J

Gamesby Mrs P
Gannon Mrs F P
Grace Mr D
Grace Mr L
Grainger Mrs T
Grassie Mrs I
Greene Mr T P
Hardwick Mrs C B
Harrison Mrs M M
Healey Mrs H
Healey Mr T E
Hitchins Mrs M J
Hodgson Mrs A M
Holmes Mrs M
Holmes Miss S
Hutchinson Mrs E
Jemeson Mrs P A
Johnson Mrs W M
Jones Mr D
Jones Mr D P
Jones Mrs V N
Jowett Mrs D
Jowett Mr W
Kelleher Mrs M T
Kenyon Mrs M
Kilbane Mrs L P
Kilgallon Mrs P
King Mrs M E
Laden Mr G
Leahy Mrs I
Leahy Mr J A
Minskip Rev D
Moffit Mrs M D
Molloy Mrs R E
Moore Mr J
Morris Miss M C
Mulgrew Mr D
Mulgrew Mrs P A
MacNamara Mstr J J
McCarthy Mrs M
McCoy Mrs A
McDonald Miss H
McDonnell Mrs A
McDonnell Mr J
McDonough Mrs A
McGee Mr J
McGee Mr R
McGee Mrs M E
McGowan Mrs E J
McGowan Mr J
McManus Mrs M
Norris Mrs C
Oliver Mrs D
Oyston Mrs M
Pattinson Mrs M R
Pierre Mr J
Pierre Mrs M C
Potter Mrs M T
Rafferty Mrs C
Rafferty Mrs M
Readman Mrs H
Ribeiro Dr A

Roe Mr C W
Ruxton Mr O
Ryan Rev J J
Ryan Rev M A
Seavers Mr E C
Seavers Mrs H M
Sharma Mrs M S
Sheppard Mrs T M
Skerry Miss A E
Skerry Mrs C M
Smith Mr D
Speight Mrs T
Stead Miss M C
Stead Miss M E
Steele Mrs M
Stobbs Mrs R
Tasker Mr A J
Tasker Mrs M B
Tempest Mr H N
Urch Mrs M T
Urch Mr J
Varley Miss E A
Varley Mrs S E
Vevers Mr C W
Waterson Mr J
Waterson Mr T
Watt Mrs D E
White Rev D J
Whittle Mrs D
Wrigglesworth Mrs V
Wright Miss M G
Wright Miss W

CTA Reps
Bassadone Mr R P
Bassadone Mrs H

1993
Bishop John Crowley
Bishop Kevin O'Brien
Allen Mr J
Amicucci Mrs K
Appleyard Ms M
Appleyard Ms T
Appleyard Ms L
Ashford Mr D
Ashford Mrs M
Ashford Mrs A
Ashford Mr T
Ashford Miss M
Bain Ms S
Baker Mr G
Baker Mrs M
Barrett Mrs C
Barugh Mrs M
Beadle Mr D
Bell Mr L
Bickerstaffe Miss M
Binks Mrs C
Bivens Ms M
Black Miss J
Boot Mrs H

Booth Mr A
Booth Mrs K
Bostock Mrs J
Boyes Mrs E
Boyes Dr W
Boyes Mrs M
Boyes Mr D
Boyes Mr M
Boyes Mr M
Boyes Mr P
Brankley Miss I
Brannen Ms M
Brennan Rev J
Brewster Mr A
Broadbent Mrs A
Broder Ms M
Brough Mr D
Brown Mr J
Brown Mrs J
Brown Mr D
Bryan Miss M
Bryan Mr S
Buxton Ms G
Callan Ms A
Carney Mrs M
Carney Mr S
Chapleo Ms W
Christie Ms B
Christie Mr A
Clifford Mrs E
Coates Ms R
Cockerill Mr A
Collins Mrs D
Collins Ms M
Colvin Mrs D
Cone-Sheffield Miss M
Cornforth Mrs M
Cowell Ms P
Crossen Mrs M
Crossen Ms M
Cuthbert Ms L
Dale Mr F
Daniels Miss M
Dasey Miss J
Davison Mr M
Davison Mrs B
Deacon Mrs N
Deakin Ms C
Denham Mrs M
Dilworth Ms M
Dilworth Miss K
Dilworth Ms M
Dobey Mrs A
Dobey Miss E
Dodds Miss C
Donnelly Mr J
Duggan Mrs M
Dunne Mr P
Durnion Mr M
Eastick Ms M
Feeney Mr J
Feeney Mrs M

Floyd Ms E
Flynn Mr M
Foy Mr J
Francis Ms R
Gallagher Mr E
Gardiner Mr F
Gilmour Mrs N
Glasby Mrs P
Glasby Mr R
Glasby Mrs M
Glenton Mr G
Glover Ms M
Goldspink Ms M
Goonan Ms E
Grace Mr H
Grace Mr D
Grace Mrs E
Grace Ms
Graham Ms S
Grant Mr S
Grant Mrs A
Greene Mr T
Griffiths Mr P
Hancock Mrs N
Hargan Ms M
Harris Mrs K
Harris Miss V
Heron Mrs M
Hickey Sr
Hitchins Mrs M
Hodgson Mr J
Hodgson Mrs A
Hodson Ms H
Hoe Mrs E
Hoe Miss R
Hope Ms E
Hutchinson Mrs D
Hutchinson Sr A
Issac Ms M
Jameson Mrs P
Jameson Mr N
Jameson Mr M
Jenner Miss P
John Dr I
Johnson Mr M
Johnson Ms M
Jones Mr D
Jones Mrs V
Jones Mr D
Jones Mr V
Keenan Ms J
Kelleher Mrs M
Kelleher Mr L
Kellett Rev Fr D
Kelly Ms K
Kilmartin Mrs J
Knox Miss M
Leedham Ms S
Lindup Mr A
Lindup Ms L
Lovell Mr M
Lovell Mrs M

Lovell Mstr B
Mageean Mr F
Manders Mrs M
Martin Miss M
McCarthy Mrs M
McCullagh Mr M
McCullagh Mrs I
McCullagh Miss H
McDonald Mrs S
McGee Ms E
McGee Ms H
McGowan Miss J
McGrogan Ms A
McKeown Mr J
McMahon Mr M
McMahon Mr B
McMahon Ms E
McManus Mrs M
McNeil Mr J
McRae Ms C
Mercer Mstr D
Miles Ms M
Mills Mrs G
Mills Mr G
Mills Ms S
Mitchell Mrs I
Moan Ms A
Moore Mr A
Moss Mrs M
Mulholland Ms O
Mullins Mrs H
Mullins Mr P
Mullins Mr C
Nicholson Rev B
O'Brien Ms S
O'Connor Fr M
O'Donnell Sr B
O'Donoghue Mr M
O'Donoghue Mrs R
Oldfield Mr T
Oldfield Ms T
O'Neill Dr J
O'Neill Mrs V
Owen Mrs M
Parker Ms M
Phillips Mrs L
Porthouse Ms H
Rainey Mr J
Rawson Mr P
Rayner Ms M
Robinson Mr P
Robinson Mrs E
Robinson Ms C
Robson Mr J
Robson Mrs A
Robson Mr M
Roe Mr C
Roe Ms K
Snaith Ms E
Somerville Ms L
Spaight Rev D
Spaight Mr C

Spaight Mrs
Sparling Miss M
Squire Miss E
Squire Mrs M
Statham Ms K
Stead Miss M
Stead Miss M
Stephens Mr F
Stewart Mr P
Sullivan Mr T
Tasker Mr A
Tasker Mrs M
Taylor Mr J
Thompsom Mrs O
Thompson Mrs F
Thornton Sr O
Tiernan Ms K
Turner Mrs M
Vevers Mr C
Walsh Ms S
Warburton Mr M
Ward Mr T
Waterson Mr J
Waterson Mr T
Waterson Mr L
Watson Miss G
Westerman Mrs M
Westerman Mr A
White Miss E
Whitfield Ms N
Whitfield Mrs
Widdowson Mr J
Wieczorek Ms P
Wilce Mr F
Wilkinson Mrs J
Williams Mr B
Wilson Mr M
Wood Mrs M
Wood Mr E
Wood Mrs P
Wrigglesworth Mrs V
Wright Ms M

1994
Bishop John Crowley
Adameck Miss C
Akerman Mrs E
Amicucci Mrs K
Andrews Mr J
Atkinson Ms N
Atkinson Mr D
Atkinson Mrs A
Atkinson Mr M
Baker Mr G
Baker Mrs M
Barnes Mr M
Barnes Mrs M
Barnett Mr R
Barrett Mr R
Barrett Ms C
Batty Mr C
Batty Mrs M

Beach Mr F
Beach Mrs E
Bell Mrs M
Bell Miss M
Bell Mrs C
Bell Miss S
Benson Mrs O
Binks Ms C
Bird Miss G
Bivens Ms M
Bonner Mrs S
Bonner Miss M
Boote Mrs H
Booth Mrs H
Borsumato Mr J
Bottom Dr S
Boyes Mrs E
Boyes Mr D
Boyes Miss L
Boyes Mr P
Boyes Dr W
Boyes Mrs B
Boyes Mr D
Boyes Mr M
Brady Mrs F
Broadbent Mrs A
Brough Mr D
Brown Mr J
Brown Mrs M
Brown Mrs J
Brown Mstr D
Bryan Mr S
Bryan Miss I M
Burns Mrs A
Burns Ms P
Burns Mr A
Burns Ms M
Burrage Mrs M
Cafferky Mrs M
Cafferky Mr J
Cafferky Miss B
Cafferky Miss A
Cahillane Mrs H
Cahillane Ms L
Callan Ms T
Campbell Mrs K
Capraro Mrs N
Carrick Mr M
Carroll Mnsgr W
Cartlege Mrs E
Casey Mrs M
Cavanagh Ms F
Chapman Ms M
Christie Ms B
Clark Ms N
Clark Mr L
Clark Mrs V
Cline Mr T
Codling Ms S
Cofinas Mrs C
Coleman Mrs L
Collins Mrs M

Collins Mrs M
Connor Mr M
Connor Ms C
Connors Miss M
Conway Mr P
Conway Mrs M
Cooper Mr B
Cooper Mrs P
Couhig Mrs S
Cowell Ms P
Cowell Mr B
Craggs Ms E
Cronin Ms U
Cronin Mr J
Cronin Miss S
Cunningham Miss J
Curtis Ms R
Daley Rev J
Daly Ms S
Dasey Miss J
Dasey Miss M
Dasey Rev G
Davidson Miss E
Davies Mr L
Davies Mr M
Davison Mr M
Deacon Mrs N
Denham Mrs M
Dinsdale Ms M
Dobbs Mr F
Dobbs Mrs M
Doherty Ms M
Doherty Dr J
Donaghue Mr S
Donaghue Mr W
Donnelly Mrs M
Duffy Mr T
Duggan Mrs
Dunn Mr J
Dunn Mrs M
Dunne Mr P
Eason Mrs A
Feeney Mr J
Feeney Mrs M
Flanagan Mrs B
Flanigan Miss R
Fleming Mrs L
Fleming Inf L
Floyd Ms E
Folland Ms P
Folland Ms M
Foster Mrs B
Fullerton Mrs
Galvin Ms E
Gamblin Ms K
Gamblin Ms L
Gannon Mr J
Garner Ms R
Gee Mrs P
Giblin Mrs D
Gilmour Mrs N
Glasby Mrs P

Glasby Mstr R
Gollogly Mr J
Grace Mr D
Grace Mr H
Grace Mrs E
Graham Mrs I
Grainge Mrs
Grainge Mr
Grainger Mrs V
Gray Ms J
Grayson Mrs L
Hall Miss T
Hamilton Ms B
Hargan Ms M
Hargreaves Ms I
Hart Miss G
Hart Miss P
Heagney Mr N
Henegan Miss E
Higgins Mr F
Higgins Miss M
Hill Mrs J
Hindmoor Ms J
Holder Mr S
Hughes Ms A
Jackson Mr T
Jackson Mr T
Jackson Mr S
Jackson Mrs G
Jameson Mrs P
Jameson Miss J
Jameson Miss C
Jamieson Miss M
Jewitt Mrs C
Jinks Mrs P
Jinks Mr T
Johnson Ed F
Johnson Mr M
Johnson Mrs S
Jones Mr D
Jones Mrs V
Jones Mr D
Keenan Ms J
Kellett Fr D
Kelly Mrs R
Kelly Mr J
Kilmarti Mrs J
Knox Ms D
Knox Miss M
Lane Ms H
Lanny Mrs M
Laville Ms C
Leahy Mr J
Leng Mrs G
Ling Mr P
Little Mr B
Lovelady Rev B
Lynn Mrs K
Mannix Mrs A
Marshall Miss M
Martin Mr T
Martucci Mrs K

Maslin Mrs N
Mason Ms E
McArthur Ms M
McCann Mr T
McCann Mrs N
McCarthy Mrs M
McCarthy Mrs M
McCreesh Miss K
McCullagh Miss H
McCullagh Mrs I
McCullagh Mr M
McCunnell Mr P
McCunnell Mrs F
McGee Ms E
McGough Mr S
McGowan Mr J
McGrogan Ms A
McLean Mrs M
McLoughlin Mr J
McMahon Miss M
McMahon Mr B
McNeil Mr J
McRae Ms C
Mendoza Mrs M
Mendoza Mr M
Middleton Ms E
Millam Miss A
Mills Mrs H
Mills Mr W
Mills Ms S
Mills Miss C
Mills Miss D
Mills Mr G
Mitchell Mrs B
Mockler Mrs T
Mockler Mr J
Moore Miss E
Moran Mrs L
Morris Mr L
Mortell Canon J
Mortimer Ms M
Mullen Mr T
Mullen Mrs V
Mundy Ms M
Mundy Mrs M
Murray Ms E
Nicholson Rev B
Nockels Ms J
Norris Ms
Noteyoung Mrs J
Noteyoung Mrs L
O'Brien Miss S
O'Connor Fr M
O'Connor N
Oldfield Mrs P
O'Malley Mrs S
O'Neill Mrs V
O'Neill Dr J
O'Sullivan Mrs T
O'Sullivan Miss A
Owen Mr T
Parker Ms M

Parry Ms A
Pennington Mrs H
Pennington Mr J
Phillips Mrs L
Pierre Mrs M
Prosser Ms T
Prost Ms C
Rainey Mr J
Rayner Ms M
Readman Mrs E
Ribee Miss M
Richardson Mr T
Richardson Mr T
Richardson Mrs O
Riley Ms L
Riley Ms T
Robinson Mrs J
Robinson Ms C
Roe Mr C
Rommel Mrs M
Rommell Mr J
Roth Ms M
Rowcliffe Ms M
Rowney Mrs N
Seavers Mr C
Seavers Mrs H
Sherwood Ms V
Sigston Mrs M
Sigston Mr D
Singleton Mr J
Smith Mr L
Smith Mrs M
Smith Miss K
Smith Mrs M
Southworth Ms T
Spaight Rev D
Stead Miss M E
Stead Mrs E
Stead Miss M C
Steele Mrs M
Stevens Mr M
Stevens Mrs M
Stewart Mrs M
Stewart Mrs
Tasker Mr A
Tasker Mrs M
Tate Mrs D
Taylor Mrs S
Taylor Mr J
Tiernan Ms K
Tinkler Miss T
Todd Ms M
Toker Miss B
Tomkins Mr K
Trett Mrs B
Twentyman Mr J
Twentyman Mrs P
Twissell Mr C
Twissell Mrs M
Vasey Mrs M
Walker Ms P
Waller Mrs E

Walsh Miss S
Walsh Miss M
Walsh Mr P
Warwick Ms R
Watson Ms S
Watson Ms F
Whalley Ms P
Whitfield Mrs
Whitfield Mr N
Williams Mr L
Williams Mrs M
Williams Mstr D
Wilson Ms M
Wilson Mr M
Wood Mr E
Wood Mr P
Wood Mrs M
Wood Mrs E
Wright Mr T
Wright Miss W
Young Mrs C

1995

Bishop John Crowley
Bishop Kevin O'Brien
Bishop
Agar Mrs M
Akerman Mrs E
Amicucci Ms K
Ascott Sr M
Atkinson Mr D
Atkinson Mrs A
Austin Mr D
Bainbridge Mrs M
Baker Mr G
Barmby Mr P
Barnett Mr R
Barr Ms D
Barrett Ms C
Bell Ms S
Binks Ms C
Binks Mr K
Binks Ms D
Binks Mr L
Bivens Mrs W M
Boardman Mrs B
Boyes Mr D
Boyes Dr W
Boyes Mrs M B
Boyes Ms E
Boyes Mr M G
Boyes Mr D
Boyes Miss L
Brennan Rev J A
Brent Ms K
Brough Mr D
Brown Ms N
Brown Mr J
Brown Mrs V
Brown Mstr D
Brown Mrs J
Brown Mrs R

Bruton Mrs E
Bruton Mr T
Bryan Miss I
Bryan Mr S
Brynoif-Trett Mrs C
Burke Mr K
Burrows Ms R
Callan Miss T
Carney Ms P
Casey Ms M E
Cassidy Ms K
Cattermole Mrs A
Cavanagh Ms F
Clark Mr L
Clark Mrs V S
Clark Mrs M T
Clarke Ms M
Clifford Ms E
Cody Mrs S
Cofinas Mrs C
Connelly Dr
Collingwood V Rev L J
Collins Mrs M A
Collins Ms D
Collins Mrs M
Hutchinson Sr
Cook Mr A
Corrigan Mrs E
Couhig Mrs S
Coyle Mrs C
Craig Ms D
Crawford Mr S
Creaven Mrs T M
Creaven Mr T
Creaven Miss L
Crossman Ms S E
Cummins Mr J
Cummins Mrs B
Cummins Mr M
Cummins Ms B
Cummins Ms J
Dahms Mr P
Dahms Ms B
Dahms Mr M
Dahms Mrs C
Dandria Dr V
Dasey Ms M M
Dasey Ms J F
Dasey Rev G M
Davison Mr M
Davison Mrs B
Davison Mr J
Davison Mrs M
Deacon Mrs N
Devine Mr J
Devine Mrs E
Dinsdale Ms M
Dobbs Mrs M
Dobbs Mr F
Donaghue Mr S
Donoghue Mr W
Dooley Ms N

Dooley Ms M
Doto Mr C
Dowling Mrs M
Downey Mr M
Duffield Ms C
Duffy Mr A
Duggan Mrs M M
Dunn Mr J
Dunn Mrs M
Dunne Mr P
Dunwell Mrs N C
Dunwell Mr G
Eves Miss M
Farrow Mrs M
Farrow Mr K
Fitzgibbon Mr P
Fitzgibbon Mrs B
Floyd Ms E
Flynn Mr E
Flynn Ms K
Folland Miss P
Folland Mrs M
Found Ms D
Fox Mr M
Fox Ms C
Gallagher Mr E J
Gallon Mr J
Galvin Mrs B
Garner Mrs R
Gibson Mr E
Gilmour Mrs N
Goodfield Mrs S
Grace Mr H
Grace Mrs E
Grace Mr D P
Gray Mrs J
Grayson Mrs L A
Gribbin Miss L M
Gribbin Rev Fr H F
Griffiths Mr P
Griffiths Ms T
Griffiths Miss C
Griffiths Mstr J
Hand Mr K
Hand Ms M
Hardgrave Mrs S
Hardgrave Mr L S
Hay Ms N
Hay Mr P
Higgins Ms M
Hodgkinson Miss C
Hodgson Ms K
Holmes Mrs M
Holmes Miss S
Hoy-Taylor Mr J
Hoy-Taylor Mr D
Hutchinson Ms F
Hutchinson Ms J
Hutchinson Sr A
Jackson Ms M
Jenner Mr P
Jinks Mrs P

Jinks Mr T
Johnson Mr M
Johnson Mr J
Jones Mr D P
Jones Mrs V N
Jones Jr Mr D
Jones Mrs P
Jones Ms C M
Keenan Ms J
Kellett Fr D
Kelly Ms M
Kelly Ms K
Kemp Mr B
Kemp Mrs
Keogh Fr
Kilmartin Mrs J
King Ms B
Kirwan Mr T
Lambert Mr K
Lambert Mrs M
Langham Mr R K
Lanny Mrs M
Leaiiy Mr J
Leonard Ms T
Lindsay Ms P
Little Mr R
Little Miss K
Lovelady Canon B R
Lowe Mrs R
Lowe Mr G
Mackinder Mrs M
Mannix Mrs A
McBride Ms R
McCarthy Mrs M
McCullagh Mrs I
McCullagh Mr M
McDermott Ms P
McDougall Ms M
McGee Miss E
McGlinchey Mrs T
McGough Mr S
McGowan Mr J
McGrogan Ms A
McGurk Miss M
McLaughlin Mrs M L
McLaughlin Mrs M
McLaughlin Mrs B
McLean Mrs M
McMahon Ms E
McMahon Mr B
McManus Mrs A P
McRae Mrs C
Menzies Mr T
Metcalfe Mr G
Metcalfe Mrs E
Mills Mrs G
Mills Miss D
Mockler Mrs T
Mockler Mr J
Morris Mr L
Nevison Ms D
Nicholson Fr B

Norris Ms C
Norris Ms T
Norton Mrs E
Oakey Mrs P
O'Brien Ms S
O'Brien Mrs W
O'Connor Mr N
O'Donoghue Mrs R
O'Donovan Ms N
O'Donovan Mr T
O'Hara Canon G
O'Hare Sr Collette
O'Hare Ms S
Oliver Ms P
O'Neill Dr J N
O'Rourke Ms S
O'Rourke Mr M
Oxley Ms S
Parker Ms M C
Patrick Ms C
Pemberton Mr M
Pemberton Ms C
Pennington Mr J
Pennington Mrs H
Poole Mrs B
Puttick Mrs N
Quigley Mrs M
Quigley Mr J
Quigley Mrs L
Rae Mrs I
Rae Mr K
Rainey Mr J F
Rathbone Mr T
Rathbone Mrs L
Rawson Mr P
Rayner Ms M
Reynolds Ms J
Richardson Mr T
Ridley Ms K
Riley Mrs T
Roberts Mr P
Robinson Mrs J
Robinson Mrs E A
Roddam Mr P
Roddam Mrs D
Roe Mr C
Ross Mr F
Rossie Mrs L
Sanderson Mrs H
Sleight Miss J
Smith Miss K
Spaight Rev D
Statham Ms K
Stead Miss M E
Stead Miss M C
Storey Mr T
Storey Ms E
Stott Ms P
Tasker Mr A
Tasker Mrs M
Taylor Mrs M
Taylor Mrs S

Taylor Mr J
Teece Mrs B
Tennant Mrs J R
Thomas Miss S
Tomkins Mr K
Vasey Mrs M A
Wade Mrs A
Waland Mrs A
Walker Ms J
Walsh Ms S
Walsh Mr P
Walsh Ms M
Waterson Mr J
Waterson Mr T
Weatherall Mrs L
Weddle Ms E
Whitefield Mr C
Whitefield Mr N
Whitfield Mrs C
Whittle Mrs D
Whittle Miss T
Wilkinson Ms J
Williams Mrs E
Williams Mrs T
Williams Ms D
Williams Mstr D
Williams Mr L
Williams Mrs M
Willmott Ms M
Wilman Miss L
Wilman Miss S
Wood Ms M
Wood Mrs S
Wood Mr E
Wood Mrs P
Young Miss C
Young Miss J
Young Mrs L
Young Ms C

1996

Bishop John Crowley
Agnes Sr
Alderson Mr R
Allinson Mr M
Allinson Mrs V
Amicucci Ms K
Armstrong Mrs J
Bage Mrs M L
Bainbridge Mrs M
Banks Mr J
Banks Mrs B
Bivens Mrs M
Bottom Dr F
Boyes Mr D W
Boyes Dr W
Boyes Mrs M
Boyes Mrs E M
Boyes Mr M
Boyes Miss A
Boyes Mr D
Boyes Miss D

Boyes Miss O
Brough Mr P
Brough Mr D J
Brough Ms J
Brown Mr J
Brown Ms M
Brown Mrs J
Brown Mstr D G
Bryan Miss I
Bryan Ms A
Bryan Mr S
Brynolf Trett Mrs C
Brynolf Trett Mr N
Burke Mrs M
Burke Miss R
Burns Mrs A
Burrage Mrs M
Cairns Mr T
Cairns Mrs R
Cairns Mstr M
Cairns Mstr J
Callan Ms T
Cansdale Mrs H
Capraro Mrs N
Chambers Mrs M
Clark Mrs M T
Clarke Mrs M
Clotilda Sr
Cofinas Mrs C
Collins Mrs M
Collins Mrs M
Collins Mrs D
Cook Mr A
Cook Mrs C
Cooksey Mr R
Cooper Mrs A
Coulthurst Mr J
Crilly Mr M
Crossen Miss K
Dack Mr J
Dale Miss J
Dasey Ms J
Dasey Ms M
Dasey Mr P
Dasey Rev C
Dawson Mrs F
Dent Sr Imelda
Dinsdale Ms M
Dobbs Mr F
Dobbs Mrs M
Donovan Mrs T
Donovan Dr D T
Dooley Mrs M
Dunn Mrs M
Dunn Mr J
Dtjnne Mr P
Evans Mrs B L
Evans Ms T
Fairweather Mr R
Fentiman Mrs I P
Fentiman Hr J D
Finucan Sr Everilda

Floyd Ms E
Folland Mrs P
Folland Mrs M
Forgan Miss R
Foy Snr Mr J
Foy Jnr Mr J
Garner Mrs R
Gilmour Mrs N
Girvan Miss I L
Girvan Ms R
Good Ms C
Goodridge Mrs E
Grace Mrs E
Grace Mr H
Grace Mr D
Grainger Dr P
Grant Mrs M
Grayson Mrs L A
Griffiths Mr P
Halliday Mrs J
Healy Sr Ita
Hei Ms C
Hemblade Mr V
Hemblade Mrs M
Hemblade Miss C M
Hemblade Mrs J
Hewitt Ms A
Higgins Miss M
Hodgkinson Mrs
Hodgson Mrs T
Hornby Ms J
Hornby Mrs V
Hunt Ms M
Jevons Mr S
Johnson Mrs A
Jones Ms C
Keenan Ms J
Kellett Fr D
Ketchin Mrs H
Kilmartin Mrs J F
Kirke Mrs F
Kirwan Mrs E
Lane Ms N
Lawler Ms J
Lawler Mr J
Leneghan Miss M
Leneghan Mr P
Leneguan Mrs C
Leonard Ms T
Lockett Sr Gabriel
Long Ms W
Lovelady Canon
Lynn Mrs K
Macdonald Mr L
Macdonald Mrs M
Manders Mrs M
Marjary Ms E
Martin Mr J
Mason Ms N
Matthews Ms T
Maughan Miss C
Maughan Mr J E

McCarthy Ms M
Nativity Sr
Michael Sr
McCullough Mrs A
McDermott Ms E
McDermott Mr W
McDermott Mrs A
McDougall Ms H
McGinley Ms E
McGinley Mrs P
McGloin Ms J
McGough Mr S
McGovern Ms T
McGrogan Ms A M
McLeary Mr B
McMahon Ms B
McMahon Mr B
McManus Sr S
McQuilling Mr G
McRae Ms C
McRae Mr J
McRae Miss V
McRae Miss S
Mennell Mrs L
Mennell Mr J
Metcalf Mrs H
Mills Miss D
Mills Mrs G
Moloney Sr M
Moody Mrs K
Morgan Mrs M E
Moss Ms F
Sr Veronica
Neesham Mr W
Neesham Mrs M
Nicholson Fr B
Norris Mrs W
Norris Mrs T
Norris Mr D
O'Brien Ms P
O'Brien Miss S
O'Gorman Mr T
O'Neill Dr J N
O'Shea Ms E
O'Shea Mr A
O'Sullivan Sr Aidan
Paley Mrs L
Paley Mr S
Paley Miss L
Paley Miss S
Parker Ms M
Pennington Mrs H
Pennington Mr J
Pybus Ms P
Quinn Mrs E
Quinn Mr B
Quinn Miss P
Quinn Miss S M
Rae Mrs I
Rae Mr K
Rainey Mr J
Richardson Mr G

Richardson Mrs
Robinson Mrs J
Robinson Ms C
Roddam Mr P
Roddam Mrs D
Roe Mr C
Rowlands Ms E
Scaife Ms K
Shell Ms S
Smith Ms K
Smith Mrs M
Smith Miss C
Smith Miss L
Spaight Rev D
Stanley Mrs B
Stead Miss M C
Stead Miss M E
Tasker Mr A
Taylor Fr D
Taylor Mrs M
Thompson Mr B
Tiernan Mrs K M
Trainor Mr J
Waterson Mr T
Watson Mrs N
Weatherall Ms L
Whitfield Mr N
Whitfield Mrs C
Whitfle Ms D
Williams Ms D
P0-Wood Ms M

1997

Bishop John Crowley
Bishop Kevin O'Brien
Adams Mr A
Akerman Mrs E
Alderson Mrs M
Alderson Mr R
Allen Ms E
Archibald Ms F
Ardern Mrs M
Aspery Mrs M
Aspery Miss K
Axford Mrs P
Baker Mr C
Barrett Mrs L
Berryman Mrs C
Binks Mr K
Binks Mrs D
Blues Mr L
Bivens Mrs W
Bonner Ms E
Bowman Mr J
Bowman Mrs N
Boyes Mr D
Boyes Mrs M B
Boyes Dr W
Boyes Mr M
Boyes Mrs E M
Boyes Mr D
Boyes Mstr J

Boyes Miss A
Boyes Mr P
Boylen Mrs K
Boylen Mr P
Bradley Mrs V
Brough Mr D J
Brough Mrs J
Brown Mr JA
Brown Mrs M T
Brown Mrs J
Brown Mstr D
Bryan Miss I
Bryan Mr S
Burns Mrs P
Burns Dr L
Burns Mrs A
Burns Mr A
Byrne Mrs B
Byrnes Mr G
Byrnes Mrs D
Cairns Ms R
Callan Miss T
Campbell Ms J
Capraro Mrs N
Carr Mrs M
Carr Mr J
Cavanagh Mrs F
Charlton Mrs TK
Christie Mr A
Clark Mrs M
Cockerill Mr A
Cofinas Mrs C
Collins Mrs M
Collins Mrs D
Connelly Mrs J
Connor Mrs C
Coughlan Mr J
Coughlan Mrs J
Cowell Mrs P
Curry Mrs K
Dahms Mr P
Dahms Mrs B
Dahms Mr M
Dale Miss J
Dasey Mr P
Dasey Miss M
Dasey Miss J
Dasey Fr G
Damson Mr P
Damson Mrs M
Delany Mrs T
Dick Ms K
Dinsdale Mrs M
Dobbs Mr M
Dobbs Mrs M
Donaghue Mr P
Donnelly Mrs M
Dorgan Mr D
Dowling Sr F
Duffy Mrs M
Dunn Ms E
Dunne Mr P

Emms Mrs A
Emms Mr A
Emms Mr J
Evans Mr N
Farnill Miss H
Farrer Fr P
Farrer Mr L
Farrer Mrs S
Fitzgerald Mr H
Fitzgibbon Mr G
Floyd Mrs E
Folland Mrs M
Folland Miss P
Foster Mrs M
Foster Mrs M A
Frew Mr J
Gallagher Mrs N
Garcia Dr E
Garner Ms R A
Gibson Mrs P
Gilmour Mrs N
Good Mrs C
Grace Mr D
Grace Mr H
Graham Mrs I
Grainger Dr P
Grainger Mrs E
Graihger Mrs T
Grayson Mrs L
Gribbin Fr H
Griffitns Mr P
Groves Mrs C
Hadfield Mrs A
Hargan Mrs N
Hargan Mrs M
Harrison Mrs H M
Harrison Mr J
Harrison Mr W
Harrison Mrs
Hawkes Mrs C
Hawkes Mr H
Hawkes Mr H J
Heslehurst Mrs I
Hodgkinson Miss C
Holder Rev S
Holmes Ms E
House Ms M
Hughes Mr J
Humble Mrs M
Hume Mrs N
Hutchinson Mrs B
James Mr A
Jennings Mr J
Jones Ms P
Jones Mrs P
Kavanagh Ms M
Keenan Ms J
Kellegher Mrs N
Kellett Fr D
Kilmartin Mr T
Kilmartin Mrs J
Kingston Mr T

Kingston Mrs D
Kirkman Ms J M
Knox Mrs D
Kosina Mrs K
Laden Mr G
Lambe Mr R
Lambe Mrs C
Lanaghan Mrs P
Lecky Mrs J
Leddy Mr J
Leigh Mrs A
Lester Mrs N
Lish Mrs L
Lohan Mr E
Loughlin Mr C
Loughran Mrs K
Lumb Mr C
Lumb Mrs M
Mailey Mrs K
Mailey Miss G
Maltby Ms A
Manders Mr J
Manders Mrs D
Marjary Ms E
Matthews Miss T
Matthews Mr J
Matthews Mr G
Maughan Mr J
Maughan Miss C
May Mrs K
McAnany Mrs C
McBride Mr K
McCabe Mr P
McCabe Mrs K
McCarthy Ms M
McCauley Ms B
McCauley Mrs E
McClurey Mr E
McCullagh Mr N
McCullagh Mrs I
McDermott Mrs A
McDougall Mrs M
McGee Miss E
McGough Mr S
McGouran Mr H
McGouran Mr K
McGowran Mrs C
McGowran Mr B
McGrogan Ms A
McGurk Mr W
McKenna Mrs E
McKittrick Mrs J
McLean Mrs M
McLean Miss K
McLeary Mr B
McMabon Mrs B
McMahon Mr B
McMahon Mr A
McMahon Mrs P
McManus Sr C
McQuilling Mr G
McRae Mrs C

Metcalfe Mrs E
Metcalfe Mr G
Miller Sr L
Mills Mrs G
Mills Mr G
Mills Ms D
Mills Mrs N
Mohan Mr J
Mohan Mrs D
Moore Mrs M
Murray Miss N
Nesbitt Mstr
Nesbitt Mrs
Nichol Ms M
Nicholson Fr B
Nicoll Ms G
Norris Ms J
Norris Ms T
Oakey Mrs P
O'Brien Ms S
O'Donnell Ms T
O'Neill Mr T
O'Neill Dr J
O'Neill Mrs V
O'Rourke Mr M
O'Rourke Mrs S
Orvis Ms N
Parker Ms M
Pattinson Mrs M
Peacock Mrs C
Pegden Miss H
Pegden Mstr T
Pegden Mstr M
Pegden Inf L
Pegden Mr
Pegden Mrs
Pennington Mrs H
Pennington Mr J
Prest Mrs L
Prosser Mrs E
Proudler Mrs R
Puttick Mrs N
Pybus Ms P
Quinn Mr A
Quinn Mrs S
Rae Mrs I
Rae Mr K
Rafferty Mrs T
Rafferty Mr L
Rainey Mr J F
Rathbone Mr T
Raynor Ms M
Robinson Mrs J
Robinson Mrs M
Robinson Ms M
Robinson Ms C
Roddam Mrs D
Roddam Mr P
Roe Mr C
Rose Mrs M
Rose Mr R
Rowcliffe Ms M

Rowlands Mr E
Savage Mr L
Savage Mrs M
Scott Mrs M
Seaton Mrs A
Seaton Mr D
Simpson Mr J
Smith Mr CW
Smith Mr D
Smith Mrs A
Spaight Rev D
Sproates Mr J
Sproates Mrs P
Sproates Miss L
Sproates Mr N
Stead Miss M C
Stead Miss ME
Stephenson Mrs RM
Stephenson Mrs B
Sutherland Mrs N
Sutherland Mr R
Tasker Mr A J
Tate Ms D
Tierhan Mrs KM
Trainor Mr J
Walker Mr C
Walker Mrs C
Walker Ms E
Walker Mrs A
Wall Mr J
Walsh Ms S
Waterson Mr T
Watters Mr CJ
Weatherall Mrs L
Welsh Sr U
Westwater Mrs M
Whalley Mrs P
Whitfield Mrs C
Whitfield Mr N
Wilmot Ms N
Wilson Mr P
Wilson Ms J
Wilson Miss N
Wood Mr K
Wood Ms N

1998

Bishop John Crowley
Bishop O'Brien
Adams Mr A
Agar Mrs
Akerman Mrs E
Alderson Mrs M
Allen Mrs E
Ascott Sr M
Askins Ms J
Atkinson Mrs A
Atkinson Mr D
Baker Mr G
Baker Mrs T
Baker Miss V
Barnes Ms D F

Barrett Mrs C
Barrett Mrs C
Barrett Miss J
Barry Rev A
Barry Mrs E
Barugh Mrs M
Battle Mr G
Baxter Mrs N
Bickerstaffe Mr J
Binks Mr L
Bivens Mrs N
Black Miss J
Bointon Mrs D
Bointon Miss A
Bottery Mrs M
Bowman Mstr R
Boyes Mr D
Boyes Dr W
Boyes Mrs M B
Boyes Mrs E
Boyes Mr D
Boyes Miss O
Boyes Mr H
Boyes Mr A
Boyes Mrs A
Bradley Mrs V
Broadhead Mrs M
Broadhead Mstr C
Bruton Mrs J
Bryan Miss I
Bryan Mr S
Bryan Mr A
Brynolf-Trett Mrs C
Brynolf-Trett Mr N
Burns Ms P
Burns Mr J
Burrage Mrs M
Byrnes Mrs D
Byrnes Mr J
Byrnes Mr D
Cairns Mrs R
Callan Ms T
Campbell Mrs S
Canavon Mr H
Capraro Mrs N
Cavanagh Mrs F
Cave Mrs E
Christie Mr A
Clark Mrs M
Clutterbrook Mrs J
Cofinas Mrs
Collingwood Canon
Collins Mrs D
Collins Mrs M
Connolly Mrs P
Coote Mrs C
Cornforth Miss L
Cowell Mrs P
Crisp Mrs B
Crowley Mr M
Currie Mrs M
Daley Mrs K

Dasey Miss J
Dasey Miss M
Dawson Mr P A
Dawson Mrs N
Devine Mrs J
Dinsdale Mrs M
Doherty Mrs B
Donegan Mr J
Donegan Mrs J
Dorgan Mr D
Duffy Fr A
Duffy Mrs T
Mr Duffy
Easton Mrs W
Farnill Miss H
Farrer Fr P
Floyd Mrs E
Folland Miss P
Folland Mrs N
Forgan Miss
Foster Mrs G
Frew Mr J
Gamesby Mrs P
Gibbins Mr A
Gibbons Mr B
Gibbons Mrs
Gilmour Mrs N
Gilroy Mrs J
Grace Mr D
Grace Mr H
Grace Mrs E
Grainger Dr P
Grayson Mrs A
Griffiths Mr P
Griffiths Mstr J
Gull Mrs D
Guy Miss L
Hargan Miss M
Hargan Mrs M
Harrison Mrs M
Harrison Mr J
Hartley Mrs B
Hawley Mrs A
Hazel Mrs T
Henman Miss C
Hodgkinson Miss C
Hodgson Mrs E
Hodgson Mr
Holmes Mrs M
Hughes Mrs M A
Hughes Mr J B
Hughes Mrs T
Hunneysett Mrs E
Hunneyset Miss E G
Jackson Mrs A
Jackson Mr J
Jackson Mrs M
Jackson Mr B
Jackson Mrs
James Mr A E
Jenner Mrs P
Jones Mrs V

Jones Mr D
Keenan Ms J
Kelleher Mrs M
Kellett Fr D
Keogh Bro A
Kilgallon Miss K
Kilgallon Mrs M
Kirby Mr M
Kirby Mr N
Mr Kirby
Kirkman Mrs J
Knight Mr J
Knight Mrs N
Larkin Mrs M
Larkin Mr G
Leader Mrs M
Leddy Mr J
Lester Mrs N
Lewis Mrs E
Lidster Mrs J
Long Mrs M
Luth Mrs A
Lynch Mr D
Lynch Mrs V
Lynn Mrs K
MacDonough Mrs A
Manders Mr J
Manders Mrs D
Mannix Mrs A
Matthews Miss T
McBride Mr K
McCarthy Mrs M
McClurey Mr E
McCullagh Mr M
McCullagh Mrs I
McDermott Ms A
McGee Mrs E
McGowran Mrs C
McGowran Mr B
McKenna Mrs J
McLean Mrs M
McMahon Mrs B
McMahon Mr B
McManus Sr S
McNaughton Miss K
McRae Mrs C
Metcalfe Mrs G
Metcalfe Mrs
Millan Mrs A
Mills Mr G
Mills Mrs G
Mills Ms D
Monks Miss H
Moore Ms A
Moore Mrs
Murphy Mr G
Murray Miss M
Nichol Mrs M
Nicholson Fr B
Normington Mr S
O'Brien Mrs S
O'Connor Fr M

O'Donnell Mr A
O'Hara Canon G
O'Neill Dr J
O'Neill Mrs V
Orwin Mrs A
Oyston Mrs M
Padley Mrs A
Parker Ms M
Pearson Mrs M
Pearson Mrs K
Pearson Mr W
Pearson Mr G
Peiper Mrs M
Pennington Mrs H
Pennington Mr J
Priddis Mrs C
Pybus Mrs P
Quinn Miss S
Quinn Mr A
Rae Mr K
Rae Mrs I
Rafferty Mrs S
Rafferty Mr J
Rainey Mr J F
Raynor Mrs M
Revill Mr D
Revill Mr P
Richardson Mrs
Robinson Mrs J
Robinson Miss A
Robson Mrs M
Roddam Mr P N
Roddan Mrs D V
Roe Mr C
Rossi Mrs L
Rouse Mrs N
Rouse Mr J
Rowlands Mr E
Salter Mr A
Salter Mr P
Salter Mrs M
Salter Mr G
Salter Mrs V
Salter Mstr B
Shakesby Mrs J
Shakesby Mr
Sill Mr H
Simpson Mr J B
Smith Mrs A
Snowdon Ms A
Spaight Canon D
Stead Miss M E
Stead Miss M C
Stephenson Mrs N
Stocking Mr S
Stocking Mrs L
Stonehouse Mr D
Stonehouse Mrs A
Sutherland Mrs M
Sutherland Mr R
Tate Mr S
Tate Mrs M

Taylor Fr D
Taylor Mrs S
Taylor Mr J
Taylor Miss L
Thompson Mrs E
Thompson Mrs T
Thompson Mr D
Tiernan Mrs K
Troy Mrs J
Tuthill Miss K
Vickers Mrs N
Wake Mr R
Walker Mr T W
Walker Mrs J P
Walker Sr D
Walker Shakes Mr J
Walker Shake Miss A
Walker Shake Mrs J
Wall Mr J
Waterson Mr T
Watters Mr C
Welford Mr J B
Welford Mrs J A
Welsh Mrs M
White Mrs R L
White Miss E
Whitfield Mr N
Whitfield Mrs C
Whitfield Mr A
Whittle Mrs D
Willey Mr J
Wilson Miss M
Wilson Miss S
Wood Mrs M
Wood Mr W
Wordsworth Mstr P
Wordsworth Mrs D

1999
Bishop John Crowley
Agar Mrs E
Akerman Mrs E
Alderson Mrs M
Appleby Miss L
Ashford Mr T
Ashford Miss M
Ashford Miss R
Ashford Mrs A
Askins Miss J
Askins Ms C
Askins Mrs P
Baker Mrs T
Banks Miss R
Barnett Mr J
Barnett Mrs E
Barrett Mrs C
Barry Rev J
Barry Mrs E
Battle Mr G
Baxter Mrs W
Bell Miss R
Bell Mrs K

Bell Mrs C
Binnington Mrs J
Bircham Mrs J
Bivens Mrs W
Boardman Mrs B
Boardman Miss L
Bointon Miss C
Boyes Mr M
Boyes Mr D
Boyes Dr W
Boyes Mrs M
Boyes Mrs E
Boyes Mr D
Boyes Mrs R
Boyes Mstr J
Boyes Miss O
Boyes Ms A
Boyes Ms H
Boyle Mrs I
Boyle Mr O
Bradbury Mrs A
Brannen Miss M
Brennan Rev J Rev
Broadhead Mrs M
Broadhead Mr K
Brown Mrs S
Brunjes Mrs B
Bruton Mrs J
Bryan Miss I M
Bryan Mr A
Burns Dr L
Burns Mrs P
Burns Ms M M
Burns Rev A
Burrage Mrs M
Byrnes Mrs D
Byrnes Mr G
Byrnes Mr D
Callaghan Mrs M
Callaghan Mr J
Callan Miss A T
Capraro Mrs N
Carr Mrs R
Carrick Mr M
Carson Rev E
Cavanagh Mrs F
Charlton Mgr R
Christie Mr A
Clark Mrs M
Clark Mr A
Clark Mrs M
Clark Mr M
Clark Mr D
Clarke Mrs
Clifford Mrs M
Clyburn Mrs K
Cofinas Mrs C
Cofinas Mstr D
Colligan Mrs E
Collingwood Canon
Collins Mrs D
Conforth Miss L

Conway Mrs M
Couer Mr B
Coughlan Mrs J
Crossman Mrs S
Crossman Inf J
Crowley Rev M
Cunningham Mrs E
Dahms Mr P
Dahms Mrs B
Dahms Mr M
Dale Ms J
Dales Ms A
Dales Ms F
Dales Mr P
Dales Mr A
Dalton Ms M
Dasey Miss I
Dasey Rev G
Dasey Mr P
Dawson Mr P
Dawson Mrs M
Dee Mr F
Dee Mrs I
Dinsdale Mrs M
Donaghue Mr P
Dowd Mrs M
Dowlin Mrs V
Downs Miss B
Downs Mr A
Downs Mrs M
Dowson Mrs M J
Dowson Mrs E
Duffy Mr J
Duffy Mrs M
Duffy Mrs T
Duffy Mr B
Duffy Fr
Duggan Mr W
Duggan Mrs R
Dunlop Mrs
Dunn Mr P
Durham Mrs M
Farnill Miss H
Farrer Fr P
Farrer Mrs S
Farrer Mr L
Fascia Mrs J
Fillingham Mr T
Fillingham Mrs M
Finucane Mrs M
Fitzgibbon Mr G
Floyd Mrs E
Folland Miss P
Folland Mrs M
Forgan Miss R
Fortune Mrs D
Freed Mrs B
Freed Mr D
Frew Mr J
Gallagher Mrs E
Gallagher Mrs A
Gannon Mrs F

Garwell Mr R
Garwell Mrs
Gill Mrs
Gilmour Mrs N
Gilroy Mrs J
Good Mrs C
Goonan Mrs E
Grace Mr D
Grace Mrs E
Grace Mr H
Graham Mrs S
Griffiths Mr P
Griffiths Mstr J
Hall Mrs M
Halley Mrs L
Hargan Mrs M
Harrison Mr I
Harrison Ms H
Harrison Mrs T
Harrison Mrs M
Hawkins Mrs P
Hawley Mrs A
Hayden Mrs R
Hayden Mr B
Hazel Mrs T
Hemblade Mr V
Hemrlade Mrs M
Hemdlade Mrs C
Hendry Mrs S
Hinman Dr N
Holder Rev S
Howitt Mstr J
Howitt Mrs D
Hume Mrs M
Jackson Mrs R
Jackson Mr B
Jackson Mrs K
Jeavons Mrs B
Jones Mrs C
Keefer Miss P
Keenan J
Kelleher Mrs M
Kelleher Miss N
Kellett Fr D
Kelly Mr T
Kelly Mrs P
Kett Mrs L
Khan Mr J
Kilmartin Mrs J
Knowles Mr B
Lacey Mr J
Lacey Mrs M
Larkin Mrs M
Lavin Mrs S
Leahy Mrs I
Lecky Mrs J
Leigh Mrs A
Lidster Mrs J
Lloyd Mrs G
Lloyd Mr K
Lohn Mr E
Lowe Mrs S

Lumb Mrs A
Lynch Mr D
Lynch Mrs V
Lynn Mrs K
MacDonald Mstr J
MacLean Mrs P
MacLean Miss J
Maginn Mrs B
Maguire Mr C
Maguire Mrs M
Maughan Mr J
Maughan Miss C
McBride Mr K
McBride Mrs P
McCarthy Mrs M
McClurey Mr E
McClusky Mr M
McCormack Mrs M
McCormick Mrs M
McCormick Mr B
McCoy Mr R
McCullagh Mr M
McCullagh Mrs I
McDermott Mrs D
McDermott Mr J
McDonagh Ms M
McDonagh Mrs N
McDonough Mrs A
McDougall Mrs M
McGee Mrs E
McGough Mr S
McGough Mr J
McGowran Mrs C
McGowran Mr B
McGurk Mr W
McKenna Mrs N
McLean Mrs M
McLean Dr K
McMahon Mrs B
McMahon Mr B
McManus Sr C
McNaughton Miss K
McRae Mrs C
Meek Miss T
Mendoza Mrs M
Metcalf Miss J
Miles Mrs M
Mills Mr G
Mills Mrs G
Mills Ms D
Milward Ms G
Moody Mrs E
Moore Miss C
Mortell Canon J
Murphy Miss M
Murphy Mrs E
Naughton Mrs J
Nicholson Rev B
Normington Mr S
O'Brien Bishop K
O'Brien Mrs P
O'Connor Fr M

O'Connor Mrs C
O'Hara Canon G
O'Neill Mrs V
O'Neill Dr J
O'Sullivan Sr C
Oyston Mrs M
Pallatta Mrs M
Pallatta Mr D
Parker Mrs M
Pearce Mrs M
Pennington Mrs H
Pennington Mr J
Pickering Mrs A
Pickering Mr D
Pollock Mrs C
Pollock Mr A
Potter Mrs M
Priddis Mrs C
Priestley Mrs K
Pybus Mrs P
Quinn Miss P
Radford Mrs D M
Radford Mrs A
Radford Ms J
Radford Ms L
Rae Mrs I
Rae Mr K
Rainey Mr J
Raynor Mrs M
Redhead Mrs M
Renshaw Mrs C
Richardson Mrs C
Rickard Mrs M
Riley Mrs V
Robinson Mrs J
Robinson Miss A
Robinson Mstr S
Roddam Mrs D
Roddam Mr P
Roe Mr C
Ruse Ms D
Savage Mr L
Savage Mrs M
Selby Miss N
Selby Mstr M
Severs Mr P
Severs Mrs B
Shankley Mr B
Simpson Mr J
Smith Ms A
Smyth Rev G
Smyth Mrs E
Snowdon Miss A
Snowdon Miss M
Spaight Canon D
Squire Mr
Squire Mrs
Stead Miss M C
Stead Miss M E
Stephen Ms F
Stonehouse Mrs B
Stott Mrs P

Summers Ms A
Summers Miss L
Summers Miss E
Sutherland Mrs M
Taylor Mrs K
Thompson Mrs E
Tillotson Mrs
Tillotson Mr K
Todhunter Mrs J
Trainor Mr R
Vasey Mrs M
Walker Mrs M
Walker Mrs E
Walker Mr J
Wall Mr J
Wardell Mrs P
Waterson Mr T
Welch Mr R
Weymes Miss E
White Miss E
Whitfield Mrs C
Whitfield Mr A
Whitfield Miss S
Whiting Mrs M
Wiles Mrs W
Wilkinson Mr T
Wilkinson Mrs M
Wood Mr E
Wood Mrs P
Wood Mrs M
Woodman Mrs M
Woodman Mr P
Wright Mr R

2000
Crowley Bishop John
Bishop Kevin O'Brien
Ablett Mr M
Ackerman Mrs E
Adams Mr J
Adams Mrs M
Adams Ms M
Adams Mr C
Agar Mrs E
Alderson Mrs M
Allen Ms E
Andrews Miss J
Andrews Mrs U
Andrews Miss C
Anthony Dr S
Armstrong Mrs E
Arnold Mr B
Arnold Mrs M
Ascott Sr M
Askins Mrs P
Askins Mstr C
Askins Mr J
Askins Mr J
Askins Miss J
Atkinson Mrs E
Atkinson Ms B
Axford Mrs R

Bainbridge Mstr A
Bainbridge Mrs V
Bainbridge Mr P
Bainbridge Mrs M
Baker Mrs T
Barrett Mrs C
Barron Mrs F
Barry Rev T
Barry Miss E
Barry Mr D
Barwick Ms R
Bates Mrs B M
Bell Mrs C
Bell Mrs M
Bell Mrs E
Bell Mstr L
Berry Mr J
Berry Mrs M D
Bivens Mrs W
Blamire Mrs N
Bointon Miss C
Booth Ms M
Boyes Mr D
Boyes Dr W
Boyes Mrs M
Boyes Mrs E
Boyes Mr M
Boyes Miss H
Boyes Miss A
Boyes Mr D
Boyle Mrs I
Boyle Mr O
Brannen Miss M
Brewster Mrs V
Brewster Mr C
Broahead Mrs M
Broadhead Mr K
Broadhead Mr K
Broadhead Mr C
Brook Ms M
Brown Mrs R
Brown Mr J A
Brown Mrs R
Brown Mrs J
Brown Mr D
Brudenell Mrs P
Bryan Mr T
Bryan Miss I
Bunting Mr B
Bunting Mrs M
Burns Rev A
Burns Mrs M
Burns Mr D
Burns Mrs D
Burns Mr S
Burns Mrs M
Burrage Mrs M
Byrnes Mr G
Byrnes Mrs D
Byrnes Mrs C
Byrnes Mr D
Callan Ms T

Capraro Mrs N
Carney Mrs N
Carney Mrs K
Carr Mrs A
Carr Mstr P
Castor Mrs M
Cavanagh Ms F
Choosey Mrs B
Christie Mr P
Clark Mrs M
Clarke Mrs M
Clifford Mrs E
Clifford Ms M
Clifton Mrs K
Cofinas Mrs
Cofinas Mr
Colligan Mrs E
Collingwood Canon
Collins Mrs D
Connelly Sr M
Connolly Mrs P
Connor Mrs C
Conway Mrs M B
Conway Mr P
Corrigan Mrs J
Coughlan Mrs J
Coverdale Ms A
Coward Ms M
Cowell Mrs P
Crosby Mrs
Crotty Mrs M
Crowther Ms M
Cunningham Mrs C
Currie Mrs K
Dahms Mr P
Dahms Mrs B
Dahms Mr M
Daniels Mr D
Darby Mr R
Dasey Miss J
Dasey Miss M
Dasey Mr A
Dawson Mr P
Dawson Mr M
Dent Sr I
Digiorgio Mrs J
Digiorgio Miss E
Digiorgio Miss F
Dillon M J
Dillon Mrs J
Dinsdale Mrs M
Dixon Mr J
Doherty Mr W
Donaghue Mr P
Dorgan Mr D
Dorgan Mrs A
Dorgan Miss E
Dorgan Miss C
Dorgan Miss M
Dowd Mrs M M
Dowling Sr M
Downs Miss B

Downs Ms M
Downs Mr A
Dowson Mrs E
Duffy Mrs M
Duffy Mr J
Duffy Miss T
Duffy Ms B
Dunn Mrs M
Dunne Mr P
Durham Mrs M
Edwards Miss J
Elsey Mrs M
Emmett Mrs J
Evans Mr
Farrer Rev P
Finicane Miss M
Fitzgibbon Mr G
Fitzgibbon Mr P
Fitzgibbon Mrs
Flanagan Mrs J
Folland Miss P
Folland Mrs M
Forgan Miss R
Foster Mr C
Foy Mr J
Foy Mrs H
Frain Sr M
Freed Mrs B
Gallagher Mrs E
Gallagher Mrs A
Gibson Ms A
Gillis Mrs J
Gilroy Mrs J
Glenton Mr G
Good Ms C
Grace Mr H
Grace Mr D
Grant Rev P
Grayson Mrs L
Griffin Mrs M
Griffith Mr P
Grimes Mr S
Hackett Miss M
Hagetstadt Ms M
Hall Mrs M
Hall Mrs E
Hall Mr D
Halley Mrs L
Hardwick Mr
Hardwick Mrs
Hardwick Mr
Hargan Miss M
Hargan Mrs M
Harrison Miss H
Harrison Mrs T
Harrison Mr J
Hawksby Mrs M
Hazel Mrs T
Heagney Mr M A
Heagney Miss G M
Henry Ms S
Hill Mrs M

Hills Mstr T
Hills Mrs C
Hinman Dr M
Hodgkinson Miss C
Hodgson Mr T
Holder Rev S
Holmes Mrs M
Hornby Ms M
Hughes Ms T
Hume Ms M
Hynes Mr F
Hynes Mrs J
Hynes Mr F
Hynes Mrs J
Jackson Mrs C
Jackson Mr A
Jones Mrs C
Jones Mr D
Jones Mrs V
Keenan Ms J
Kelleher Ms M
Kelleher Mrs N
King Miss M
Larkin Mrs M
Larwood Mr C
Larwood Mrs S
Leahy Mrs I
Lecky Mrs J
Leddy Mr J
Leigh Mrs A
Leng Mrs G
Lidster Mrs J
Lincoln Mrs H
Ling Mrs P
Lingings Mrs P
Lingings Mr M
Lloyd Mr K
Lloyd Mrs
Lohan Mr E
Longstaff Mrs S
Luby Mrs T
Lynn Mrs K
Main Mrs E
Marshall Mrs
Massey Mrs E
Mathieson Mrs M
Mathieson Mr R
Matterson Mrs M
Maxfield Mr
Maxfield Mrs
May Mrs L
McBride Mr G
McBride Mrs M
McBride Mr K
McBride Mrs V
McCabe Mrs B
McCann Miss T
McCarthy Mrs M
McClean Dr C
McClurey Mr E
McCluskey Mrs M
McCluskey Mr M

McCormick Mr B
McCormick Mrs M
McCullagh Mrs I
McCullagh Mr M
McCune Mrs M
McCunnell Ms F
McDermott Miss A
McDonagh Mrs A
McElvaney Mrs K
McGeary Mrs P
McGeary Mr B
McGeary Mrs E
McGeary Inf C
McGeary Mr M
McGee Miss E
McGill Mrs J
McGlinchey Mrs T
McGowran Mr B
McGowran Mrs C
McGrath Mr K
McGrother Miss M
McGurk Mr W
McKenna Mrs A
McLean Mrs M
McMahon Ms B
McManon Mr B
McManus Sr C
McNicholas Mrs K
McRae Ms C
Metcalfe Miss J
Metcalfe Mrs E
Miller Ms G
Milson Ms A
Moore Mrs S
Moore Ms A
Moran Mrs R
Morgan Mrs G
Morrissey Mr M
Morrissey Mrs B
Mount Miss A
Murphy Mrs E
Murphy Miss M
Murray Mr R
Murray Mrs C
Murray Mrs M
Naughton Mrs J
Newton Ms R
Newton Miss K
Nicholson Rev B
Normanton Mr
Norris Mrs H
Norris Mrs L
O'Brien Mrs P
O'Brien Mrs P
O'Connell Rev T
O'Connor Rev M
O'Connor Mr K
O'Connor Mrs P
O'Donnel Mr A
O'Donoghue Mrs R
O'Hara Canon G
Oliver Miss M

O'Neill Dr J
O'Neill Mrs V
O'Sullivan Sr M
Oyston Mrs M
Pardoe Mrs M
Pearce Ms M
Pearson Mrs M
Pennington Mrs H
Pennington Mr J
Phillips Mrs L
Plumtree Ms M
Potter Mrs M
Power Mrs D
Priddis Mrs C
Proudfoot Mrs F
Pybus Ms P
Quinn Miss S
Quinn Mr S
Quinn Miss P
Rae Mr K
Rae Ms I
Raine Mrs M
Rainey Mr J
Raynor Ms M
Riley Mr V
Ritchie Mrs S
Roberts Mrs V
Roberts Mstr M
Robertson Mr D
Robertson Mrs S
Robinson Mrs J
Robinson Miss A
Robinson Ms T
Roddam Mrs D
Roddam Mr P
Roe Mr C
Roe Mr C
Rossi Mrs E
Rudd Mrs P
Ryan Rev M
Ryder Mrs J
Salt Mrs J
Savage Mr L
Savage Mrs M
Seavers Mrs H M
Selby Miss N
Selby Mstr M
Sellers Rev M
Severs Mrs P
Severs Mr P
Shippey Mrs E
Shuttleworth Mr B
Shuttleworth Mrs M
Simpson Mr J
Sindall Mrs
Skidmore Mrs A
Small Mrs M
Small Mr A
Snowdon Miss M
Snowdon Miss A
Spaight Canon D
Spark Mrs M

Spark Mr F
Stayman Mrs M
Stead Ms M
Stead Ms M
Steele Mrs M
Stephenson Mrs N
Stephenson Mrs N
Stewart Mrs M
Stonehouse Ms B
Stubbs Mrs J
Stubbs Miss R
Stubbs Mstr J
Summerhill Mr R
Summerhill Mrs E
Summers Mrs A
Summers Miss L
Summers Miss E
Sweet Ms E
Sweetman Ms M
Tate Mrs D
Teece Mrs B
Thomas Mrs S
Thomas Mrs C
Thompson Mrs S
Tillotson Mr K
Trainor Mr R
Treacy Mr A
Treacy Mrs P
Turner Mstr L
Twomey Sr C
Vasey Mrs M
Walgate Mr G
Walker Ms E
Walker Mrs M
Warburton Mrs J
Ward Mr T
Ward Mr B
Ward Mrs B
Wardell Mrs V
Waterson Mr T
Watts Mr J
Webb Rev C
Webb Mrs P
Welch Mrs C
Weymes Miss E
White Miss M
White Mrs L
White Mr R
Whitfield Mrs C
Whitfield Mr A
Whitfield Mr N
Whittingham Mrs A
Whittle Mrs D
Wiles Ms E
Wilkinson Mrs J
Williams Mrs A
Wilmott Miss M
Wilson Mrs P
Wilson Miss M
Wilson Mr V
Wilson Mrs I
Wing Mrs E

Wood Ms M
Woods Mrs T
Wright Rev W
Young Mrs C

2001

Bishop John Crowley
Bishop Kevin O'Brien
Adams Mr J
Adams Mrs M
Agar Mrs E
Akerman Mrs B
Alderson Mrs M
Allen Ms E
Andrews Miss C
Andrews Miss J
Andrews Mrs U
Appleby Mr C
Appleby Mr J
Appleby Ms C
Appleby Mr R
Arnold Mr B
Arnold Mrs F
Askins Miss J
Askins Mrs P
Askins Mr M
Atkinson Mrs E
Axford Mrs P
Bainbridge Mrs M
Bassett Ms E
Barrett Mrs
Barrett Ms K
Barron Mrs F
Barry Rev A
Barry Mr D
Barry Ms E
Beach Mrs E
Beach Mr F
Beckenkrager Mr E
Beckenkrager Mrs P
Bellis Ms J
Bellis Mr M
Bellis Mr B
Bickerstaffe Mgr T
Bickerstaffe Mrs M
Binks Mrs K
Birch Mrs H
Birch Inf T
Bivens Mrs
Bointon Miss C
Boland Mr J
Boland Mrs M
Boyes Dr W
Boyes Mrs M
Boyes Mr T
Boyes Mr D
Boyes Mr D
Boyes Mrs E
Boyes Miss A
Boyes Miss H
Boyes Mr M
Boyle Mrs I

Boyle Mr O
Brady Miss S
Broadhead Mr K
Broadhead Mrs M
Broadhead Mr C
Broadhead Mr K
Brookfield Mrs P
Brown Mrs V
Brown Mr J
Browning Mrs V
Brudenell Mrs P
Bryan Mr A
Bryan Mrs M
Bryan Miss I
Bulai Sr M
Burns Dr L
Burns Mr M P
Burns Mrs M M
Burns Rev A T
Burns Mrs A
Burns Mr A
Burrage Mrs M
Byrnes Mr G
Byrnes Mrs D
Byrnes Mr D
Callan Ms T
Calvert Mrs C
Campbell Park Miss J
Capraro Mrs N
Carhill Mrs A
Carr Mr P
Carr Mrs A
Casey Mrs B
Casey Mstr C
Cavanagh Ms F
Cave Mrs P
Chambers Mr A
Chambers Mrs M
Charlton Mgr J
Charlton Rev W
Choosey Mrs B
Christie Mr A
Christie Mrs B
Clark Mrs N
Clarke Mrs M
Clarke Mrs M
Clarke Ms L
Clifford Ms M
Close Ms J
Close Ms L
Cofinas Mrs C
Cofinas Mstr D
Coleman Mrs C
Coleman Mr G
Coleman Fr A
Colligan Mrs E
Collings Rev L
Collings Mrs E
Collins Mrs D
Collinson Miss C
Connor Mrs M
Connor Miss K

Costello Ms A	Gallon Miss C	Kelleher Miss N	McKeown Mr G
Coughlan Mrs J	Garcia Dr E	Kelleher Ms M	McKeown Miss C
Coverdale Ms A	Gillis Mrs J	Kett Mrs L	McLean Dr K
Cowell Mrs P	Gilroy Mrs J	King Miss S	McLean Mrs M
Cox Mrs M	Glancy Ms K	Knowles Mr W	McMahon Mr B
Cox Mr J	Golligly Mrs B	Knox Ms D	McMahon Ms B
Craig Mrs J	Good Ms C	Lacey Mrs M	McManus Sr S
Crowther Ms M	Graham Mrs S	Lacey Mr J	McRae Ms C
Cummins Mrs B	Gray Mr C J	Larkin Mr J	Merckx Mrs A
Cummins Mr J	Gray Mrs R	Lawson Mrs P	Merckx Mr S
Cunningham Mrs M	Griffiths Mr P	Lawson Mrs E	Merryweather Mrs M
Dahms Mr P	Griffiths Mstr J	Leahy Mrs I	Metcalfe Ms E
Dahms Mrs B	Gunn Mrs L	Leigh Mrs A	Metcalfe Ms J
Dasey Miss J F	Halley Mrs L	Leng Mrs G	Mitchell Mrs B
Dasey Mrs P	Harding Mrs P	Lester Mrs N	Mortell Canon
Dasey Mr A	Hardy Mrs W	Lidster Mrs J	Moxon Mstr G
Dasey V Rev G	Hargan Mrs	Ling Mrs P	Murphy Mrs B
Davison Mrs G	Hargan Mrs M	Lloyd Mr K	Murphy Mrs E
Dawson Mr P	Harkness Mr D	Lloyd Mrs M	Murphy Miss M
Dawson Mrs M	Harris Mstr S	Lodge Mrs I	Murray Miss E
Dicicco Mrs A	Harris Miss R	Lohan Mr E	Murrison Mstr E
Dixon Mr J	Harrison Miss H	Longstaff Mrs S	Naughton Mrs J
Dodds Mr N	Harrison Mrs A	Loughlin Rev J	Naylor Mrs W
Doherty Mr W	Harrison Mr J	Luby Mrs T	Neal Mr E
Donaghy Mr F	Harrison Mrs T	Lynch Mrs V	Neal Mrs C
Donaghy Mr P	Harrison Inf P	Lynch Mr D B	Nestor Mr C
Dowd Mr B	Hart Miss G	Main Mrs E	Nestor Mrs M
Downs Miss B	Hart Miss P	Maloney Ms M	Nestor Miss L
Downs Mr A	Harwood Mrs P	Manning Ms C	Nestor Mr R
Downs Mrs M	Hayes Miss T	Manning Ms D	Nestor Rev D
Dowson Mrs M	Hazel Mrs	Martin Mr J	Nestor Miss J
Duffy Mrs M	Heaney Mr J	May Mrs J	Nicholson Rev B
Dunn Mr P	Heaney Mrs D	McBride Mr K	Normington Mr S
Durkin Miss M	Heslehurst Mrs I	McBride Ms V	Norris Miss L
Edwards Miss J	Hill Mrs M	McBride Mrs P	Norris Mrs M
Ellis Mrs B	Hill Miss N	McBride Mr G	O'Connor Fr M
Everett Mrs D	Hipkins Mrs D	McBride Mrs M	O'Connor Mrs P
Eves Miss M	Hipkins Mstr C	McCabe Mrs K	O'Connor Miss H
Farnill Miss H	Hodgkinson Miss C	McCabe Mr J	O'Donoghue Mrs R
Farrer Fr P	Hodgkinson Mrs	McCabe Mrs C	O'Hara Canon G
Fascia Mrs J	Hogan Mgr D	McCarthy Mrs M	Oliver Miss M
Ferens Mrs I	Holder Rev S	McClurey Mr E	O'Neil Dr J
Field Mrs J	Hollinrake Dr	McCunnell Ms F	O'Neill Mrs V
Findlay Mrs P	Hollinrake Mrs	McDermott Mrs L	O'Neill Mrs M
Finucane Miss M	Home Mrs J	McDermott Miss A	Oyston Mrs M
Fixter Mstr T	Horner Mrs E	McDonagh Mrs N	Parker Mrs M
Fixter Mrs S	Hornshaw Ms S	McDonald Mstr D	Pearson Mrs M
Flynn Ms J	Houlden Ms E	McDonough Mrs A	Pennington. Mrs H
Flynn Ms M	Hughes Mrs M	McGeary Mr M	Pennington Mr J
Flynn Mr D	Hughes Mrs T	McGeary Mrs E	Phillips Mrs L
Flynn Mr J	Hughes Mrs M	McGeary Infant C	Pickering Mr D
Flynn Mrs K	Hume Ms M	McGeary Mr B	Pickering Mrs A
Flynn Mr T	Jayasuriya Ms C	McGeary Mrs P	Plant Mrs A
Flynn Mrs L	Jennings Mr J	McGough Mr J	Potter Mrs M
Folland Mrs M	Johnson Mr S	McGough Mr S	Priddis Mrs P
Folland Miss P	Jones Mrs A	McGovern Ms T	Proctor Mrs M
Forgan Mrs R	Jones Mr P	McGowan Mr B	Quinn Mrs J
Fortune Mrs D	Jones Mrs C	McGowan Mrs C	Quinn Miss S
Foster Mr C	Keenan Ms J	McGowan Inf M	Quinn Mr S
Frederick Miss K	Keitch Mrs M	McGuirk Mrs A	Radford Mrs C
Gallagher Mrs G	Kelleher Mrs J	McKenna Mrs A	Radford Miss L
Gallagher Mrs E	Kelleher Mstr L	McKeown Mrs M	Radford Miss J

Rae Mr K
Rae Mrs I
Rainey Mr J
Rathbone Mrs L
Raynor Ms M
Raynor Mrs M
Read Mrs D M
Reading Miss K
Regan Mrs K
Richardson. Mrs C
Richardson Mrs G
Richardson Mrs G
Richardson Mstr J
Rigg Mrs T
Riley Mr V
Robertson Miss S
Robertson Mr D
Robinson Rev G
Robinson Miss A
Robinson Miss J
Robinson Mrs J
Robinson Mrs K
Robinson Mrs T
Robinson Miss L
Robinson Mrs T
Robinson Mr G
Robinson Inf S
Roddam Mrs D
Roddam Mr P
Roe Mr C
Roe Mr K
Roe Mrs M
Rooks Miss R
Ross Mr I
Ross Mrs M
Rowell Sr D
Rowell Mrs P
Rudd Mrs M
Russi Mrs H
Rutherford Ms B
Ryder Mrs J
Salmon Mrs M
Savage Mrs M
Scannell Mr A
Selby Miss N
Selby Mstr M
Shearer Ms C
Simpson Mr J
Skidmore Mrs A
Slade Ms J
Snowdon Miss A
Snowdon Miss M
Spaight Canon D
Spencer Mrs M
Spencer Ms A
Stead Ms M
Stead Ms M
Stephen Ms F
Stewart Mrs M
Stonehouse Ms B
Stott Mrs P
Summerhill Mr R

Summerhill Mrs E
Summers Mrs A
Sweetman Ms M
Taylor Mrs K
Thomas Mrs K
Thompson Mrs K
Thompson Mrs E
Thompson Mrs P
Thompson Mrs S P
Thompson Mr M
Thompson Mrs J
Thompson Miss K
Tillotson Mr K
Tobin Miss S
Tolliday Miss M
Tolliday Mrs J
Toolan Mrs B
Trainor Mr R
Trotter Ms L
Turner Miss L
Usmar Ms N
Wall Mr J
Warrior Mrs M
Waterson Mr T
Watson Miss S A
Watson Mrs S
Watt Mr C
Watt Mrs D
Weymes Miss E M
Whalley Mrs P
Whelan Mr N
Whelan Mrs K
Whinstanley Mrs
White Miss E
Whitfield Mrs K
Wittingham Mrs A
Williams Mrs A
Williams Mrs J
Wilmott Ms M
Wilson Miss M
Wintie Mrs D
Wood Ms M
Wright Mrs J

2002
Bishop John Crowley
Adams Mrs M
Adams Mr J
Akerman Mrs E
Akerman Miss S
Alderson Mrs M
Alderson Mrs M
Allen Ms E
Anthony Dr K
Arnforth Mr J
Askins Mrs F
Askins Miss J
Bainbridge Mrs M
Baird Dr M
Barnett Mrs S
Barry Mr D
Beckenkrager Mrs P

Beckenkrager Mr E
Beddow Ms K
Belbin Ms C
Belbin Mr H
Binks Mrs K
Binnington Mrs A
Binns Mrs D
Birch Mrs H
Birch Mstr T
Bivens Mrs
Blanchard Mrs J
Blanchard Mstr T
Bottom Dr S
Bowen Mrs M
Bowen Mr
Bowen Mrs
Boyes Mr M
Boyes Mr T
Boyes Mr D
Boyes Dr W
Boyes Mrs M B
Boyes Mrs E
Boyes Mr D
Brekon Mrs M
Brennan Rev J
Brown Mrs R
Burns Fr A
Burns Mrs M
Burns Mr M P
Burns Mrs M P
Burns Mr T
Burrage Mrs M
Byrnes Mr D
Cahill Mrs A
Callan Ms T
Capraro Mrs N
Carr Mrs A
Carr Mr P
Casey Ms M
Cassidy Mrs K
Cavanagh Ms F
Chew Miss S
Chilver Mrs T
Chilver Mstr L
Christie Mr P
Clarke Mr T
Clifford Ms M
Colligan Mrs E
Collins Mrs M
Collins Mrs D
Collins Mrs M
Collins Mr D
Collins Mrs N
Connor Mrs C
Conway Mrs
Coppinger Mrs A
Cosgrove Mrs V
Coscrove Mr A T
Coward Ms M
Cowell Mrs P
Cox Mrs M
Cox Mr J

Cox Mrs C
Cox Mr N
Cresswell Mr M
Crowther Mrs M
Cunningham Mrs M
Daley Rev J J
Davies Ms M
Dawson Mr P
Dawson Mrs M
Dawson Mrs R
Dent Ms E
Dillon Mr M
Docherty Mrs V
Doherty Mrs C
Doherty Mstr D
Donkin Mrs M
Donnegan Mrs M
Dooley Mrs T
Dowson Mrs D
Doyle Mr P
Doyle Mrs G
Duffy Mrs E
Dunhill Mrs V M
Dunhill Mr S J
Dunne Mrs M
Dunne Mr P
Dunne Mrs E
Durkin Miss M
Durkin Mr J
Edwards Mrs M
Farnhill Miss H
Farrer Mr A
Farrer Mrs S
Farrer Fr P
Fletcher Mrs K
Forgan Miss R
Gallon Miss C
Gardiner Mrs E
Garside Mr J
Garside Mrs J
Gibson Ms A
Gillis Mrs J
Gilroy Mrs J
Glenton Mr C
Grayson Mrs A
Greenheld Mrs K
Griffiths Mr P
Griffiths Mrs S
Hackett Mr J
Hainsworth Ms A
Hall Mrs M
Hargan Miss M
Harrison Mr J
Harrison Mrs T
Harrison Inf P
Harrison Miss H
Hart Mrs A
Hazel Mrs T
Hemblade Mr V
Hemblade Mrs M
Hemblade Miss C
Hemblade Mstr R

Hodge Mrs R
Hodge Mstr J
Hodge Miss N
Hodgson Mr J
Hodgson Mrs A
Holmes Mrs M
Hume Ms N
Jackson Ms F
Johnson Ms M
Johnston Mrs M
Kavanagh Mrs P
Keenan Ms J
Kett Mrs L
Kieran Mrs A
Kilmartin Mrs J
King Miss M
Kirby Mrs A
Knowles Mrs D
Knowles Miss C
Larkin Mrs M
Larkin Mstr A
Leahy Mrs I
Leake Ms S
Leng Mrs G
Lester Mrs N
Lewis Mr F
Lewis Mrs D
Lidster Mrs J
Ling Mrs P
Lloyd Mrs M
Lloyd Mr K
Longbone Mr G
Longbone Mrs F
Loughran Mr J
Loughran Mrs S
Luby Mrs T
Maloney Ms N
Marshall Ms A
Massie Rev W
McCann Miss T
McClurey Mr E
McCunnell Ms F
McDermott Mrs L
McDermott Miss A
O'Flynn Mr B
O'Hare Sr C
Oliver Mrs C
Oliver Miss S
Oliver Mstr C
O'Malley Mr G
O'Neill Mrs V
O'Neill Dr J
O'Neill Dr P
O'Neill Mstr D
O'Sullivan Ms H
Oyston Mrs M
Peggs Mrs S
Pennington Mrs
Pennington Mr
Phillips Mrs L
Potter Mrs M
Pybus Mr F

Pybus Ms P
Quigley Mr B
Quinn Miss S
Quinn Mrs J
Quinn Mr S
Rae Mrs I
Rae Mr K
Rainey Mr J
Ramsay Ms K
Rawlinson Mrs M
Raynor Mrs M
Rice Barnet Miss Z
Rice Mrs A
Rice Barnet Miss I
Robertson Mr D
Robertson Miss S
Robinson Mrs K
Robinson Fr G
Robson Mrs M
Roddam Mrs D
Roddam Mr P
Roe Mr C
Rossi Mrs L
Rossi Mr B
Rowell Mrs P
Rowell Miss R
Rowell Miss P
Russell Inf L
Scott Mrs M
Selby Mr M
Selby Miss N
Selby Mrs G
Serplus Fr B
Shepperson Mrs V
Simpson Mr J
Smith Mrs I
Smith Mrs M
Smith Mrs A
Snowdon Miss A
Spaight Canon D
Stead Ms M
Stead Ms M
Stenburgh Ms C
Stephenson Mrs N
Stockwell Mrs V
Stockwell Miss B
Stott Mrs P
Sua Sr L
Sullivan Mrs A
Summers Mrs A
Taylor Ms N
Thompson Mrs C
Thompson Mr J
Thorpe Mr M
Thurlow Mr P
Thurlow Mstr O
Thurlow Mrs J
Thurlow Miss A
Tillotson Mr K
Tobin Miss S
Tolliday Miss M
Tolliday Mrs J

Trotter Mrs B
Trotter Miss R
Wales Mrs B
Walton Mr A
Waterson Mr T
Wattan Mrs M
Weatherall Mrs L
Whittle Mrs D
Wilkinson Mrs B
Wilkinson Miss M
Williams Mrs A
Willmott Ms M
Wilson Miss M
Wood Ms M
Wordsworth Mrs D
Wordsworth Mr P
Wordsworth Mr P
Wordsworth Miss M
Wright Miss K
Wright Mrs T

2003

As of March 27th
Bishop John Crowley
Bishop Kevin O'Brien
Adams Mrs M
Alderson Mrs M
Andrews Miss J
Andrews Mrs U
Andrews Miss C
Atkinson Mrs E
Bainbridge Mstr A
Barrett Mrs C
Bell Mrs C
Berry Mr J
Berry Mrs M D
Bivens Mrs W
Blamire Mrs N
Boyes Mr D
Boyes Dr W
Boyes Mrs M
Boyes Mrs E
Boyes Mr M
Boyes Miss H
Boyes Miss A
Boyes Mr D
Boyle Mrs I
Boyle Mr O
Brewster Mrs V
Brewster Mr C
Broadhead Mrs M
Broadhead Mr K
Broadhead Mr K
Broadhead Mr C
Brown Mrs R
Brown Mr J A
Brown Mrs R
Brudenell Mrs P
Bunting Mr B
Bunting Mrs M
Burns Rev A
Burns Mrs M

Burrage Mrs M
Byrnes Mr G
Byrnes Mrs D
Capraro Mrs N
Carney Mrs N
Castor Mrs M
Choosey Mrs B
Clark Mrs M
Clifford Mrs E
Clifton Mrs K
Colligan Mrs E
Collins Mrs D
Connelly Sister M
Connor Mrs C
Conway Mrs M B
Conway Mr P
Corrigan Mrs J
Coughlan Mrs J
Coverdale Ms A
Crosby Mrs
Crowley Rev M
Cunningham Mrs M C
Dasey Miss J
Dasey Miss E
Dasey Mr A
Dent Sr I
Di Giorgio Mrs J
Di Giorgio Miss E
Di Giorgio Miss F
Dowd Mrs M M
Dowling Sr M
Downs Miss B
Dowson Mrs E
Duffy Mrs M
Duffy Mr J
Dunn Mrs M
Dunne Mr P
Edwards Miss J
Elsey Mrs M
Emmett Mrs J
Farrar Rev P
Finicane Miss M
Flanagan Mrs J
Folland Miss P
Folland Mrs M
Forgan Miss R
Foy Mr J
Foy Mrs H
Frain Sr M
Freed Mrs B
Gillis Mrs J
Grace Mr H
Grace Mr D P
Grant Rev P
Grayson Mrs L
Griffin Mrs M
Griffith Mr P
Hackett Miss M
Hall Mrs M
Hall Mrs E
Hall Mr D
Halley Mrs L

Hargan Miss M
Hargan Mrs M
Harrison Miss H
Hazel Mrs T
Hodgkinson Miss C
Holder Rev S
Holmes Mrs M
Hornby Ms M
Hunneysett Mrs E
Jackson Mrs C
Jackson Mr A
Jones Mrs C
Jones Mr D
Jones Mrs V
Leahy Mrs I
Lecky Mrs J
Leigh Mrs A
Leng Mrs G
Ling Mrs P
Linings Mrs P
Linings Mr M
Lloyd Mr K
Lloyd Mrs
Longstaff Mrs S
Luby Mrs T
Lynch Mr D
Lynch Mrs V
Massey Mrs E
Matterson Mrs M
McBride Mr G
McBride Mrs M
McCarthy Mr D
McCarthy Mrs M
McCluskey Mrs M
McCormick Mr B
McCormick Mrs M
McDermott Miss A
McDonagh Mrs A
McElvaney Mrs K
McGill Mrs J
McGowran Mr B
McGowran Mrs C
McGrother Miss M
McKenna Mrs A
McNicholas Mrs K
Metcalfe Miss J
Moore Mrs S
Morgan Mrs G
Mount Miss A
Murphy Mrs E
Murphy Miss M
Naughton Mrs J
Nicholson Rev B
Norris Mrs M
Norris Mrs L
O'Connell Rev T
O'Connor Rev M
O'Donoghue Mrs R
O'Neill Mr T
O'Sullivan Sr M
Oyston Mrs M
Pearson Mrs M

Pennington Mrs H
Pennington Mr J
Phillips Mrs L
Potter Mrs M
Power Mrs D
Proudfoot Mrs F
Quinn Miss S
Raine Mrs M
Rainey Mr J
Ritchie Mrs S
Robertson Mr D
Robertson Mrs S
Roddam Mrs D
Roddam Mr P
Roe Mr C
Rossi Mrs E
Rudd Mrs P
Ryan Rev M
Seavers Mrs H M
Selby Miss N
Selby Mstr M
Sellers Rev M
Severs Mrs P
Severs Mr P
Shippey Mrs E
Skidmore Mrs A
Small Mrs M
Small Mr A
Snowdon Miss M
Spaight Canon D
Spark Mrs M
Spark Mr F
Stayman Mrs M
Steele Mrs M
Stephenson Mrs N
Stewart Mrs M
Summerhill Mr R
Summerhill Mrs E
Teece Mrs B
Thomas Mrs S
Thomas Mrs C
Treacy Mr A
Treacy Mrs P
Twomey Sr C
Walker Mrs E
Warburton Mrs J
Wardell Mrs V
Waterson Mr T
Watts Mr J
Webb Rev C
Webb Mrs P
Welch Mrs C
Weymes Miss E
White Miss E
White Mrs L
Whittle Mrs D
Wilkinson Mrs J
Williams Mrs A
Wilson Mrs P
Wilson Miss M
Wing Mrs E
Young Mrs C

Bibliography

Cranston Ruth, *The Miracle of Lourdes*, Doubleday, London 1988

Todd Oliver, *The Lourdes Pilgrim*, Matthew James Publishing, Chelmsford, 1987

Harris Ruth, *Lourdes: Body and Spirit in the Secular Age*, Penguin, London 1999

Ravier A, *Lourdes*, Lourdes Press

Lorentain Rene, *Bernadette Speaks*, St Paul Books, Boston, 1999

Sharpe Mick, *The Way and the Light*, Arum Press, London 1988

Target George, *The World of Pilgrimage*, AA Publishing, London, 1997

A Pilgrim, *Bernadette and Lourdes*, St Bernard Press, Coalville

Cousineau P, *The Art of Pilgrimage*, Element, Dorset, 1999

Markham J, Ed, *Keeping the Faith: 700 years of Catholic Life in Hull*, Highgate, Beverley, 1999

Brown Donfried Fitzmyer Reumann, *Mary in the New Testament*, Paulist Press, New Jersey, 1978

Cramer Anselm, *Ampleforth: The Story of St Laurence's Abbey and College*, Ampleforth Abbey, 2001

Storey A J, *Mount Grace Lady Chapel*, Highgate, Beverley, 2001

Appleyard E, *Zest for Life*, Caedmon Press, Whitby, 1999